Politics and Theater

STUDIES ON THE HISTORY OF SOCIETY AND CULTURE
Victoria E. Bonnell and Lynn Hunt, Editors

Politics and Theater

The Crisis of Legitimacy in
Restoration France, 1815–1830

Sheryl Kroen

UNIVERSITY OF CALIFORNIA PRESS
Berkeley · Los Angeles · London

Portions of chapters 2, 5, and the conclusion were
originally published as "Revolutionizing Religious
Politics during the Restoration," in *French
Historical Studies*, vol. 2, no. 1 (winter 1998).

University of California Press
Berkeley and Los Angeles, California

University of California Press, Ltd.
London, England

Library of Congress Cataloging-in-Publication Data

Kroen, Sheryl, 1961–

   Politics and theater : the crisis of legitimacy in
      restoration France, 1815–1830 / Sheryl Kroen.
      p. cm. — (Studies on the history of society
      and culture ; 40)
   Includes bibliographical references and index.
   ISBN 0-520-22214-8 (cloth : alk. paper)
      1. France—History—Restoration, 1814–
   1830—Political aspects. 2. France—History—
   July Revolution, 1830—Theater and the
   revolution.   3. Molière, 1622–1673. Tartuffe—
   Influence.   4. Legitimacy of governments—
   France.   5. Monarchy—France—History—
   19th century.   6. Democracy—France—
   History—19th century. I. Title. II. Series.
   DC256.8 .K76 2000
   944.06—dc21
                                    99-048330

For my mom:
Irene Stern Kroen, 1928–1998

Contents

List of Illustrations ix

Preface xi

Introduction: Staging Monarchy in a
Postrevolutionary World 1

PART I. POLITICS AS THEATER 21

1. The "Counterrevolutionary" State and the Politics
of *Oubli* (Forgetting) 39
2. The Missionaries: Expiation and the Resacralization
of the King's Two Bodies 76
3. Competing Commemorations: The Problem of
Performing Monarchy 109

PART II. THEATER AS POLITICS 155

4. "Practicing" Politics in an Age of Counterrevolution 161
5. Popular Anticlericalism: Defining the Sacred in
Postrevolutionary France 202
6. Tartufferie 229

Conclusion 285

Notes 307

Bibliography 375

Index 387

Illustrations

1. "Down with Charles X, Down with the Catholic Clergy, Long Live Liberty . . . !"   179
2. Fleur-de-lis foldup   192–193
3. Bonapartist suspenders   194
4. "Liqueur de Béranger"   195
5. The "Jesuit-king" in a gingerbread cookie   223
6. The "Jesuit-king" in a defaced coin of the realm   225
7. *Tartuffe:* "Oh, from here the work is marvelous!"   254
Map. Geographical distribution of *Tartuffe* incidents   257

Preface

This book analyzes the fifteen years of the nineteenth century when the Bourbons were restored to the throne in France after twenty-five years of revolution, war, and, arguably, the most ambitious experiment in popular democracy the world has ever known. The portrait of the Restoration which it brings into focus, however, bears little resemblance to the caricature of reaction and reversal which most of us have been taught to expect. But then nothing I had learned about the Restoration prepared me for what I found when I first went to the archives. This book reimagines the Restoration as a period of extreme crisis, when the state and the church, in their own competing fashions, were forced to reassert their legitimacy, precisely in relation to the events of the previous twenty-five years. This period was not defined by a renewed alliance between the altar and the throne. Indeed the church and state were continually at odds about the conception of monarchy which should rule France, and their struggles over the fifteen years of the Restoration consolidated rather than reversed the secular gains of the Revolution and the Concordat. Far from being a period of political stability or quiescence, when the majority of the population was suddenly excluded from the political sphere, the Restoration witnessed the continued expansion of politics into everyday life which had begun during the revolutionary decade. Excluded from the voting box, men and women turned to their town squares, marketplaces, cafés, churches, and theaters; they penned and posted placards, uttered seditious cries, sang revolutionary songs, trafficked in the illegal accoutrements of the revolutionary and imperial past, attacked crosses and busts of kings, and organized charivaris against unpopular priests and civil officials. Through this wide range of practices French men and women forced the state to take steps to subjugate the church; they kept the ideological alternatives to Christian monarchy alive and vital; and ultimately they brought down the fragile monarchy in 1830, leaving France with a legacy of the Revolution now altered by the specific struggles of the counterrevolutionary Restoration.

The road I have followed from my first days in the archives to this moment has been full of surprises and unexpected twists and turns. While I always intended to focus on the understudied early nineteenth century, and my goal was to understand the legacy of the French Revolution in the process, I never expected to write a book solely about the Restoration. I never expected half of it to be about religion; nor did I ever dream that I would be casting my whole interpretation of this period through the prism of Molière's seventeenth-century comedy *Tartuffe*. The archives forced these things upon me. In my unexpected intellectual journey I was far from alone; this book has been shaped by many generous people whom it gives me great pleasure to acknowledge publicly.

For those people who have read different incarnations of this book, offered criticism, citations, and encouragement, please accept my warmest thanks: Marjorie Beale, Jonathan Beecher, Martyn Lyons, Peter McPhee, Jo Burr Margadant, Ted Margadant, Jeffrey Needell, Edgar L. Newman, Jeffrey Ravel, Maria Riasonovsky, Mary Louise Roberts, Sylvia Schafer, and Alan Spitzer. I would like to offer special thanks to Colin Jones and Catherine Kudlick whose feedback helped me to understand the importance of fraudulence and Tartufferie for making sense of the Restoration. I owe a special debt to Timothy Tackett for his tireless efforts to turn a panel he organized into a forum for *French Historical Studies*. Thomas Kselman, who reviewed my contribution to the forum for the journal, helped me improve both that article and this book by encouraging me to connect the struggles between the church and state in the Restoration with analogous struggles in the Old Regime. For sharing their unpublished manuscripts on related subjects, I thank Susanna Barrows, Elisabeth Fraser, David Higgs, and Darrin McMahon. For their helpful criticism I am thankful to the two anonymous reviewers at the University of California Press, my careful and helpful copyeditor, Eleanor Gates, and my editor, Sheila Levine. For shepherding my book through the publication process, I thank Mark Reschke.

The initial research for this book was funded by grants from the Chateaubriand Foundation, the Mellon Foundation, and the Humanities Council at the University of California at Berkeley. I was able to go back to the archives several times to do additional research on the missionaries as a result of generous funding by Pomona College, a National Endowment for the Humanities summer grant, and a travel grant from the University of Florida. For the time to integrate new archival material on the missions and to reframe and reconceptualize my understanding of the Restoration I am very grateful to the National Endowment for the Humanities and to the University of Florida. In France many archivists and specialists at the libraries have been extremely helpful. In particular I would like to thank Mademoiselle Le Brigand from the museum associated with the National Archives and Sylvie Bléton at the Bibliothèque de l'Arsenal.

My intellectual debt to Lynn Hunt is palpable throughout this book. Her own work and approach to the Revolution of 1789 inspired me in the first place to go off on my quest to understand its legacy in the nineteenth century. But she has also modeled for me the art of being a mentor and a frank, critical colleague and friend. Many other professors have inspired me, read with me, argued with me, and given me the great pleasure of becoming their colleagues: I hope I can give in some small measure to my own students what Susanna Barrows, Thomas Laqueur, Robert Linn, and Michael Rogin have given to me.

While teaching at Pomona College I had the pleasure and privilege of knowing two historians, Pamela Smith and Helena Wall, who offered endless intellectual as well as emotional support during my first years of teaching. Julie Liss's careful reading of the introduction and her continuing emotional support throughout this process have been precious to me. Margaret Waller was a wonderful gift Pomona gave me; while team-teaching, researching in Paris together, reading and rereading draft after draft of everything we did, it became difficult to sort out where her ideas stopped and mine began. At the University of Florida I have many accomplished and generous colleagues. As I worked out different aspects of my argument, conversations with Swapna Banerjee, Alice Freifeld, Holly Hanson, and Rebecca Karl were invaluable. Louise Newman read an early draft of the manuscript and, demonstrating her extraordinary talent as a reader and teacher, helped me to see where I was going and how to get there. Susan Hegeman read and listened to much of this book and was invaluable in helping me hone my theoretical arguments.

Michael Gorham, a specialist on the Russian Revolution and literature, read every page of the manuscript with extraordinary care and intelligence, and helped to make it a much clearer book. Kathryn Burns, my dear neighbor and friend, was my closest writing partner. There isn't a page she hasn't read in many drafts, nor an idea she hasn't heard many times over a Leo's waffle. I don't know how I could have written this book without her love, support, and intelligence. The cast of colleagues at Florida who helped me would not be complete without my students. On two separate occasions I subjected my undergraduates to French history through the prism of *Tartuffe,* and their encouragement, enthusiasm, and good ideas propelled me along as I rewrote this book.

Clearly I've had intellectual support aplenty, but I've had much much more. I have been so rich in my friends and my family, whose confidence, love, and unending support made everything possible. Aside from the friends already mentioned, I want to thank Finnette Fabrick, Carla Hesse, Maura O'Connor, and Rebecca Rogers. My children, Leana and Joshua, born at different stages of this project, have given me the perspective and the joy to see it through. Armida Gallindo, Kristi Barfield, Aurélie Maignet, and Melissa Poblete cared for my children over the years, enriched all of our lives, and allowed me to do my work. Thank you with all my heart. Peter Hirschfeld, the love and anchor of my life, has been everything a person could dream of in a loving, supportive partner. But more than anyone, it was my mother whose total and unconditional love gave me the faith and the passion to do this and everything else in my life. It is to her memory that I gratefully dedicate this book.

Staging Monarchy in a Postrevolutionary World

There may be nothing particularly new or radical about treating the writing of history as a sort of "staging" or history itself as theater.[1] But for the French Restoration the theatrical metaphor is not merely useful or suggestive as an approach to history; it holds the key to making sense of this fifteen-year period and to explaining its central place in the emergence of a modern democratic political culture in France. The theater stands at the heart of my interpretation of early nineteenth-century France, and at center stage is one particular play: Molière's seventeenth-century comedy *Tartuffe*.

Two cartons of police reports at the National Archives originally focused my attention in this direction: first, on the theater, and, more specifically, on *Tartuffe*. Cartons F7 6692 and F7 6693 contain police reports and copies of songs and seditious writings seized during "troubles in the theater" which shook France between 1825 and 1829 in over twenty different departments, in the context of more than forty separate incidents. Men and women went to their local theaters, plastered the walls with placards, distributed flyers, disrupted other plays, and when evicted from the theater took to the streets outside the theater—all to demand a performance of Molière's *Tartuffe*. In some communities the play was banned; this often resulted in audiences refusing to allow any other play to be performed until *Tartuffe* was permitted. When the play was performed, certain lines became the focus of intense political expression. The police knew when to prick up their ears, the audience knew when to laugh, boo, and hiss. This politics of the theater often spilled into the streets, where posters were hung, songs sung, and people congregated until the wee hours of the morning. These incidents ranged in duration from the length of one performance to up to a full month of continuous agitation. Participation ranged from what the authorities called "a few troublemakers" to a majority of the local population, including people of all political persuasions and social classes. Wherever such incidents took place, the language and images of Molière's play found their way into popular political expression. Local and national events came to be seen through the prism of *Tartuffe*.

Why, of all public places, did people go to the theater to express their views? And why, of all plays, did they choose Molière's *Tartuffe*? The plot, the characters, and especially the themes of this seventeenth-century comedy made it the perfect vehicle for expressing anxiety and discontent regarding the central religious and political issues of the early nineteenth century. Seeing so many things around them as signs of "Tartufferie," the "troublemakers" in the theater encouraged their fellow citizens and opponents to view their world in a particular way. In so doing they left behind a trail of documents which inspires a similarly original and illuminating new perspective for me, the twentieth-century historian looking back. Following the troublemakers' cues, thinking seriously about the characters to whom they drew attention, and the issues which led them to take to the theaters and to invoke Molière's comedy, I too take seriously theatricality and its particular incarnation in "Tartufferie" as a means of making sense of history.

Molière's play features a confidence man, a swindler, and a hypocrite by the name of Tartuffe, who, by feigning to be an ascetic and pious man, is taken into the household of the good, if misguided, bourgeois Orgon. The "piety" of Tartuffe is a farce and provides for a good deal of comedy: while living with the family he tries to impose a rigid moral code, even as he himself indulges in the life-style of a wealthy bourgeois and does everything in his power to acquire his benefactor's wealth. The comedy is driven by the efforts of the weaker characters—the wife, Elmire; the daughter, Mariane, and her fiancé, Valère; the son, Damis; the brother-in-law, Cléante; and the most outspoken of all, the maid, Dorine—to get the father to see Tartuffe for the fraud he is. From the very beginning their ability to see the truth is proclaimed through the voice of Dorine, who, in act 1, scene 1, denounces Tartuffe to her superior, Orgon. "You see him as a saint. I'm far less awed; / In fact, I see right through him. He's a fraud."[2] Orgon refuses to heed the warnings of those around him and through the first four acts of the play signs over all his wealth to Tartuffe, and even promises his already-betrothed daughter's hand in marriage to this swindler. In his support for the hypocrite he is egged on by the only other character on stage who is taken in by Tartuffe, Orgon's pigheaded and detestable mother, Madame Pernelle. Having failed in their direct efforts to make Orgon see the truth, the other characters finally band together and plot to get Tartuffe to reveal his treachery to Orgon by means of staging a kind of "play within a play." Knowing that Tartuffe lusts after Orgon's wife, the characters set up a tryst between Tartuffe and Elmire in a room where Orgon can see them. In a particularly comic moment, Tartuffe proceeds to try to seduce Elmire right on top of a table under which her husband is hiding! At long last, Orgon accepts the truth about Tartuffe, but alas! it seems it is too late. He has not only deeded his entire estate to the swindler; he has also made him privy to a secret which could land Orgon in jail. In the final scene, when it appears that everything is lost, the king's bailiff arrives, but much to everyone's delight, instead of arresting Orgon he turns to the good bourgeois and his family and pronounces:

> Rest easy, and be grateful.
> We serve a Prince to whom all fraud is hateful,
> A Prince who sees into our inmost hearts,
> And can't be fooled by any trickster's arts. . . .
> With one keen glance, the King perceived the whole
> Perverseness and corruption of [Tartuffe's] soul, . . .[3]

Thus the play ends with a classic *deus ex machina,* perfectly suited to its context at Versailles under Louis XIV, with the all-seeing, all-knowing king acting to save the day.

If one reads through the songs, placards, and broadsheets circulating in the context of *Tartuffe* incidents, the applicability of this particular play to the local and national events in the 1820s becomes startlingly clear. If *Tartuffe* became popular in the years after 1825, it was because it was the perfect vehicle for criticizing the religious politics of church and state in this period. Tartuffe himself had long served as a stock figure in anticlerical literature.[4] But during the Restoration the church was spearheading a religious revival, orchestrated by zealous missionaries preaching an austere, almost puritanical variety of Catholicism which many people found oppressive. At the same time, churchmen seemed to be enjoying greater favor from the restored Bourbon monarchs. So while preaching austerity, the church and its representatives appeared to be growing richer and more powerful. Therefore, what could be better grist for the anticlerical mill than the somber ascetic who sneaks satisfying glimpses of exposed cleavage while inveighing against women's revealing fashions, the man who grows fat on the opulent cuisine he so readily criticizes and who lines his pockets with the wealth he argues is so terribly corrupting? Equating the missionaries of the Restoration with Molière's main character, Tartuffe, made perfect sense. Insults in the songs and placards were hurled most often at local curés and archbishops who, in language reminiscent of *Tartuffe*, "seduced more than one fair maiden" or "lined their own pockets with gold." [5]

The year 1825, when "troublemakers" began taking to the theater to demand *Tartuffe* with some regularity, is hardly an innocent date. As the year when Charles X (the more religious brother of the recently deceased King Louis XVIII) marked his ascension to the throne with an elaborate Old Regime–style coronation, 1825 seemed a perfect year to begin using Molière's comedy to question the clear-sightedness of the new king. Was *this* king, who many suspected of being a secret bishop, capable of acting as responsibly as the Prince in Molière's comedy? Given his purported role in a clerical plot to place the reins of government secretly in the hands of the men of the collar, could the people of France rest assured that "[the King's] love of piety" would not "numb his wits / And make him tolerant of hypocrites"? Could they expect that "With one keen glance, [this particular king would] perceive the whole" and work to protect the people from the wiles of Tartuffe and priests of his ilk? [6] It is no wonder that the lines that most excited audiences all over France after 1825 were the two in which the bailiff pronounced, "Rest easy, and be grateful. / We serve a Prince to whom all fraud is hateful." [7]

In reaction to a wide range of specific provocations—from the arrival of missionaries to the publication of a local prelate's pastoral letter, from the passage of the controversial Sacrilege Law (1825) to the local celebration of the elaborate coronation at Reims (also 1825) or the Papal Jubilee (1826)—men and women in different parts of France turned to *Tartuffe* to express their dissatisfaction with unpopular men of the collar, their suspicions of local civil officials, or their uncertainty about the identity and the authority of their king. Tens of thousands of cheap copies of this play were sold with prefaces which directly instructed readers to "oppose the Tartuffe of the stage with the Tartuffes of the world." [8] Through such prefaces, as well as placards, broadsheets, and songs, people in the 1820s encouraged those around them to see themselves as characters on a stage or to see those around them as other characters, but, most important, to listen to the warnings and messages of Molière's play and to apply them to their world.

What I do in this book is follow the lead of the so-called trouble-makers and adopt the prism of *Tartuffe* to make sense of French history in the early nineteenth century. Just as in Molière's *Tartuffe,* where the "play within the play" helped reveal the truth to Orgon, I believe that heeding the "play within the play" which was orchestrated in and around the theaters of France in the 1820s offers new insights into the Restoration and the political culture of postrevolutionary France. Paying close attention to the specific events in an around theaters in the late 1820s directs our attention to particular issues of religion and politics which have received too little attention from historians. The religious revival of these years, the perception of a clerical plot at all levels of government reaching as high as the king, and the rise of a popular anti-clericalism in response to both (which was ultimately fatal for the regime) are the most important among them. If seeing through the prism of *Tartuffe* did nothing but force us to focus on these unexplored areas, its use would be justified. But *Tartuffe* is even more important because it offers a vocabulary for talking about the quandary in which the Restoration regime found itself and to which it was forced to respond in the early nineteenth century. Unlike the Prince in act 5 of Molière's comedy, who could be accepted by everyone at the court of Versailles as the natural and legitimate ruler of France, when Louis XVIII was returned to the throne in 1815, in the wake of the French Revolution, the Napoleonic Empire, and the recent Hundred Days, the king could hardly claim a natural and exclusive right to rule. *Tartuffe* has long been known by historians and literary critics as a play which participated in the "fabrication" of monarchical authority at its apogee under Louis XIV;[9] but this book demonstrates that it is also fitting (although until now, *not* well known) that this play should have been revived in the 1820s to proclaim and help bring about the ultimate demise of legitimate monarchy in France.

In 1669, when Molière finally slipped *Tartuffe* past the royal censors and played Orgon in the performance of his comedy at court, he and his play were part of the vast and spectacular machinery through which monarchy was produced under Louis XIV. In the context of the court culture of the Sun King, Molière's play offered his patron an ideal portrait of monarchical authority, particularly in its oft-quoted (and recently added) fifth act. But the plot and themes of this comedy also contained a critique of monarchy. The characters of Tartuffe and Orgon,

first of all, offer models of imperfect rule. Tartuffe rules entirely as a result of deception or "theater." Orgon, on the other hand, clearly has
some right to rule in his realm; yet his blindness and his susceptibility to
deception make him a flawed leader, a fact which makes it possible, indeed necessary, for his "subjects" to plot against him to restore the
proper order of things in the household. Furthermore, the device of the
"play within the play" arguably expressed a more serious critique of
monarchy. Just as Dorine and the other characters plotted to stage the
love scene between Elmire and Tartuffe to reveal the deception of the latter, so could the staging of *Tartuffe* be seen as an effort by Molière to reveal the theatricality of Louis XIV within the context of his elaborate
court at Versailles. The words of the wife, Elmire, to her husband, regarding the scene she was about to perform, "Whatever I may say, you
must excuse / As part of that deceit I'm forced to use. / I shall employ
sweet speeches in the task / of making that impostor drop his mask;" [10]
could easily have been applied to describe what Molière was doing, especially as he added his act 5, with its "sweet speeches" about his Prince,
in an effort to finally get the censors to allow *Tartuffe* to be performed.[11]
How were the people at court, caught up in the vast and elaborately ritualized theater of power which was Versailles, supposed to "see" this
supposedly ideal portrait of monarchy?

If the play offered a subtle critique of monarchy, its unproblematic
performance in 1669 stands as testimony to the strength of Louis XIV's
rule at that time and to his unquestioned claim to legitimate authority in
France. By the time of the Restoration, however, a number of historical
events had served to challenge the legitimacy of the Crown, opening the
Bourbons to more serious attack inspired by this same comedy. Over the
course of the eighteenth century the continued distancing of the monarch from his subjects, the dechristianization of the kingdom in general,
the struggles between church and state regarding jurisdiction over spiritual matters, and the related rise of critical opinion in a new "public
sphere" all contributed to what historians have called the "desacralization of the monarchy."[12] But nothing, of course, challenged the monarchy more than the events of the French Revolution and the subsequent
fifteen years under Napoleon. When the Bourbons returned to France to
rule in 1815, Louis XVIII could not merely present himself as the only
"natural," "legitimate" ruler of France; the previous twenty-five years
had taught his subjects precisely the opposite lesson, namely that legitimate authority could be constructed out of many different elements, sustained by different symbols and legends, and based on different ideolo-

gies. When the Bourbons returned they faced nothing less than the task of reclaiming their exclusive right to rule France, in a world where such a right no longer existed.[13] Possessing no natural or divine claims to legitimacy, the restored Bourbon monarchy found itself wide open to the critique that, like the main character of Molière's comedy, it relied for its existence on fabrication, deception, in short, on theater.

The first part of this book, "Politics as Theater," demonstrates how this crisis was both enacted and exacerbated during the Restoration by examining those venues where different scenes were carefully scripted and staged, not by actual playwrights, directors, and actors, but by churchmen and government officials who regularly orchestrated spectacles throughout the period. Town squares, streets, and churches became the sites for the careful staging not of a fictitious and only subtly political comedy but of something much more overtly political and contentious, the restored Bourbon monarchy. In chapters 1 and 2, which present the ceremonies orchestrated by the state and the church respectively, one of the most basic assumptions about this period comes crashing down. Far from being perfectly allied in their counterrevolutionary zeal, representatives of the state and the church dramatized and promoted very different conceptions of monarchy in their public ceremonies. Even at the top, monarchy was clearly in crisis, but the competing ceremonies of the state and church did not merely illustrate this fact; they also publicized it and offered the population surprising ways of participating in the public negotiation over the nature and terms of legitimate authority in this period.

Chapter 1 looks at the two public ceremonies by which the regime defined and sought to relegitimize itself in relation to the previous twenty-five years. The first ceremony took place in public squares in every city, town, and village of France between Napoleon's fall after the Hundred Days and the summer of 1816. Following orders from the minister of the interior in Paris, local officials enacted the symbolic *mise-en-place,* or putting-into-place, of the Restoration by rounding up, inventorying, and finally destroying the "unnatural" and "corrupt" emblems of the Revolution and Empire. The regime also pursued its "politics of forgetting" every year, on the 21st of January and the 16th of October, in the way in which it represented the most problematic events of the Revolution, the executions of Louis XVI and Marie Antoinette. In the simple masses required for commemorating these solemn events there were no direct references to the act of regicide; in fact, orders from Paris explicitly forbade speeches evoking lurid details of these events. Likewise, the regime

consistently avoided direct representations of regicide in the commemorative coins and monuments designed for these occasions. Thus, by looking at both its *mise-en-place* ceremonies and its reluctant approach to
commemorating regicide, this chapter demonstrates that in order to reassert its legitimacy the regime clearly saw the need to erase the revolutionary and imperial interludes from the collective memory and thereby
return the population to a world where monarchical sovereignty *was* still
a given.

Missionaries orchestrating a religious revival in these years also used
their public spectacles to reassert the legitimacy of the Bourbon monarchy; however, their approach, which is the focus of chapter 2, could not
have been more different from that of the regime. In their four- to eight-
week-long revivals, culminating in processions which were truly the mass
spectacles of the Restoration, the missionaries worked day and night to
reconvert the population into practicing Catholics. Intimately woven
into this religious mission, however, was the very political goal of enabling their monarchs to resume their role as leaders of the Christian
world. Resurrecting monarchy along these lines involved more than
merely "ignoring" or "forgetting" the revolutionary interlude: indeed, it
required that the missionaries do everything possible to make their congregations *remember* the Revolution as vividly as possible. Equating the
martyrdom of Louis XVI with the crucifixion of Christ, encouraging
communal confession and expiation for the sins of the nation, and turning the sacred Host and especially mission crosses into political symbols
representing Christ *and* their king, the missionaries engaged the population in a mass movement which reasserted a conception of monarchy
modeled on the Eucharist that had not reigned in France since the seventeenth century.[14] More than anything the state did in these years, the missionaries worked to unmake the political and cultural legacy of the Revolution. Looking closely at the missionaries and their efforts, this chapter
demonstrates how these clergymen directly transposed the struggles of
the revolutionary era to the Restoration, and sets the stage for understanding how and why it was during the Restoration that "the transferral of sacrality to the secular and liberal principles of the nation" was
finally accomplished.[15]

The third and final chapter of Part I depicts the Restoration as a period of continuous negotiation over the nature of monarchy as defined
between the poles of "secular" and "Christian" monarchy. The laws and
national ceremonies of the kings over a fifteen-year period are analyzed
to demonstrate this continuous effort to define and redefine the nature

of the monarchy. While the regime generally showed itself to be a defender of secular monarchy, after the passage of the Sacrilege Law in 1825, which explicitly equated attacks on the body of the king with attacks on the sacred Host, Charles X's extravagant coronation in 1825, and his participation in the expiatory processions associated with the 1826 Papal Jubilee, there was good reason for many to question whether there was any difference between the regime's and the missionaries' way of conceiving of monarchy. It was the behavior of local state officials vis-à-vis visiting missionaries which brought this question home for the majority of French citizens. While potential or real disorders occasioned by the missionaries led the state in some instances to discipline these churchmen, in other cases state officials lent their support to the missionaries and thereby fueled the growing perception after 1825 that the government and the king himself were part of a massive plot to make the missionaries the arbiters of France's future. Drawing upon the correspondence which passed between civil and ecclesiastical officials regarding the tricky problem of the missionaries, this chapter evokes the terrain in which the population at large was incited to participate in negotiations as to the nature of monarchy in this period.

If Part I, "Politics as Theater," analyzes the contentious efforts of the church and state to stage monarchy between 1815 and 1830, Part II, "Theater as Politics," turns to the audiences for whom their spectacles were intended. Guided primarily by the police reports regarding seditious activities, this section leads us into marketplaces, town squares, churches, bookstores, cafés, and even the homes of individual citizens. If roundups of revolutionary memorabilia, the reluctant commemoration of regicide, and the erection of massive mission crosses are used in Part I to evoke the ways in which the state and church tried to constitute monarchy in this period, Part II considers symbolic sedition which defied the regime's "politics of forgetting" and the many tactics protesters used to prevent, disrupt, or control the spectacles of the missionaries. Like the extravagant theatrical efforts of the church and state, the practices by which French men and women supported and protested against these two pillars of the Restoration exposed the crisis of legitimacy suffered by the Bourbons in the postrevolutionary period. But in its detailed analysis of these practices, Part II also demonstrates that the citizens of France forged a path toward resolving this crisis. Chapter 4 focuses on the "unofficial politics" of the Restoration, and provides an overview of the repertoire of practices by which the men and women of France supported, subtly undermined, and overtly opposed the church

and state during the Bourbon Restoration. Establishing the calendar
which governed popular protest, it considers the importance of national
political holidays (such as the king's day), traditional celebrations (such
as carnival), or local events (a mission, or local patron saint day) in determining the timing of popular protest. Then, looking at where these
political activities were practiced, this chapter maps the geography of
local protest during the Restoration. The largest section in this chapter
focuses on "how" the people expressed themselves: looking at written, oral, iconographic, and gestural forms, this section provides a rich
analysis of the placards, songs, seditious cries, pamphlets, and broadsheets by which a public sphere was constituted during the Restoration.
This chapter ends with a brief analysis of who tended to participate in
this unofficial political realm.

Chapter 5 is devoted to popular anticlericalism because the majority
of practices which comprise the "unofficial politics" of the Restoration
fall under this general rubric. The strictly religious agenda of the missionaries is discussed at length because it is impossible to understand the
widespread and growing dissatisfaction, distrust, and outright disgust
which the clerics engendered in these years without attending to the
ways in which their new religious order directly affected the men and
women of France. But the "religious" motivations for anticlericalism
cannot be neatly separated from their political motivations or consequences. Thus, as this chapter surveys the wide range of practices by
which men and women protested against the missionaries and other
men of the collar, it is always with an eye to situating these acts within
the political context of the postrevolutionary period. Attacks on holy
objects within churches, disruptions of sermons, mockeries of sacraments in cafés, attacks on mission crosses, and calls for performances of
Tartuffe are all conceived as a spectrum of practices which the people
developed for determining the power of priests in their lives, the stance
that the regime should adopt vis-à-vis the church, and, consequently, the
very nature of monarchy which should rule in France. Nothing illustrates more clearly the central political significance of popular anticlericalism than those practices which evoke the specter of a clerical plot.
Was there a difference between the real and apparent power relations in
the Restoration? Was the king in charge? Or was the government in the
hands of counterrevolutionary clerics like the missionaries? The unease
about this apparent clerical plot reached a feverish pitch between 1825
and 1826, when suspicion settled on the person of Charles X, who was
said to be a clandestine bishop. A wide range of seditious practices were

deployed to question the actual identity and therefore the legitimacy of the monarch himself. Such acts, when placed alongside other anticlerical practices, allow us to understand how the very nature of sacrality, and therefore of legitimate authority, was being negotiated in these years.

Chapter 6, "Tartufferie," is a culmination of the previous chapter on anticlericalism. Many of the practices which occupy our attention in the general discussion of popular anticlericalism proliferated in the context of *Tartuffe* incidents since Molière's comedy was particularly suited to the task of criticizing the religious agenda of the missionaries. But after 1825, this play allowed people to expose and express anxiety about the illegitimacy of the regime. This chapter opens with an analysis of the *Tartuffe* incident in 1825 in Rouen, where, like the characters in Molière's comedy, the protestors used the theater to reveal and reverse the pernicious power of the clerics in their town, in the name of the proper, legitimate authority of the secular authorities. The next section explores the nature of "Tartufferie" as it erupted all over France in the 1820s, highlighting in particular the means by which it spread. While all of these *Tartuffe* incidents illustrate anxiety about the crisis of legitimate authority prevailing in this period, this section argues that they also produced the means of resolving this crisis of legitimacy and representation. For as men and women took to the streets and theaters, as they sang their songs and posted their seditious placards in public, they developed tactics by which they could and did control their civil and ecclesiastical officials. This final argument about the consequences of Tartufferie was made most clearly by lawyers arguing for the troublemakers charged for their role in a *Tartuffe* incident in Brest in 1826.

With this discussion of "Tartufferie" the main body of the book is complete; however, the conclusion lays out the historiographical consequences of recasting the Restoration through the prism of *Tartuffe*. In particular, by presenting an interpretation of the Revolution of 1830 which comes directly out of my research on the Restoration, I indicate lines of inquiry which could be profitably applied to later periods. A significant part of this section completes the argument developed in chapter 3, namely that the "counterrevolutionary" Restoration regime, although quite sympathetic to the state religion, ironically developed mechanisms for policing and controlling the church which consolidated the secular legacy of the Revolution. Here I look at the overtly anticlerical July Monarchy's response to the widespread violence against mission crosses between 1831 and 1834. It is quite clear that, like the seditious acts against these crosses which mimicked practices conceived in the Restoration, the local government officials who dealt with these violent anticlerical acts were merely perfecting and applying tactics that had been honed for fifteen years under the Restoration government. I also consider the benefits of applying to the July Monarchy the same set of questions which defined my efforts to understand the restored monarchy of 1815: how could Louis-Philippe constitute himself as a legitimate monarch in 1830? What role did the population play in constructing legitimate authority outside the still limited "official" politics of the July Monarchy? I also raise questions about French history since 1830, thinking in particular about historical moments in which crises of legitimacy produced similarly contentious acts of commemoration, and in which a focus on cultural practices, defined quite broadly, might enrich our understanding of the past. Taking my final cue from the "Tartufferie" of the 1820s, I conclude this book with a discussion of the usefulness of thinking about the emergence of democracy in relationship to theater.

Restaging the Restoration

The staging of the Restoration presented in this book emphasizes characters, sets, and plots which have not traditionally been the focus of histories of this period. At center stage are officials of the regime, in particular those representing the king, his ministers, the legislature, and their policies at the local level. Representatives of the Catholic church and, in particular, the itinerant missionaries orchestrating a religious revival are likewise given leading roles. Alongside these organizers of the competing spectacles of the church and state are the men and women of France who attended their performances passively, or, more interestingly, engaged as active participants and supporters of the missions, or as authors of seditious practices directed against the missionaries, the representatives of the monarchy, or both. Certain settings dominate my rendering of the Restoration: the public spaces where the state and church orchestrated their respective versions of France's past, present, and future figure largely, as do those venues which became favored sites of opposition, such as marketplaces, cafés, churches, and especially theaters. While Paris is important as the place from which orders were given to local officials, where laws were passed, and where the king resided and presided over special ceremonies, my emphasis is on the provinces, the context in which most French citizens witnessed, made sense of, responded to, and played a role in shaping the history of the period. The action or "plot" which dictated my analysis is, in Part I, the ceremonial representations of the church and state, and, in Part II, the diverse practices comprising the "unofficial politics" of the Restoration. While key national events such as the accession of the new king, Charles X, or the passage of the Sacrilege Law figure in my narrative, they are there to explain local perceptions and actions. Debates in the legislative chambers or the results of national elections are less important, for example, than the increasingly "national" repertoire of practices deployed against the missionaries and the regime, whether in the form of mockeries of the sacraments, disruptions of church services by stink bombs, command performances of *Tartuffe,* or representations of Charles X as the Jesuit-king in cookies, puns, or the disfigured coins of the realm.

This is hardly the Restoration that has been presented to us by historians in the past. Histories of the period 1815–1830 have tended to focus on those figures who participated in national, official politics: the kings, their ministers, other members of the royal family, leaders of national political factions, and the small fraction of the population that was enfranchised.[16] Works which focus on political ideology and political debates of this period go beyond this limited repertoire of characters to imagine the students hearing lectures at the Athenée from the likes of Victor Cousin, contemporary historians offering competing interpretations of the Restoration, elite men taking advantage of the expanding network of "cabinets de lecture," and the broader reading public brought into national political debates by the pamphlet wars and massive propaganda campaign which became especially important after 1825.[17] One recent book on the Fédérés who supported Napoleon's final gambit in 1814, and who remained involved in politics throughout the Restoration, points to a broader oppositional coalition.[18] Various books on illegal political activity allow us to imagine the world of politics beyond the ballot box, but they tend to focus on small, organized groups, or short-lived movements.[19] Only studies of anticlericalism have allowed us to envision a broader participation in the political arena, but even there the tendency is to focus on published sources, and on liberal propaganda campaigns orchestrated from above and from Paris, rather than on the popular anticlerical practices of the population at large.[20] With the exception of two recent books on the Revolution of 1830 which explicitly look back to the 1820s to make sense of the Three Glorious

Days, the broader population of France only rarely appears on the historical stage during the Restoration in discussions of matters concerning politics.[21]

The "settings" which have dominated prior treatments of the Restoration are related to the narrow conceptualization of politics that informs them. Earlier works tend to focus on institutions of government, such as the chambers, the ministries in Paris, the king's palace; the headquarters of national newspapers; the meeting places of organized political groups, whether legal or illegal; reading rooms created by such competing political and religious groups; university amphitheaters; and banquet halls and public meeting places during preelection periods. The sites of the Missions to the Interior are invoked, as are the theater riots of the post-1825 period; but these are treated as secondary phenomena, useful for illustrating the church-state alliance of the period, the rise of anti-Jesuitism, or liberal anticlericalism.[22] Those who have focused their attention on the Missions to the Interior have tended to emphasize their religious or intellectual aspects, and while political considerations are not absent, they are certainly not central to the analysis.[23] The struggles in churches, carnivalesque mockeries in cafés and town squares, and violence against mission crosses have begun to attract the attention of historians, particularly those interested in understanding the antecedents to the anticlerical and carnivalesque practices associated with the Revolution of 1830; but these have never been the focus of a full-scale analysis which tries to link up such venues and practices with a broader understanding of the ideological dilemmas and political culture of the Restoration.[24]

In preceding interpretations the Restoration has been analyzed primarily in relation to the Old Regime to which it was apparently a "return" or as part of the narrative concerning the right wing in France, which includes other periods when elements of the right wing came to power, such as the July Monarchy, the authoritarian Second Empire, or the Vichy regime in the twentieth century. If integrated into a discussion of the rise of democracy in France, it is only in narrow institutional terms which focus on voting practices, parliamentary procedure, ministerial responsibility, and which present the Restoration as a kind of apprenticeship in constitutional monarchy. Two of the most recent books on the Restoration illustrate this perfectly: Emmanuael de Waresquiel and Benoît Yvert's *History of the Restoration, 1814–1830: The Birth of Modern France* (1996) along with Pierre Rosanvallon's *The Impossible Monarchy: The Charters of 1814 and of 1830* (1994) argue that this period must be integrated into the political history of modern France, but both focus narrowly on official politics, using debates in the chambers and shifts in constitutional thought and practice to make their points.[25] The Restoration is excluded from histories which chart the emergence of democratic or republican political culture in France.[26] Contrary to the interpretation which I offer, the Restoration is generally portrayed as a step backward, an embarrassing interlude in the progression toward modernity and popular democracy. There are two critical exceptions to this. The first is Tudesq's analysis of the social consequences of the Revolution, which analyzes the society of notables which came into being by the 1840s.[27] The second is Isser Wolloch's recent study, *The New Regime: Transformation of the French Civic Order, 1789–1820s,* which clearly tries to integrate the "reactionary" Restoration into our understanding of the legacies of the French Revolution. Like de Toqueville's corresponding study of the Old Regime, Wolloch's analysis beautifully illustrates the importance of looking for continuities and progressive changes that took place in spite of the political discontinuities which have preoccupied historians until now. His critical study of lawmaking, formal political practices, the state bureaucracy, primary education, the justice system, and conscription anticipates many of my conclusions regarding the Restoration.[28]

The simplest explanation for the disparity between my own and previous interpretations of the political history of the Restoration is that the Restoration has simply been ignored for a very long time; a whole wave of historiography which has transformed the way we understand politics as *political culture* when thinking about the Old Regime, the Revolution, and much of the nineteenth century after 1830, and especially after 1848, has simply never been brought to bear on this period. The three-volume series entitled *The French Revolution and the Creation of Modern Political Culture* beautifully illustrates the contrast between the thorough rethinking of the politics of the Old Regime and of the French Revolution as "political culture" in the first two volumes and the relative paucity of scholarship attempting the same for the early nineteenth century.[29] Despite its misleading title, the third volume, *The Transformation of Political Culture, 1789–1848,* demonstrates that there is a new vogue in early-nineteenth-century political history (especially in France), but its interest is political theory, not political culture. In the introduction the editors, François Furet and Mona Ozouf, explain that the articles in their volume "study the ways in which the French Revolution has been portrayed in European thought and how its legacy influenced the development of political philosophy in the nineteenth century."[30] Even the American scholars included, whose previous works had more of a focus on political culture, turned their attention to the intellectual historical aspects of their topics in their contributions to this particular volume.[31]

Several tendencies in the historiography of nineteenth-century France explain why this new approach to political history has not yet been applied to the Restoration. First, as I have already mentioned, revolution and counterrevolution are not studied together, but rather are segregated into two separate discussions; historians have either studied the right wing in France, and the periods of reaction associated with its development, or they have focused on the "republican tradition" in periods during which republicanism, and democracy in general, were presumed to have made progress.[32] The shift toward rethinking the political history of the nineteenth century as political culture has characterized recent inquiries into the left wing in France and its development during the July Monarchy and the Second and Third Republics, but the Restoration has played a minor role in such discussions. This is related to a second tendency in the literature on the nineteenth century, which is to exclude the Restoration from the more general discussion of the rise of modern political culture in France because the period between 1799 and 1830 is seen as "premodern" and therefore outside the discussion of the many factors which "modernized" politics in France. Whether historians have focused on the economic, social, or cultural changes which politicized French peasants and integrated them into a national political discourse, their analysis has rarely strayed to periods earlier than 1830. The Restoration could be ignored in discussions of the political legacy of the Revolution because it has been wrongly assumed that the "republican tradition" had no relevant history in this period, and that politics, especially national politics, was simply not a part of most French men's and women's lives before 1830.

The tendency to ignore periods of reaction when discussing the legacy of the political culture of the Revolution is clear in recent studies of the symbolic forms and practices which came to comprise the republican tradition over the course of the nineteenth century. These studies focus only on periods when this symbolic system was officially accepted and used by the various regimes; they also tend to point inexorably toward the Third Republic, when republican festivals and symbols finally "came to power."[33] Studies of republican festivals, for example, focus only on the Revolution (1789–1799), the July Monarchy (1830–1848), the Second Republic (1848–1851), and the Third Republic (1871–1940) and disregard the intervening reactionary periods.[34] The same pattern can be seen in the volume of Pierre Nora's series on the collective memory of France devoted to *The Republic;* while there are four articles dedicated to such cultural inventions of the revolutionary decade as the tricolor flag, the republican calendar, the "Marseillaise," and the 14 juillet, they all focus on periods when governments acknowledged them as part of their legacy.[35]

In his *Marianne into Battle,* which traces the fate of this feminine representation of the republic from 1789 to 1880, Maurice Agulhon specifically underscores the importance of the symbolic struggle between revolution and counterrevolution in France; yet this struggle does not occupy a defining place in his analysis. Agulhon argues that the First Republic's cultural revolution left the French nation with "two political movements [Revolution and Counterrevolution] and two systems of thought, but also, and consequently, two symbolic systems." He goes on to say that this "accounts for one striking characteristic of French history: over a long period of time the most serious political conflicts are accompanied by a counterpoint of conflicting symbols." The evidence presented in this book bears out Agulhon's suggestion: clearly during the Restoration the church and state actively, if differently, confronted the symbolic systems of the republic (as well as the empire), and gave new meaning and significance to the republican and Bonapartist symbolic sedition which figured so prominently in the unofficial politics of this period. Yet Agulhon's own discussion of the Restoration period is limited to one anecdote about the political struggle of 1814–15 also being "a struggle between different flags and even more between different flowers."[36]

For historians interested in the other system of thought or symbolic system, namely the ceremonial and symbolic trappings of monarchy, the same tendency can be seen to ignore those cultural practices and ideologies with which they were in conflict. Wacquet's *The Royal Festival during the Restoration, or the Old Regime Rediscovered* fits squarely within this schema, since it presents the Restoration regime only in terms of its efforts to hearken back to the festive practices of monarchs of the Old Regime, consistently eschewing any discussion of the ideological quandaries produced by the Revolution which made such a "return" impossible. Like the emblems and festive practices associated with republicanism, the ceremonial trappings of monarchy are set apart, outside of the struggle with opposing symbols and practices which gave them new historical significance and meaning in this period.[37] An exception to this general rule can be found in the work of two art historians, Anne Wagner and Elisabeth Fraser, who in their respective studies of sculpture and painting of the Restoration explicitly treat the complex problem of representing monarchy in light of the revolutionary and imperial legacies.[38]

In the 1960s and 1970s the focus of political history shifted to the middle of the nineteenth century, to the moment when conditions were assumed to be ripe for the emergence of modern, democratic political culture. Historians in France focused on demography and on the social and economic history of different regions, and accented the modernization and growing integration of the French nation by mid-century.[39] Historians in the United States were more interested in questions concerning political modernization.[40] Led by Charles Tilly, who tried to distinguish modern from traditional forms of violent protest, historians produced a series of studies focusing on different ways in which politics was "modernized" in the nineteenth century—all of them ending in the Second Republic.[41] For Ted Margadant economic changes combined with the development of a network of national political organizations to create a movement capable of challenging the state in the insurrection of 1851.[42] For Edward Berenson it was the development of "modern" propaganda techniques, used by democratic-socialist ideologues and militants, which explained the politicization of the French peasantry and their integration into a national political discourse between 1830 and 1852.[43]

This veritable renaissance in the study of the Second Republic has left us with a wonderfully rich portrait of popular political culture in the period 1848–1851.[44] But it has only emphasized the scarcity of information we have about this realm in other periods of French history of the nineteenth century, particularly those cast as periods of reaction. Susanna Barrows, speaking of the Second Empire, notes that the 1850s, for example, "maintain an eerie silence in the face of the ruthlessly efficient 'authoritarian' empire."[45] The extraordinary politicization of the Second Republic is presumed to have disappeared, as if it were possible for French men and women who had risen up against the state in 1851 suddenly to suffer "collective amnesia in their political consciousness."[46] If it was the extraordinary repression of the Second Empire, so meticulously studied by John Merriman, which explains the lack of attention to the period after 1851, it is the presumption of "premodernity" which precluded the discussion of popular political culture and consciousness during the Restoration.[47]

In the currently accepted interpretation of the nineteenth century, the economic, social, and political changes which explained the politicization of the peasants of 1848 became important only after 1830. According to this view, national politics simply did not touch the everyday lives of most French peasants before this historical juncture; these men and women lived according to the rhythms of the seasons and according to the demands of local customs and folklore. This assumption is what led Maurice Agulhon, one of the leading scholars of the nineteenth century, to make the following statement about the place of politics in rural France before 1830: "One could say, simplifying things somewhat, that this place is nonexistent (*nulle*) before 1830, modest between 1830 and 1848, important, even massive, and decisive after 1848 and the establishment of universal suffrage."[48]

By presenting Agulhon's self-proclaimed "simplification" of the political situation in France prior to 1830, I do not mean to imply that he and other historians have completely ignored evidence to the contrary. In fact, in his own *Republic in the Village* Agulhon shows himself to be ever sensitive to folkloric practices and the ways in which struggles over matters such as burial rites and carnival rituals eventually led French men and women to embrace the secular and liberal values associated with the republic; but for him, this process did not make significant progress until the years preceding the Second Republic. As my chapters 2, 3, and especially 5 demonstrate, if this perspective has reigned it is largely because historians interested in politics have not taken seriously the national religious revival orchestrated by the missions or the political struggles they engendered. In a short piece written on the theater incidents of the Restoration, Alain Corbin acknowledges the importance which the missions may have had in the political history of this period when he says, "The Restoration is the time of the great missions; it would be without a doubt fruitful to place these theater riots in the context of the great processions of the [missions]."[49] But tellingly, this comment is relegated to a footnote, and underscores the fact that the missions, like the popular struggles of the Restoration more generally, have until now not been considered central for explaining the emergence of a modern, national democratic political culture in France.

This book attempts to bring the new ways of thinking about political culture to bear on the early nineteenth century, and to avoid some of the biases which have led to the many silences and weaknesses in the historiography outlined here. My restaging exposes the critical role of this

"counterrevolutionary" period in transforming and securing many legacies of the revolutionary period. Far from being a mere step back, this
book shows how the regime's politics of *oubli* combined with the missionaries' project of expiation to transpose the struggles of the revolutionary period to the nineteenth century. The many practices deployed
against the missionaries and the regime are proof that this was a period
defined by an increasingly national, public struggle over the problem of
legitimate authority, a process in which the general population engaged
in surprising ways, and not always for political reasons, but which
nonetheless had clear political and ideological consequences. This interpretation reimagines the Restoration as a kind of ideological crucible
which left a tangible legacy of practices as well as ideals which would
constitute the political culture of France in the nineteenth century.

In addition to reinserting the Restoration as a critical link between
the Revolution of 1789 and the rest of the nineteenth century, this book
demonstrates how useful it can be to use the Restoration to turn back
and think critically about the Old Regime. Again, it was *Tartuffe* that
pushed me in this direction. In order to explain why the very same comedy could have served in the 1660s to consolidate the absolute rule of
Louis XIV and after 1825 to expose the illegitimacy of Charles X's
reign, I was forced to think seriously about what had changed in the
intervening years. In this enterprise I could rely upon a rich historiography on the early modern period. I present this literature in brief introductions to each of the two parts of this book in order to show quite
concretely how the Restoration came to secure the legacy of the fires of
revolution, but also how both "from above" and "from below" the Restoration was the culmination of centuries of practices by which monarchy was both constituted and ultimately undermined.

PART I

Politics as Theater

The main action of "Politics as Theater" takes place in the fifteen years of the Bourbon Restoration, and the leading roles are played by representatives of the church and state who, in different ways, set about the difficult, and ultimately impossible, task of reasserting the age-old legitimacy of the monarchy in France. Yet before we enter the town squares and churches where these officials represented monarchical authority to the people of France between 1815 and 1830, or make sense of the struggles which erupted around their ceremonies, we need to step back and take a longer view of the whole history of legitimate monarchy in France, of which the Restoration was but the final act. In particular we need to survey the repertoire of legal, symbolic, and ceremonial practices by which monarchy had been constituted over the centuries so as to understand the choices made by the missionaries and civil officials during the Restoration; for the struggles that erupted between them were the result of the complex and often contentious relationship between the church and state and, more broadly, between religion and politics, which over the centuries helped to strengthen the monarchy, and ultimately to erode its legitimacy.

The King's Two Bodies

According to Ernst Kantorowicz's analysis of the theological origins of absolute monarchy, to understand the nature of legitimate monarchy in France at its height in the seventeenth century we need to turn our attention back to the medieval period, when, borrowing the pontifical model of the church, the new nation-states began the long and complicated process of fashioning monarchy around "the king's two bodies." Ascribing to themselves the mystical powers previously reserved for popes and bishops, rulers of the late medieval and early modern period elevated the secular state to the sphere of mystery at the same time as they made themselves into Christlike embodiments of this new kingship.[1]

To explain the development of the notion of the "two bodies of the king," Kantorowicz turns to the ecclesiastical realm where this model initially appeared in the connection between the body of Christ and the spiritual body which was the church. Here the first critical shift took place in the twelfth century when "the Church was compelled to stress most emphatically not a spiritual or mystical, but the *real* presence of both the human and the divine Christ in the Eucharist." [2] Finally culminating in the dogma of transubstantiation by 1215, this new emphasis on the real presence of Christ in the sacrament gave rise to "the development of the term *corpus mysticum* as a designation of the Church in its institutional and ecclesiological aspects." [3] "In short, the expression 'mystical body' which originally had a liturgical or sacramental meaning, took on a sociological content." [4] Hence we arrive at the twelfth-century formula for the "two bodies of Christ" on which the two bodies of the king would be based: "Two are the bodies of Christ: the human material body which he assumed from the Virgin, and the spiritual collegiate body, the college of the Church." [5]

As soon as the designation of *corpus mysticum* emerged in the religious realm it was adopted in the secular realm: "When in the twelfth century the Church, including the clerical bureaucracy, established itself as the 'mystical body of Christ,' the secular world sector proclaimed itself as the 'Holy Empire'. . . ." [6] It was not long before rulers were equating themselves with Christ, in particular in relationship to the "body politic," which was now also imbued with mystical qualities. Articulated by the Tudor judges in England, but also serving the French monarchs of the same period, the secular rendering of the two bodies of the king is summarized in the following:

> The King has two bodies, the one whereof is the Body natural . . . and in this he is subject to Passions and Death as other Men are; and the other is the Body politic and the Members thereof are the subjects, and he and they together compose the corporation and he is incorporated with them, and they with him, and he is the Head, and they are the Members; and this Body is *not* subject to Passions and Death, for as to this Body, the king never dies. [7]

Between the thirteenth and the sixteenth centuries the French monarchy constituted itself according to these two distinct and yet related bodies of the king. That the king, like Christ, was God's physical, corporeal representative on earth was expressed ceremonially with each coronation, with every procession which featured the physical body of the king, and especially in the ritual of touching for scrofula which physically demonstrated the sovereign's godlike power to heal. Indeed, as Marc Bloch has shown, this royal touch was practiced in France up to the time of Louis XVI and attested to the fact that the sovereign's power was supernatural, and that both his authority and his person were sacred.[8] That the model for the relationship between this "sacred" body of the king and the other body, the body politic, was likewise derived from the pontificalism developed since the twelfth century is clear from Lucas de Penna's description of the French monarchy from the sixteenth century: "And just as men are joined together spiritually in the spiritual body, the head of which is Christ . . . , so are men joined together morally and politically in the *respublica,* which is the body the head of which is the Prince."[9] The mystical, sacred quality of this "second" body of the king, and its distinct identity from the first, was most clearly demonstrated in the funerals of the French Renaissance kings.

Over the three centuries between the reigns of Phillip III and Louis XIII, the French dramatized the existence of the two distinct, but related, bodies of the king in the peculiar funeral rituals performed on the occasions of the deaths of the monarchs. Their historian, Ralph Giesey, has emphasized the ceremonial apparatus used between 1270 and 1610 to distinguish between, on the one hand, the dead king and his successor (the physical, mortal body of the king) and, on the other, the immortal *dignitas,* or kingship, which was ritually invested in an effigy that literally "reigned" during the "ceremonial interregnum" existing between the death of one king and the coronation of the next. Legally, the new king had full power at the moment of his predecessor's death, but the "mantle of dignity" did not cover him until he was crowned, and for the Renaissance kings this coronation did not take place until many weeks after the death of the previous monarch. During these intervening weeks both the mortal remains of the dead king and the physical body of his successor were kept from view, and all rituals focused on the wooden or waxen likeness of the deceased king, who was served meals, received visitors, and was even given a joyous entry. During this "ceremonial interregnum" the king was still alive, albeit not in the corporeal sense: hovering around the effigy of the king was the *mysticum* or *magnitus* of a king which *ne meurt jamais,* or "never dies." In Giesey's words, "The effigy was the basis for the speculation of the royal Dignity, separate from both the deceased king and the king-elect, . . . The royal Dignity does not die. . . ."[10]

Geisey underscores the eucharistic quality of the effigy when he likens the royal funeral ceremony in Renaissance France to a "mystery play of the royal cult, kindred in spirit to the religious dramas of the Gothic period," and offers the direct connection between "the royal funeral procession, where the effigy was carried under a canopy, and the *Corpus Christi* procession where the host was similarly borne," a connection he notes was made by fifteenth-century chroniclers of these processions.[11] Of the two bodies of the king, these ceremonies seemed therefore to emphasize the succession of *magnitus,* of the body politic, embodied in the hostlike effigy. But the dramatization of the distinction between the two bodies of the king gave way in 1610 to a new model of kingliness, which invested the physical body of the new king with the immortality and eucharistic qualities previously reserved for the effigy alone. For in this year, the new king, Louis XIII, assumed the full dignity of kingship within days of the death of his predecessor, not at a coronation orchestrated after weeks of ceremonies performed around an effigy of the dead king, but immediately, in a *lit-de-justice* performed just after his predecessor's demise. In a move that betrays the absolutist pretensions of this and future kings, the "ceremonial interregnum," signifying the reign of *magnitus,* separate from the physical body of the living king, was closed; what emerged in its stead was a new model of kingship which acknowledged that "each king is 'perfect king' instantly upon the demise of the living king,' . . . the dignity must be immanent always in the living king and in him alone." [12]

The closing of the gap between the two bodies of the king, the insistence upon the immortality of kingliness *not* separate from but inherent in the mortal body of the new living king, was emblematically portrayed in the device used to represent the succession of the new boy-king, Louis XIV, in 1643. In his designs for the medal which would commemorate the *lit-de-justice* marking the new king's succession, the royal artist chose the symbol of the phoenix. As Giesey explains, it was the perfect emblem for the ceremony which had eclipsed the funeral rituals of the Renaissance kings and had consolidated the full power, mystery, and sacrality of kingship in the person of the living king.

> . . . the emblematic image is apt, and speaks for itself: the royal power passes instantaneously from the dead to the living, from the Corpse of Louis XIII, who on May 14th was laid to repose on his *lit funèbre* at St.-Germaine-en-Laye, to the infant Louis XIV reposing four days later on the *lit-de-justice* in the Parlement of Paris. The scene is reminiscent of the fabulous Phoenix, who set fire to his nest, which was his funerary bed, to be consumed in the flames while hatching himself to rise in a new incarnation from the ashes. What better metaphor to symbolize the perfect dynastic continuity which Bourbon absolutism had achieved? [13]

The next seventy-two years, during which Louis XIV and his supporters would erect a veritable cult around the body and image of the Sun King, would demonstrate how powerful this new mode of representing monarchy could be.

The Portrait of the King

Louis XIII's ceremonial innovations of 1610 pointed in the direction of Louis XIV's consolidation and perfection of a conception of kingship which transformed the mortal, flesh-and-blood body of the king, and any image thereof, into a perfect representation of kingship according to the model of the Eucharist. This new logic of kingship motivated the fundamental changes in the monarchy's ceremonial and symbolic practices during the reign of Louis XIV. What we see, in particular, is a two-fold shift over the course of the seventeenth century: public ceremonies involving the physical presence of the king declined at the same time as the image of the all-powerful king, physically absent but, in the manner of the Eucharist, in his absence still present, proliferated throughout the realm, and became ever more effective at securing his subjects' loyalty to and identity through his rule.

On the level of ceremonial, Louis XIV progressively abandoned those rites of state by which his predecessors had regularly represented themselves directly before their subjects. In 1660 the king held his last royal entry on the occasion of his marriage; after 1673 he held no *lit-de-justice*. The rituals of touching for scrofula, receiving petitioners, of celebrating events within the royal family all took place within the confines of his court at Versailles. Certainly Versailles was not "private," for within the context of the court at Versailles Louis XIV regularly exposed his person to a public ritual without end; yet there was a difference between directly participating in mass spectacles in the streets of his kingdom and participating in the rituals at court which were publicized to the kingdom at large only through the engravings, medals, and wall almanacs produced expressly for this purpose. Increasingly, the people of France witnessed the public representation of monarchy through ceremonies and objects which invoked the king's presence in spite of his more or less continuous absence from public view.[14]

The widespread use of the fairly new ritual of the *Te Deum* exemplified, in the realm of ceremony, the new tactics adopted by the monarchy to represent itself throughout France. As Michel Fogel has shown, the *Te Deum* was introduced in 1587 by Henry III: it took the hymn of praise to God, which had been a part of rituals in which the king had directly participated—his coronation, or his entry into a city—and turned it into the nucleus of an autonomous ceremony, no longer requiring his presence. Combining the song of celebration of God with the reading of a psalm and prayers said for the king, the *Te Deum* was celebrated simultaneously throughout the kingdom to mark the historical triumphs of the monarchy. Thus, the birth of a successor, a military victory, or a peace which was profitable to the realm all became occasions to bring together all the orders and the bodies of society to offer thanksgiving to their king, even though he was not physically present at the ceremony. Proliferating his image, tied to a specific narrative of historical events, this ceremony could "render present everywhere that unique personage, the incarnation of the state, at the very moment when not deigning to show himself to his people, he chose absence."[15] Celebrated with increasing frequency over the course of the seventeenth century, the *Te Deum* beautifully illustrates the shifting tactics used to represent monarchy in the age of absolutism.[16]

Just as the *Te Deum* focused attention on the historical events punctuating the life and reign of the monarch, so did images of Louis XIV in this period surrender the Christian and allegorical symbols, which had represented past kings, in favor of a more real and historical representation of the king. In particular, after the 1670s, one sees a decline in the solar and Apollonian myths previously used to represent the Sun King in favor of "real allegory," that is, a system of emblematics which represented "the king in his own likeness and illustrating the history of his reign."[17] At Versailles itself this was evident in the themes chosen for decorating the palace: in 1674 the Stair of the Ambassadors was decorated with a mural showing the great deeds of the king since his ascension to the throne, just as in 1678 the vaulted ceilings of the *Galerie des Glaces* represented the many triumphs of the monarch. Rather than rely on Christian and mythological symbols and fables to attach glory and sacrality to the person of the king, "the history of the king dismissed fable, to become its own fable."[18]

Real historical images of the king proliferated throughout the kingdom during the reign of Louis XIV not only in the ceremony of the *Te Deum* but also in the broadsheets, wall calendars, commemorative medals and coins, and even marriage charters which brought historical representations of the reigning monarch right into the homes of his

French subjects.[19] These images, or "portraits of the king," became the most effective media through which the monarchy expressed and consolidated the new conception of kingship perfected during the reign of Louis XIV. Under the king who declared, "L'Etat, c'est Moi," we see the full and perfect transposition of the eucharistic model into the juridical and political realm. Just as the utterance "This is my body" produced a sacramental body of the species of bread and wine, visible on the altar as the real presence of Jesus Christ and as a representation of the spiritual body of the church, so did the portrait of the king, which expressed "It is Louis," constitute the sacramental body of the monarchy while at the same time celebrating the king's historical body and representing the king as the state, as the body politic, as the fictive body of the kingdom. In Louis Marin's words, the transposition of the eucharistic model to the juridical and political domain, a transposition which brings to light the historical gesture of absolutism, endowed the body of the king with the threefold visibility of Jesus: "as sacramental body it is visibly *really present* in the visual and written currencies; as historical body it is visible as *represented*, absence becomes presence again and again as 'image'; as political body it is visible as *symbolic fiction signified* in its name, right, and law."[20] Finally joining in one flesh-and-blood body the two bodies of the king dramatized by the Renaissance funeral ceremonies, "the king's portrait in its mystery, would be the sacramental body that would at once operate the political body of the prince and lift the historical body up into the political body."[21]

What Louis XIV thus accomplished at the height of his power was a system of political persuasion whereby his subjects' belief in the king, and loyalty to, and identity with the whole system of monarchy could be ensured by the mere propagation of his image, devoid of all symbolic or allegorical camouflage. The countenance of the king—whether on a coin, a broadsheet, or a marriage charter—or the invocation of his name and his triumphs in a *Te Deum* all functioned to consolidate his absolute power over his subjects not by state violence but by "the submission of their captured imaginations." If the portrait of the king could function as a "well-oiled machine for producing obedience without using brutal constraint," it was because the system of practices and beliefs which prevailed in the seventeenth century offered a solid foundation for monarchy to be so construed.[22] Correspondingly, when the legitimacy of monarchy constituted according to the eucharistic structure failed in the eighteenth century, it was because changes in the institutional relationship between the church and state and the religious practices of the subjects of the monarch had combined to weaken this foundation.

The Spiritual and Institutional Foundations
of Christian Monarchy

Whether in its Renaissance incarnation as two separate and distinct bodies, or in its absolutist version of the portrait of the king, the legitimacy of monarchy rested on a belief system which accepted the sacred nature of the king and the increasingly sacramental quality of his mere image. This belief system was promoted by an arrangement whereby the church and state sustained one another, depended upon one another, and collaborated to produce a system of laws and institutions which made it possible for subjects to accept the sacrality of kingship connected to the eucharistic model. The representatives of the Catholic church participated in state rituals such as the coronation or the *Te Deum,* led their congregations in prayers for the sovereign, and exhorted them to obey his edicts, which bore the hallowed formula "King by the grace of God."[23] Clerics and jurists reaffirmed the religious character of the French monarchy in sermons, treatises, and polemics; they argued that Catholicism unified the country and legitimized the social and political order. As the bishop of Troyes explained, "the entire social system [comes] back to a great and single center, God, the principle and origin of all things, the sacred source from which derive both the prerogatives of authority and the duties of dependence."[24] Unequivocally representing the Most Christian Kings of France as "the visible images of the Divinity," the clergy exhorted their parishioners to obey all of their superiors in the social and political order extending up the hierarchy to their king and then God, thus resting the entire network of authority and subordination "upon the foundation of the ancestral faith of the realm."[25] The Crown correspondingly lent its support to the church. In Merrick's words, "Since religion not only marked the way to salvation but also preserved social order, the crown made Catholicism a collective obligation rather than a private option in France. The divinely ordained king and his magistrates accordingly collaborated with the clergy and defended the national faith through enforcement of sacramental conformity, censorship of unorthodox opinions, and punishment of irreligious and immoral conduct."[26] Royal legislation made civil status dependent upon sacramental conformity: it required parents to send their children to cathechism; it compelled subjects to attest births, marriages, and deaths through participation in the baptismal, matrimonial, and mortuary rites of the national faith.[27] The very constitution of the politico-religious order thus made Christian monarchy possible: the divine ordination of the Crown, the identification of the sovereign community with the person of the king, and the definition of French citizens as Catholic subjects were all corollaries of the collaboration between church and state which made it possible for the monarchs of France to rule absolutely by the seventeenth century. However, throughout the eighteenth century a combination of the "dechristianization" of the population and the prolonged disputes between the church and state over their appropriate jurisdiction in the spiritual and temporal spheres progressively undermined the juridical principles of kingship "by the grace of God."

By whatever standard one adopts, it seems clear that by the eighteenth century the laws regarding religion and morality had fallen into disuse. Historians have demonstrated quantitatively that this century saw more delayed baptisms, a growing indifference concerning burials, and omissions of religious invocations and intercessary clauses from wills. Novels, newspapers, historical and scientific works, and unorthodox books were on the rise, while the number of theological books in print declined. One saw a higher incidence of Sabbath-breaking, blasphemy, suicide, premarital sex, illegitimate births, abandoned children, contraception, adultery, and prostitution; at the same time there was less regularity in attendance at Sunday masses and fulfillment of paschal obligations, fewer confraternities and ordinations, and more friction between clergy and laity over tithes, ecclesiastical fees, parish expenditures, administration of the sacraments, observance of holy days, and standards of moral conduct.[28] Many historians blame this trend on the Counter-Reformation of the seventeenth century, which was aided and abetted by the Most Christian Kings. Characterized by a more rigorous application of the sacraments, which ultimately excluded many parishioners from access to Holy Communion and absolution, the (usually Jansenist) curés doubtless turned a number of penitents away from the confessional and the Eucharist.[29] With their collaborators in the state, the Counter-Reformation clerics also made a clear distinction between official Catholicism and the popular practices of their parishioners. Forbidding unauthorized pilgrimages, suppressing popular holy days, carefully differentiating between the sacred and profane by enclosing cemeteries, traditionally used for grazing, marketing, dancing, elections, and assignations, and, generally, by condemning the vulgar revelries of the peasantry, this movement underscored the difference between Catholicism in its official character and the practices embraced by the faithful. According to Merrick, "Inasmuch as it made the clergy (tonsured, celibate, educated, and more commonly from outside the parish) more alien, and Christianity more repressive than before, the Counter-Reformation probably aggravated anticlericalism and caused disaffection from the rites of the national religion." [30] But this dechristianization can only be understood in the context of the struggles between the church and state which further undermined the role of Catholicism in the construction of kingship in the same period.

The works of Dale Van Kley and Jeffrey Merrick on the religious controversies of the eighteenth century agree that the protracted disputes involving the monarchy, the parliaments, and the clergy over the appropriate jurisdiction of the church and state in temporal and spiritual matters generally eroded the sacrality of monarchy by weakening the religio-political foundation on which it rested.[31] Both authors look closely at controversies from the eighteenth century in an effort to demonstrate how specific arguments made by clergymen, parliamentarians, and magistrates served to undermine the foundations of Christian monarchy. In other words, "secularization" and "dechristianization" were not, for these historians, the fruit of the Enlightenment, or some abstract shift in this direction, but rather the end result of a complex series of negotiations over the details of administering the kingdom in the eighteenth century which gradually desacralized monarchy by "disrupting the conjunction between religion and politics, discrediting divine ordination, and secularizing citizenship." [32]

In theory, the relationship between church and state as regards the spiritual and temporal lives of the subjects of France was clear; yet over the course of the eighteenth century, as a result of skirmishes over specific issues, one sees the practical extension of the state and its representatives into the spiritual sphere. In theory, purely spiritual matters clearly fell within the jurisdiction of the clergy. "The clergy alone formulated and interpreted the doctrines that embodied the work of God and administered the sacraments that dispensed His grace," and this fact was attested to by the royal legislation of 1695, which declared that all strictly spiritual matters "belonged to the ecclesiastical courts." [33] The king had always "unsheathed the temporal sword of coercion to enforce the doctrinal decisions and disciplinary judgment of the clergy," [34] but the decisions remained the prerogative of the men of the collar. But over the course of the eighteenth century, the state and its representatives did more than merely support the church or "enforce" its decisions. In practical terms, they increasingly meddled in "spiritual matters": they demanded the wholesale accountability of the clergy to the monarchy and its magistrates; the judges circumscribed ecclesiastical jurisdiction in matters of doctrine and discipline by means of the *comme d'abus*, which allowed for appeals to the royal court in religious cases. Stepping in to prevent excommunication, or to insist on the giving of the sacraments, the magistrates invoked the standard of *externality*, arguing that "subjects could not be excluded from the community of the faithful without being excluded from civil society as well." [35] In other words, rather than seeing the church and Catholicism as the key to social order and therefore defending the clergy's autonomy in the business of constituting the spiritual body of the nation, the government by its increasing meddling in spiritual matters showed that it had a new vision of the body politic as potentially disrupted by the divisive and exclusionary practices of the Catholic church.

In harmony with this new vision of the social and political order, the eighteenth-century state generally undermined the church's role in constituting the sovereign nation by progressively severing citizenship from Catholicity and by retreating from its role as the guardian of public Catholicism. Parliamentarians increasingly argued that men and women were "born citizens before becoming Christians," a position eighteenth-century legislation underscored as the Crown progressively broke the connection between civil status and religious conformity: first circumventing the necessity of ecclesiastical certification of death in 1736 (then turned over to the police), then tacitly recognizing the legitimacy of Protestant marriages in the second half of the eighteenth century, the state finally completed the disjunction of Catholicity from citizenship when, in 1787, Louis XVI provided for the secular registration of births, marriages, and deaths.[36] If French subjects were civil citizens first, and Catholics later as a matter of choice, their government also refrained from prosecuting French men and women for the infraction of laws concerning irreligion and immorality. The Crown censored fewer and fewer works which could be deemed blasphemous. "Treatises on *police* in the second half of the eighteenth century acknowledged that blasphemy, if not sacrilege, had become 'very common among ordinary people' and admitted that the magistrates, who considered the laws too harsh, rarely punished it . . . . " If occasional, spectacular demonstrations of the state's willingness to defend the ancient religion of France still took place, the application of corporal punishment, and even execution for blasphemy, was increasingly the exception rather than the rule.[37] Inclined to regard Sabbath-breaking and blasphemy as evidences of crudeness rather than criminality, "judges of the last decades of the *ancien regime* no longer shared Louis XIV's assumption that such offenses against God automatically threatened society and required exemplary retribution in this world."[38] Thus, "[t]he punishment of irreligion and immorality, like the enforcement of sacramental conformity, and the censorship of unorthodox opinions, declined in the eighteenth century."[39] At the same time that French men and women turned away from the rites of Catholicism, the state increasingly defined its subjects as citizen-members of a secularized body politic.

Controversies concerning religion and politics also served to erode the sacrality of kingship by exposing the monarch himself to criticism and by questioning the givenness of the relationship between the king and his kingdom.[40] When, in the eighteenth century, bishops and parliamentarians engaged in various controversies, they did not repudiate kingship by the grace of God in principle; however, they did directly attack the king's ecclesiastical and fiscal policies. They justified their critiques by invoking standards of orthodoxy and lawfulness, and in the process undermined the assumed unaccountability of the Crown. If, in the seventeenth century, kings regularly declared it blasphemous to dispute the absolute prerogative of the Crown, in the eighteenth century, as a result of the king's controversies with the clergy and the Parliament, criticizing the king and his policies came to assume the status of a right. Throughout the eighteenth century not only the specific policies of the king but also his personal behavior and character became the focus of widespread attacks. Whether reiterating the political arguments of parliamentarians in broadly diffused pamphlets, or attacking the purportedly licentious behavior of the king and queen, or publicizing what the monarchs of the eighteenth century themselves acknowledged as a failure to live up to the religious standards of the Most Christian Kings, the increasingly widespread criticism of the eighteenth century served to desacralize the monarchs, setting the stage, as it were, for the demise of the first of the king's two bodies.[41]

Kingship, the sovereignty of the nation as embodied in and through monarchy (or the second body of the king), was similarly undermined in the eighteenth century. When parliamentarians and clergymen alike, although on different sides of many debates, claimed to represent the "public interest" in their disputes with the Crown, or demanded respect for royal authority on the basis of its benefits to the kingdom rather than "the duties of religion," or when they insisted that taxation required the consent of the nation, they fundamentally challenged the very nature of kingship which had reigned in France for at least five centuries. All of these arguments "nurtured the concepts of sovereign community disengaged from the person of the monarch."[42] Not only, according to these arguments, was the kingdom no longer coterminous with the sacred body of an individual living king; these disputes moved French citizens in the direction of imagining that they could be "joined together morally and politically in the *respublica*," a sacred body politic possessing the full mystery and sacrality of kingship, without a king.[43]

The "Ceremonial Interregnum," 1789–1815: The Demise of the King's Two Bodies

If the king's flesh-and-blood body had been subjected to criticism over the course of the eighteenth century, the execution of Louis XVI on the scaffold in 1793 clearly marked the ultimate demise of the corporeal body of the king of France. The connection between the criticism which desacralized the body and the actual act of execution which ended its life has been demonstrated by historians who have charted the sharp rise in attacks on Louis XVI and Marie Antoinette in the years leading up to 1793, as bad fathers and mothers and as despotic, traitorous rulers whose very existence threatened the life of the fully separate and indeed more important "body politic." This was especially true after the flight to Varennes in 1791 forced the nation to question its ruler's devotion to kingship as it had been reconceived, since 1789, as constitutional monarchy.[44] With his beheading on the scaffold on January 21, 1793, the French people finally killed the king's mortal body, and for the first time since 1610 there was a "ceremonial interregnum": explicitly denying the possibility that the *magnitus* of the body politic resided in either the dead body of Louis XVI or any royal successor, the revolutionaries spent the next seven years orchestrating its embodiment in the nation and working to transfer the mantle of dignity through the new secular rituals and symbols of republicanism.[45]

Recent work on the cultural politics of the revolutionary decade has shown that the revolutionaries tried to complete a process, begun earlier in the century, of transferring sacrality from the eucharistic body of the king, sustained by the religio-political foundations of Christian monarchy, to the secular nation, constituted through the new calendar and civic rituals of republicanism. Just as absolute monarchy had "hallowed" kingship over the centuries, and gradually engendered the loyalty and quasi-religious devotion of its subjects, first as Catholics, but increasingly as citizens, so did the revolutionaries continue the "dechristianization" of France, at the same time as they used oaths, symbols, and festivals to tie the people to the nation through the new secular religion of republicanism. The second "body" of the king was thus not killed so much as transformed beyond recognition: if it possessed the *magnitus* and mystery of Old Regime "kingship," it was now defined by the new universals of "liberty, equality, fraternity," symbolized by tricolor flags and liberty trees, and enacted in festivals celebrating the historical events of the fledgling revolutionary nation, all of which combined to "sacralize" this radically different body politic.[46]

In their efforts to find the proper symbols, forms of dress, and festivals by which to transform Christian subjects into citizens, and transfer the sacrality of Christian kingship to a secular republican nation, the revolutionaries promoted a proliferation of practices which would endure as a critical challenge to monarchy. For almost a decade French men and women lived in a world where sovereignty had been thoroughly severed from any king or notion of kingship, and their daily lives were full of tangible reminders of this new order of things. During the following fifteen years, under the rule of Bonaparte, the multiplication of symbolic alternatives to Old Regime monarchy continued, now with imperial and new dynastic claims mixed in with the new sacrality of the republican, sovereign nation-at-arms. Over the course of the twenty-five years which comprised the "ceremonial interregnum" between the last Bourbon monarch of the eighteenth century and the next of the nineteenth, the givenness of monarchy had thus been thoroughly undermined. As viable alternatives organized the social and political order, first during the Revolution and later during the Consulate and Empire, ideology was brought into being.[47] The physical and mental landscape of France, thoroughly transformed by the experience of these twenty-five years, bore testimony to this enduring legacy of the Revolution.

Tartuffe or Politics as Theater

Molière's *Tartuffe,* written and performed at the height of absolutism, offers both a powerful example of the working of the "portrait of the king" in the late seventeenth century and a way of understanding its decline, which I have just traced. Hovering about the play, but never actually appearing on stage, was the image of the king. Despite his continuous absence from the scene, the king clearly ruled, "by the grace of God," a fact which was proven by his omniscient ability to see all that went on his kingdom and to step in, when necessary, to ensure its proper functioning. The resolution to the crisis in Orgon's little kingdom, made possible by the clear-sighted intervention of the Prince against Tartuffe in act 5, makes the play a testimonial to the benefits of absolutism under a king whose justice and responsible paternalist rule protects his subjects and ensures that the proper order of things will always be maintained. Yet, at the same time that Molière's play offered a language for applauding the divinely ordained absolute monarchy of Louis XIV, its depiction of the well-meaning but despotic father, Orgon, and the perverted and deceptive reign of the hypocrite, Tartuffe, offered a critical language which could be applied to question a ruler who failed to live up to the standards still clearly maintained by the absent "Prince." Furthermore, the role the characters on the stage played in organizing against their despotic ruler, Orgon, in the name of restoring proper order to their kingdom, clearly severed the absolute connection between king and kingship and underscored the possible separation of sovereignty from the person of the king should he fail to properly fulfill his role as a benevolent ruler of his subjects. Clearly these two critical perspectives on monarchy—that individual monarchs could err and be deserving of criticism, and that the sovereignty of any king was dependent on his satisfying the needs of his subjects, and must therefore be an expression somehow of their "will"—were both widespread and honed throughout the eighteenth century in the context of specific disputes between the Crown, the parliamentarians, the magistrates, and the clergy.

If Molière's comedy foreshadowed the critique of monarchy that would dominate in the eighteenth century, and ultimately contribute to the fall of the king in the Revolution, it was more prescient still in its articulation of the crisis of legitimacy facing the Bourbon monarchy when it returned to the throne in 1815. It was Molière's critical attention to the gap which all too often existed between appearance and reality that was relevant in this regard, for by underlining the often theatrical quality of authority he gave his audience the tools for questioning the very representation of monarchy. Could the "portrait of the king" represented in his absence on the stage be taken as exactly equivalent to the real, flesh-and-blood king living at court in Versailles? Did the vast spectacle of kingship produced at Versailles serve as a mask which distorted the real nature of kingship? While these questions had resonance for some in the late seventeenth century, and for many more in the eighteenth century, it was after the Revolution and the Empire that the full value of this critique of monarchy would be appreciated. For what could be more relevant for the citizens of France between 1815 and 1830 than Tartuffe's own words when applied to their monarch? "Why, after all, should you have faith in me? / How can you know what I might do, or be? / . . . Ah, no, don't be deceived by hollow shows. / I'm far, alas, from being what men suppose; / Though the world takes me for a man of worth / I'm truly the most worthless man on earth."[48] If monarchy could exist at all after the events of the past twenty-five years, it could do so only as the result of an elaborate staging: the efforts of the church and state to represent monarchy would illustrate this point and, in response, the subjects of the monarch would turn to Tartuffe both to expose and to reconcile themselves to this reality of modern political life.

CHAPTER ONE

The "Counterrevolutionary" State and the Politics of *Oubli* (Forgetting)

On the 17th of June in 1816 in Yvetot, a small city in the north of France, the subprefect organized a public ceremony in honor of the marriage of the king's nephew, the duc de Berry. The festivities of the day began in the church, where a mass was said in honor of the royal wedding. After the mass, those assembled were escorted by the local National Guard to the city hall, in front of which the subprefect made a long speech explaining the next part of the day's ceremony: the destruction by burning of "sinister emblems of revolutionary times" which the authorities had been collecting over the previous six months. As he pointed to tricolor flags and cockades, busts of Napoleon, and other revolutionary reminders, the speaker pronounced, "Let us destroy forever these signs of agitation which introduce, among us, discord, license, and unhappily the taste, or at least too great an indifference to crime." [1]

The subprefect went on to contrast these symbols with those of the restored monarchy. Where revolutionary symbols stood for all that was evil, impure, and bloodthirsty, those of the monarchy represented all that was good and peaceful. He focused at length on the shortcomings of the tricolor flag as compared with its pure white equivalent. "What demon, in effect, could imagine substituting three colors, which go together so badly, for the simple and unique color which, until then had united us all under the sweetest of regimes? Why this mixture of red and blue, emblems of bloody furor, with white which has always been the image of candor?" He lauded the return of the *drapeau blanc,* so simple and pure, representing "by its innocent color the most lovable and sweetest qualities."[2] The speech, according to the subprefect, "was welcomed by unanimous acclamations of a large crowd, representing people of both sexes and all ages, brought together to witness the destruction of these proscribed objects."[3]

As he spoke of the fire which would soon destroy these sinister emblems, the subprefect revealed the many purposes of the ceremony he was orchestrating—the purification of the political landscape of revolutionary symbols, the removal from the hearts and minds of his onlookers of the very memories and feelings such objects evoked, as well as the rekindling of their passion for the true and legitimate leader of France. "May the flames which we are about to ignite to destroy these impure objects, be themselves the emblem of that sacred fire which is making daily progress in our hearts, and consuming there that mélange of lugubrious memories and sentiments which continue to rob many among us of the happiness they could enjoy if they could appreciate all that providence has deigned to do for us in returning our legitimate King!"[4] As the subprefect ended his speech against the background of the crackling fire, the crowd screamed, "Long Live the King!" while the National Guard "played the most loved songs of the French."[5]

This ceremony is known to us because the subprefect of Yvetot sent a report carefully describing the proceedings as well as a copy of his speech to the prefect of his department. He was proud of his initiative, of his original scheme for organizing a public burning of revolutionary reminders on a day commemorating a great royal wedding. However, if the timing of this official's ceremony was distinctive, or if the contents of his speech were particularly edifying, in his orchestration and extensive account of a public destruction of revolutionary and imperial emblems in the summer of 1816, this subprefect showed himself to be a typical, if particularly enthusiastic, local representative of the Second Restoration government, following orders regarding the *mise-en-place,* or "putting-into-place" of the regime, in the wake of the Hundred Days.

The Symbolic *Mise-en-Place* and the Many Meanings of *Oubli*

In keeping with Article 11 of the Charter of 1814, the First Restoration government (in power until the Hundred Days) was guided by a spirit of *oubli*—oblivion, disregard, or forgetting—with regard to the past. This important article read, "All investigations of opinions and votes expressed before the Restoration are forbidden. The same disregard [*oubli*] is demanded of both the courts and the citizenry." [6] In practical terms, this translated into an effort during the First Restoration to revive the symbols, the calendar, and many of the rituals of the Old Regime, but without a direct confrontation with their revolutionary or imperial counterparts. But Napoleon's return in the Hundred Days proved that this conciliatory policy was far too dangerous. It became impossible simply to "pardon" the past loyalties of given individuals or to "ignore" the power of tricolor flags, revolutionary songs, or busts of Napoleon to rally together opposition to the government. So in direct contradiction to the spirit of Article 11 of the Charter, the Second Restoration government embarked upon an active campaign to accomplish another kind of *oubli* with regard to the period before 1815: compulsory forgetting.

Immediately upon his return to France after the Hundred Days, King Louis XVIII indicated the first shift away from the original policy of *oubli* in a speech wherein he revealed his intention to prosecute the instigators of the recent plot against the government. The government could continue to ignore the actions of the majority of "misguided Frenchmen," but could do the same for the organizers of the Hundred Days only at its own peril.

> I promise . . . to pardon those misguided Frenchmen for all that has happened since the day that I left Lille, . . . But the blood of my children has been spilled as a result of a treason such as the world has never seen. . . . I must therefore, for the dignity of my throne, for the interest of my people, for the peace of Europe, exempt from pardon the instigators and authors of this horrible trauma. They will be subjected to the vengeance of the laws.[7]

This singling out of "instigators" of the Hundred Days was soon broadened, however, to include bureaucrats who overzealously performed their duties under Napoleon's government. The purges of from one-third to one-half of all officeholders affected any individuals whose pasts were tainted by revolutionary activities.[8] Likewise, the disbanding of the military and the creation of a huge population of soldiers placed on "demipension" fit squarely within this policy of protecting the realm from potential traitors.[9] But where the Second Restoration government truly abandoned its initial policy of oblivion with regard to the past was in its extraordinary attack upon the symbols, rituals, and practices which reminded the population not only of the recent return of Napoleon but also of the full twenty-five years during which the Bourbon monarchs had ceased to reign in France.

Early in the fall of 1815 we see evidence of the first steps in the direction of this ambitious campaign in the scattered local efforts to root out every symbol or practice that carried some reminder of any regime other than that of the present king. In September and October of that year, local officials began to order their police commissioners and gendarmes to watch out for and severely punish any expression of public support for Napoleon, either by public pronouncements ("Long Live the Emperor" being the most common) or by the distinctive emblems people wore, "such as tricolor cockades and eagles." [10] But as the *arrêté* (decree) of the mayor of Bordeaux from October of 1815 demonstrates, officials did not stop at prohibiting public, individual expressions of direct support for the past emperor. Rather, anticipating the kind of effort which would be adopted nationally by November of the same year, the mayor requested: first, that everyone possessing objects, placards, or writings decorated with signs of Napoleon, or any government other than that of the present king, bring them to the Hôtel de Ville within five days; second, that those with such articles in their stores likewise turn them over to the authorities within the same five-day period; third, that after five days the police commissioners make visits to the homes of those people who, because of their profession, might have such objects in their possession, and if such objects were found, to seize them immediately; and fourth, that merchants or others who tried to sell such objects were to be arrested immediately and brought before the police tribunal "for having provoked citizens to revolt." [11] In the majority of cases, local officials did not begin to prosecute offenders of such seditious acts until after November, when, in response to a series of laws and directives from the national government, the *mise-en-place* was pursued in earnest.

On the 11th of November the national government passed a law "related to the repression of seditious cries and provocations to revolt," which clearly outlined the legal basis on which local officials could pursue "troublemakers" seeking to disturb the current order of things by drawing attention to the signs and emblems representing any government other than that of the current king. It was declared illegal to don tricolor cockades, carry tricolor flags, sing revolutionary songs, or keep images of the usurper or symbols of the Empire in public places. [12] The penalties threatened for infractions were to be stiff, much stiffer than the sentences handed down for analogous offenses under Napoleon. Seditious acts considered to be mere misdemeanors under Napoleon were treated as crimes in the Second Restoration, and the penalties were correspondingly tougher. Whereas a "down with Napoleon" during the Empire would have earned an offender a sentence somewhere between five to six days and six months, in 1816 a "down with Louis XVIII, long live Napoleon," the waving of the wrong flag, or trafficking in goods with republican or Bonapartist emblems would have merited between three months and one to five years in prison.[13] In theory, therefore, a strict ban on public representations of anything but the current regime was in place by November of 1815. However, in its early efforts to secure the future of the fragile monarchy, the Second Restoration government went well beyond stiff laws which rendered illegal the accoutrements of Bonapartism.

In the fall of 1815 the minister of police ordered public officials all over France, in big cities and in the tiniest communes, to gather together all reminders of the terrible years of revolutionary turmoil and destroy them. In a circular sent to November to all prefects, the minister of police focused first and foremost on the need to remove busts and portraits of Napoleon still standing in public places. Later in the letter, the minister broadened the range of objects to be seized: "These measures must extend to all prohibited signs such as flags, cockades, etc. Take care to make disappear from all public places and their surrounding areas all emblems of the same genre." In what should be seen as a tribute to the presumed potency of these revolutionary objects, the minister stressed the inadequacy of merely concealing them from the public: "They have been it is true, concealed from public view, and relegated to storage rooms. But their conservation is itself a scandal which must be stopped. For it maintains the criminal hopes of the government's enemies; it serves as a text for malevolent commentaries." Thus the minister informed the prefects of their duty to make such "monuments of adulation entirely disappear. . . . Give the promptest orders in your district that they be transferred without delay to the capital of your prefecture, and as they arrive, you will take care to destroy them."[14]

As concerned as the minister of police appeared to be to root out and destroy every physical reminder of all governments other than the reigning monarchy, his further instructions demonstrate his appreciation of the need for discretion in carrying out this campaign. The minister encouraged prefects to see that an "enlightened sensibility preside in these destructions." In particular, he seemed concerned that the prefects differentiate between "works of art" and "tasteless objects which attest at once to the baseness and incapacity of their authors." The prefects were to set aside potential works of art, signal the minister regarding their existence, and wait for orders regarding their fate. Care was also to be taken when encouraging private individuals and private establishments to give up their seditious objects, although the private sphere was not exempt from the officials' orders. The minister instructed his prefects that "your surveillance must not be limited to public establishments." But here again the minister qualified his instructions, distinguishing between the treatment to be accorded individuals who possessed such objects, but were not using them as political weapons against the government, and those people who were using them to keep the revolutionary spirit alive. Echoing the speech of the king from July of 1815, the minister recommended leniency for the masses (or in the words of the king, the "misguided Frenchmen") for whom such objects were *not* the signs of political protest, as opposed to the instigators or troublemakers who were likely to use them to bring down the regime. The former group was to be treated well, their objects were to be respected as private property, and persuasion alone was to be employed in their confiscation and/or destruction. "Invite the people who are likely to have in their homes cockades, engravings, stamps, imperial seals, etc. to turn them in to the authorities." But the latter group deserved no such treatment: "This consideration you owe only to those who wouldn't use these proscribed images badly; you must, on the contrary, treat with severity those who would use such objects as a means of stirring up the spirit of opposition." [15]

The task set before the prefects was immense. Removing and destroying tricolor flags and busts of Napoleon which adorned public buildings and replacing them with appropriate monarchical symbols and statues already required a significant amount of work and money. But the goal of collecting *privately* owned revolutionary and imperial memorabilia was extraordinarily ambitious. During the Revolution the government consciously multiplied the symbols and objects by which the people of France could identify with and become attached to their new government. Adding a new repertoire of imperial symbols, Napoleon did the same. During both the Revolution and the Empire the selling of such objects was big business. The articles of everyday life—plates, chamber pots, tobacco cases, fabric—were adorned with emblems of liberty, eagles, and other examples of *signes prohibés*," and sold by merchants all over the country for twenty-five years. The task which the minister of police set before the prefects of France in 1815 was nothing less than the collection and destruction of this vast quantity of public and private objects.

This simple circular of November 1815 set an extraordinary administrative effort into motion: prefects obeyed the orders issued by the minister of police, sent circulars to their subordinates, the subprefects, who, in turn, communicated with their subordinates, the mayors, police commissioners, and gendarmes, who saw that the orders were executed in communes all over France. In response to this order the symbolic *mise-en-place* was carried out in most French towns between the fall of 1815 and the summer of 1816. The police archives bear precious evidence of this extraordinary campaign: correspondence between public officials, inventories of seditious objects collected and destroyed, reports on local ceremonies including, occasionally, the texts of speeches offered on these special occasions—all offer an extraordinary glimpse into the nuts and bolts of reasserting legitimate monarchy in the wake of the Revolution and Empire.[16]

The differential zeal with which local officials carried out the *mise-en-place* can be gleaned from the instructions they conveyed to their subordinates. For example, in a letter addressed to the mayors of his city, the subprefect of Rouen (less than two weeks after the initial order from the minister of police to his prefect) reiterated his superior's instructions but took the initiative to see that public establishments received the utmost attention since they were known to be important centers of political opposition. Thus he ordered: "If you learn that such objects exist in private homes but especially in public establishments such as inns, cabarets, and cafés, you can . . . demand their destruction."[17] While this subprefect seemed to share the minister of police's desire to respect private property when trying to persuade such individuals to give up their possessions, he apparently did not agree with his superior's distinction between people making good or bad use of the seditious objects. Rather, like the mayor of Bordeaux who began a similar campaign back in October, the subprefect wanted a report in *all* cases where individuals did not turn them over to government officials. "You will use, first, all manner of persuasion, and if in spite of your invitations, someone refuses to destroy these emblems of an abhorred government, you will let me know immediately."[18] But usually the orders from prefects to subprefects and from subprefects to mayors were less zealous and merely recapitulated the orders of the minister of police, stressing only the minimum actions required. Typical was the circular from the prefect of the Dordogne to his subordinates, sent out more than a month after receiving his own orders from the minister, requesting merely that they "take the measures necessary to see that the emblems representing the past regime are effaced and replaced by those of the legitimate government."[19]

Throughout the spring of 1816 the minister of police continued to write to prefects all over France, following up on his initial orders of November. In some cases the letters simply requested a report: "I would like for you to inform me, upon receipt of this letter, of the results of the measures you have demanded, . . . and especially if you are sure that the tricolor flag has been destroyed in all of the communes in your department."[20] But often the follow-up letters to the prefects suggested noncompliance on the part of local officials and the fact that someone in the local arena had informed the minister of the continued display of revolutionary and/or imperial symbols. In February, for example, the minister of police reprimanded the same prefect in a letter which began, "I am informed that tricolor flags which have been removed from public edifices are being conserved in some city halls."[21] In another example, from the Dordogne, one mayor vehemently denied the reproach contained in a previous letter from his superior regarding a failure to destroy a local liberty tree.[22]

What was actually involved when these orders were translated into action? In general, it seems clear that the authorities focused most of their attention on those *signes prohibés* found on official government buildings, town squares, and other key public gathering places. We know this because local officials often prepared careful lists of all objects collected, and they only rarely mentioned objects which had been privately owned.[23] To make sure that such objects were removed from all public places, search teams composed of gendarmes were sent from town to town "to know whether or not there still exist emblems or signs of the government of the usurper."[24] Occasionally a special effort was made to seek out a specific article, in the event of a denunciation. For example, in April of 1816, the mayor of Buchy in the Seine-Inférieure informed his prefect that "we went to the home of Monsieur le Curé of our town, having been informed of the continued existence of two little tricolor flags which were used in processions for public holidays."[25]

Similarly, in the Oise, gendarmes were sent to a church in Beauvais which was said to house emblems of the previous government.[26]

Local officials often wrote in to their prefects, and even to the minister of police, to ask for advice on specific objects. The curator of the art museum in Rouen wrote to his prefect requesting guidance in sorting out what was seditious in his collection from what was true art.[27] The prefect of the Marne asked for similar instructions concerning three busts of Napoleon, while the prefect of the Nord asked for advice about a painting of Napoleon by Robert LeFebvre which might be considered "art."[28] Despite the clear instructions about confiscating private property, one local gendarme asked his prefect what he could do about a huge eagle he found publicly displayed in a local café without infringing upon the owner's property rights. The prefect instructed him to suggest that the café owner remove the eagle from public view. The gendarme did so and the café owner complied.[29]

The problem of merchants selling revolutionary and imperial objects was alluded to in local *arrêtés,* but was not discussed very much in official correspondence in the first year of the Restoration. Booksellers were mentioned in regard to one particular genre of publication—catechisms and books of religious songs. Special circulars were sent out to prefects concerning a catechism "in use in all churches in France, in which a whole chapter is consecrated to the devotion and attachment due to Napoleon's person."[30] The texts with the problematic chapter were already in use in churches and schools, but were also still being sold in bookstores all over the country. To rectify this situation subprefects and mayors were respectively informed to "be sure that visits are made immediately, in your entire district, to publishing houses, to bookstores, and to any merchant selling books, either by the commissioner responsible for inspecting bookshops, or by any other officer of the police."[31] Once at the bookstores, the officials were supposed to find the catechisms and *cartonner* (remove) the problematic chapter. From the reports sent in by various officials, it is clear that this vague instruction was interpreted in at least two different ways. In some cases the catechisms were actually destroyed. But in most cases it seems that the seditious chapter was crossed out, or the pages lacerated; thus "rectified," the books were then left on the shelf to be sold. The "rectification" of texts was also carried out in schools and churches where the catechisms were already in use.[32] Similar actions were taken with regard to song books containing pieces in honor of Napoleon or his family. In these cases single pages were simply torn out.[33]

Once officials all over France had collected busts of Napoleon and tricolor flags, lacerated the appropriate chapters of catechisms, and given a careful accounting of what they had found, what they chose to do with the *objets proscrits* varied widely from place to place. That the objects were to be collected and not just concealed, but actually destroyed, was clear enough in the instructions from the minister of police. But the precise form this destruction was to take was never clearly specified. Nowhere, in any of the government directives, was a ceremony of the type evoked at the beginning of this chapter recommended. In fact, within the wide range of activities one finds described in the rich correspondence between local officials and their superiors in this period, the subprefect of Yvetot's public ceremony comes out looking extremely zealous.

This is especially true if that ceremony is compared to the actions of an official such as the mayor of a small town in the Dordogne who not only failed to report on any such elaborate public burning but did not even bother to replace the tricolor flag with a *drapeau blanc*. He explained in a report that the weather had made this unnecessary: "upon the return of our King Louis XVIII, the tricolor flag was almost completely destroyed by the temperament of the weather; all that remained was the white piece in the middle, so we removed the red and blue pieces which were next to it." [34] A somewhat more enthusiastic destruction of revolutionary symbols took place in another small commune where a town council meeting spontaneously became the occasion for the burning of a recently discovered tricolor flag. At the meeting the mayor announced the continued existence of "an old tricolor flag from the time of the Terror." The mayor had already shredded the flag but suggested in the meeting that it be burned. The members of the town council, "by a spontaneous movement, demanded that a fire be ignited immediately before the city hall, and in their presence; this was carried out to the unanimous cries of Long Live the King." [35] There was apparently no speech, no advance notice, and so no large crowd—just a simple burning of one flag by the assembled city council. Within the city of Rouen, one of the mayors organized the destruction of busts of Napoleon with a similar lack of pomp. A specialist was hired to destroy the sculptures and their molds in the courtyard of the city hall, but the only ones present other than the officials were the "crowd of curious onlookers" who happened to be in the neighborhood at the time. [36]

Most often the reports sent in to the prefects, and then later to the minister of police in Paris, resemble that of the subprefect of Dieppe, who merely assured his superiors that he had carried out his orders and enjoyed "the certitude that not a single sign which would serve as a reminder of the government of Bonaparte could be found, anywhere in my *arrondissement,* and that all such emblems had been destroyed by fire." [37] Prefects often spoke for their whole department when they summarized the results of the ceremonies; the report of the prefect of the Marne is typical, with its simple declaration that having followed the orders forwarded to him on the 24th of November, "busts were destroyed, along with seals and stamps representing the eagle, tricolor flags were burned publicly in many places to the cry of Long Live the King." [38] It is hard to glean from such a formulaic report exactly what that burning was like. Was it planned in advance as a big public spectacle as in the case of Yvetot? Did the official in question simply decide on the spur of the moment to burn whatever objects were in his possession? Were special days chosen for these events? What was said as the fire was ignited? How many spectators were there? How many of them really said "Vive le Roi"? What were people thinking as they watched these events?

It is not possible to say exactly how the symbolic *mise-en-place* was carried out or received in every town throughout France between the fall of 1815 and the summer of 1816. But based on these reports it is possible to sketch a "typical" ceremony, as well as some variations added by different officials. Using the lists officials prepared of the seditious objects which they collected, it is possible to give an idea of what was hauled before spectators to be burned or otherwise destroyed. Drawing upon the reports of local officials, the few speeches which were actually recorded and saved, and the initial orders from their superiors in Paris, it is possible to reconstruct the logic which guided these ceremonies. Figuring out how spectators actually responded to such ceremonies is a more difficult proposition. It was hardly in the interest of any given official to admit a negative response, and indeed what one finds almost universally in these reports is the assurance that everyone assembled unanimously shouted "Long Live the King!" Yet the richness of the archival material on the ceremonies themselves, the inventories of the objects collected, and the reports on seditious acts proffered against the regime in the years that followed this campaign all combine to allow us to imagine even these elusive responses to the *mise-en-place.*

For the public ceremony which represented the culmination of months of efforts on behalf of the *mise-en-place,* burnings in the town square were most common, although in some cases burnings were carried out in the places where the offending reminder was found. The ceremonies often began with a mass, as in the case of Yvetot. Or news of the ceremony was announced in the church where sermons about the *mise-en-place* were also given.[39] The whole community was allegedly present, although the *procès-verbaux* of these ceremonies, when read closely, reveal that only those civil servants required to come were usually in attendance. A procession was common, often leading from the church to the town square, as was a speech by the most important official present, replete with the language of the need to "purify" France of its past. Music and bands of the type described in the Yvetot ceremony seemed to have been rare. But in almost all cases, whether a fire was ignited or busts of Napoleon smashed, cries of "Vive le Roi" were purportedly emitted by the assembled crowd. Some reports were more enthusiastic than others, as in the case of the prefect of the Charente-Inférieure, who not only noted that everywhere in his department the proscribed symbols were destroyed, but that in many places, "their destruction was a real public festival, and furnished the inhabitants with an occasion to manifest their joy at the return of their Legitimate King, their love for this excellent monarch, and their sincere devotion to his august Dynasty."[40]

The dates chosen for these ceremonies demonstrated some creativity. The ceremony in Yvetot, as described earlier, took place in conjunction with a royal wedding. One ceremony in the Dordogne took place on the 14th of July. Someone had tried to fly a tricolor flag on Bastille Day in 1816, and the local authorities were quick to publicly destroy it where it was hung.[41] Anniversaries of important events in the Hundred Days were seized by many officials as an opportunity for a *mise-en-place* ceremony. Both the prefect of the Loire and the prefect of the Somme chose the 20th of March, in the words of the former, "the day of odious memory, for the destruction of all of the signs of revolution, assuming that if this destruction were public and solemn, it could have a salutary effect on the spirit of the people."[42] In the Gers the prefect chose a date marking the local history of the Hundred Days in Auch. On the 5th of April in 1816, he described the ceremony in the capital of his department: "Yesterday was the anniversary of the fatal day when [local military authorities] substituted the colors of Bonaparte for the flag of the King. . . . I believed it necessary to choose this day to solemnly destroy all revolutionary and imperial signs."[43] Later in his letter he proclaimed his ceremony a success: "I expect that the sincere and boisterous joy of this day will impose silence for a long time to come on those rumormongers and prophets of doom" who would otherwise trouble our peace and security.[44]

Broad participation in these ceremonies was explicitly encouraged, according to various reports by local officials. In a small town in the Basses-Pyrénées, the mayor not only encouraged his citizens to personally deposit their proscribed emblems representing "anarchy and despotism" at the city hall; he also "required each inhabitant to bring his own portion of wood necessary for producing the bonfire in the public place where these emblems would be destroyed." The ceremony itself was apparently very successful. Officers of the Departmental Legion followed their chief in a gesture reminiscent of the Old Regime, when they "unsheathed their swords as if to swear their lives in support and defense of the throne of our kings." Later in the evening the civil and military officials in the town hosted a banquet where toasts were proffered "to legitimate monarchy, and to each of the Princes and Princesses of the Royal Family." [45] Other reports from the same department underscore the apparent popularity of these ceremonies. In Bayonne it seems that the burning of seals, flags, and other signs of the usurper became the occasion for spontaneous dancing: "hardly had the flame been ignited when the cries of *Vive le Roi* were heard with a new enthusiasm, and several members of the National Guard, who were by then accompanied by their wives, abandoned their arms in order to dance some rounds around the fire." The whole crowd soon followed suit: "the entire population of Bayonne was soon on their feet, attracted by the unanimous desire to see these last emblems of our unhappiness, doomed to execution, disappear." [46]

Local officials varied in their views about how useful it was to expose the population to the *signes prohibés* which had been collected over the months since November. At one extreme of the spectrum was the ceremony from Orthez (another enthusiastic example from the Basses-Pyrénées), where the mayor organized a special procession to carry the "impure signs" to the Place St-Pierre, where they were placed "in state," as it were, for the population to come and view them for two hours before their destruction: "The emblems, having been placed on the pyre [at 2 o'clock], remained exposed to the gaze of the public until 4 o'clock, the hour at which we left the *sous-préfecture* [and orchestrated their ceremonial destruction]." [47] The prefect of the Saone-et-Loire chose, on the contrary, not only to avoid laying out the objects for public scrutiny but also to avoid any public ceremony around their destruction. His reasoning interestingly was related to the extremely small quantity of such objects which had been turned in. He thought a public display of their destruction "might have offered a very good example if one had to throw on the flames a considerable mass of objects, . . . but that it would produce a very bad effect, being executed with only a small number of articles." He chose instead to have some articles destroyed with no pomp whatsoever, and then did what he could to make the remaining objects useful, as in the tricolor scarves made of wool, which he had separated into three parts (blue, white, and red) or dyed and then turned over to charities.[48] In the Haut-Rhin, the prefect likewise avoided a public display of seditious objects and any ceremony organized around their destruction, although his reasoning had to do with the political complexion of his department and the effect such a ceremony was apt to produce. He explained to the minister of police, in a letter from February of 1816: "In many departments in the North, in the Midi, in the West, noted for their devotion to the royal cause, the signs of the usurpation have been publicly destroyed by burning. This measure had the double benefit of frightening the small number of troublemakers and satisfying the right-thinking majority by the public triumph of a cause for which they had made sacrifices, or for which they had shown themselves ready to make." Unfortunately, he went on to explain, in Alsace the very different political persuasion of the majority of the citizens must deter the public administrators from engaging in these kinds of ceremonies. For in his department there was but a very small group who *did not* take an active part in supporting the Hundred Days, and even they ended up following its laws. Everyone had taken an oath to the usurper's government, almost everyone had signed the "*acte additionnel.*" In light of this, "if we were to make of the destruction of the tricolor flags, etc., a public ceremony, either it would have no spectators, and our goal would not be achieved, or there would be no others than the same Royalists who rallied around Napoleon just six months ago." He saw therefore no advantage to be achieved from such a public ceremony, but rather the possibility of opening the royal cause to overt criticism, and so opted to burn the proscribed objects in the courtyard of the prefecture.[49]

What objects were actually destroyed in these ceremonies? Most of the objects were public property. Emblems, busts, seals, and flags were removed from schools, academies, city halls, court buildings, and *bureaux de police;* prints, paintings, and statues were removed from museums. In one of the most extensive lists put together by officials in this period, only one of 120 objects was privately owned; that was "an eagle painted on wood, coming from a tobacco shop."[50] Most of these objects derived from the reign of Napoleon. However, for those French citizens who came to watch such ceremonies, it was clear that the history and symbols which they were supposed to forget stretched back before Napoleon to the beginning of the Revolution.

The particular objects which were paraded before the spectators often bore witness to the historical changes of the previous twenty-five years. One *drapeau tricolore*, for example, from a commune in the *arrondissement* of Rouen, had been embroidered in different corners with insignia and words which told the story of the successive governments in France since 1789. A fleur-de-lis and the date "1791" attested to the period of the constitutional monarchy; the words *la Nation, la Loi, la République* and little liberty caps attested to the republican period of the Revolution and the Terror. The words *Garde Nationale de Bonville, District de Cadebre* attested to its continued use by the National Guard of this one town throughout the period from as early as 1791 to 1815.[51] Because Napoleon had adopted the tricolor flag of the Revolution, any flag stood as a reminder of the Revolution itself; but this was usually underscored in the inventories of seditious objects which described tricolor flags and ties, for example, as "having served the National Guard under different revolutionary governments and under that of Bonaparte."[52] Flags which came specifically from the period of the Terror were often given special attention. As we saw above, such a flag often got a burning of its own.[53] As the people stood and watched objects thrown onto the pyre, they saw liberty caps mixed with eagles, seals from the various revolutionary governments mixed with the imperial laurel, liberty trees mixed with busts and sculptures of the emperor. The inventory from the Loiret, followed by an explicit description of how these objects were destroyed, demonstrates this point perfectly. A large majority of the objects destroyed (either by fire, when possible, or by specialists hired to break and melt them down) were Napoleonic; but flags and seals and other objects often represented different governments from the previous twenty-five years: included fourth on the list were "576 seals of many types, either representing the republic, or the eagle, coming from diverse administrations," and thirteenth on the list were "two liberty caps."[54] If the onlookers thought about the Revolution as separate from the Empire, these ceremonies were designed to demonstrate that they were undeniably linked.

This symbolic message was seconded in speeches, which argued that the Revolution and the Empire should be seen together as one horrible nightmare from which the French nation had only just begun to rouse itself. Talking about the tricolor, the subprefect of Yvetot asked the citizens of his town to consider what about the various governments it represented was worth remembering: "Would it be the Rebellion against the ill-fated Louis XVI . . . ? Would it be the carnage, the havoc which was wrought all over the land under this banner? Would it be its terrifying return which plunged us into an abyss of disaster?"[55] When the same subprefect advised all the mayors in his district, "Let us abolish, without any hope of returning, all that can make us remember this epoch . . . " he was referring not only to the most recent Napoleonic adventure but to the twenty-five years of revolutionary turmoil *en bloc*.[56] The same message was underscored in the report by the mayor of Orthez describing the ceremony in his town orchestrated around the destruction of "all the signs of the usurpation as well as all the emblems which bring to mind the calamitous times of despotism and anarchy." Directly linking the "usurpation" or the memory of the Hundred Days with that of the Revolution, and especially the Terror, this mayor underscored the relationship between the particularly warm reception granted this ceremony in his town and the recent arrest of some troublemakers in a neighboring department who, in his words, "during these calm and happy days dream of nothing but overthrows and disorders, and hope only to reawaken those extinguished passions, and to reorganize the murder and the pillage . . . . to put France back under the yoke of the usurpation, in order to put us back under the blade of the executioners of 93."[57]

The ceremonies often combined attacks on revolutionary and imperial symbols with the erection of symbols representing the new (old) regime. *Drapeaux blancs,* fleurs-de-lis, busts and portraits of the new king, and Christian symbols—statues of Christ or merely crosses—were resurrected on the facades of public buildings and in town squares. Ceremonies were not always orchestrated to celebrate these changes. A French citizen might have noticed that public officials in his town had changed the color of their scarves and belts from red to white, but no one seemed to celebrate such minor changes.[58] But the erection of flags and busts did often merit a local celebration. In one small town a subprefect conducted a ceremony in which a tricolor flag from the time of the Terror was burned on a day set aside for celebrating the erection of a bust of Louis XVIII.[59] While the direct substitution of a white flag for a tricolor flag, of a bust of Louis XVIII for a bust of Napoleon, or of a fleur-de-lis for an eagle was often carried out immediately, occasionally the local officials had to wait a while for the new symbols to arrive. In Neufchâtel the subprefect reported that the "signs of the past government" had disappeared by the 21st of December 1815, but on the date when he wrote his report to his prefect, on the 25th of the same month, he was still waiting for a bust and portrait of the new king to arrive from Paris. He also informed his prefect of his intention to adorn the town square with a statue of Christ.[60] Likewise, in a small town in the Dordogne, a liberty tree was chopped down and permission was immediately given to the local curé to erect in its place a huge stone cross. But the substitution was not immediate; the clear replacement of one set of symbols for another was not acted out for the local population of this town.[61] Sometimes the substitutions were more subtle. In another town in the Dordogne a mayor turned over the wood from the town's liberty tree to the curé to be used to repair the presbytery. The liberty tree was not transformed into a cross, but the message that the new regime was lending its material support to the Catholic church—a clear reversal of the revolutionary position—must not have been too difficult for most people to ascertain.[62]

Some public officials stressed the religious aspect of the *mise-en-place* more than others. In some ceremonies the change of regime was portrayed as providential, an ultimate delivery from the evils of the Revolution. The erection of religious symbols was as important as the erection of monarchical symbols. In some cases the symbols were seen as inseparable. In the small town of St-Gilles de Crelot in the Seine-Inférieure, for example, the mayor organized a ceremony in the local church around the raising of a white flag. The flag was intended "as a sign of gratitude that Providence had wanted to return to us, Louis le Desiré, by the name of Louis XVIII, ..." He arranged for the local National Guard to bring the flag into the church, where it was "then placed triumphantly in the sanctuary to be a souvenir and a sign of the most devoted love and attachment on the part of the inhabitants of this commune to legitimate authority and to the Bourbon family." The local priest took advantage of the large gathering of officers of the National Guard and the other inhabitants of the town "to remind them of their most sacred duties to God and to his Religion, and to a cherished monarchy which God in all his grace has restored to us after twenty-five years of turmoil and Tyranny, ..."[63]

Some local officials turned visits by members of the royal family into occasions for spreading this particularly religious message. In Toulouse, for example, the separate visits of the duke and the duchess of Angoulême, in July 1815 and September 1815, respectively, were turned into occasions for public processions and prayers. The symbols of the new government were paraded through the streets. The starting point and the ending point of the processions were churches, where public prayers were offered in expiation for the sins of the Revolution and in thanks for the Second Restoration.[64] Such ceremonies became the mainstay of the Missions to the Interior, long after the summer of 1816, when government officials ceased to conduct such ceremonies themselves. In the *mise-en-place* ceremonies orchestrated by state officials, this expiatory message was rare. These officials did not evoke memories of a lugubrious past in order to inspire a massive reconversion to Christianity and legitimate monarchy; if they encouraged remembering at all (and even this was rare), it was to encourage the population to appreciate and embrace the peaceful, happy alternative which monarchy offered to the reign of disorder and anarchy.

The king's speech upon his return after the Hundred Days certainly expresses this logic. Alluding to the horrible twenty-five years when the Bourbons did not rule in France, the king explained: "My subjects have learned, through a cruel ordeal, that the principle of legitimate monarchy is one of the fundamental bases of the social order, the only one on which one can establish among a great people, a freedom at once prudent and orderly (*sage* and *bien-ordonnée*)."[65] Not explicitly denying that other "fundamental bases for the social order" could exist, but only stressing the obvious benefits of legitimate monarchy, the king's speech articulated a logic which many of his officials orchestrating *mise-en-place* ceremonies seemed to embrace. The subprefect of Yvetot's circular to the mayors of his arrondissement clearly emphasized this value of evoking and destroying reminders of the past twenty-five years. In his words, "Let us destroy, without return, all that can remind us of this epoch when the most humiliating tyranny weighed upon our beautiful France. We remember this past only in order to be more *sage* and to rally with our hearts and our souls around the *plus sage* of Kings."[66] Surely everything about the ceremony in Yvetot underscored this logic. This is why the local official seized the occasion of a royal wedding to evoke images of the revolutionary past: casting the emblems of the past twenty-five years as contrived and unnatural, as bringing nothing but evil and violence to France, how could anyone present *not* want to embrace the "natural" symbols of the Bourbons, which promised peace, sagacity, and virtue? Just as "th[e] bizarre amalgamation [of blue, white, and red] seemed to be the sad prognosis of all the confusion of our ideas and the profanation of all that has been, until now, the object of our respect," so did the return of the *drapeau blanc* promise a peaceful, hopeful future. A similar logic must have inspired the mayor of Orthez to make twenty-five years of emblems available for viewing for two hours before their destruction in his *mise-en-place* ceremony. But running through this subprefect's speech is a related logic which I would argue is more prevalent in the staging of the *mise-en-place* across France. If remembering those "unhappy times" when citizens were "deprived of the presence of [their] cherished monarch" was necessary, the ultimate goal of this exercise was to forget: if the unnatural tricolor flag deserved a prominent place in the ceremony, it was to mark the moment when it and other symbols of its kind would be destroyed "without return."[67]

Of course this was the stated intention of the government: destroying (and not merely removing from public view) the *signes prohibés* was essential to the security of the regime in the face of potential enemies, but this speech, and the whole project of the *mise-en-place,* reveals a deeper ideological purpose—namely, the effacement not only from the public landscape but from the very memory of the population of any alternatives to legitimate monarchy. In other words, by eliminating reminders of and therefore any *retour* (return, or comeback) of republicanism and Bonapartism, then using speeches to demonstrate the "natural" superiority of the representations of Bourbon rule, the representatives of the Restoration regime participated in a national campaign to undo the major accomplishment of the Revolution—the creation of ideological difference.[68] The very existence of Napoleonic and revolutionary symbols threatened the Bourbon monarchy not only because they were capable of rallying the regime's enemies but because they represented alternatives, which revealed Bourbon legitimacy to be one among many ways of organizing the social order; monarchy was but one of many "constructed" ideologies. The only way around this political truism was to deny the very events that made it true; this required nothing less than the physical and spiritual "purification" of France. Destroying actual reminders in the hope of purging the collective memory is what these ceremonies were meant to accomplish.

The language of purification which dominates both the correspondence about this campaign and the speeches made in the context of these ceremonies makes sense in this regard. The minister of police himself claimed that the mere preservation of proscribed objects threatened to "corrupt the public spirit."[69] When a mayor from the small town of Gouy responded to his prefect's orders, he echoed the language of many of his fellow civil officials when he assured his superior that "the commune was entirely *purified (épurée)*."[70] Some local officials went to extraordinary lengths to *cleanse* the French landscape. In the Dordogne one mayor went so far as to burn the pole to which a tricolor flag was attached lest the pole *pollute* the white flag he was erecting in its place. He explained that he raised the new flag "with a new pole, not wanting the white flag to be *souillé* [defiled, sullied, polluted, blemished] by a pole which had served the tricolor flag."[71] But the best evidence that most officials used this ceremony as an act of purification was the fact that while they were directed by the minister of police merely to destroy the seditious objects they collected, almost all of them opted to destroy the corrupting reminders by fire.[72]

It was an official from the Basses-Pyrénées who combined the language of purification with that of forgetting in a speech which beautifully summarizes the regime's approach to representing revolutionary events and symbols in the context of these *mise-en-place* ceremonies. As he threw onto the fire what he called "these last emblems of our political errors," he proclaimed: "May this fire in consuming them, efface, destroy *to the very memory* of our long misfortunes, . . . May these projects, as absurd as they were criminal, these crazy and guilty hopes, evaporate, dissipate with this impure smoke, charged with the last traces of their abhorrent symbols." The need for this destruction, and its relationship to the future of the regime, were both explained as the official described all that would remain once this "purification" was complete: "That the royal lily without stain (*le Lys sans tache*), that the Panache of the good Henry, be forevermore the *only* signs of rallying, and that on festive days, as on days of combat, our voices can utter *only* the cry from the heart, this cry of love and of glory, VIVE LE ROI (Long Live the King)."[73]

The Failure of Compulsory Amnesia

Gauging the response of the French population to this elaborate campaign is no easy task. Reports of protests during individual ceremonies were rare. But they did happen. On the 21st of July 1815, the day a bust of Louis XVIII was to be set up in a lycée after a procession through the streets, young students screamed "Vive l'Empereur!" and booed, hissed, and whistled as others tried to say "Long Live the King."[74] However, since most of the evidence we have of the *mise-en-place* ceremonies comes from reports which were formulaic, and stressed the positive response of the assembled crowds, and since direct opposition of the above variety was rare (or rarely reported), assessing the actual response to the symbolic *mise-en-place* of the Restoration requires a certain degree of imaginative effort. We need to think about what was not said or done at these ceremonies. What was *not* confiscated by the police? What objects were *not* burned? Who did *not* go to these ceremonies? Where were they when they were taking place? What effect might the ceremonies have had?[75]

Despite my efforts to tease out the logic guiding this national campaign, it is hard to know exactly what the government hoped for in organizing its *mise-en-place*. If in its call for the purification of France the government wanted the kind of spontaneous popular attacks on symbols which were common during the Wars of Religion, it was probably sadly disappointed. Except in the regions of the White Terror, the symbolic *mise-en-place* was at best stiff, formulaic, and ineffective. There is no evidence that these ceremonies made people believe in the sacrality of the resurrected monarchical and Christian symbols, or that they had become convinced of the "corruption" of their revolutionary counterparts.[76]

The government's goal was, at the very least, to make people "forget"—to remove reminders of the previous twenty-five years from their sight, to burn them, and thereby to prevent them from rallying citizens against the new government. But certainly the actions of local officials also drew attention to these objects. The officials themselves spent hours, even days, poring over such articles as the tricolor flag described above, which bore a full narrative of the Revolution and the Empire. As they wrote their detailed reports, what were they thinking? What was their personal experience over the past twenty-five years? Did thinking about the different governments or the campaigns of Napoleon jog their memories, even make them think fondly of certain moments? No document in the archives confirmed such an eventuality, but one can find evidence of efforts by local officials to minimize compliance with the minister of police's orders, as we saw in the many examples of such officials either following orders with a minimum of pomp or having to be reminded repeatedly to remove and destroy the *signes prohibés*. What effect did the roundup of seditious objects have on the inhabitants of a given town? We saw above an example in which the local police asked advice on a case concerning an eagle in a local café. The officials ultimately asked the owner to remove the eagle from public display, which he did. Who was present when the gendarmes came in to talk to the café owner? Where was that eagle stored? Was it ever pulled out of storage to become the focus of good stories about the gendarmes and the Restoration government? or the good old days of the Empire?[77] Who might have been present when police officers showed up in bookstores and began tearing out pages of catechisms? What did the inhabitants think and feel, and how did they respond when they viewed the pile of seditious objects before they were burned on the pyre in the town of Orthez?[78]

On the most basic, material level, we know the campaign was at least a partial failure. Even where the *objets proscrits* were successfully replaced with appropriate monarchical and Christian symbols, is it not conceivable that the new objects served as reminders of what they had replaced? There were so many objects and sites which represented layers of memory. When the people in St-Saud in the Dordogne went to their town square and saw the new stone cross put up by the curé, did they ever think of the liberty tree which had stood there before?[79] When the people of Rouen walked into the central room of their city hall they would have seen a statue initially created to represent Minerva that had been transformed during the Revolution into a goddess of liberty. After much discussion, it was finally decided in January of 1816 that the statue was to be "returned to its original state" and left standing in the city hall.[80] This statue was removed for a short time in order to be appropriately stripped of its revolutionary attributes. Would the visitors to the city hall have noticed the change? When people went to church, to school, or into a bookstore, and used or bought a prayer book, they may have seen catechisms whose pages containing passages referring to Napoleon were shredded, or the offending passages crossed out. But seeing the missing pages or the black marks was also a reminder of what the regime was currently defining itself against. The goal of the regime's *mise-en-place* campaign was the total eradication of reminders of the Revolution and a purification of the political landscape. But the ability of even appropriate monarchical and Christian objects to jog people's memories about past regimes undermined the basic project.

From the reports it is clear that the government could not even claim to have wiped out all *public* examples of the *signes prohibés*. There are many examples of officials claiming that their "commune is entirely purified . . . ." Most reports confidently assure the minister of police that the officials in question "can certify that no [seditious objects] exist in the whole area of their department."[81] But at the same time, their reports also indicate the continued existence of objects they had not been able to locate. In one small town in the Seine-Inférieure, the mayor, thinking his campaign to clean up revolutionary symbols was at an end, learned that members of the local National Guard had simply turned their tricolor cockades inside out, and since there was white fabric on the inside they now "appeared" to be white cockades. In a postscript to his report he reassured his superior that he discovered that the tricolor cockades had been conserved *not* in a "spirit of opposition," but in an effort to economize, which made it more excusable.[82] For whatever reason they were conserved, these tricolor emblems, hidden on the undersides of the appropriate white counterparts, stood as evidence that the past had certainly not been erased without the possibility of *retour*. Other examples cited throughout these pages—such as the scarves which one prefect chose to separate into their component blue, white, and red parts to be given to charity—offer the same kind of tangible evidence of the past. In another case, involving the seal of the city of Bosquerard, the mayor explained, "the eagle still exists on the seal of the mayor's office; but when I am obliged to use it, I do so in such a way as to prevent the eagle from appearing, so that one sees only the words, 'Mairie du Bosquerard.'"[83] A little pressure in the wrong direction while applying the seal, and the eagle would have appeared—either accidentally or intentionally. How many such objects, having the outward appearance of monarchical emblems but concealing revolutionary emblems, remained in circulation?

Where the project was truly a failure was in the realm of private possessions. Flags and busts adorning public facades may have been effectively removed from view (or appropriately transformed), but the same cannot be said of the innumerable everyday objects bearing the prohibited signs which had been proliferating in French households for twenty-five years. As already noted, inventories of objects collected rarely refer to privately owned objects. Although some local officials, like the prefect of the Jura, took special care to assure his superior about the absence of privately owned seditious objects, ("very few busts and portraits of Bonaparte are to be found in the homes of private individuals"), usually this was not discussed. Evidence of widespread symbolic sedition from later on in the Restoration demonstrates that such "privately held" objects were very much in circulation. This leaves us with certain nagging questions regarding these *mise-en-place* ceremonies. What did it mean for a person to watch his or her local public official burn tricolor flags and make long speeches about the need to purify the landscape, and then to go home and eat dinner from a plate bearing scenes from great imperial victories, sit on a chair (or chamber pot) with liberty caps, take tobacco from a tricolor case and smoke it in a Napoleonic pipe? This is not merely a rhetorical question, for court records and police reports from the period 1816 through 1830 bear witness to the continued, if not renewed, importance of such revolutionary reminders in the daily lives of French people.

"The Old Flag," a song by Pierre Jean de Béranger from December of 1821, evokes the image of the hidden (in this case, Napoleonic) emblem preserving memories of more glorious days, and private hopes of political change:

> My old Companions in our days
>   Of glory greet me here;
> Drunk with remembrances, the wine
>   Hath made my memory clear:
> Proud of my own exploits and theirs,
> My flag my straw-thatched cottage shares.
>   Ah! when shall I shake off the dust
>   In which its noble colours rust?
> Beneath the straw where, poor and maimed,
>   I sleep, 'tis hid from view: . . .[84]

But is this what holding on to objects with insignia from the Revolution and the Empire meant for most French citizens? Perhaps it was simply a way of thumbing one's nose at authority. Or perhaps it was a way of remembering personal experiences with which they were associated. But perhaps it did represent an attachment to, or faith in, a political ideology in just the way that the revolutionaries had hoped it would some day. If so, to what ideology were they showing their allegiance? To Bonapartism? To republicanism? What did various symbols mean?

Of course the tricolor flag hidden away by the veteran of the Napoleonic campaigns was only the most glaring example of the kind of material reminder of the past which overtly threatened the regime; the whole range of material "reminders" evoked here—from the stone cross which had replaced the liberty tree, to the white cockades merely concealing their tricolor underside, to the extraordinary diversity of seditious objects among the private possessions of the population—all these tangible reminders revealed the failure of the politics of *oubli*, the utter impossibility of returning to a world where legitimate monarchy was a given, or the only alternative available. Indeed local officials furthered the revolutionaries' project by attaching new layers of political meaning to the now prohibited signs dating from the "ceremonial interregnum" when the Bourbon monarchs did not rule France: their *mise-en-place* ceremonies identified the symbols and practices of the Revolution and the Empire as the perfect vehicles for remembering, and eventually for opposing the current regime.

The Reluctant Commemoration of Regicide

The second public ceremony by which the regime practiced its politics of forgetting involved the commemoration of the executions of Louis XVI and Marie Antoinette. Just as representatives of the state did not use the *mise-en-place* ceremonies to evoke, but rather to efface, the memory of the Revolution, so did they *not* use the 21st of January and the 16th of October to condemn the French people for their actions in 1793 but rather to distance them from the single act which most seriously challenged the Bourbons' claim to legitimacy. Everything about the way in which the regime commemorated regicide underscores this fact, from the procedure followed in the annual days of mourning celebrated on the 21st of January and the 16th of October, to the nature of the monuments and coins produced in memory of these events. Even more than its *mise-en-place* ceremonies, the regime's reluctance to commemorate regicide clearly articulates the conception of monarchy put forth by the state in the postrevolutionary world. Avoiding as it did any allusions to the physical bodies of the king and queen, or the actual death of the "first body" of the king (and queen), the regime focused on the challenges posed by the temporary death of the "second body" of the king, the body politic in its monarchical incarnation, and simply avoided any evocations of the relationship between this and the mortal, "executed" body of the king.

In the fall of 1815, after the second return of the Bourbons, a proposal was put forth in the Chamber of Deputies for an annual celebration of the 21st of January, the anniversary of King Louis XVI's execution. The proposal itself denied the legitimacy of the assembly which voted to kill the king in 1793, denied the culpability of the French people in the "crime" of the execution, and asked for a ceremony that would give the people of France an opportunity to formally distance themselves from this crime. The proposal read:

> Given that this House is the first assembly legally elected under a legitimate government, which has freely exercised its powers since this unhappy epoch; given, that the only way to free the French from a crime of which they were never guilty, is to attest to their profound pain by a solemn act; given that the disavowal of this crime is a heartfelt act in which the entire French population would want to participate, I ask that his Majesty be asked to propose a law in which two things will be required: 1) A solemn service be conducted in every church in France to consecrate the painful memory of the 21st of January; 2) the same day be declared one of general mourning, to attest to the eternal regrets of all of the French.[85]

The proposal was well received and debate on the issue only concerned practical details, such as whether or not statues should also be erected in memory of King Louis XVI and other royal victims of the Revolution.

That this ceremony and the monuments to be erected were designed to reassert a particular conception of monarchy is clear from the language of the debate around it. In particular, a proposed amendment to the above law, which referred specifically to the erection of a monument for Louis XVI, recommended that a declaration be engraved on the monument which denied the role the nation played in the "parricide" committed on the 21st of January 1793. Furthermore, it contained an oath of fidelity to the legitimate monarchs of France, and to the fundamental and sacred right of primogeniture, from male to male, established by God in the family of Saint Louis, Henry IV, and Louis XVI. All of the members of the chambers were to sign this declaration and oath. The original text read:

> In the presence of God and our fellow men, we, the deputies of the French Nation declare, affirm that this nation, so long unhappy and captive, was not complicitous in the parricidal execution committed on the 21st of January 1793. . . . It is by the blood of this most august victim that, in front of God and our fellow men, on behalf of ourselves, our children, our nephews, and the France which we represent, we swear unshakable fidelity to our legitimate kings, regarding as a sacred and fundamental principle, the unalterable, imprescriptible right of heredity by primogeniture from male to male, of Henry IV, and of Louis XVI.[86]

Thus in the very framing of this ordinance we see the direct connection between reasserting loyalty and unshakable fidelity to legitimate monarchy and the erasure of the act of regicide, the exoneration of the population from the single act which overtly challenges "the unalterable, imprescriptible right of heredity by primogeniture . . . ." which this commemorative act was meant to solidify. On the 19th of January 1816, Louis XVIII signed and promulgated an abbreviated version of this law, making the 21st of January a day of mourning for the whole kingdom and requiring the celebration of a solemn service in every church in France in memory of the king. The law also stated that in "expiation for this unhappy day" a monument would be erected to Louis XVI.[87] The failure to actually erect such a monument, and the repeated efforts of the regime to exonerate the population from complicity in this crime, to evade graphic representations of violence, and to stress forgiveness rather than the need for expiation, demonstrate that if the regime employed the language of "expiation" in this law, this was certainly not the spirit which guided its approach to handling regicide.

The nature of the annual commemoration of the 21st of January prescribed by the king and carried out all over the country clearly illustrates this point. For the 21st of January, the government required only a modest ceremony in memory of the executed king, as a part of a mass in churches all over France. All civil servants were expected to attend this ceremony and to dress appropriately in black. Since the day was to be treated as a national day of mourning, all administrative offices were to be closed, as were stores, cafés, and cabarets. What is interesting is that the ceremony was explicitly *not* to include a sermon, but only a reading of the last will and testament of the late king. In the words of the circular sent to the archbishops of France in December of 1815, "It is the desire of the King, that on the 21st of January there be no funeral oration in the church, but only a reading of Louis XVI's Last Will and Testament; this is the most noble manner in which to remind the French of the great virtues of this Prince, and to renew the profound affection which these painful memories excite."[88] There were to be no speeches evoking the lurid details of the event, no condemnations from the pulpit of the French population's part in the act of execution; instead, the people would hear only Louis XVI's noble plea that his nation forgive and forget. The most important sections of the will to be read on this occasion underscored the king's own willingness to forgive. Referring to those who had imprisoned and were planning to execute him, the king wrote, "I pardon, with all my heart, all those who have made themselves my enemies without my having given them cause, and I pray that God will also pardon them, and I also pardon those who by a false zeal, or a misguided zeal, have greatly wronged me." Later in his will the message of forgetting and forgiving was addressed in particular to his son, the future king: "I recommend to my son, should he have the unhappiness to become King, to think of all that is required for the happiness of his fellow Citizens, that he must forget all hatred and all resentment and especially all that has any relation to the misery and grief that I am suffering."[89] What this translated into, in practice, was a ceremony which contained only the most abstract references to the act of regicide itself.

The same general principles shaped the commemoration of Marie Antoinette's execution: the 16th of October, like the 21st of January, was treated as a day of mourning, when people were expected to wear black, and when civil servants were expected to be present at a mass in the local church. Again, no sermon was to be read; but in this case the reading matter chosen was particularly interesting. For it bespoke an effort to use this occasion to clean up the image of the late queen. Portrayed as a libertine before the Revolution in the pornographic *libelles* which spread rumors of her sexual promiscuity, during her trial even the queen's sexual relationship with her own son was raised by the prosecution.[90] This was clearly a useful ploy, since the revolutionaries were trying to portray her as a doubly bad mother—of her nation as well as of her own child. Marie Antoinette's sister-in-law, Madame Elisabeth, was also implicated in this alleged incest. During the Restoration the reading the government chose for the ceremony commemorating Marie Antoinette's execution was the letter she wrote to this sister-in-law on the eve of her death, which explicitly denied the accusation of incest. The relevant passage of this letter apologized for the testimony of her son at her trial. "I have to talk to you about something which gives me great pain. I know how much this child must have made you suffer! pardon him, my dear Sister; think of how young he is, how easy it is to make a child say almost anything, especially about something he doesn't understand." Once the sexual crime was thus denied, the remainder of the letter emphasized the religiosity of the queen, for in the last passages of her letter she expressed her commitment to the Roman Catholic church and her desire to settle her sins with God before she died.[91] After 1824, when the death of Louis XVIII introduced the need for another day of mourning in October, the queen's memorial was shifted to the 21st of January, and the reading of her letter was suppressed. Thereafter, only the late king's demand for forgiveness and forgetting was intoned annually on the day set aside for commemorating the regicides of 1793.

On the local level some officials went beyond the minimum orders issued by the minister of the interior and celebrated the day of mourning for Louis XVI with considerably more pomp. In Marseilles, in 1818, bells were rung in all the churches, and a cannon fired on the eve of the anniversary as the sun set over the town. First thing in the morning on the 21st, the same sound was heard as all the vessels in the port lowered their flags to half-mast.[92] In the department of the Manche, a circular sent out by the prefect required the organization of a procession to the church in any town where the National Guard was organized.[93] In Troyes, inhabitants of the town were invited to hang white flags outside their homes, marked with black ribbons as a sign of mourning. A special invitation was also extended to all the inhabitants in the town to come to the church dressed in black—not just the usual civil servants.[94]

Everyone seemed to adhere to the minister of police's requirement that stores and especially cafés and cabarets be closed, but some required that they remain closed only for the duration of the church ceremony, while others extended the period of official mourning for up to a whole weekend.[95]

But in an extraordinary initiative from the local level, we find the resuscitation of the revolutionary practice of communal oath-taking, only this time used for counterrevolutionary ends. During the Revolution the oath of loyalty was a critical ritual because it underlined the contrast between national sovereignty, borne of the general will, and the authority of kings.[96] During the Restoration we find local officials using the same practice of the oath, but this time to reassert the king's sovereignty. In many cities registers were circulated, offering citizens of France the opportunity to take a solemn oath attesting that they had never participated in the initial killing of the king, and that they supported the legitimacy of the new monarch. The municipal council of Dieppe, for example, requested authorization from its prefect to open such a register in 1816, which members described as "a public register in which each of the inhabitants of this city could attest, by the addition of their signature, that he is completely innocent of the spilling of the blood of the unfortunate Louis XVI, and that he wishes to abandon to public execration that band of troublemakers and plotters upon whom alone the blame for such a crime should fall."[97] In the Drôme the prefect recommended that the subprefects and mayors of his department encourage the citizens of their towns and villages to take the oath, which was supposed to serve as the inscription for the monument to Louis XVI. The citizens of the department were supposed to go to their churches, approach the altar, offer remorse and tears, and take the following oath to God: "we swear unswerving fidelity to our legitimate kings, regarding the principle of hereditary primogeniture from male to male as a fundamental, sacred, and inalienable right, established by God in the family of Saint Louis." The prefect added another important vow of his own: "We promise him that we shall never again allow a usurper to rise amongst us."[98] The most successful register campaign seems to have taken place in the Manche, where the prefect claimed to have collected the signatures of over 60,000 people, expressing "horror, inspired by the murder committed against the sacred person of His Majesty the King, Louis XVI."[99] The language of this last prefect's report seems to stray the farthest from the national government's manner of commemorating regicide. Drawing attention to the "sacred person" of the king, this one local exception underscores how much the national government and most of its local officials used the commemoration of regicide to avoid evoking the bodies of the king and queen, and, when acknowledging the act of regicide, to associate it with a band of troublemakers acting outside of and against the general will.

Most of the reports on the local celebrations of the 21st of January were formulaic, and simply stressed the solemnity of the church service. A few officials were more enthusiastic. The prefect of the Hautes-Alpes, in a particularly positive report, explained that it was not surprising that the inhabitants of his department were extremely happy to have this pious ceremony, considering that during the Revolution "the deputies of this department showed themselves to be wholly loyal, and not one of them figured among those who saved their own skin by sacrificing that of the royal victim." [100] Some "positive" reports were clearly designed to reassure the national officials who were concerned about political opposition in certain towns. One letter from the prefect of Aisne proudly reported that the 21st of January was celebrated all over his department with "solemnity and the most sincere expressions of regret." In one town in particular, he added, "a spacious church was filled by the entire population of the town, ... I saw old people leave their retirement, and throw themselves at the foot of the altar, demanding God's pardon for a crime which they hadn't committed." But the rest of the letter throws some doubt on the veracity of this report. The prefect seemed to be responding to questions about "disturbances" which had plagued these ceremonies in his town before when he noted, "Seditious cries are becoming rarer; bringing some troublemakers before the local prosecutors, and seeing that rapid and severe justice was done, I clearly spread the message that such crimes would never rest unpunished, and the frequency of such acts immediately diminished." [101] One has to wonder if he did not exaggerate the enthusiasm of the retirees in his department to compensate for the seditious acts about which the minister of police was so concerned.

Occasionally reports directly indicated the unpopularity of this solemn occasion. The prefect from the Côte d'Or admitted just how badly a ceremony in his department went in 1816. "Last year the funeral celebration of the 21st of January had a chilly reception. Many churches were deserted, and the people appeared to be unmoved by the memories which this sad occasion evokes." But the prefect was pleased to report that the popular response was much improved the following year. "I have the great satisfaction of announcing to your Excellence, that the funeral was celebrated in a totally different manner this year." The churches in 1817 were apparently filled and "tears were shed in abundance" as the testament of the late king was read. It seems that some farmers got so upset during this part of the ceremony that they lost consciousness.[102]

In a number of cases, civil servants refused to participate, even though they were required by law to take part in the ceremony. In one town of the Bas-Rhin the justice of the peace, several key members of the city council, and other city officials did not show up at the ceremony. The prefect interpreted this as "a plot on the part of these civil servants to show their scorn for the august Bourbon family."[103] Similarly in the Lot-et-Garonne, one primary school teacher refused to attend the ceremony as he was supposed to, accompanied by his students. The teacher was suspended from his position for his insolence.[104]

For the ceremony of mourning orchestrated for the late queen the regime seemed to have more problems getting people to participate. The commissariat in Corsica complained: "In spite of the number of individual invitations which were proffered in the city, in spite of the ringing of the churchbells which, beginning the night before, solemnly announced this sacred service, the inhabitants did not come, and there were only a small number of women, mostly the wives of civil servants."[105] But it was not only in areas where people were known to support the ex-emperor that this ceremony was unpopular. In Le Havre the subprefect explained that the ceremony was attended by all of the officials in town, but that the local population was completely uninterested in the celebration. "[A]ll the civil servants came . . . but as to the part which the inhabitants of the city as a whole played in this ceremony, very few appeared at the church, and this day of mourning produced nothing but a sentiment of complete indifference among the masses."[106] There were some cases in which the civil authorities, required by law to attend, refused to participate.[107] In the Haut-Rhin the president of the local tribunal publicly refused to take part in the commemoration. When the prefect saw that he was absent from the ceremony, he sent a detachment of soldiers out to escort him to the church. When the soldiers reached his home they were informed by the president that he had no intention of going to the ceremony. They had no choice but to go back to the church without him.[108] More often, if the civil authorities chose not to attend, they did so less overtly. In Chateauroux, in the Indre, the officers of the National Guard, who were supposed to attend the ceremony, sent their subofficers to replace them. The prefect was

"scandalized" by this and required the officers to take part in the ceremony after all.[109]

In Rouen in 1822 the authorities expected critics of the regime to use
the occasion of the 16th of October to make "seditious cries against the
king." Special surveillance was established at the church, but no incident
followed.[110] The ceremonies in memory of the king and queen organized
by state officials did not always excite enthusiastic participation, but despite the occasional fears of the authorities, they also did not become
privileged occasions for the critics of the regime to perpetrate seditious
crimes. These, as we shall see in later chapters, were reserved for the
spectacles of the missionaries, who used the commemorations of the
21st of January and the 16th of October to attack the revolutionary
legacy more harshly, to evoke the guilt of the French population, and to
cement a new bond between the people and their Most Christian Kings.
To *these* commemorations there were quite passionate responses, both
for and against.

It is only after we compare the commemoration of regicide prescribed
by the state with the fervent, participatory spectacles of the missionaries
in the next chapter that the modesty of the regime's approach, its reluctance to represent the executions of the king and queen, will become
clear. From the archives of the police, from the reports of local functionaries on the official days of mourning on the 21st of January and the
16th of October, it is the *silence* which is deafening—silence about the
events of the Revolution, nationally or locally; silence about the violence
of the Terror; silence about the actual deaths of the king and queen. If
this silence can only be fully appreciated after we look carefully at the
expiatory denunciations of revolutionary violence conducted by the missionaries, the reality of the regime's reluctance to represent regicide can
be demonstrated by closely examining its other commemorative efforts
in the realm of monuments and coins.

The law of January 1816, which required the celebration of the 21st
of January and the 16th of October, included the stipulation that a
monument be erected on the site where Louis XVI and Marie Antoinette
were executed in "expiation" for these events; the consistent reluctance
on the part of the regime to actively represent regicide is demonstrated
by its repeated failure to carry out this project. After the first stone of
the monument had been put into place on the Place Louis XV in January of 1815, with a plaque which read "A Louis XVI, le 21 janvier,"
plans for the erection of a full-scale commemorative statue were dropped.
When Charles X came to the throne, he conceived the notion of finally

erecting this monument in the context of the Jubilee celebration in 1826; the monument representing regicide was to be the last of four stations where special expiatory prayers for the sins of the nation would be conducted. While the willingness of the new king to use the commemoration of regicide in this way bespeaks a logic closer to the missionaries and heretofore foreign to the state, in actuality the project was never achieved. The regime did not begin construction on the monument until 1827, and then the project was abandoned, supposedly because of squabbling over costs.[111] But the fact is that in spite of Charles X's inclinations, the regime never did support the use of commemorating regicide for anything but its politics of forgetting. Its failed effort to erect an expiatory chapel at the Madeleine illustrates the same point.

In 1816, Louis XVIII issued instructions that the Madeleine, the church refashioned under Napoleon as a "Temple of Glory," be turned into an expiatory church to the memory of Louis XVI, Marie Antoinette, and Madame Elisabeth. "Their statues in white marble had a place reserved for them," and for the altar was conceived "a statue of Saint Mary Magdalen, represented as a personification of France in an attitude of repentance."[112] Barthelemy Vignon, the architect hired by Napoleon to build the Temple of Glory, was given the task of transforming the Madeleine into an expiatory monument. As was true for the monument to regicide on the Place Louis XV, the Church of the Madeleine was never transformed into a monument of expiation. When Vignon died in 1828, he was buried in a vault under the church porch, but his ideas were never put into effect because of squabbles over finances and disagreements with the director of fine arts. It was not until after 1830 that a successor to Vignon was named, and clearly by then the impetus to commemorate regicide was past; in fact, for a short time the July Monarchy considered consecrating the building to the victims of the Three Glorious Days.[113] If these failed expiatory monuments tell us something about the regime's reluctance to represent regicide, the one successful commemorative site—the Conciergerie—demonstrates beautifully the logic the regime endorsed throughout its fifteen years in power when it came to representing the events of 1793.

The Conciergerie, the prison where Marie Antoinette was kept between August and October of 1793 while she awaited her trial and execution, was the one site which the Restoration regime successfully transformed into a "lieu de mémoire" for the Revolution.[114] Everything about the transformation of this site expressed the logic of *oubli* which guided this regime's commemoration of the Revolution. While called an

"expiatory chapel," this monument, as it was actually constructed under direct orders from King Louis XVIII, did, in fact, remain true to the
regime's politics of forgetting. The site was not used to evoke the horrific
events of August through October of 1793; indeed every change worked
to efface the traces of these tragic moments and to replace them with edifying emblems of the need to forget and forgive the events which transpired there. It was only in the context of the bicentennial of the Revolution that the Conciergerie was restored to its historic state; from 1816
until 1989 this monument and museum expressed the message which
the Restoration regime consistently uttered regarding the events of the
previous twenty-five years. The current guidebook to the Conciergerie
describes the changes effected during the Restoration in a way that un-
derlines this fact.

> In the form in which it was created this expiatory monument radically trans-
> formed the prison cell of the queen, even in its very essence. From a miser-
> able, bare place, it became a fully-furnished, almost luxurious private chapel;
> from a closed and anguished space, it became an annex or prolongation of
> the prison's chapel, a site for prayer. Many people have accused Peyre [the
> architect responsible for these changes] of having acted without nuance, with
> a serious lack of archeological scruples. This is to forget the fact that his
> changes were supported and directed by the desire of Louis XVIII to suppress
> or do away with the dungeon; this wretched site was supposed to have dis-
> appeared in order to re-emerge in a completely different form, at once more
> banal (but more bearable) and idealized. Worries about historical integrity
> played no role at all in the construction of this monument; the only thing that
> mattered was the clear and coherent political and religious goal it was meant
> to achieve.[115]

What, precisely, were the changes made? Before the transformation,
Marie Antoinette's cell was part of a larger room, also shared by her
guards, and separated by a wall from the adjacent chapel. When the
room was remade in 1816, a wall was erected between the queen's space
and that of the guards, and the wall dividing her from the chapel was removed. The actual bed in which Marie Antoinette slept in her cell was
removed, and in its place was erected an altar, equipped with a crucifix
given by Louis XVIII, which was supposed to have been used by the late
queen during her time in this prison. Thus all physical traces of the
queen's incarceration were removed from what had been her cell: the
guards were gone, the bed was gone; and the space she occupied was
sanctified by the altar, by the crucifix, and by the new connection with
the adjoining chapel.[116]

The cenotaph made of marble, erected in the original chapel of the prison, completes the message of cleansing, pardoning, and forgetting which the transformation of the cell accomplished. It bears two inscriptions: the upper half, written in Latin by Louis XVIII, says:

> On this site, Marie Antoinette, Jeanne of Austria, the widow of Louis XVI, after the death of her husband and the removal of her children, was thrown into prison, where she remained for seventy-six days in anxiety, mourning, and abandon. But strengthened by her courage, she showed herself to be, in chains as she was on the throne, greater than her fortune. Condemned to death by criminals, awaiting her death, she wrote an eternal monument to piety, courage, and all the virtues on 16 October 1793. All who come here, adore, admire, and pray.[117]

The second excerpt is in French, and reiterates the plea from Louis XVI's last will and testament, to which the queen's final letter alludes:

> That my son never forget the last words of his father which he repeated explicitly for him, that he never try to avenge our death. I pardon all of my enemies for the ills they have done to me.[118]

The decorations commissioned for the chapel offered an expiatory narrative to make sense of the events which transpired there. Of the three paintings chosen to adorn the three walls of the chapel, the first featured the queen in her cell, looking peacefully out the window; the second showed her being separated from her family at the Temple (where they were all imprisoned until August of 1793); and the third showed her taking communion in her cell. None of the paintings actually refer to her execution, and the final canvas represents an historically impossible scene, for the queen is represented as receiving the sacraments from a refractory priest, the Abbé Maguin, in full regalia. This third painting, interestingly, replaced an original commissioned for the site, a canvas which represented the queen at the moment when she wrote to the august princess the letter which was read at her funeral commemorations between 1815 and 1824.[119] According to one art historian, the three scenes do much more than evoke three historical moments in the life of this royal prisoner; taken together "they retrace the sufferings and the torments of the queen who, in the name of faith, accepts to sacrifice her own innocent blood and to pardon her executioners. . . . in this way her sacrifice is paralleled to that of Christ. By her martyrdom, Marie Antoinette cleanses the crimes committed during the Terror, she becomes France's redemptress."[120] This message was common fare in the expiatory spectacles of the Missions to the Interior. But for the regime it was quite exceptional, and within this very monument the expiatory message was less important than the transformations to the site itself which emphasized erasure of the past, forgiveness for the acts commemorated there, and the general effort to rehabilitate the queen's image in a positive light.[121]

As a rule, the regime either avoided erecting monuments in expiation for the executions of the king and queen, or when they succeeded they used them as an opportunity to encourage forgetting and forgiveness. The same reluctance to commemorate regicide can be seen in the way in which the regime chose to represent this act in medals. The regime issued medals in commemoration of most of the important occasions marking this period.[122] The regime issued seven medals on the subject of the executions of the king and queen. None of them featured any direct reference to the act of regicide which was mourned annually. On one medal engraved by the Baron de Puymaurin, who was *directeur de la Monnaie* from 1816 to 1830, the deaths of the king, his sister, and the queen were commemorated, but without reference to their execution. The front of this coin featured the joined busts of Louis XVI in uniform, with Marie Antoinette and Madame Elisabeth in court dress, and contained an inscription around the edge which read, "Louis XVI, Marie-Antoinette D'Aut., P.M.H. Elisabeth de Fr." The reverse side contained an inscription between two palms which read, "Son / of Saint Louis / rose to heaven / 21 January 1793 / 16 October 1793 / 10 May 1794." All the other medals drew attention to the regime's commemorative efforts rather than to the executions they actually commemorated. One medal featured the exhumation of the remains of the Bourbon monarchs, while another showed the transfer of their ashes to Saint-Denis. Another medal commemorated the setting of the first stone of the monument in the Place Louis XV (which was never completed). The last medal struck celebrated the construction of the expiatory chapel at the Eglise de la Madeleine (even though, as we have seen, the chapel itself was never achieved).[123]

Just as we will compare the expiatory celebrations of the missionaries with the restrained days of mourning organized by the regime, we need only compare these medals with those by which émigrés commemorated the killing of members of the royal family in order to recognize the degree to which the Restoration regime avoided graphic references to the acts of the Revolution which directly assaulted the institution of monarchy.[124] Most of the émigrés' medals featured guillotines and the royal victims, either being transported to the executioner's block or after they had been killed, and included such inscriptions as "Cry and seek revenge!" [125] One represented France as a beast with the head of a sow and the tail of a serpent lancing its venom, with one paw resting on the severed head of Louis XVI.[126] A medal commemorating the killing of the queen featured a madwoman with an ax in one hand and a torch in the other marching and trampling a field of royal lilies. The inscription read, "Second victim of a regicidal people." [127] In a set of medals commemorating the execution of other family members—Madame Elisabeth and Philippe Egalité—the people of France were represented, in one, as a pack of wolves attacking a dove and, in the other, as a serpent encircling a crown, a scepter, and a sword.[128] The contrast between these violent and judgmental medals and those issued by the Restoration regime is striking.

But in its approach to regicide, as in its approach to the whole range of events and reminders which were the legacy of the past twenty-five years, the regime showed itself to be remarkably consistent and steadfast; if it was to confront the "ceremonial interregnum" when the Bourbons did not reign in France, it was only to encourage its subjects to forget it. If its *mise-en-place* ceremonies and its reluctance to commemorate regicide dramatized the regime's politics of *oubli,* its commitment to this policy will become clearer still when we examine the efforts of local government officials to contend with their supporters in the church who, throughout the Restoration, adopted a radically different approach to casting the revolutionary past in relationship to monarchy and its future.

CHAPTER TWO

The Missionaries

Expiation and the Resacralization
of the King's Two Bodies

In 1820, between the 2nd of January, when a procession featuring 3,000 *pénitents* marked the opening of a mission in Marseilles, and the 27th of February, when an even more extravagant procession and ceremony marked its close, the inhabitants of Marseilles were invited to participate in a religious revival.[1] Led by eighteen clergymen from the national Missionaries of France, with Charles de Forbin-Janson at their head and five missionaries from a regional society, the revival was made possible by the assistance of local clergymen, urged on by the vociferous support of the archbishop of Aix. Instead of the usual commercial activities and festivities associated with the carnival season, the city of Marseilles was transformed for eight solid weeks by the spiritual efforts of these zealous missionaries, intent upon returning its inhabitants to a strict adherence to the sacraments, too long abandoned by this increasingly incredulous or at least nonpracticing population.[2]

The extensive efforts of the clergy assembled in Marseilles to bring the parishioners back into their churches, to confess their sins, and to reconsecrate their lives to Christ by the taking of the sacraments are attested to by the exhaustive and exhausting labor of the priests, who worked daily from 4 o'clock in the morning until 8 o'clock at night, scheduling church services, confessions, and retreats at all hours in an effort to make themselves available to a majority of the population. Their message was an austere one: they denounced simple pleasures such as dancing and the theater; they inveighed against the immoral and irreligious writings of Voltaire and Jean-Jacques Rousseau, and against the many "dangerous" novels they accused of "poisoning" the local population. They willingly employed terrifying tactics, such as preaching from a cemetery over an open grave, surrounded by bones and with a skull in their hands, to threaten those outside the kingdom of Christ with eternal damnation.

While "private" sins were addressed in the priests' sermons and services, "communal" sins, particularly those committed during the course of the Revolution, often provided the focus for their efforts. By their own account, the most successful of their services was held on the 21st of January, when "evoking at the same time the Passion of the Son of God and the suffering of the martyr-king Louis XVI," the Père Guyon succeeded in provoking the wave of confessions that would bind the people of Marseilles both to their God, through the sacrifice of his son, Jesus Christ, and to their new king, Louis XVIII, the successor to the martyr, Louis XVI.[3] This critical religious and political message was repeated regularly throughout the mission—at the end of separate retreats for men, women, and soldiers, and in larger outdoor ceremonies, when the priests led their followers in the *amendes honorables,* or the public confessions for sins against God and their king, practices common under the reigns of the Most Christian Kings of the Old Regime, but newly resurrected in the religious and political expiatory ceremonies of these missionaries.

The specific connection between the need to expiate for the Revolution and the reassertion of the legitimate authority of the resacralized kings was made clear in sermons as well as in rituals and symbols at the center of the mission. In sermons, priests preached against every aspect of the Revolution: the killing of the king and queen, of course, but also practices which implicated their auditors more directly, such as the traffic in *biens nationaux,* the oaths taken by constitutional priests to the revolutionary state, and the civil ceremony for marriage. Missionaries in Marseilles used their ceremonies to invoke the public landscape of the Revolution, particularly drawing attention to its most violent episodes. The final procession was carefully orchestrated around two sites where the guillotine had stood during the revolutionary period: at the first a communal confession was organized; at the second, Forbin-Janson gave a rousing sermon which ended with the invocation, "No more victims. No more executioners." This ceremony was concluded with the erection of a massive cross, requiring 3,000 men to carry it; the site of the cross was carefully chosen, again to evoke the local geography of the Revolution, and particularly the violence turned against the Catholic church.[4]

After weeks of debating potential sites for the cross, the missionaries agreed upon the spot where a cross had been violently destroyed during the Revolution.[5]

If the missionaries evoked the revolutionary period and reminded the population of its part in the sinful events of the previous twenty-five years, it was in order to use their confessions and expiation for these events to reestablish the sacred bond linking the people to their king and their God, and to make possible, once again, the reign of their Most Christian Kings, according to the model of the Eucharist. If the *amendes honorables* intoned throughout the mission made this point clear, it was in the final erection of the mission crosses that this conception of monarchy was symbolically achieved in a way which left lasting traces for the inhabitants of Marseilles. In preparation for the final procession and erection of the cross, the inhabitants were encouraged to decorate their homes with a mixture of Christian and monarchical emblems: white flags and crosses greeted the procession as it snaked its way for eight hours through the city of Marseilles. As it went by, spectators were exhorted to repeat the cry "Long live Jesus! and Long live the King!"

The activities of the missionaries incited minor opposition, but nothing so serious as to compromise the essential success of the mission of 1820. One placard posted in the middle of the night threatened the arrival of troops who were purportedly preparing an attack on the women taking part in the exercises in the church; but before it could have any impact, this incitement to rumor and panic was quickly taken down by the authorities. Early in the mission some troublemakers disturbed the opening exercises in the church when they threw stones and dead and living cats into the middle of the congregation. In spite of the missionaries' harangues against the sinful pleasures of the theater, the police reported that "the theater is frequented, as usual, and it does not appear that the mission has deprived it of its regular devotees." The theatergoers also turned this venue against the missionaries when they requested a performance of the anticlerical *Tartuffe*, a request which was granted, giving the audience the opportunity to mock the visiting priests directly by greeting some of the passages of the play "with a bit more applause than was customary."[6]

A local liberal paper, *Le Phocéen*, attacked every aspect of the missionaries' efforts. Reprinting a brief letter from bakers, the paper gave voice to the material concerns of citizens whose livelihoods were threatened by the missionaries' determination to supplant local festivities associated with carnival. Another letter, this time from a bookstore owner,

played with the epithet of "poisoner" used by clergymen to describe the
philosophes, and turned it against the missionaries themselves: evoking
the discord and disorder sown by the mission, the article appealed to
public reason to decide "at this moment upon whom should justly fall
the odious title of public poisoners?"[7] Echoing the language of *Tartuffe*
already directed against the missionaries in the theater, the paper ridi-
culed the spectacular tactics of the so-called "sacred jugglers," whose
"profane pomp" had succeeded in "seducing" even the well-educated
population, who should have known better than to fall victim to the
trickery of "impostors" and "hypocrites." Linking the efforts of the missionaries in Marseilles to the national campaign of these so-called "apostles of the counterrevolution," the paper concluded with a letter from
the Isère, which evoked memories of the worst violence of the revolutionary period in its chilling portrait of the dangers of the current religious revival:

> People who lived in Brittany in [17]93, recognized in the ceremonies of these
> traveling priests, the same gestures, the same signs of rallying which were in
> the departments of the West, when priests were at the head of the insurgents
> of the Vendée. . . . Armed fanatics, who with a candle in one hand and a red
> cross in the other, seemed to demand blood more than the remission of their
> sins; . . . all of this creates consternation in the spirit of good citizens.

The national threat posed by the missionaries, and the fact that their activities could be read as a plot to undermine the solid and peaceful foundations of the realm, were evoked as the author enjoined his readers
to be vigilant and to help foil the plot of these so-called "Jesuits" by
addressing themselves directly to their king: "If the representatives of
France aren't careful, the bands of Loyola will have done irreparable
harm. A religious civil war is imminent in our region, and if courageous
voices don't warn the throne in time, this scourge produced by the missionaries will spread rapidly and touch all the points of the realm."[8]
This threat seemed serious to inhabitants of Marseilles, a city which was
particularly divided and violent between 1792 and 1794, but also more
recently during the White Terror of 1814–1815.

There is no evidence that the majority or even a significant minority
of the population of Marseilles was involved in the protests against the
missionaries, or shared the histrionic fears expressed in this particular
newspaper; however, the belief that this could come to pass, that such
an interpretation of the missionaries' campaign could come to dominate
local consciousness, led the local prefect into continuous negotiations

with both his superiors in Paris and the members of the local church establishment regarding the pressing need to manage the mission. Even before the missionaries set foot in Marseilles, this Catholic and royalist prefect found himself in the embarrassing position of trying to block the mission from taking place; when that failed, the prefect focused his energy on policing the missions and on doing what he could to clearly differentiate the actions and views of the missionaries from those of the local civil administration, and thereby obviate any interpretation of the mission which could support fears of a clerical plot. The prefect tried, without success, to respond to protests concerning the timing of the mission by encouraging the missionaries to postpone their revival until after the carnival season. He tried to restrict the missionaries to the interiors of churches, to block evening services, and to prohibit special ceremonies, such as those held in the cemetery, from taking place. When outright prohibition failed, the prefect turned to more discreet measures to control and contain the mission's message and potentially pernicious consequences. He placed secret agents at the ceremonies and negotiated with the priests over the contents of their sermons and other details, such as the placement of the mission cross, always working to prevent the missionaries from sowing discord and giving troublemakers opportunities to express their overt opposition. Invitations from the clergy to participate in the mission were regularly refused by civil officials who saw the necessity of avoiding the public impression that the missionaries enjoyed their sanction. This was true for every one of their processions, but it was regarding the commemoration of the 21st of January, when the missionaries most clearly deviated from the regime's official policy of *oubli,* that the prefect explained to the minister of the interior the need for the administration to distance itself from the mission: "The President of the Tribunals, the Mayor, and I were invited to the [missionaries' religious ceremony on the 21st of January], but since among the public one would suppose that this ceremony was a continuation of the morning's funeral service, . . . we thought it appropriate not to appear at the missionaries' commemoration." [9]

The archbishop of Aix, Monseigneur de Bausset-Roquefort, vociferously defended the missionaries in Marseilles, opposing every effort on the part of the civil authorities to intervene in the revival; in the correspondence through which he voiced his opposition to the prefect's measures one can see the deeper political issues at stake in the orchestration of the mission. Inherent in the defense made by the archbishop was the portrait of a Christian nation, finally reunited under the spiritual guidance of its priests, with the official sanction and support of the restored Christian king. In response to quite specific problems raised by the prefect—that evening services offered occasions for disorder, that external processions and mission crosses offered opportunities for critics to attack the church and therefore to sow disorder—the archbishop consistently denied the existence of any real opposition to Christianity resuming its proper role as the public religion, linking its members in a devotion to their God and king. Categorically denying any space for controversy, the archbishop simply refused to acknowledge any of the events of the past century which had served to make the relationship between religion and politics, between church and state, an arena for struggle. Refuting the prefect's fears that the mission would sow discord, he explained: "Religion, very far from destroying order and public tranquility, has always contributed to the maintenance of both." He saw in the local administrators' efforts to police the mission nothing less than a return to the worst persecution of the revolutionary decade. The archbishop argued that to yield to any of the local officials' demands, and to eliminate from the missions "all that is meant to touch, to edify, to attract, and to convert," would be to lose for "a second time, a part of the spiritual advantages which we have had the happiness of recovering with the return of our very Christian king, and the grandson of St. Louis." [10]

The struggles between local and ecclesiastical officials were publicized to some extent by the liberal newspaper, which applauded the efforts of the local administration to temper the mission; but, according to police reports, the missionaries themselves made manifest their disagreements with the prefect and his subordinates, and flaunted their determination to carry on in the name of the higher authority of their king. Responding to the prefect's request that the missionaries avoid preaching in the cemetery, Forbin-Janson apparently announced "that he had no need to heed the local authority, that he had in his pocket orders from the king that permitted him to do anything he believed appropriate." The police report acknowledged "that it is not certain that Monsieur de Forbin-Janson spread this news, but it is certain that he has always acted in a manner which would make everyone believe it." [11] In a later report, quoting a supposedly reliable source, the prefect offered a portrait of the mission and the way it was being perceived in Marseilles, which gave him great cause for concern, and which obviously motivated his vigorous efforts to control the missionaries. The view that was circulating through town was that "since the Mission of France was authorized and recognized by the Government, the missionaries had powers which were so extensive, that when they arrived in a town to exercise their ministry, the local ecclesiastical authorities [and civil authorities] had no authority." [12]

At issue in the struggles between civil and ecclesiastical officials over the staging of the mission in Marseilles was the deeper question of the appropriate jurisdiction of missionaries, of the established church, and of the state (both the king and his representatives in the local arena) in spiritual and political matters. That spiritual matters were explicitly political was articulated in the sermons, rituals, and symbols of the missionaries, which consistently reiterated the message that the religious reconversion of the inhabitants of Marseilles was part of a broader political restoration of Christian kingship in France. The archbishop's defense of the mission, and his refusal to yield to intervention on the part of the civil authorities, only emphasized the political stakes involved in this religious revival. Likewise, the prefect's efforts to manage the mission, his sensitivity to the way in which the inhabitants of Marseilles might interpret the public spectacles of the mission, in particular in relationship to the civil authorities and the government in general, all bespeak an awareness of the political significance of the religious revival. For the prefect, the mission was a "political" problem because it threatened public order, because it sowed fears that the civil order, extending up to the king, was under the control of so-called "Jesuits," and because the vision of the political order defining the missions was directly at odds with the vision the regime he represented was trying to propagate and enforce. As was true for many of his colleagues working within the civil administration, the prefect was trying to manage the staging of monarchy on the local level.

Far from being exceptional, the key features of the mission of Marseilles were reproduced all over France, in the context of more than 1,500 revivals staged in cities, smaller towns, and in the countryside over the course of the Restoration. This religious revival, generally supported by the church establishment, was a mass movement which touched a majority of French men and women and which had profound political significance and consequences. Truly the mass spectacles of the Restoration period, drawing crowds in the tens of thousands, these missions helped to define the political culture of this period, offering as they did a particular conception of monarchy and its relationship to its past and present subjects. Working to do nothing less than reconstruct the juridical, religious, and ceremonial foundations of monarchy "by the Grace of God," under assault in France since the seventeenth century,

the missionaries staked out a vast terrain in which the complex negotiations over the nature of legitimate authority would be played out over
the fifteen years of the Restoration.

The Missions to the Interior of the Restoration have been the focus of
an ambitious study by the historian Ernest Sevrin, published in two volumes in the 1950s.[13] The first volume offers an overview of the missions,
while the second covers the period between 1815 and 1822 in detail, going mission by mission. The author intended to follow this up with another volume on the rest of the Restoration but died before this work
could be completed. While Sevrin acknowledged the political intentions
and consequences of the missionaries' efforts, this was secondary to this
primary objective of documenting the spiritual goals and accomplish-
ments of their national religious revival. In the following analysis I draw
liberally upon the research already accomplished by Sevrin, particularly
where the organizational history of the missions is concerned, and for
the early missions of the period. But this is complemented by my own archival research, which is especially important for the years Sevrin did not
complete. When I do use Sevrin's material it is primarily to demonstrate
the political ambitions and consequences of this religious movement.[14]

Restoration France:
A Spiritual Desert in Need of Missions

Just as in Marseilles, where the mission of 1820 was requested by local
ecclesiastical authorities and orchestrated in order to return the inhabitants of this city to the practices and beliefs of the national faith too long
abandoned by its population, so was the national missionary movement
of the Restoration inspired first and foremost by the pressing need to administer emergency aid to a country whose religious state was considered to be disastrous from all points of view. When the Bourbons re-
sumed the throne in 1814 the Catholic church was in a weakened state,
and the population was distanced from the practices and teachings of
the national faith. Having lost its material base during the Revolution,
when church lands and the lands of their émigré benefactors were sold
off as *biens nationaux,* the church also suffered an acute crisis of personnel in the early nineteenth century: in 1815, 7,000 of the 50,000
ecclesiastical posts were vacant, and given the rate of deaths and ordinations, this number was expected to rise to 25,000 vacancies by 1820–
21.[15] In some dioceses as many as one-third to one-half of ecclesiastical

posts were empty, making it impossible for the population to practice the rites of Catholicism properly, even if the people were so inclined.[16] But according to commentators from the period, the events of the previous century had also weakened this inclination. In the early years of the Restoration, the leading Catholic periodical, *L'Ami de la Religion et du Roi,* offered a portrait of the religious state which demonstrated the pressing need for a revival. Apparently the rites of Catholicism had fallen into disuse where many women and, in some regions, the vast majority of men abstained from the sacraments. A large number of young people and adults had not been confirmed, had never followed catechism, or had never taken their first communion; some had never even been baptized. Work on Sunday and blasphemies of all sorts had become common. Irregular unions, invalid marriages (performed by constitutional priests), or marriages contracted on a purely civil basis during and after the Revolution had multiplied. This portrait of a nation of Christians, wandering on their own in a spiritual desert, led many to see missions as the sole means of saving France.[17]

As early as 1814, when one of the future leaders of the Missionaries of France, Forbin-Janson, went to see the pope to discuss his plans for a mission to China, the pontiff encouraged the priest to focus his energy at home: "Your project is good, but it is necessary first to offer our aid to the populations which surround us. France needs missions for its people and retreats for its clergy."[18] Forbin-Janson immediately returned to France, and, together with his colleagues Jean-Baptiste Rauzan and René-Michel Legris-Duval, presented a "Memoir for the King on the Establishment of Missions for France" to launch this much-needed religious revival. Underscoring the desperate need for a revival in their country in 1814, this memoir opened with the suggestion that "perhaps there is no nation whose political and moral state demands the aid of a spiritual mission more imperiously than France."[19] This proposal contained a specific program for a national missionary organization, with independent funds to respond especially to the large number of vacant ecclesiastical posts, and also for the reestablishment of the Calvary of Mont-Valérien outside Paris as their operational base, a venue long favored by the royal family for its spiritual exercises, and a site where during the Revolution the calvary itself had been destroyed, the resident priests chased away, and the church attacked. Louis XVIII apparently read this memoir with interest, accorded an audience to its authors, and generally approved their plan, acknowledging that when he was in exile he had himself conceived of the project of rechristianizing France through missions. The budgetary details were avoided in these early negotiations, but the king immediately gave his support for the plan to restore Mont-Valérien.[20] By 1815 the founders of the Missions of France, having recognized the Abbé Rauzan as their leader, submitted their project for a missionary movement to the most distinguished priests in Paris; the *vicaires capitulaires* of Paris approved their plan on the 9th of January 1815, arguing "that missions would be the most favorable means, perhaps the only means, to shore up at the same time religion and the social order."[21] They needed money, they needed recruits; to publicize their project and get both, they published a prospectus in *L'Ami de la Religion et du Roi*. They established a committee of women, patronesses of the missions, to help with fund raising. Because Mont-Valérien was still in ruins in 1815, and therefore uninhabitable, the missionaries took up temporary residence in Paris, in a house at 8, Rue Notre Dame des Champs; the rent for this first transitional year was liberally covered by the king. Although they began to organize revivals immediately in the areas surrounding Paris, the Hundred Days interrupted the missionaries' plans, which were taken up anew as soon as Napoleon was defeated a second time.

Between January and September of 1816 Mont-Valérien was restored, first the calvary, then the three chapels; the inauguration of all these was celebrated on the 14th of September 1816 at the Festival of the Exaltation of the Holy Cross. Thereafter, services were conducted regularly, with curés from Paris accompanying their congregations to this site to renew the ancient devotion of previous kings and their Parisian subjects to this particular cross. But in order to make Mont-Valérien the center of a national missionary organization, a proper seminary for training and organizing missions for the whole of France, Rauzan submitted a request for legal authorization, which he believed would encourage bishops to send him recruits, and also garner for his organization the financial base the missionaries needed to operate. Therefore a new memoir was penned by Rauzan, with the intention of firmly establishing his Society of Missionaries. Louis XVIII responded favorably, and in an ordinance signed on the 25th of September 1816, he accorded the missionaries legal status.

The text of this ordinance is interesting, because it clearly expresses the king's support for the missions on the grounds of their necessity, related explicitly to the severe shortage of ecclesiastical personnel in

France. In the king's words, "the small number of priests attached to particular churches being insufficient to attend to the needs of the dioceses of our realm, and the Society of Priests of the Missions of France, offering a powerful assistance to the curés and parishes deprived of pastors . . . [this society] is hereby authorized." But even in this early ordinance, the king clearly circumscribed the missionaries' action, insisting that they were always to operate with the explicit "authorization of the archbishops and bishops of our realm," and that missions could furthermore be sent out only in response to "the demands of bishops in the dioceses where they would operate, and after our authorization."[22] Thus, while acknowledging the need to minister to the population's spiritual needs in light of the large number of vacant ecclesiastical posts, the king carefully limited the missionaries to working under the auspices of the established church, and with his, the king's, express authorization.[23] These terms would become extremely important over the course of the Restoration, when a variety of organizations orchestrated their missions with or without this national organization being approved by the king, and when the missionaries in general began to exceed their initial, modest spiritual mission of attending to their flock in the absence of pastors.

If the Missionaries of France was the only society to enjoy official royal authorization, many other associations of priests worked in concert with this group as well as on their own to rechristianize France between 1815 and 1830. The Jesuits constituted the most important group to assist in the national missionary movement in these years, although, by direct orders from the king, they were to do so, "not in the name or the habit of their order," but under the authority of bishops, who were free to use them liberally as educators or as missionaries.[24] Given the long history of distrust vis-à-vis the Jesuits, this was clearly a prudent measure; but as we already saw in the case of Marseilles (where Jesuits were *not* involved), it did not prevent critics of the missions from associating the revivals of these years with the Order of Loyola, the hated *hommes noirs* castigated throughout the Restoration by the liberal press and by popular songwriters such as Pierre Jean de Béranger. Particularly after the Père Guyon, one of the most important leaders and orators serving the Missionaries of France, became a Jesuit in 1821, it became easier to associate the missions of the Restoration with this hated order, presumed to be operating under direct orders from the pope in spite of the king's efforts to contain their spiritual ministries within the framework of the missions authorized and approved by the French church hierarchy.[25]

The other groups of missionaries which participated in the national movement were regional, or restricted to a diocese. The Oblats de Marie, for example, which cooperated with the Missionaries of France to organize the mission of Marseilles in 1820, led missions throughout the Restoration under the leadership of the Abbé Eugène de Mazenod, but they restricted their activities to the southwest of France. Likewise, missionary organizations in Besançon, Lyons, Tours, Toulouse, and Rennes worked in concert with the national organization, but mainly orchestrated missions in their respective regions. This is not because some of the leaders of these regional organizations did not have a vision or ambitions to train missionaries for a national movement; in fact there were many efforts to found such seminaries, but they all failed.[26] There were many other smaller organizations aiding in missions restricted to a single diocese or even a single parish; Sevrin identifies more than forty-five such organizations at the local level.[27] Generally these were not long-standing organizations but rather fleeting associations of missionaries brought together for individual missions. These were often organized by bishops who took advantage of the funds made available by the king to pay for auxiliary priests, or *prêtres de secours*.[28]

While a huge variety of priests, of different ages, regions, and orders, participated in the missionary movement, there are certain features they all shared, which undoubtedly gave this revival a certain spirit. Most important, the older missionaries had almost all been in exile or hiding during the Revolution, and if they returned during the Empire they were usually battling against the Concordat as they tried to orchestrate missions in those years. The younger missionaries, while having no direct experience of the Revolution, or even the Empire, tended to share the radical counterrevolutionary stance typical of the older priests and émigrés. In general they were driven more by moral fervor than by intellectual or scholarly prowess.[29] In their efforts to orchestrate local revivals they were supported by a church hierarchy which was increasingly noble and outspokenly opposed to the legacy of the French Revolution.[30]

Between 1815 and 1830, over 1,500 missions were orchestrated in France.[31] Of the eighty dioceses in France in 1821, only one, Cambrai, was untouched by missions. Some regions were more favored by missionaries than others, with Provence, Brittany, and the Lorraine enjoying the most active and repeated revivals. While missions in departmental capitals, capitals of *arrondissements,* and bishoprics figure most largely in the archival evidence and periodical press, the majority of missions appear to have taken place in the countryside.[32] The number of people participating in these missions was prodigious, by all accounts. Missionaries recorded the numbers of people confessing and participating in mass communions, as well as the numbers of people participating in or at least attending their outdoor processions; as civil officials tried to keep track of the missionaries' activities and preserve order, they too regularly reported on participation in different aspects of the mission. The numbers of those confessing and taking the sacraments stretch from the hundreds into the thousands depending on the mission and the size of the local populations. The churches were usually filled to capacity throughout the mission, and even in towns where the missions were declared "less successful" by their supporters the participants and spectators for the outdoor procession as much as doubled the populations of towns. When a particularly talented orator (such as the Père Guyon) gave a sermon the crowd could swell to 60,000, as it did in Avignon in 1819.[33] If audiences of that number were rare, crowds between 10,000 and 20,000 were quite common. In Arles there were reports of 12,000; in Blois, 14,000; in Carcassonne and Clermont-Ferrand, 20,000; and in Cherbourg, 25,000.

Ascertaining the relationship between the missionaries, sent out by a wide variety of organizations, and the established church during the Restoration is a complicated matter; however, in general, the rules set up by the king in his authorization of the Missionaries of France in 1816 held sway throughout the period, and the missions were therefore only permitted with the explicit authorization of the local church hierarchy. In large cities missions took place because they were requested by the bishops, or at least approved if the initiative did not come from them. In Sevrin's analysis of the missions, he identified only two of the 118 resident bishops who were openly hostile to the missions, 22 whose opinion is unknown, and 94 who requested or authorized the missions.[34] Hostility to the missionaries seemed more widespread at the lower levels of the church hierarchy: parish clergymen often opposed missions, or sided with their congregations in criticizing specific aspects of the missions once they were under way.[35] But overall, it would be impossible to explain the sheer quantity and geographical range of the missions without assuming the basic material and spiritual support of the established church at the local level.

While the variety of organizations involved in orchestrating the missions and the particularities of the contexts in which they were conducted necessarily distinguished individual missions from one another, there was sufficient consistency among them to justify talking about them together as constituting a national movement. If Ernest Sevrin separated his monumental analysis of the missions into two separate volumes, one of which looked at the missions taken as a whole, it was precisely because there was a "mass of details which characterized all of the missions." [36] Everywhere, one sees the same daily rituals in churches and retreats; the same extravagant ceremonies (similar in their timing, their content, and the ways in which they were orchestrated); the same content in sermons and, most important, the same religious and political message which all these tactics were deployed to propagate. It is precisely by attending to such "details" that it will be possible to understand how this national mass movement shaped the political culture of the Restoration in ways which hitherto have been unappreciated.

Rechristianizing France: Remaking the Body of the Church

Conceived with the intention of ministering to a population in desperate need of spiritual guidance, the missions of the Restoration, in Sevrin's view, had first and foremost a religious goal: to reintroduce an increasingly incredulous population to the teachings of the national faith, to administer the sacraments too long ignored, in short, to convince the people of France to accept Jesus Christ as their savior and to live their lives in accordance with the sacramental requirements of the Catholic church. Missionaries "multiplied catechisms, commentaries on scriptures and simple instructions, interactive sermons, retreats; even their ceremonies were examples of the doctrine in action"; everything the missionaries did was with the intention of "introducing the knowledge of religious truths, forgotten by some, and never known by others." [37] This educational agenda was central to the missionaries and is evident in the wide range of tactics they adopted when orchestrating individual missions. Morning services were usually aimed at the lower classes, those with little if any education and exposure to catechism; instruction in this context was straightforward, and communicated through simple, engaging stories and anecdotes. Formal catechism was aimed at all social groups, at children, of course, but also at adult men and women deprived of religious education in their childhood, and requiring basic instruction before they could participate in their own communion during the course of the mission.[38] Commentaries on biblical texts and explanations of basic Christian truths were included in special retreats aimed at particular groups, such as women, prisoners, or soldiers, and were reiterated in general sermons throughout the mission. Evening lectures were aimed at the more educated population, presumed to have been turned away from Catholicism by the teachings of the philosophes. In this context the missionaries directly addressed the challenges issued by writers like Voltaire and Jean-Jacques Rousseau, insisting upon the existence and attributes of God, the necessity of revelation, the authenticity of the Holy Scriptures, and the value of their prophecies; they preached about the life and miracles of the Savior, his resurrection, the distinct character of his Church and the superiority of his doctrine over those of other religions.[39] They suggested books their followers could read and offered to discuss further points of doctrine with individuals interested in working through their doubts. Instruction in the truths of the Catholic religion as against the teachings of the previous century, or simply in relation to the usual doubts which kept men and women from accepting Christ as their savior, were also orchestrated in the context of *conférences dialoguées,* or interactive sermons. Here one missionary would present a basic teaching of the church, only to be challenged by another priest, carefully placed among the auditors for this purpose.

The goal, however, was not merely to instruct the population in the forgotten teachings of the Catholic church, but to convert. "One preached, one catechized only to convert, to resuscitate a Christian vitality in the souls, in the family, in society itself."[40] Conversion could not be accomplished merely by offering instruction in the teachings of the church and by appealing to reason; what was necessary, above all, was to move the population, to appeal to its emotions, to incite faith and a belief in the need to accept the body of Christ. This related but far more important goal inspired the pomp and theatricality of the missions. During the six to eight weeks of a typical mission, extraordinary efforts were made to engage a majority of the population in a moving spectacle of piety and public devotion to Jesus Christ. Upon arrival, missionaries immediately solicited recruits for their choirs. They distributed and sold booklets of canticles, and willingly borrowed profane melodies to make their sacred message more appealing to their followers. While they assiduously pursued their instructional efforts in services and retreats, they also deployed enormous resources to orchestrate more spectacular demonstrations of their message. For processions, members of the community were enjoined to decorate their homes with appropriate monarchical and Christian emblems, often sold in the context of the mission by traveling salesmen who accompanied the missionaries. Large groups of men were recruited to carry the massive mission crosses; thousands of followers were incorporated into these processions; and temporary scaffolding was erected to allow thousands more to participate in choirs, or merely to witness these extravagant spectacles of piety.

But the most important thing was to get the population to take the sacraments and renew their devotion to Christ; to this end the missionaries tended to employ threats and terrifying tactics. While this was represented most clearly in their infamous ceremonies in cemeteries, where they preached before an open grave with a skull in hand about the horrors of eternal damnation, fire and brimstone sermons which underscored the consequences of living outside the church constituted a regular feature of all the missionaries' religious services. The goal of the preachers was to make their auditors tremble, to shock their listeners, and thereby to move them to accept the teachings of Christ.[41] But even as they clearly articulated the need for people to accept the Host and devote their lives to Christ, their austere moral message made it difficult for most French men and women to confess and enter the ranks of the saved. In contrast to missionaries in the eighteenth century who were afraid to go against the habits and practices of the population, who combined a positive view of the dogma and principles of Catholicism with a kind of complacency about the morality of their auditors, the "missionaries of the Restoration knew no such timidity. Whatever their audience, they preached dogma and morality integrally."[42] The missionaries declared war on popular festive culture—on "pagan" celebrations of saints' days, on the excesses of carnival, on dancing. They denounced all forms of nonreligious entertainment as debauchery, attacking more private forms of leisure such as the reading of novels, as well as public pleasures enjoyed in cafés, cabarets, and theaters. The missionaries did not only preach against these sins in the abstract; they willingly made examples of individuals in the congregation, singling them out during their sermons and posting names of sinful members of the community in town squares. While they were in town they tried to have the theater season suspended, and to have cafés and cabarets closed; whenever possible, they scheduled their missions to interrupt the "sacrilegious" festivities associated with carnival.

In Brittany, where the tradition of celebrating the festival of the dead was more popular than elsewhere in France, the service in the cemetery was always the preferred occasion for missionaries to bring home their severe message. The following sermon, given by the famous Abbé de La

Mennais in 1819, gives a sense of the tenor of these terrifying ceremonies. As the *terrible prédicateur* took one skull after another into his hands and interrogated them before his listeners, he evoked the whole range of sins which could condemn one to eternal damnation:

QUESTION: You, Who are you?

ANSWER: I am a father, an honest man.

QUESTION: What is your situation?

ANSWER: I am in hell.

QUESTION: Why?

ANSWER: I had children. I neglected to instruct them and to have them baptized; they are lost; God holds me responsible. I am damned.

QUESTION: And you, who are you?

ANSWER: I am the wife of this man; I shared his errors, I share his punishment. I am damned.

QUESTION: And you?

ANSWER: My father and my mother have responded to you: I am damned.

Throwing the three skulls back into the grave, back to the hell from which they will never return, the Abbé de La Mennais turned his attention to the evil rich man, the evil poor man, the usurer, the young woman dead at twenty who assiduously practiced the sacraments but was too vain, too attached to dancing, and the working man who got drunk after mass on Sunday. Ending with a positive example, the preacher showed the way to avoid the fate of these skulls:

QUESTION: You, the last, who are you?

ANSWER: Just a poor wretch; I sinned my whole life, but I have made penitence, and so I am saved!

MORAL: Hear that, sinners, and rejoice! Let this fill your hearts with hope! We have all sinned; I perhaps more than you; but let us repent, and we will be saved. Let us swear to repent on the tombs of the dead! [43]

This austere moral message was seconded by many within the church establishment who penned pastoral letters during the Restoration, or *mandements,* which clearly articulated the stricter requirements of what many came to call the "new Catholicism" of this period.[44] These contained provisions which had a direct impact on the personal lives of Catholics for they laid down strict rules limiting access to the sacraments of baptism, first communion, marriage, and extreme unction. The *mandement* of the archbishop of Rouen, published in 1825, was typical in this regard. It threatened parishioners who had not recently taken the sacraments with excommunication; it prevented noncommunicants from acting as godparents; children of civil, but not religious, marriages were declared bastards; local curés were encouraged to post the names of noncommunicants and those living in sin (or in "concubinage") on the church wall. This religious "rigorism," as Sevrin called it, or "fanaticism," as critics called it, was central to the missionaries' message. If members of the church establishment such as the archbishop of Rouen were equally avid in their support of this rigorism, it was with the missionaries that this "new Catholicism" was indelibly associated during the course of the Restoration.[45]

Not all members of the church establishment agreed with the missionaries' moral crusade. Some merely questioned the sagacity of employing threats and terrifying tactics, arguing that sweeter methods often led to more durable results. Many questioned the excessive attacks of the missionaries on the simple pleasures of the people. For example, Monseigneur Salmon du Châtellier, the bishop of Evreux, responded to his grand vicar's request to invite the Missionaries of France to give a mission in his diocese with the following reservations: "I fear, my dear Matthew, that the missionary goes overboard in his rigorism. . . . For example, where dancing is concerned, even the most rigorous missionaries acknowledge that dancing is not by nature evil. Yet they forbid it absolutely, and exclude from the sacraments everyone who does not take a solemn vow to renounce this practice forever. This is what I call a pious scandal, and I would prefer to renounce any hope of having missions rather than allow them to reproduce this scandal in my diocese."[46]

The missionaries' combination of rigorism and terrifying tactics is what prefects often cited as what was most dangerous about the revival. Complaining about the mission in Nevers in 1817, the prefect reproached the missionaries for "too readily employing somber images and religious terror."[47] The prefect of the Saône-et-Loire described the missionaries preaching in Autun in the same terms: "they are all alike in the ardor of their invectives, in the exaggeration of the threats by which they terrify their auditors."[48] But it was the following report from the Allier in 1817 which best evoked the dangers posed by the religious intolerance of the missionaries as the writer conjured an image of their sowing discontent all over the country:

> Diverse reports have come in on the effect produced by the missions of Nevers, Bourges, Clermont and Grenoble, and these are ever less reassuring since they come from reasonable people, worthy of our faith. It is especially the religious intolerance of the missionaries, . . . the prohibition to bury, the

invitations to rebaptize those who were first baptized during the Revolution, . . . which generally produce a bad effect on the population.[49]

Not since the Counter-Reformation of the seventeenth century had the population of France experienced a protracted effort on the part of the clergy to restore a strict adherence to the sacraments, in combination with such an austere moral order.

The parallels and contrasts between the revival of the nineteenth century and that of the seventeenth is apt on many levels. As in the seventeenth century, the missionaries' efforts did produce a wave of conversions and a renewed attachment on the part of the population to a rigorous practice of Catholicism.[50] But as was true for the Counter-Reformation, the religious revival of the Restoration also produced the opposite effect, driving many French men and women away from the rites of Catholicism. Especially because the missionaries often came from outside the parish, and were seen to represent a Catholicism which did not conform to local mores and practices, a strand of anticlericalism emerged from this movement; a kind of nostalgic view of an "old" Catholicism came to prevail as people grew more overtly critical of the "new" Catholicism of the missionaries, so easily characterized as "foreign" to the true practice of their faith.[51]

If their severe moral message made it clear that embracing Christ was no easy task, in strictly religious terms, the missionaries also propagated an explicitly political message: consecrating one's life to Christ also required a renunciation of the events and legacies of the past century associated with the Enlightenment and especially the French Revolution. Or, said another way, the missionaries sought to cleanse the spiritual body of anyone who bore the sinful stain of these events. Thus the sacraments were also denied to those who remained attached to the ideas of the philosophes, had fought on behalf of the Revolution and the Empire, or remained unrepentant about their participation in any aspect of the Revolution from acquiring *biens nationaux,* to taking an oath to the revolutionary government (if one was a priest), to accepting the sacraments from such "illegitimate" priests. In spite of the fact that the pope himself had accepted the *biens nationaux* and the constitutional priests as legitimate when he accepted Napoleon's Concordat of 1801, the missionaries remained intransigent on the "political" sins which justified excluding parishioners from the Kingdom of Christ.[52] The road to salvation charted by the missionaries required taking a clear political stance: there was no middle ground. Either one confessed and repented for every aspect of this sinful past and actively embraced Christ, or one did not.

In their sermons, the missionaries constantly inveighed against this wide range of political sins. In the words of the prefect of the Hautes-Alpes:

> The evils of the Revolution constitute the text of their sermons. In front of the military personnel of the garrison, most of whom were officers or soldiers under Napoleon, the army is represented as having exercised nothing but plunder and brigandage; those who participated in the war against the counterrevolutionary Vendée heard themselves called cannibals. In a sermon on restitution, people who had legally repaid their debts with assignats were invited to cover the difference which resulted from the depreciation of this paper.[53]

Everywhere the missionaries went they denounced *biens nationaux;* they preached against those who participated in the "sacrilegious" traffic in church lands, and they actively encouraged restitution, serving as mediators in local negotiations between acquirers of *biens nationaux* and their original owners. Constitutional priests, another sinful blot in France's history, were singled out in sermons, particularly in towns where such priests continued to minister to the local population. Missionaries regularly identified individuals with known ties to the revolutionary cause in order to dramatize their message that there was no possibility of joining the ranks of the saved if one did not publicly confess for past political sins connected to the Revolution. In Arles, for example, visiting missionaries made a public display of overriding the decision of the local curé and refusing to grant one prominent member of the community burial rights, because in spite of his public support for the king and his clear disdain for the emperor, he had nonetheless participated in the Revolution and made no effort to conceal his continued commitment to the ideals of the philosophes. In spite of efforts by local civil and ecclesiastical officials to intervene in his behalf, he was denied the rites of extreme unction and a proper Christian burial.[54]

The campaign of the missionaries against "irregular unions" offers a good example of the spiritual path from individual revolutionary sinfulness to salvation, and of the tactics employed by these priests to purify the spiritual body of the church. Both couples who had been married by constitutional priests and couples who had only contracted their unions civilly were encouraged to remarry with the benediction of a proper priest. The missionaries made it clear that those who refused to do so would be denied the sacraments and would not be able to act as godparents and that their children would be deemed illegitimate. The missionaries had some spectacular successes, as in the town of Salies-de-Béarn in 1818, where 238 couples, previously married in civil ceremonies, presented themselves at the church to receive matrimonial rites. All over the country, couples renewed their vows with the benediction of the church because it was the only way to salvation.[55]

As they made their way around France, teaching the forgotten truths of Catholicism, the missionaries at once encouraged parishioners to participate in the baptismal, matrimonial, and mortuary rites of the faith, and excluded from the sacraments all who refused to renounce either their personal immoral pleasures or their political connections to the Revolution and its legacy; in so doing, the missionaries sought to purify and remake the body of the church, and they also gave this "cleansing" a clear political spin.[56] But their political ambitions extended far beyond separating individual sinners from their past political errors in order to ensure their salvation; their efforts point to the more ambitious goal of purging the nation of the communal sins committed over the course of the eighteenth century in order to enable the monarch to reign in France "by the Grace of God." The public sphere, secularized over the course of the eighteenth century and brutally dechristianized during the revolutionary interlude, had to be remade in a Christian mold: mass confessions for the sins of the past, a thorough purging of the symbols and artifacts of this period, and an active rechristianization of the landscape were all necessary corollaries of this more ambitious project.

Remaking the Body of the Nation: The Imperative of Expiation

For the missionaries orchestrating this national revival, the return of the Bourbons did not merely represent an opportunity to rechristianize the kingdom under the auspices of a regime sympathetic to their spiritual mission; for them the restoration of their monarch corresponded to the deliverance of the nation from the grip of the Antichrist, and offered the possibility of building a true Christian kingdom on earth. At the heart of their campaign was an eschatological interpretation of French history of the previous centuries, voiced in popular prophetic literature of the period, and constantly reiterated and dramatized in the missionaries' sermons and ceremonies: France had sinned during the Enlightenment, was chastised during the Revolution, and in 1814 was finally delivered back into the hands of the Bourbon kings, who could at last resume their role as leaders of the Christian world.[57] It is impossible to understand the nature of the religious revival of the Restoration without recognizing that helping the monarch to realize this prophecy was absolutely central to its mission. This spiritual and fundamentally political quest created two critical imperatives for the missionaries. First, if the people of France were to enjoy the fruits of deliverance they would first have to purge themselves, not merely as individuals but, more importantly, as a nation, of the sins which had produced their nation's fall; in short, deliverance required confession and expiation for the sins of the past and especially for the sins committed during the Revolution. Second, in addition to leading the nation in cleansing citizens' souls and the landscape of all signs of this sinful episode, the missionaries had to work to reconstitute a spiritual and juridical framework which would allow Christian monarchy to flourish. This double imperative, of expiation for the revolutionary past and a thorough restoration of the foundations of Christian monarchy, imbued the revival with a radical counterrevolutionary mission.

Certainly the time seemed ripe for a thorough remaking of the body politic: a Bourbon king had just been restored to the throne, and Catholicism to its status as the religion of the state. The king himself seemed to support the missionaries' quest to rechristianize France. Yet the political vision at the heart of the missions was radically different from that of the state: a huge chasm separated the moderate intentions of the king to rule over France under the auspices of a modern, secularized form of monarchy, and the missionaries' more radical desire to restore monarchy "by the Grace of God." Publicly the missionaries never acknowledged the differences which distinguished them from the regime they so ardently supported; on the contrary, they did everything in their power to give the impression that they were faithfully representing their king in the context of their missions. If civil officials tried to interfere with missions in the name of social order, citing the very real disorder which missionaries appeared to be stirring up, missionaries and their supporters in the church simply behaved and spoke as if the officials in question were exaggerating the problems caused by the missions and falsely representing the desires of their ruler. Again and again they would make arguments of the sort we have already seen in the archbishop's defense of the mission in Marseilles: first, that religion, far from creating disorder, always helped to ensure social peace; and second, that to limit their ceremonies in any way, to temper their counterrevolutionary message, would be, on the one hand, to submit themselves once again to a kind of persecution they had not known since the Revolution, and, on the other hand, to relinquish the hope of achieving the full benefits of the return of "our very Christian king, and the grandson of St. Louis." [58]

The critical emphasis the missionaries placed on their outdoor, public ceremonies must be understood in the light of their determination to use their missions to dramatize the fact that for them, Article 6 of the Charter, which restored Catholicism as the religion of the state, represented the dawn of a new age, when France as a nation could finally be returned to Christ its Savior. In general, the missionaries' insistence upon spectacular outdoor processions and their consistent efforts to integrate civil officials and the local population served the same purpose: they enabled the missionaries to speak for the monarch and his government and to define the spiritual and political body of the nation.[59] It was by taking over the public space, with the apparent sanction of the state, that they put into effect their radical counterrevolutionary project of remaking the body of the nation according to a Christian model.

It was the bishop of Strasbourg, in an 1825 *mandement* announcing the arrival of a mission in his town, who expressed the political ambitions involved in the outdoor ceremonies of the missionaries when he explicitly compared them with the "odious" and "impious" festivals of the French Revolution. "As for the processions, the singing of canticles, the festivals of the missions, are these ceremonies not as noble, as useful as the bizarre processions of impiety . . . from the disastrous times of the Revolution?" [60] Recalling the festivals of the revolutionaries, the bishop underscored the violence and unhappiness into which this sacrilegious project had plunged France. He did so in order to emphasize the peace and healing which proper religious ceremonies would make possible. But at the same time he drew attention to the ambitious agenda at the heart of the revolutionaries' festive project, namely, the effort to remake France in a republican mold and to transfer the sacrality of Catholicism and monarchy to the secular terrain of the Republic.[61] In evoking the political goals of the revolutionaries' festival project, the bishop also acknowledged the ongoing political battle in which he and the soon-to-arrive missionaries were engaged. His *mandement* was defensive; the "odious" spectacles of the Revolution may have become a thing of the past, but the spirit which guided them, the philosophy which enthroned the deity of Reason, continued to stand in the way of the reconsecration of the public sphere to God. In his words:

Philosophy proclaimed these odious ceremonies, disgusting for their impiety and cynicism, to be the triumph of reason; it substituted for the hymns of our temples revolutionary songs which foretold the slaughter of a misguided people. And after dragging us through the mire and blood, it dares to continue to censor our ceremonies, dedicated to Christian worship, where everything breathes of piety and peace, and which brings man closer to God, and leads him to practice his duties. Oh! it should cry for all the ills it has made France suffer instead of insulting the religion which can heal our wounds and efface the traces of our sufferings.[62]

The specific aspect of "philosophy" which the bishop was contending with was the freedom of religion, the tolerance of the Charter which, in a town like his, with a significant Protestant and Jewish population, made public spectacles of Catholicism of questionable legality. The Concordat clearly stated that in towns with significant non-Catholic populations it was up to the civil authorities to determine whether outdoor public ceremonies threatened the freedom of religion which the state was committed to protecting. It was this law that administrators continually cited in their efforts to prohibit the outdoor ceremonies of the missionaries.

In fact, there was a disingenuousness in the bishop's depiction of the ceremonies of the missions as bringing nothing but peace, as merely allowing the state religion to represent itself on the streets in public. His comparison of these ceremonies with the festivals of the French Revolution was more apt, as it acknowledged the huge stakes involved in the public spectacles of the missionaries, as well as the huge wounds and controversies which they were designed to reopen. For just like the festivals of the revolutionary years, the ceremonies of the missionaries were self-consciously deployed to encourage the population as a whole to participate in rites and rituals that would reconfigure the sacrality of the public sphere—only this time in response to the "sacrilege" of recent decades. Like the "odious" festivals of reason, these ceremonies offered songs, symbols, and particular communal rituals, organized around a revived Christian and monarchical calendar, all to counter the ambitious cultural project of the revolutionary decade. But their spiritual mission required nothing less: for if they were to save France, and enable their monarch to resume his role as leader of the Christian world, they had to remake the body politic, and that required first and foremost a public confrontation with the Revolution and its legacies.

At the heart of their missions, and most beautifully expressed in their public, participatory ceremonies, was the imperative of expiation: to enable France to achieve salvation, to make it possible for the king to rule "by the Grace of God," the nation as a whole had to accept responsibility for the sins of the Revolution, publicly confess, and erect symbols of repentance and renewed devotion to the true God and his representative on earth, the king. Expiation required *remembering* the sins of the past in detail because without remembering there could be no repentance and, therefore, no salvation. What this translated into in practice was a religious revival in which missionaries traveled around France doing everything they could to remind the population of the revolutionary interlude in chilling, graphic detail. They raised the specter of the Enlightenment so that it could be defeated in brilliant autos-da-fé. In town after town they reopened old controversies: between constitutional and refractory priests and their congregations, between acquirers of *biens nationaux* and the owners whom they had despoiled, between supporters of the Revolution (local representatives to the Convention who actively participated in the Revolution, military personnel who fought in the revolutionary or imperial armies) and royalists (especially those who had led the White Terror of 1815). Missionaries evoked the local geography of the past twenty-five years, erecting mission crosses where a cross had been violently attacked during the Revolution or, more commonly, where the guillotine had stood during the worst period of revolutionary violence. Sites where liberty trees or statues honoring revolutionaries stood also served as appropriate venues for reconsecrating the landscape to Christ and their king. Again, for the missionaries, the point of this graphic remembering was to make national redemption possible; true social peace and reconciliation could come only after confrontation with and repentance for the sins of the past. If the missionaries saw the opening of wounds and the revival of painful memories as a necessary evil on the road to salvation, civil officials in the Restoration were less sanguine, and in their reports they were more blatant and rueful about the political ramifications of the missionaries' spiritual quest. They complained about "cinders being ignited" and fresh wounds being reopened, and they expressed concern that the missions exacerbated rather than resolved the complex struggles which dated back to the revolutionary period. The prefect of Allier expressed such fears in a letter to the archbishop of his diocese in 1819:

> Given the actual state of spirits, still heated and embittered by long dissensions, opposed interests, animosities which have not yet died out, shouldn't we be afraid that a public animated discussion of several delicate and controversial issues will produce disquiet and reawaken disorder and hatred?

When it is necessary to make an effort to encourage union and peace, shouldn't we avoid anything which goes against our simple habits, any sort of spectacle which seeks to inflame the spirit of the people?[63]

If the missionaries and the prelates supporting them denied such pernicious effects, and repeatedly reiterated the spiritual justification for their expiatory project, a closer look at the missionaries' public ceremonies, in combination with the civil officials' reports on their consequences, allows us to see the degree to which the public spectacles of the missions constituted a full-scale, counterrevolutionary response to the ambitious cultural agenda of their revolutionary predecessors. Right in its evocation of the contrast with the festivals of the French Revolution, the bishop of Strasbourg's depiction of the public ceremonies of the mission helps us to appreciate that in the context of the Restoration it was not the regime but the missionaries participating in this national religious revival who responded most directly, most vociferously, to the counterrevolutionary imperative to undo the cultural and political damage done by the revolutionary period and to thoroughly remake and resacralize the public sphere in the name of Christ and their king.

If the revolutionary epoch was the sinful period for which the nation had to accept responsibility and to repent, the sinful spirit of the Enlightenment had led France into the grip of the Antichrist, and so it too had to be evoked, denounced, and purged if the nation was to find its way to salvation. Although the missionaries regularly condemned the poisonous eighteenth-century writings from the pulpit, pointing in particular to the writings of Jean-Jacques Rousseau and Voltaire, they dramatized the spiritual significance of their assaults in the expiatory rites orchestrated around their public destruction. As Martyn Lyons has shown, missionaries staged autos-da-fé throughout the Restoration in which *mauvais livres* were voluntarily handed over to the missionaries so that they could be publicly destroyed by fire. The church establishment clearly supported this assault on *mauvais livres*, particularly in light of the cheap new editions of the philosophes which were appearing with great frequency after 1817: the *vicaires-generaux* of the Paris diocese issued a Lenten *mandement* condemning philosophical works.[64] Indeed the missionaries even asked the king to step in and censor the new editions of the philosophes, and thereby revive his proper role as definer and defender of the sacred in his kingdom. In fact, the king refused, but by orchestrating their expiatory autos-da-fé, as often as possible with the participation of local civil officials, and by concluding their ceremonies with the *amendes honorables* for sins against God and their king, the missionaries brought home the message that if the king was not in fact punishing blasphemy and sacrilege in the manner of his forefathers, they would perform such rites on his behalf.[65]

Like the *mauvais livres,* the wide range of sins committed during the revolutionary period had to be attacked from the pulpit; but more important, they had to be given tangible form so that participants in the mission could take responsibility for them and publicly repent. Like the real books that owners voluntarily handed over to the missionaries for public expiatory rites, individuals with direct ties to the revolutionary period were singled out so that they could serve as living embodiments of sinfulness, repentance, and redemption. In Valence, for example, much publicity was given to the conversion of M. Marbos during the course of the mission precisely because he had been a constitutional priest risen to the level of a bishop and because he had served in the Convention which condemned the King to death, although he had not himself voted in favor of regicide.[66] In towns with military garrisons, missionaries preached especially vociferously against the soldiers who had served during the Revolution and Empire, "fighting against the army of their God and their King," and they made special efforts to get officers from the army and from the National Guard to participate in the mission and wear the sign of the revival, the little cross, on the lapels of their uniforms.[67] Purchasers of *biens nationaux* were encouraged to offer reparations to their prior owners, and public spectacles were conducted around reconciliations. In Salies-de-Béarn, for example, "restitutions were made and then those who had been enemies publicly reconciled, some inside the church itself."[68] In Avignon in 1819, a more dramatic example of the same was cited by a missionary: "one citizen, whom another had wronged during the Revolution, said to him, 'I congratulate you, and I pardon you for all your wrongs against me, as I hope that God will pardon me.'"[69] Whenever possible, individuals repenting for revolutionary crimes were integrated into public processions in ways which evoked the specific nature of their crime. In the case of the mission of Bordeaux in 1817, for example, the prefect reported that "among the number of people that the mission converted, one noticed some revolutionaries who had participated in the worst violence of 1793 . . . they helped to resurrect the cross [in 1817] that they had once destroyed."[70]

While they had some success in integrating such participants in revolutionary excesses into their ceremonies, the police reports remind us to think about the many citizens of different towns with similar links to the revolutionary period who did not participate in the mission, and for whom the public dramatization of the specific divisions within their town and within their families must have caused considerable pain or at least discomfort. Most often cited by the prefects were cases in which constitutional priests continued to minister to the local population. Describing the mission in Rennes, for example, where the bishop and many of his subordinates had taken the oath to the government during the Revolution, the prefect asked the minister of the interior to "imagine the embarrassment of the old bishop and the irritation of [the other constitutional priests who serve him] when one or two of the Missionaries of France threw into doubt the validity of their absolutions or the marriages which they had sanctified since the Revolution."[71] The assault on constitutional priests must have pained many in the population, particularly if one considers the number of parishioners who had received the sacraments from them which were later deemed illegitimate. But it was their assault on *biens nationaux* which prefects saw as most troubling for the population. For every spectacular public reconciliation that the missionaries described, there were many more French citizens who chose neither to take advantage of the missionaries' councils of arbitration nor to publicly repent for this particular sin. Describing the repeated attacks by missionaries on the *biens nationaux* in the context of the mission in Briançon in 1818, the prefect of the Hautes-Alpes echoed the concerns of many of his fellow administrators when he explained: "this subject touched upon speculations declared inviolable, but in spite of the force of the law which clearly defended [the *biens nationaux*], one can easily imagine the discomfort and disquiet which such discourse excites."[72]

If identifying individual sinners and incorporating them into the expiatory rituals was a part of their project, the missionaries' spiritual quest led them to cast their net more broadly and to implicate the entire population in the sins committed during the course of the previous decades, whether or not they had actively participated in the worst violence and sacrilege of the revolutionary years. Underscoring this particular message of the missionaries, the prefect of the Bouches-du-Rhône summarized their sermons in the following terms:

> In the majority of their discourses the missionaries, and principally the director inveighed against the partisans of the revolution, the liberals, the philosophers of the century, the nonbelievers, and the excesses of the revolutionaries, . . . but the director also made a point of pronouncing that *each person by his or her Sins was complicitous in the Revolution.*[73]

The Abbé Fayet's sermon, given in the context of the mission at Clermont in 1818, made the point more poignantly by stressing the collective guilt which must be acknowledged for the carnage produced during the Revolution and the Empire.

> Your crimes are the cause of the disaster which has afflicted France these thirty years. It is to punish you for the anarchy which devoured you that God sent you that evil genius [Napoleon], . . . I don't wish to open a wound still raw and bloody, but without your crimes, without your impious enthusiasm for this miserable nonbeliever, would you have had to suffer the disastrous deaths of your children, sent to slaughter by this madman? . . . You are menaced with still greater ills if you do not convert yourselves in good faith.

There was nothing unusual about this general indictment or the evocation of the spiritual stakes for France of mass expiation and redemption. As Sevrin tells us, "where the crimes of the Revolution were concerned, the disorder in mores, and the necessity of doing penance, the Abbé Fayet used the language of the preachers of his era."[74]

If the population as a whole was complicit by its sins in the horrors committed during the previous thirty years, there was one sin which stood at the symbolic center of these missions, and that was the killing of the monarchs in 1793. Whenever possible, expiatory rites were conducted on the 21st of January or the 16th of October, and the same message of communal sin was intoned particularly on occasions devoted to remembering and denouncing this particularly sacrilegious crime. Clearly not everyone had voted for the executions of Louis XVI and Marie Antoinette, but on the 21st of January missionaries made a point of "dwelling on the crimes committed during the course of the Revolution, and attributing them to the mass of the nation, without explicitly naming names or specifying facts."[75]

If their sermons explained their vision of sinfulness and necessary repentance, it was through their public rituals that the missionaries dramatized the meaning and the consequence of this communal expiation. Every mission culminated in the same set of communal rites: mass confessions for the sins of the Revolution, *amendes honorables* for the collective sins of the nation, and the erection of mission crosses. Taken together, these rites did not only constitute an effort to *unmake* the legacy of the eighteenth century, and especially the Revolution; rather, the missionaries' vehement assault on the revolutionary past was merely a necessary step on the road to *recreating* a conception of monarchy which had not reigned in France since the seventeenth century.

Resacralizing the King's Two Bodies: The Eucharistic Conception of Monarchy in the Nineteenth Century

Presiding at all the ceremonies of the missions was the sacred Host, given a place of honor on the altar, whether in the church or in external processions. To add to the solemnity and mystery of occasions orchestrated around this physical embodiment of Christ, missionaries encouraged participants to arrive bearing candles and wearing little crosses on their lapels; with their moving sermons they enjoined their followers to prostrate themselves before Christ, literally to throw themselves body and soul into their spiritual exercises. The service orchestrated in La Rochelle on the 21st of January in the context of a mission in the Charente-Inférieure in 1818 was typical in this regard. According to the prefect's report:

> [The missionaries] had informed the population on the eve of this ceremony that no one would be able to enter the church without a candle. The catafalque [was] placed in the middle of the cathedral, at a height of more than twenty feet. . . . The Host was given a place of honor on this altar, and surrounded with a prodigious number of candles. . . . Our bishop climbed up by means of a ladder, and gave his benediction. The Seigneur Guyon profited from this occasion to launch his condemnations to the impious and the nonbelievers who did not recognize the true God. More than 1500 women and 25 men were in attendance with their candles.[76]

Just as their exhausting daily routine was motivated by a desire to get the people of France to confess, take communion, and thereby accept the body of Christ, so were their public spectacles organized around the sacred Host, dramatizing the significance of the Eucharist, and telling and retelling the story of Christ's mortal sacrifice for his fellow man.

The processions of the missionaries were dedicated to reenacting the crucifixion, reiterating the eucharistic narrative at the center of Catholicism. In Provence, missionaries cast themselves as Christlike victims, and led processions in bare feet, with ropes around their necks, to the site where the calvary would be erected, and where "their" crucifixion would be symbolically enacted.[77] Those carrying the cross were likewise enjoined to walk without shoes through the rocky streets and, as they bloodied their own feet, reenact in a small way the suffering of Christ, their savior. None of this was particularly unusual, however; this was standard fare for Corpus Christi festivities, long celebrated in France. What was new, and what gave the spectacles of the missionaries political significance, was that the missionaries tied this ancient narrative of

Christ's mortal sacrifice to that of Louis XVI and Marie Antoinette. The following account of the end of an expiatory ceremony in Brittany, where the practice was not to parade a calvary through the town but to affix Christ to the cross at the end of the procession, evokes the transposition of the eucharistic narrative to the events of the Revolution. When a sailor was invited to attach the representation of Christ to the cross, he refused, saying "that he had already crucified enough people during the Terror." If the missionaries retold this story in their description of this particular mission, it was because it perfectly expressed the central point of such ceremonies, namely that to achieve salvation the population, as individuals and as a community, had to take responsibility for the violence of the Revolution, particularly for the "crucifixion" of the innocent Louis XVI and Marie Antoinette.[78]

At the symbolic center of their expiatory eucharistic spectacles were the bodies of the king and queen executed during the course of the Revolution. The message, as we saw in Marseilles, was always the same: the sacrifice of the mortal bodies of Louis XVI and Marie Antoinette was to be understood as analogous to the sacrifice of Jesus. Like the body of Christ, the bodies of the dead king and queen were celebrated throughout France in a continual eucharistic festival, and the ultimate meaning of this festival was clear. The crosses planted all over the kingdom, adorned with the emblems of the Bourbons, represented the reign of Christ in France, through his mortal and yet divine representative on earth, the king of France. The subjects of France, by participating in expiatory rites, by confessing for the sins committed by the nation against Louis XVI and Marie Antoinette, reconstituted the spiritual body of the church as the political body which was the nation, joined in devotion to Christ and their king.

The Host, or a cross bearing a likeness of Christ, was carried through the streets by missionaries, but if their followers were themselves enacting the suffering of their savior in order to dramatize the narrative of Christ's sacrifice, it was through streets adorned with a mélange of Christian and monarchical emblems. The streets and windows along the procession route were decorated with white flags, adorned with fleurs-de-lis and crosses. Spectators along the procession route and participants in the cortèges wore the same mixture of Bourbon and Christian emblems on their lapels, or carried white flags, candles, and little crosses in their hands. The procession route reenacted the stations of the cross, but it was the sins of the Revolution committed in a particular town which determined the course that the procession would follow, the specific sites where participants would stop and offer prayers. When the cross was finally erected, and the missionary gave his final sermon, he evoked not the general sins for which Christ had sacrificed himself on the cross but the specific sins by which the French brought about the mortal sacrifice of their king and queen. And as they led the tens of thousands of participants in mass confessions for these sins, the missionaries did not merely offer prayers of repentance to God but *amendes honorables* for their crimes committed against their God and king. Finally, when they erected their massive calvaries on sites of revolutionary excesses, they did not use simple crucifixes but eucharistic symbols laced with the emblems of the restored monarch of France. As they raised these symbols they encouraged their auditors to join them in cries of "Long live Christ! Long live the King," and led them in singing canticles which likewise stressed the concurrent reconquest of France by Christ and their king: "Long live France / Long live the King (*le Roi*) / Always in France / the Bourbons and the Faith (*la foi*)." [79]

The conception of monarchy dramatized in these mass spectacles, far better attended than any commemorative festival organized by the regime in these years, was founded on the principle of divine right and based on the model of the Eucharist. Not since the seventeenth century had the people of France participated in spectacles which were designed to emphasize the sacred nature of the body of their king and the equivalence between the emblems representing Christ and the symbols of their monarchs. Not since the funerals of the Renaissance kings had the streets of France been organized around Gothic-style venerations of the effigy of the Christlike king, meant to evoke both the mortal body of the king (which does die) and his *magnitus* (which does not). [80] While no effigies were present in the ceremonies of the missionaries, the physical sacrifices of Louis XVI and Marie Antoinette were continually evoked—in the timing of the ceremonies (on the 21st of January), in the contents of their sermons, and in the emblems of the monarchy which adorned the streets and the eucharistic symbol of the calvary itself. Unlike the commemorations of the state which consistently avoided evoking the bodies of the king and queen, these mortal but ultimately sacred bodies were ever present in the expiatory rituals of the missionaries. [81]

Sevrin, in his eloquent tribute to these missionaries, takes great pains to distinguish their august spiritual mission from any sordid, earthly "political" gambits on behalf of the Ultras or any secret society such as the Congregation; if the message in the missions was political, he argues, it was part and parcel of their spiritual quest. There is no question that

Sevrin was right. If critics of the missionaries were quick to accuse them of representing the Ultras or secret societies, there is no reason to assume such a connection in order to understand the nature of their missions, and especially the political agenda which apparently informed them. It is clear that the missionaries' view of the world, inspired entirely by their religious vision, shaped their perspective on the eighteenth century, the Revolution, as well as the future of monarchy. That they should have figured the past and future of France in terms of an expiatory narrative, that they should have reimagined and worked to reconquer France in the name of a monarch who should rule, like Christ, according to the model of the Eucharist all makes perfect sense, and certainly does not need to be understood by resorting to narratives of conspiracies and plots on behalf of radical right-wing parties.

Yet the nature of the missionaries' ceremonies, the radical counter-revolutionary agenda at the heart of their revival, and the visible support they received as they went from town to town did create talk of such conspiracies. Their austere moral message and their assault on the revolutionary legacy combined to engender popular anticlericalism in defense of both an "older" Catholicism and the secular legacy of the eighteenth century and the Revolution. More than any of the modest ceremonies of the Restoration regime, it was the expiatory spectacles of the missionaries which shaped the battleground on which struggles over France's future would be waged. As they traveled across France invoking the personnel, geography, and the songs, symbols, and festivals of the revolutionary period, they directly undermined the regime's efforts to encourage *oubli*, and offered their critics the perfect tools to use to defend their own notion of the sacred which should govern in postrevolutionary France.

CHAPTER THREE

Competing Commemorations

The Problem of Performing Monarchy

All over France civil officials responded with alarm to the missionaries and wrote to their superiors in Paris for guidance and assistance about how best to contain the disorder engendered by their national revival. Literally thousands of letters were exchanged between local civil administrators and their superiors in Paris about the critical question articulated most clearly by the mayor of Toulouse, who in 1818 asked the minister of the interior:

> Mustn't one take away from the missionaries the possibility of becoming the arbiters of France's future? Is it prudent to let a handful of men who could be misguided by a false zeal, exercise such enormous influence on the prodigious crowds which they attract in all of the cities of France which they visit? [1]

Few local officials put the question so baldly. In their regular correspondence with their superiors in the civil administration they tended to dwell on the logistical details which would merely enable them to ensure order in the context of visiting missions. Yet what this mass of documents makes clear is that what was at stake in the minutiae of orchestrating the religious revival at the local level was nothing less than the contentious and complicated matter of representing, or literally "staging," monarchy in France. The missionaries posed a real problem for civil administrators during the Restoration: the potential or real disorder they occasioned put civil administrators in the awkward position of having to decide exactly how they were to handle these men of the collar, authorized, after all, by the king himself, and leading a revival on behalf of what was now the state religion. Should these representatives of the government censor the missionaries, and rely upon the Charter, the Civil Code, and the Concordat to defend the juridical legacy of the Revolution by which the regime was legally constituted? Or should they lend their support to the missions, ensure order in their processions, and even participate in them, in spite of the fact that the missionaries' sermons and spectacles articulated a conception of monarchy which was at odds with the one the regime apparently supported? What role should the population play in determining the fate of the missionaries? Should the local population participating in or actively organizing against the missions also be granted the status of "arbiters of France's future"? It was by their decisions on a host of minor questions that local officials offered their complicated responses to these fundamental issues.

This chapter will carefully consider the policies that civil administrators ultimately adopted vis-à-vis the missionaries during the course of the Restoration because it allows us to appreciate the way in which the regime constituted itself at the local level, in the context of controversies which raised fundamental questions about the nature of the monarchy and the spiritual and temporal order it was supposed to defend. By contrasting the spectacles of the missionaries and the state, the previous chapters have broadly outlined the competing conceptions of monarchy performed all over France in this period. Now, as we turn our attention to the practical matter of governing the kingdom and, in particular, to the struggles which erupted between civil and ecclesiastical officials over the mechanics of ruling under a "Christian" versus a "secular" monarchy, we can demonstrate the degree to which a continuous public and participatory negotiation over the nature of legitimate authority defined and ultimately destroyed the regime.

The Juridical Foundations of Monarchy

In legal terms, there is no question that the Catholic church benefited from the restoration of the Bourbon monarchy. The Charter itself proclaimed Catholicism to be the state religion, marking an improvement over the Concordat of 1801, which regarded Catholicism as merely "the religion of the great majority of Frenchmen."[2] However, if Article 6 of the Charter granted Catholicism this status, it stood beside Article 5, which promised freedom of religion; as we shall see, this religious tolerance was consistently defended by the state, and severely curtailed the privileges which could be enjoyed by the Catholic church in spite of its new and improved official status.

A veritable wave of clerical legislation was passed in the first two years of the Restoration. Many of the liberal measures adopted during the Revolution, and not reversed under Napoleon, were attacked. The law permitting divorce was removed from the Civil Code. Married priests were deprived of their pensions. While full restoration of church properties was not possible due to the financial straits of the new regime, an ordinance was passed in 1814 facilitating gifts to religious establishments. Strengthening church control over education, an ordinance of October 1814 permitted bishops to open an ecclesiastical school exempt from university control in every department. In December of the same year the government legally reaffirmed the sanctity of Sundays and religious holidays. The ultraroyalists tried to replace the Concordat of 1801 negotiated by Napoleon with the Concordat of 1516, which would have given the church more power than it had had in 300 years. This effort failed, however, and the agreement signed in 1817 was hardly the radical document the ultraroyalists had hoped for. Some new dioceses were created, and the pope succeeded in appointing some bishops, but the basic subjugation of the church to the state and the defense of the revolutionary settlement, including the acknowledgment of *biens nationaux* and the validity of constitutional priests and their sacraments, were all maintained in the Concordat of 1817. In practical terms, the Concordat of 1801 held sway.

In many respects the legal framework of the Restoration disappointed those who sought to reassert the juridical foundations of Christian monarchy as against the secular monarchy consolidated over the eighteenth century. The failure to reestablish the Concordat of 1516 was one example of this, and the abortive campaign to return the responsibility for civil registers from justices of the peace to the priests was another. Unlike in the seventeenth century, when being considered a member of the body politic required attending catechism, or attesting to birth, marriage, and death through participation in the baptismal, matrimonial, and mortuary rites of the national faith, by the late eighteenth century, civil status had been fully severed from sacramental conformity. Efforts to undo this critical shift in the first year of the Restoration were foiled when the House of Peers rejected the proposal. Religion had become a private option rather than a public obligation, and by preserving the role of the justices of the peace in maintaining the civil registers the

Restoration regime made clear its determination to maintain this particular secular legacy from the eighteenth century.

In its willingness to control the verbal space of the kingdom on behalf of the national religion, the monarchy also showed itself to be the successor of the eighteenth-century monarchs of France rather than of their seventeenth-century counterparts. Whereas in the seventeenth century monarchs not only censored "blasphemous" literature but also had their magistrates perform "ritual tearings and burnings of condemned books in order to avenge violations of conventional norms and purge their errors from public consciousness,"[3] over the eighteenth century such public expiations fell into disuse, as did censorship in the name of religion. Despite repeated efforts by the missionaries to get the king to support their campaign against *mauvais livres,* especially after the massive reprintings of the writings of the philosophes which began in 1817, Louis XVIII consistently cited the Charter's freedom of the press and refused to intervene and turn the state against the publishing houses. Certainly the state orchestrated no autos-da-fé. In fact, the regime did have censorship laws which explicitly protected the Catholic church against attack; however, these were not very strictly enforced. In May of 1819 press laws were passed proscribing offenses to public morality and religion. Such famous individuals as Pierre Jean de Béranger and Paul Louis Courier were imprisoned under the law, although it was still only applied in rare cases. On the 17th and 25th of March 1822, stricter bills were introduced, providing for the suppression of any publication that "by its tendency or its spirit diminished the respect due to religion."[4] While the vagueness of the law opened many newspapers to attack, it was never really enforced. In fact, in total there were only three victims of the law of 1822.[5]

In the seventeenth century, French jurisprudence protected the sacred character of persons, places, objects, and ceremonies as well as times consecrated to God. The monarchy of the eighteenth century moved away from punishing citizens for such acts of sacrilege, although the laws on the books still made it possible for the government to act otherwise, and very occasionally it did so; in spite of some laws that the Restoration government passed which put it in a position to define and punish sacrilegious acts, it followed its eighteenth-century predecessors by avoiding their enforcement.[6] An ordinance of December 1814 reaffirmed the sanctity of Sundays and religious holidays, but there doesn't seem to be any evidence that this law was enforced. In 1825 the regime passed a quite controversial law on sacrilege, which seemed to signal a

clear return to the juridical practices of its seventeenth-century ancestors. In April of 1824, when the Sacrilege Law was initially proposed, it
was withdrawn by the minister of justice on the grounds that such a
metaphysical term as *sacrilege* had no place in secular law. Yet in January of 1825 the bill was reintroduced. Under the proposed bill, thefts
committed in churches were to be punishable by hard labor for life or
with solitary confinement, while profanation of the sacred vessels or the
Host was to be punishable by the same sentence accorded to criminals
convicted of parricide. The condemned person was to be led to execution with his feet bare and his head covered with a black cowl. Before
infliction of capital punishment, his right hand was to be amputated.[7] In
fact, the final version of the law that was promulgated omitted reference
to parricide and limited the punishment for this crime to a combination
of capital punishment and an *amende honorable* for crimes against God
and King. In practical terms the passage of the law raised the specter of
religious persecution against Protestants and nonbelievers, which the
monarchy had clearly renounced in the eighteenth century. Rumors immediately circulated that not only violent attacks and profanations
within churches but even the failure to decorate one's home, or respectfully kneel before passing religious processions, would provoke the vengeance of this law. Although the worst fears of its critics were never actually realized, the mere fact of this law's passage led many to conclude
that the government was abruptly changing course and moving toward
establishing a theocracy in France. In the words of one of its staunchest
opponents in the chambers, Pierre-Paul Royer-Collard, "Not only does
[the proposal] introduce into our legislation a new crime, but what is
even more extraordinary, it creates a new principle of criminality, an order of crimes which is, so to speak, supernatural. . . . As such the law
throws into question both religion and civil society, their nature, their
ends, and their respective independence . . . governments, should they be
successors to the apostles?"[8] If the content of the law was sufficient to
excite widespread concern and protest, the apparent turnaround of the
government on this issue between 1824 and 1825 and the growing conviction (even among monarchists on the right) that its suspicious passage could only be explained by the secret machinations of the Knights
of Faith led many to see this law as but the first sign of an extensive clerical plot to secretly put the reins of government in the hands of those
working to resurrect the kind of theocracy described by Royer-Collard.[9]
    The Sacrilege Law, more than any other single piece of legislation
passed during the Restoration, completely contradicted the consistent

policy of the regime to differentiate sacramental conformity from citizenship, to avoid ascribing to itself the role of definer or defender of the sacred, in short, to constitute monarchy in strictly secular terms. This law, which clearly evoked the equivalence between the sacred Host and the person of the king, and which revived the ancient practice of the *amende honorable,* was the sole legal act of the Restoration to offer the eucharistic conception of monarchy which was common fare in the revival of the missionaries. That the profanation of the Host, which represented the body of Christ, was conceived in the early version of this law as "parricide," and analogously as "regicide," demonstrates the degree to which the eucharistic model of monarchy was at work in the framing of this law. In the final version of the law, attacks on the sacred Host were not automatically interpreted as attacks on the body of the king; since the law required proof that the culprit committed the act "voluntarily, publicly and by hatred and contempt for the monarchy," it imagined the possibility of a sacrilegious act that had nothing to do with the king. Yet the apparent support by the government for a law which contained at its core a conception of monarchy that equated the king with God, and his body with the sacred Host, was sufficient to provoke widespread controversy and protest. The law was, in fact, never applied. Its only victim, as one historian has argued, "was the regime crazy enough to accept responsibility for it." [10]

A central issue which contemporaries regarded as a sort of barometer in church-state relations was the question of the *biens nationaux.* While émigrés were also concerned in this critical matter, the church obviously had an interest in legislation concerning this particular legacy of the Revolution, and critics of moves to offer restitution or undermine the legality of the *biens nationaux* often focused on its clerical dimension. In 1815 the regime passed a law that provided for the restitution of all properties which the government had acquired as *biens nationaux,* but which had never been "alienated" to individual citizens. It was not until 1825 that this thorny issue was resolved by a law which did not punish acquirers of *biens nationaux* or challenge the inviolability of property acquired in this way, but which did acknowledge the rights of those "despoiled" during the Revolution and afforded them reparations. While the *milliard des émigrés* provoked a broad reaction among many critics who saw this as a return to the injustices of feudalism, even this legislation clearly did not challenge the validity of the *biens nationaux.* In the matter of *biens nationaux* the regime showed itself to be the inheritor of the secular monarchs of the eighteenth century whose magistrates regu-

larly enforced laws which echoed the logic of an anonymous pamphle-
teer of that period who declared that there was "nothing more sacred in
the order of civil things than property." [11] If in the eighteenth century the
magistrates enforced this view by protecting the property of Jansenists
and by ceasing to punish religious crimes like suicide with the confiscation of property, the Restoration monarchs perpetuated it in their consistent insistence upon the legality of the *biens nationaux*.

In addition to the Sacrilege Law and the new law offering reparations
for *biens nationaux*, the government promulgated two other clerical
laws in 1825, one giving priests more power in education and the other
recognizing the right for women (but not men) to organize in *petits
séminaires;* taken together, this series of laws represented a high point in
legislation favoring the church, and offering a conception of monarchy
like that regularly proffered by the missionaries. So severe was the reaction to this clerical thrust that the government was forced to explain itself in order to assuage the widespread fears that France was becoming
a theocracy, increasingly, if clandestinely, ruled by men of the collar. In
May of 1826, Denis-Luc Antoine Fraysinnous, the minister of ecclesiastical affairs, gave a long speech on the religious politics of the government, emphasizing in particular the vast gap that existed between the actual state of affairs in France and the "myth created by propaganda"
which led people to believe that society was increasingly controlled by
priests, and in particular by Jesuits. Fraysinnous offered statistics, such
as the fact that in education the Jesuits ran only 7 out of 100 seminaries, and that those were but a small fraction of schools training the
young, including 60 communal colleges and 800 private institutions. [12]
The regime remained on the defensive regarding ecclesiastical matters,
as anticlericalism continued to swell throughout the kingdom until
1828, when it finally promulgated a law which represented a clear acknowledgment that it had to back off on its policies supporting the
church. The Ordinances of June 1828 responded in particular to fears
that the priests, and especially the Jesuits, were gaining control over primary and secondary education by placing both under the strict surveillance and control of the university. The church establishment was opposed to this act, and a committee of seven bishops drew up an official
letter of protest, signed by seventy prelates. Charles X had to seek the
intervention of the pope (which was granted) to get the clergy to fall into
line with the regime on this matter. [13]

Thus, in terms of its legal efforts to define the relationship between
church and state, the Restoration divides easily into three periods. First,

in the years up through 1824, the regime generally supported the church, and enabled it to recover somewhat from its weakened position, but consistently maintained the juridical foundation established over the eighteenth century and strengthened by the Revolution and especially by the Concordat of 1801. The years 1825–1826 represent a high point of clerical legislation, epitomized by the Sacrilege Law, which offered a vision of monarchy completely inconsistent with the regime's general practice, but perfectly consonant with the vision of monarchy put forth by the missionaries. Finally, the years 1827–1829 mark a shift away from this position, first a defensive posture and rhetorical efforts to assuage fears of theocracy, and finally the law of 1828 actually curtailing the power of the church in the domain of education. Regardless of these specific legislative thrusts and reversals, which did play a role in shaping the way people perceived this regime, the government was, in fact, remarkably consistent in defending the secular vision of monarchy honed over the course of the eighteenth century. Its consistent efforts to retain the separation between citizenship and sacramental conformity, its intransigence as to the inviolability of the *biens nationaux,* its continuous reluctance to prosecute for blasphemy and sacrilege, even once these things were on the books, all demonstrate its commitment to this legacy.

The Ceremonial Foundations of Monarchy

If, in spite of some spectacular exceptions, the Restoration regime proved itself to be the successor to the secular monarchy of the eighteenth century in legal terms, in ceremonial terms the conception of monarchy which defined the regime over fifteen years was far less clear. From the beginning of the regime, Louis XVIII showed himself to be willing to reintegrate the church into the state's public ceremonies, and to place himself at the head of the national religion by promoting and participating in religious ceremonies and rites. After 1825 the image of a resurrected Christian monarchy became much more powerful once Charles X ascended the throne. His coronation, coupled with his active participation in the expiatory services associated with the Jubilee of 1826, sent a strong message to the nation that in spite of the legal framework of the nation (also changing in alarming ways at the same moment), the monarchy *was* returning to its seventeenth-century Christian incarnation. The apparent contradiction between these two aspects, the legal and the ceremonial foundations of monarchy, fanned the discourse of plots and conspiracies from which the regime would suffer until its fall in 1830.

On the level of the ceremonial trappings of the Restoration regime, historians are most justified in calling this period a "return to the Old Regime." Françoise Waquet's *La Fête Royale sous la Restauration, ou l'Ancien Régime retrouvé* is devoted entirely to demonstrating this point.[14] Whether by looking at the personnel hired to ensure the faithful reproduction of Old Regime ceremonial, the festive calendar adopted by the restored Bourbons, the decorations designed for these events, or the way in which the church was reintegrated into the business of representing the monarchy to its subjects, Waquet repeatedly underscores the continuity between the Restoration monarchy and its predecessors of the early modern period. Considered against the backdrop of the revolutionary campaign to dechristianize France and to use secular, republican (and later imperial) festivals to remake the nation and its people, there is no doubt that the Restoration's festival project betrays an effort to restore an older conception of the relationship between the people and its rulers, which included a return to the rhythms of a Christian calendar, punctuated by the critical personal and political events in the lives of the reigning monarchs.[15] Explicitly religious celebrations comprised eight of the ten regular festivals orchestrated annually by the regime; these included funeral ceremonies for Louis XVI, Marie Antoinette (until 1825), the duc de Berry (after 1820), and Louis XVIII (after 1825)—all of which were celebrated as masses—as well as the ceremony of the Last Supper, the procession of Corpus Christi and its Octave, the procession of the Vow of Louis XIII (August 15), and the mass in honor of the Holy Ghost.[16] Other annual festivals focused attention on events in the lives of the kings or other members of the royal family: these included the saint days of Louis (25 August) and later Charles (4 November), the royal entries of Louis XVIII and Charles X into Paris, and births, marriages, and deaths within the royal family. Like their predecessors, the restored Bourbons combined an extensive ritual at court with local festivals celebrated all over the nation, in which they did not directly interact with their subjects but through which their images were disseminated and shaped. In prints, medals, and busts (which were themselves ceremonially inaugurated and then served as stand-ins for the absent monarch), in speeches by local officials, in theater performances carefully chosen for their complimentary portraits of the king, and in *Te Deums* celebrated in churches, images of the distant king were presented to the people in the context of regular, local celebrations.

Yet if we analyze more closely the range of ceremonial practices deployed to represent the monarchy during the Restoration, it becomes clear that if the regime emulated its monarchical ancestors, it was the very recent monarchs of the eighteenth century who had already turned away from many of the rites and rituals which stressed the "sacred," "divine" nature of kingship. The whole range of rituals that were common in the reigns of the most Christian monarchs because they attested to the sacred quality of his person, or because they clearly dramatized the equation between king and kingdom, and the very Christian nature of that kingdom, were either avoided or proved very problematic for the Restoration monarchy.[17] The main ceremony devoted to underscoring the sacred quality of the monarch, the coronation, was not performed for Louis XVIII. During Louis XVIII's reign there were repeated efforts to orchestrate a coronation, but they were consistently foiled by disastrous events. The initial plan for the coronation in 1814 was put off because of Napoleon's return in the Hundred Days. A new project for a coronation in the winter of 1818–19 was canceled because of the assassination of the duc de Berry. Again plans were drawn up for a coronation in 1823, a plan which, interestingly, tried to avoid Notre Dame with its memory of the imperial coronation in favor of the smaller Eglise Saint-Geneviève. But these plans were also dropped, because of the king's infirmities. Thus Louis XVIII sat on his throne for ten years without any religious ceremony sanctifying his kingship in the ritual manner performed regularly by his ancestors in the Old Regime. As with the consistent failure to erect expiatory statues for Louis XVI and Marie Antoinette, one can always interpret the failure to perform a coronation in terms of circumstances. But in fact this ceremonial omission fits squarely with the conception of monarchy that Louis XVIII seemed committed to supporting. Indeed, in eschewing the coronation, he followed the practice of his eighteenth-century predecessors, who had likewise placed less and less emphasis on a ritual that no longer seemed necessary or appropriate for constituting monarchical authority. What is extraordinary and noteworthy, in fact, is less Louis XVIII's failure to resurrect the practice of the coronation than Charles X's determination to have one, with many of the trappings of his seventeenth-century predecessors. The august and spectacular ceremony performed at Reims, and celebrated simultaneously in local festivals throughout the country, represents a critical shift in the way in which the regime publicly constituted itself. While the king did acknowledge and publicly proclaim his continued support for the Charter, and integrated new prayers and oaths into this ritual acknowledging these new aspects of monarchical authority, Charles X participated in a public anointment in which the officiating bishop referred to him as "he whom God has given us as king." This king also practiced the ancient rite of "touching for scrofula," further underscoring the divine origin of his person.[18]

In the following year, 1826, Charles X actively participated in public expiatory processions in the context of the Papal Jubilee; in so doing he cemented the message propagated by his coronation that the conception of monarchy which he believed in was more akin to that being dramatized by the missionaries than that apparently adhered to by his predecessor and brother, Louis XVIII. Dressed in purple, the color of mourning for the kings of France, Charles proceeded on foot with a candle in his hand, casting himself as one of the tens of thousands of French subjects participating in such expiatory rituals throughout the nation. But this particular spectacle gave rise to a widespread rumor that the king was in fact a bishop, secretly working to place the reins of power in the hands of the clerics. While historians have all concurred on the critical role of this particular Jubilee spectacle in the growing obsession with the clerical plot, I would argue that this way of interpreting the event only makes sense when put in the context of the religious revival which regularly orchestrated such expiatory spectacles throughout the Restoration. In the previous chapter, I spoke of the extensive participation of civil officials in the expiatory rituals of the missionaries. Actively encouraged by the priests, and necessary to give their ceremonies the appearance of public sanction, the regular participation of uniformed members of the National Guard, the army, and civil officials served to solidify the view that the regime seemed to be supporting a conception of monarchy and a view of the secular legacy of the eighteenth century and the Revolution which was, in fact, at odds with its laws. Many civil officials refused to participate on precisely these grounds; but more often they added their numbers to the spectacular processions of the missionaries, participating most frequently in the planting of the cross, the final expiatory ritual of the missionaries. If such participation led local populations to assume that their government was falling under the control of the priests, when Charles X himself participated in the extravagant expiatory spectacle in conjunction with the Jubilee it gave national currency to this obsession with a clerical plot.

While provoking controversy from the beginning of the Restoration, it was after 1825—after the coronation, the passage of the Sacrilege Law, and the king's participation in the Jubilee of 1826—that such fears precipitated a huge wave of anticlerical protest against the missionaries and the king; this groundswell of protest led the regime to become more careful about its public image and, in particular, to take steps to assuage the fears of a theocracy. Just as the public pronouncement of Frayssinous in 1826 and the June Ordinances of 1828 constituted clear efforts by the regime to quell such fears, so did the decline in national religious services between 1827 and 1829 correspond to a clear effort on the part of the regime to demonstrate that it did not support the missionaries' conception of monarchy, but in fact was willing to defend and represent itself as the legitimate successor to the secular monarchs of the eighteenth century.[19]

The chronology of the ceremonial foundations of the Restoration regime dovetails with the shifts noted in the discussion of its legal framework. Between 1814 and 1824 a cautious secular monarchy reintegrated the church into its ceremonies, but avoided a coronation or any ceremony which clearly figured the monarch himself as sacred. The years 1825 and 1826 represent a peak in the apparent "return" of Christian monarchy of the seventeenth-century type, when the coronation and the king's participation in the Jubilee evoked a vision of kingship perfectly consonant with that put forth by the missionaries. Between 1827 and 1829, the decline in religious ceremonies associated with the regime marks an effort to sever the public connection between the actual monarch and this more radical vision. But in the local context of a visiting mission, where public political authorities often attended the missionaries' autos-da-fé, mass confessions for the sins of the Revolution, and processions culminating in the erection of their enormous calvaries, this chronology was less than perfectly clear. If debates over clerical laws and major national ceremonies such as the coronation and the Jubilee played a major role in shaping the public debate over the relationship between church and state in the constitution of monarchy in the Restoration, it was the protracted struggles between missionaries and civil officials at the local level which brought the issue home for the majority of French men and women. While all historians of the Restoration allude to the missions, and evoke in a general way the anticlerical sentiment they aroused, no one has ever looked closely at the complex, public negotiations precipitated by this revival, even though they offer a privileged vantage point from which to see the working out of the revolutionary settlement regarding church-state relations in this critical period.

Struggles Over the Missions

In many ways the following discussion of the struggles between missionaries and their supporters in the church and the Restoration regime continues the line of inquiry opened by Dale Van Kley in his studies of Jesuits and Jansenists and advanced by Jeffrey Merrick's analysis of related controversies at the end of the Old Regime. Both authors investigated struggles over religious issues in the eighteenth century in order to demonstrate how protracted disputes over the appropriate jurisdiction of the church and the state in temporal and spiritual matters gradually eroded the foundations of Christian monarchy. In Merrick's words, "Jurisdictional conflicts disrupted the collaboration between [the church and state] and the secular authorities effectively renounced any visionary attempt, as one functionary put it, 'to make society into a monastery.'" [20] The analysis of the struggles between missionaries and civil officials that follows continues this discussion on the other side of the revolutionary chasm, when the religio-political foundations of monarchy were being sorted out in the wake of the cataclysmic events between 1789 and 1815. During the Restoration it was over the minutiae of organizing missions that local government officials articulated the regime's relationship to the church. From this vantage point it is clear that far from marking a return to the Old Regime of its seventeenth-century ancestors, the Restoration regime furthered in juridical and bureaucratic terms the secularization which took place over the eighteenth century. Honing arguments, laws, and tactics which could be deployed to discipline the missionaries, the "reactionary" Restoration clearly consolidated the secular settlement prefigured during the Revolution, expressed in the Concordat of 1801, and fully applied after the Revolution of 1830.

In the eighteenth century, monarchs and their magistrates progressively saw a separation of Catholicity from citizenship as essential to social peace—unlike their seventeenth-century predecessors, who had seen sacramental conformity and obedience to the laws of the church as constitutive of the social order. Yet controversies over Jansenists and Protestants led increasingly to the view that to preserve social and political tranquility, spiritual matters had to be consigned to the private sphere; the government should not defend the church, or define the sacred, or in any way construe the citizenry in religious terms. Indeed, so far did the pendulum swing that the government increasingly saw the need to intervene in ecclesiastical matters on behalf of citizens who were being denied the sacraments or having land confiscated because of religious crimes. In other words, by the end of the eighteenth century, monarchs stopped defining the body politic in Christian terms, and they went so far as to intervene in spiritual matters in the name of the more important, and quite separate, public interest. During the Restoration the correspondence between civil and ecclesiastical officials over the missions recapitulates this essential eighteenth-century debate. On the one side, we have representatives of the state making the practical argument about the need to prohibit or carefully monitor the religious revival in the name of social order, while, on the other side, we have the missionaries and their supporters in the church trying to resuscitate the older argument that religion does not challenge but rather helps to cement social order.

In their requests for guidance and assistance from their superiors in Paris, local civil officials portrayed the missionaries as a fundamental challenge to public tranquillity on many levels. Some administrators made this point merely by evoking the broad contrast between the regime's commitment to forgetting regarding the delicate problem of the revolutionary past and the missionaries' determination to foment passions through their emphasis on remembering. In the words of the prefect of the Hautes-Alpes, in a letter written in 1818: "This maxim of *oubli* and *union,* so eminently religious, that the government spreads to its subjects by the voice of its administrators, is nowhere the rule of these missionaries." [21] Echoing the same point a few months later, but referring more explicitly to the pernicious consequences of the missionaries' approach, a police report from Valence in Provence commented ruefully, "it is painful to see ministers of religion refusing to cover the past with a veil of *oubli,* and by design, stirring up passions with their sermons." [22] Administrators did not, however, restrict themselves to abstract discussions of the virtues of *oubli;* they revealed the multiple dangers posed by the missionaries in more concrete terms. Whether by drawing attention to the missionaries' repeated assaults on the juridical framework of the existing monarchy, or their tendency to stir up painful memories of the White Terror, which had hardly had time to heal, or the unpopularity of their explicitly religious message, civil officials evoked the specter of disorder to which they, as administrators and defenders of social peace, were obliged to develop an effective response.

A commissioner of police from Dijon in the Côte d'Or explicitly raised the problem of the missionaries' assault on the legal foundations of the regime:

> The missionaries could even become quite dangerous if they try to propagate principles contrary to the Charter, or to throw doubt on the inviolability of properties which we call national; principles which we know they have integrated into their sermons in many cities where they have already been.[23]

If their direct attacks on the laws and the Charter made them appear subversive and dangerous, the missionaries' determination to use their expiatory ceremonies to remind the population of the horrors of the Revolution seemed to many administrators to carry a danger of its own, particularly in areas so recently torn apart by the violence of the White Terror. This, as we saw, was the case for the prefect of the Bouches-du-Rhône trying to preserve order in Marseilles in 1820. It was also true for the prefect of the Côte d'Or, who echoed the sentiments of the police commissioner just mentioned, and tried to block a mission from taking place the following year in Beaune. His depiction of the missionaries was more inflammatory, shaped by a language of plots and conspiracies which characterized a good deal of the criticism of the revival in these years. His fears were also more specific to the context of his department, in light of the horrors of the White Terror experienced there only four years before the missionaries were trying to come to his town.

> The missionaries are nothing other than very active agents of secret societies who are trying to provoke a counter-revolution by the means of persuasion and the propagation of fanaticism. That which the nobles couldn't accomplish in 1815 and 1816, by force and by violence, the Priests and their auxiliaries want to bring to fruition with their conferences and their preaching.

Depicting his town as finally having calmed down in the wake of those terrible events, he begged for the minister of the interior's support in preserving peace:

> You cannot imagine the effect which these missionaries produce on women, and on weak spirits, and if they don't manage to provoke a civil war in France, it's only because the elements for it don't exist. . . . We mustn't allow them to agitate the population in this way, and it is within your power to extinguish them. This is a service which you could provide for the nation, and which will earn you our gratitude.[24]

The prefect of Allier, in his letters both to the minister of police and to his local prelate from the period 1818–1819, beautifully summarizes the range of threats posed by the missionaries, as well as the obligation of the civil administration to intervene in the revival in the name of social order. His correspondence reiterates the view that missionaries were to be seen as "outside the law," as consistently setting themselves against

the juridical foundations of monarchy set up by the regime. While it is
for this reason that the prefect implies that they are stirring up discord,
his letter also touches on the exclusively religious content of the missions, which could be equally problematic politically because of its unpopularity. Although this particular official stopped short of justifying
police intervention in strictly spiritual matters, he expressed the kind of
logic which enabled many of his colleagues in the administration to do
so in other contexts.

> I do not pretend here, to examine to what degree it is acceptable that the law
> of the church finds itself continually in opposition with the laws of the state,
> and that preaching publicly violates that which civil laws and the edicts of
> our sovereign permit; I pretend even less to scrutinize questions such as de-
> ciding whether or not in the excess of their zeal some ecclesiastics don't in-
> terpret the . . . evangelical . . . in a manner much more extreme than what
> it should mean; . . . these theological questions do not fall within the juris-
> diction of the civil administrator; it is sufficient that a thing be more destruc-
> tive than it could be useful, and that in order to produce an uncertain success
> it produces real bad consequences that he should try to protect those he
> administers.[25]

In his letter to the bishop of Clermont the prefect reiterated this final
point, explaining that it justified his efforts to block a mission from taking place in one of the towns in his jurisdiction. "It is in light of this obligation that I believe it is my duty to ask you to not consent to the missionaries coming to Moulins, and to write in the same sense to His
Excellence the Minister of the Interior."[26]

Again and again administrators framed their arguments for prohibiting the missions, or limiting them to the interiors of churches, or controlling their timing or their content in terms of their commitment to preserving public tranquillity. In spite of the careful wording of the prefect
of Allier, which seemed to disqualify public officials from meddling in
strictly "theological" matters, members of the civil administration elsewhere did try to pressure missionaries to offer the sacraments and to temper their explicitly religious message in the name of social order. The following explanation of the disorder produced by the missionaries in Arles
implies the right of the administrator to step in and try to enforce religious "tolerance" and "moderation" on precisely these grounds: "Public tranquillity is again at the point of being troubled by a circumstance
that one could have predicted, and that those who inspired it could have
avoided with more tolerance and moderation."[27] Here it was a question
of denying absolution and the last rites to an ex-revolutionary, and the

civil administrators justified pressuring the local priest to administer the sacraments in the name of social peace. The majority of prefects, sub-prefects, and mayors did not go so far as to meddle in religious matters, but they did regularly intervene in the missions, and the argument was always the same: it was the job of the public administrator to ensure so-cial peace, and if religious men were "troubling public tranquillity" then it was the civil official's job to control them.

Not surprisingly, members of the church establishment saw the situa-tion quite differently. They consistently denied the general allegation that the missionaries were a threat to social order. They articulated the kind of argument made by the archbishop of Aix in the context of the mission at Marseilles that "far from destroying order and public tranquillity, [re-ligion] has always contributed to the maintenance of both." [28] In so doing they were echoing the arguments of prelates from the Old Regime, who consistently made the case that religion played a critical role in cement-ing the social order, in ensuring obedience to all authority. But as was the case in the Old Regime, as controversies over religious matters began to divide the citizenry and produce social unrest, the administrators work-ing on behalf of the regime saw controlling the churchmen as the solution to the problem. In the Restoration, in the face of civil unrest, civil officials turned their attention first and foremost to controlling the missionaries. The prelates of this period criticized this tendency of the regime to turn its might against the church and its representatives instead of the trouble-makers disrupting the missions. The archbishop of Aix criticized the dis-ciplinary measures suggested against the missionaries in Marseilles in precisely these terms, asking the regime ruled by the Most Christian King Louis XVIII why it didn't use the full power of the state against the "small number of people who seek to interrupt the mission?" Mocking those lib-eral newspapers which accused the missionaries of "disturbing public tranquillity," he asked the state to step in *not* on behalf of the trouble-makers but in defense of the sacred religion of France and its right to orchestrate elaborate outdoor ceremonies which do nothing but move and edify their participants. Refusing to cooperate with any of the pre-fect's demands to enclose the ceremonies inside churches, the archbishop summarized the ironic position of the regime vis-à-vis the missionaries: "I am surprised that the French government, which sees these missionar-ies bearing the standard of Christ in this land of infidels, wishes to ban these sacred and touching ceremonies in this very Christian realm." [29]

If prelates used all manner of argument to turn the civil adminis-trators against the "infernal troublemakers" creating disorder in the context of the missions, the representatives of the national government in Paris repeatedly adopted the suspicious stance of its prefects and encouraged them to take the measures they deemed necessary to ensure public tranquillity and peace. What this translated into in practice was not prosecutions against troublemakers on behalf of the national religion but repeated efforts to control and discipline the missionaries. Indeed the extraordinary system of surveillance and censorship put into place to control the missionaries led their main historian, Ernest Sevrin, to offer the following depiction of the Restoration regime, which departs from historians' assumptions about the inclinations of this supposedly "reactionary" and "clerical" regime:

> People have been wrong to believe that the Restoration offered the missionaries protection, either officially or clandestinely, or that it made of them an instrument of its rule. Whatever might have been the personal sympathies of Louis XVIII for this revival, his ministers of the interior, and of the police always had toward the missions an attitude which was more than reserved, often distrustful, and honestly painful to the bishops. Their policies tended constantly to enclose their religious exercises in the churches, and to ban, whenever possible, the great outdoor processions; . . . Charles X, as devout as he was, and having a minister of the right, shared this same manner of seeing the missions.[30]

The government, as Sevrin rightly points out, certainly did *not* rely upon these missionaries as an instrument of its rule; quite the contrary, because of the nature of the missionaries' message and the widespread disorder their revival provoked, this "counterrevolutionary" and supposedly "clerical" regime honed tactics for disciplining and controlling the priests which, over the long term, ironically secured the secular legacy of the Revolution.

The Revolutionary Settlement in Action

The bureaucratic apparatus in place between 1815 and 1830 which contended with the controversies stirred up by the missions was inherited from the Revolution: the Ministry of the Interior, with its hierarchy of prefects, subprefects, and mayors; the Ministry of Police, with its auxiliary hierarchy of commissaires de police; and the Ministry of Ecclesiastical Affairs, communicating directly with the church hierarchy. These constituted the web of civil and ecclesiastical officials who negotiated over the problem of the missions. The regime did not rely only upon the administration inherited from the revolutionary period to handle problems associated with the missions; it also relied upon laws dating from this period to justify intervention in the revival. In practical terms, therefore, the negotiations over specific aspects of the missions involved putting into force the administrative and legislative apparatus for defining the relationship between church and state set up during the Revolution and consolidated by the Concordat of 1801.

There was no clear national policy on the missions proclaimed by the government as of 1815 and carried out consistently over the course of the Restoration. Local officials often clamored for a uniform policy that they could follow, as illustrated by the following letter from the prefect of Allier:

> It is greatly desired that there be adopted with regard to the missionaries a precise and uniform set of rules which, while combining prudent and conciliatory measures would allow us to prevent tumult and scandal, and also the inconveniences which arise from the exalted and virulent preaching among the inhabitants and also the disagreement and misinformation among the authorities.[31]

No such national policy was ever issued. Rather, the national Ministries of the Interior and Police (eventually combined) generally left it up to local officials to assess the situation within their jurisdiction and determine how to act vis-à-vis the missionaries. In the words of a "Note" from 1829, summarizing the measures taken over the course of the regime, "The government has never given any general instructions on these issues, and we have almost always left it up to local authorities to determine what measures needed to be taken to maintain good order during the course of the religious exercises which were in question."[32] Yet through their continual correspondence with local officials, the national government did, in fact, arm administrators with a uniform set of laws and practices which they could and did use in contending with the missionaries.

The letters between local officials and their ministers in Paris reveal an army of bureaucrats trying to ascertain precisely what laws from past decades should be applied as they dealt with the problems posed by visiting missionaries. What power did they actually have to police the missionaries, and on the basis of which laws could they justify their intervention? Were laws dating from the revolutionary period still valid? In other words, the questions of local officials and the responses of their superiors dramatize in very practical terms the complexity of negotiating the relationship between church and state in this postrevolutionary period. The prefect of Allier, for example, requested advice concerning the applicability of Articles 45 and 49 of the Convention of 29 messidor year 9, which was part of the law of 18 germinal year 10. These two articles gave administrators limited rights to restrict religious ceremonies to the interior of churches, either in the case of a large Protestant population or where civil unrest was a possibility.[33] The prefect of the Seine-and-Marne addressed the minister of police in the following year regarding the possibility of applying Articles 13 and 14 of the law of 7 vendemiaire year 4, which banned all religious exercises outside of churches.[34] While the minister only responded directly in the latter case, explaining that "the law of Vendemiaire year 4 was obviously not in harmony with our present legislation," he argued that the principle implicit in (both) laws, that civil officials had the right to police religious ceremonies and restrict them to the interiors of churches in the name of social order, was certainly inherent in the first article of the Concordat, which could and should be applied vis-à-vis the missionaries. This important article read, "The Catholic religion will be liberally exercised in France. Its cult will be public, conforming to the rules which the Police and the government will deem necessary in order to maintain public tranquillity."[35] Combined with the ordinance by which the missions were authorized by the king in 1816, which required the local bishop's approval, this article from the Concordat gave the local prefect and his subordinates the right to initiate negotiations as to whether a mission should take place at all, and if it did, to determine what measures were necessary to ensure social peace throughout its duration. If this article generally established the principle that civil administrators had jurisdiction over the Catholic church and its public manifestations, other laws suggested by national officials in Paris justified more rigorous and specific forms of police action which could be deployed against the missionaries.

To contend with the problem of the content of their sermons, and in particular the missionaries' explicit attacks on the Charter, the *biens nationaux,* and the practice of civil marriage, Parisian officials repeatedly invoked three different laws. Article 201 of the Penal Code threatened with three months to two years of imprisonment "any Minister of Religion who speaks publicly against the government or a law of the government, or any act of public authority."[36] Other correspondence cited the law of 9 November 1811, article 8, as, for example, a letter from the prefect of the Hautes-Alpes to the minister of the police from 1818 which repeated the advice he had offered to the subprefect of Briançon regarding priests who had spoken against the *biens nationaux:* "there is no other measure to take but to attest, by a *procès verbal,* the infraction defined by the law of 9 November 1811, article 8, and to denounce the perpetrator to the judicial authorities."[37] Finally, the law on sedition passed in 1815, which was designed to prevent Bonapartists and republicans from speaking out against the monarchy, was broad enough to be relevant to the counterrevolutionary excesses of the missionaries. While the major part of this law alludes to attacks on or menaces against the person or authority of the king, and to the public use of symbols and signs other than that of the reigning monarchy, article 5 of this law also explicitly exposed to prosecution "those whose speeches, given in public places, . . . tend to excite disobedience to the King *and to the Constitutional Charter.*" Clearly this article was of relevance to the missionaries and their sermons, as was article 8, which declared "guilty those seditious acts of people who spread or accredit rumors relating either to the inviolability of properties that one calls national, or to the supposed reestablishment of the dîme or feudal rights."[38] These different laws empowered civil officials to use a wide range of disciplinary tactics against the missionaries, including advance negotiations with prelates over the content of sermons and ceremonies, the placement of secret agents in churches to listen for infractions, forced departures of missionaries who violated these laws, and even the prosecution of offenders.

The final law which came up repeatedly in the correspondence between civil officials regarding the missions was the law of 24 messidor year 12, which empowered state officials to refuse to participate in any public ceremony not explicitly orchestrated by the regime. Keenly aware of the need to differentiate the civil administration from the messages propagated in the context of the missions' expiatory spectacles (particularly on the 21st of January), the government again offered local officials a legal means to do so. As with the article from the Concordat and the laws on sedition, local officials varied in the zeal with which they applied this particular law. In 1817, the local official acting in the absence of the prefect of the Drôme wrote to the minister of police to applaud the decision of a mayor in his jurisdiction not to allow the National Guard to participate in the erection of the mission cross. A few years later in the same department, the prefect condemned a different mayor for adopting the opposite course and allowing public authorities to participate in the mission. In the latter context he specifically cited the mayor's decision as an infraction of the law of 24 messidor year 12.[39]

As they were informed of various measures which could be used to en-sure order in the context of the missions, a certain degree of uniformity was achieved, at least in the options clearly available to local adminis-trators. One enterprising prefect tried to turn the successful handling of the mission within his jurisdiction into a sort of model to be reproduced all over the country. The prefect of the Loire-Inférieure wrote to the min-ister of the interior in May of 1827, lauding the measures adopted by his subordinates and recommending the following list of tactics to be adopted elsewhere to ensure the tranquillity which reigned during the mission in his town of Nantes.

> It would be useful to prescribe [in concert with the ecclesiastical authorities where it concerns them]:
>
> 1. That in the interior of churches, and during all exercises, the two sexes should be separated by a barrier, and that everyone should remain seated;
> 2. That there shall be constantly, in every church, during the exercises, a *commissaire de police* with two other gendarmes at the disposition of the curé or head of the mission;
> 3. That all of the sermons given in public, or in meeting places, and espe-cially in outdoor ceremonies, be communicated in advance to the municipal authorities charged with the responsibility of ensuring order;
> 4. That the missionaries be invited to abstain from appealing directly to any official corps or the national guard or any other, without having gotten in advance, the consent of competent authorities; they should be invited, as well, to abstain from naming in their sermons, individuals accused of repre-hensible acts, leaving to magistrates alone the job of exercising calm and im-partial judgments as they pursue legal repression;
> 5. Finally, that the local authorities severely execute laws regarding the profession of bookselling, especially regarding *colporteurs* [peddlers of reli-gious books] operating without official permission.[40]

In his response the minister of the interior thanked the prefect of the Loire-Inférieure for his initiative and his suggestions, and promised to send them on to the minister of ecclesiastical affairs along with a letter recommending that his precautions be adopted more generally.[41] Al-though the minister of ecclesiastical affairs replied to his colleague that "we have every hope that the suggestions of M. the Prefect will be use-fully applied," there is no evidence that this set of precautions was adopted in a general way.[42] Rather, local civil administrators seemed to pick and choose among the various tactics at their disposal, based on the battery of laws made known to them in their personal correspondence with their superiors in Paris.

Everywhere the missionaries went they were held to the requirement of the Ordinance of 1816 that the residing bishop actually requested the mission. Critics of the missionaries quickly seized the initiative to block a mission if there was any evidence that the local bishop had not approved their arrival, and correspondence between the prefects and the ministers demonstrates their willingness to block a revival on these grounds.[43] Once it was clear that the requirement of a bishop's official invitation had been met, it was up to local civil administrators to determine (on the basis of Article 1 of the Concordat) what "rules the police and the government will deem necessary in order to maintain public tranquillity." At the very least, civil administrators required that they be informed of all that the missionaries planned to do so that appropriate security measures could be taken. But the demands of security often led to quite severe measures against the missionaries: civil officials tried to block missions entirely, control their timing, or restrict their preaching to the interiors of churches. The concern for public tranquillity justified censoring the content of sermons, placing police spies in churches, and even chasing missionaries from town in the case of infractions. Prefects, subprefects, and mayors tried to determine the placement of mission crosses to ensure order in the processions in which they would be erected and to allow for surveillance after the missions, when they expected the cross to be the site of public congregations and prayers. In every case the precise measures adopted by local officials depended on popular opinion regarding the missionaries and the nature and seriousness of protests against them; but they also depended on the personnel within the local church establishment and the civil administration, as well as the composition of the missionaries themselves, since some were more or less popular than others. Also important was the religious and political history of the local site of the mission. For instance, the presence of a large Protestant population (as around Nîmes), or the recent history of struggles during the White Terror (as we saw in Marseilles), or the presence of a large, practicing Catholic population (as in Brittany) all determined the behavior of the missionaries and the civil authorities trying to preserve order in the context of the religious revival.

Whatever the specific measures ultimately adopted on the basis of all these complex considerations, it is clear that from the beginning to the end of the Restoration civil officials did regard the missions with distrust and sought consistently to control them. The laws and the administrative procedures to be relied upon to this end were identified and honed among the civil officials governing the realm in these years. However clear this was to those working within the civil administration, to the missionaries and members of the church establishment, and to historians reading their correspondence, for the people witnessing the missions a more complex message was transmitted. For in practice the missionaries more often than not evaded the efforts of civil administrators. They avoided informing local authorities of their plans, in spite of the official requirement that they do so; they flouted the efforts to censor the content of their sermons, or to prevent outdoor ceremonies, often with the vocal support of local prelates.[44] If the missionaries' intransigence prevented the civil officials from prevailing in the local orchestration of the revival, more practical, material problems also stood in the local administrator's way. The slowness of communication, for example, often meant that clear instructions from Paris to ban a mission or to chase missionaries from town were simply not received until the missionaries were safely on to their next destination. Thus, even in cases where the civil administrators responded to anticlerical protests by policing the revival, the missionaries were able to orchestrate their ceremonies as they saw fit.

Whatever the popular response to the missionaries, whatever the measures ultimately adopted by local administrators, and whatever the form that local missions ultimately assumed, it is clear that struggles over the details of the revival as it was performed in the local context provided the focus of a very public, nationwide negotiation over the capital political issues of the Restoration. Who should be the arbiters of France's future? The missionaries? Local officials armed with a bureaucracy and set of laws dating from the revolutionary period? Supporters or protesters organizing for or against the missions? Who was actually in power in France? The king, ruling through his local administrators on the basis of the Charter, or the priests, eminently capable of imposing their own vision of France in spite of the disciplinary efforts of local officials? While no clear, long-term resolutions to these issues emerged in the local contexts in which they were negotiated, the struggles over the missions at this level gave rise to certain practices and ways of seeing which would ultimately set the stage for such a resolution at the national level.

Negotiating the Staging of Monarchy

Whenever civil officials sought to intervene in the public spectacles of the missionaries it was in response to local protests. Only rarely did local officials initiate negotiations with missionaries about the content and the staging of their revival without local provocation. Even in these cases, their efforts were usually based on the knowledge of disorder provoked by missionaries elsewhere and were therefore designed to prevent such eruptions within the area under their jurisdiction.[45] The point to underscore here is the essential role of the local population (or like populations elsewhere) in the negotiation over the missions. The full range of anticlerical practices deployed against the missionaries will be considered separately, in chapter 5; however, it will be clear within the discussion in the pages that follow that the "negotiation" which I am evoking here was not merely between the representatives of the church and of the state, but explicitly involved local populations who clearly demonstrated support for or opposition to the missionaries.

A wide range of consequences resulted from this public negotiation over the missionaries. In some cases the anticlerical protesters prevailed in no uncertain terms: missions were banned, prevented entirely as a result of anticlerical demonstrations. But in other cases the local administration clearly exerted the law on behalf of the missionaries, even threatening to apply the full vengeance of the newly available Sacrilege Law. The vast majority of cases which will be considered fall between these two extremes. In the ultimate measures adopted at the local level, the majority of civil officials showed themselves willing neither to embrace the expiatory counterrevolutionary agenda of the missionaries nor to pursue these priests to the full extent of the law. As a result, the vision of monarchy performed for the vast majority of French citizens in this period was contradictory, and this, as we shall see, was ultimately fatal for the regime. Ernest Sevrin beautifully evokes the problematic nature of this contradictory, middle ground in this period: "Let us not forget . . . the double aspect of the revolutionary crisis for the men of this period: symbol of impiety and anarchy for some, of liberty and justice for others, the *juste milieu* was difficult, and easily suspect. This is the drama of the Restoration; it is also, to a small extent, the drama of the missions." [46] It is not only "to a small extent" the drama of the missions, for in the majority of cases it was precisely the *juste milieu* that was dramatized in the missions which most French men and women witnessed. This *was* suspicious, and played a central role in fanning the discourse of plots and conspiracies which mobilized the population to defeat the regime by 1830.

Brest, 1819: Chasing the Jesuits in the Name of the General Will

In the fall of 1819 the city of Brest became the scene of a public negotiation regarding the missionaries in which the anticlerical protesters defending the secular principles of the Charter clearly won the day. Missionaries already orchestrating revivals in towns nearby, and arriving to begin preaching in the town of Brest, were finally sent away by the bishop of Quimper and the prefect of Finistère in response to extensive and well-organized protests. A wide range of tactics were deployed by the anticlerical protesters in Brest, tactics that would become common in struggles against missionaries throughout France during the Restoration. Songs and caricatures mocking the missionaries circulated in the early days of October, setting the stage for public mass demonstrations against the missionaries once they arrived at the end of the month. Between the 26th and 28th of October two to three thousand citizens of Brest assembled and orchestrated repeated charivaris outside the bishop of Quimper's residence, screaming, "No mission! Down with the missionaries! No perturbation of the peace of families! Our own pastors suffice!" to the noise of "bells, whistles, clarinets, flutes, and voices."[47] Simultaneously, hundreds of *pères de familles* joined the meeting of the municipal council to express their opposition to the arrival of the missionaries in Brest. Appointing a deputation of fourteen citizens (including the mayor, encouraged to join the crowd by a special charivari addressed to him the previous night) to express their opposition formally to the bishop, they also drew up a petition against the missionaries which was signed by at least 186 men participating in the meeting.[48] On the night of October 28th there was a well-attended command performance of *Tartuffe*. At the end of these three days of agitation, the bishop conceded to the local population, and the missionaries were chased from the town of Brest. For weeks after this successful opposition to the missionaries, pamphlets circulated in the town of Brest publicizing the triumphant events of October and even making public some of the documents written by the bishop, the municipal council, and the local and national police officials as they tried to make decisions regarding the mission of 1819. In this way the case of Brest is of peculiar interest, because the "negotiations" with officials in Paris, between civil and ecclesiastical officials within Brest, and between the organized opposition and these officials were all "public" to an exceptional degree.

From the very beginning, the prefect of Finistère showed himself to be suspicious of the missionaries and deeply concerned about the potential dangers of their planned revival in Brest. However, initially he did nothing to block the mission since he believed he had no legal basis for doing so as a result of the law protecting freedom of religion.[49] By October the prefect's fears were reconfirmed by reports from his subprefect that songs and caricatures were circulating against the missionaries. He forwarded two songs to the minister of the interior, both of which derided the spiritual goals of the missionaries and encouraged the people of Brest to defend themselves against priests who seek to create divisions within their families, who attack the beloved writings of Voltaire and Rousseau, and who subvert the very laws of the realm. These songs depicted the missionaries as the representatives of the devil, organizing ceremonies in churches where "one sees not a single family united / The wife, here, declares war on her husband; / she is then beaten up by her spouse. . . . The Devil laughs, hell rejoices." It is for such "miracles" that the missionaries work; but they also extend their efforts against certain rights: "For a long time such a hope devours them." "These priests are only severe," continues the song, "against the acquirers [of *biens nationaux*], their wives, daughters, and sisters." "Such is the spirit of the men who are sent to you, the people of Brest; a Monseigneur, who sees nothing to fear, guides toward you these devils incarnate." To such threats the authors of the song respond, "but we have our Charter, our laws . . . "[50] The obvious threat implicit in such songs, the efforts to garner opposition as the "Monseigneur" guided the missionaries toward Brest, led the prefect to go and see the bishop to prevail upon him to abandon his plans to have a mission. The bishop of Quimper, as the prefect explained in a letter from the 8th of October, refused to concede to this demand and offered the following, rather typical defense of the mission.

> The Bishop came to see me yesterday to announce the fact that his decision was irrevocably taken, and that the mission would take place; that after scrupulously examining the objects which I presented, he believed that the dangers about which I was concerned would be by far compensated by the advantages which religion always offered; if these dangers menaced him or his clergy, that they knew how to suffer when religion commanded them to do so; that the priests, preaching peace and union, couldn't be a source of division and of quarrels; that after having promised for so long a mission to the inhabitants of Brest it would be cowardice to cede to fears of outrage; and finally, that he was waiting to receive from the Minister either orders to ban the mission, or at least, his thoughts on the matter, but that he would never

cede, and the will of the king himself would not lead him to yield to my request.[51]

In light of the bishop's refusal to ban the mission, the prefect tried to imagine other measures he could adopt, and in this letter expressed his intention to order the military leaders in his town to prohibit their men from participating in the exercises of the mission.

The arrival of the missionaries quickly placed the leading administrator of Brest in a defensive posture. Charivaris outside the bishop's residence on the nights of October 26 and 27, and the meeting and delegation of the municipal council and the *pères de familles* of his town, confronted the prefect with a city that had erupted into full-fledged revolt against the missionaries. Suddenly the minister of the interior, initially supporting the prefect's efforts to ban the missionaries, began to send letters criticizing local officials for having yielded to local troublemakers and demanding that the prefect seek to prosecute the principal organizers of the disorder in Brest.[52] The prefect consistently defended the actions of the protesters as well as the leniency which his subordinates in the local administration adopted toward them. In his descriptions of the charivaris, the prefect stressed the fact that "in the middle of this large crowd," comprised primarily of respectable people, "not one seditious cry was emitted"; that in spite of the numerous assemblage, the people committed "neither excess nor violence," but in fact "maintained a kind of order, or measure within their disorder"; and that, in fact, "the name of the king himself was constantly invoked, making it impossible to treat this as a seditious population." His narrative of the events presents a carefully organized population, doing the minimum necessary to express its views within the bounds of acceptable, legal practice. While it is true that the people ignored efforts by the subprefect and other police officials to disperse them, and in that sense directly disobeyed the local authorities, after each charivari they did disband peacefully, and between these "organized disorders," the missionaries and the bishop "appeared alone, and on foot in the streets, and were never once insulted."[53] If the prefect was disinclined to prosecute the inhabitants of Brest on the basis of the reasonable and limited nature of their disturbance, he also stressed to the minister of the interior the impossibility of identifying leaders in a crowd which reached 2,000 to 3,000 members, as well as the undesirability of pursuing citizens who were clearly the leading members of the community. The minister of the interior was also distressed by the illegal and inappropriate use of the municipal council in this context, which had been turned into a directly democratic instrument, expressing the voice of the entire population of the town.[54] Again, the prefect disagreed, stressing the orderly and legal manner in which the *pères de familles* proceeded, getting the mayor to accompany their deputation to the bishop, and accomplishing, by peaceful and organized measures, that of which he himself had been unsuccessful, namely convincing the prelate to cancel the mission.[55] The prefect was not, however, insensitive to the real security problems posed by the example of his population's behavior. As he said, "Without doubt a dangerous example has been given; there is reason to fear that this manner of enforcing the general will will find imitators, and may be employed in more difficult circumstances." But within the area under his jurisdiction he was satisfied that the members of his administration had reason to "congratulate [them]selves that more guilty disorders did not follow, and that the only result was the abandonment of a project which was imprudent from the outset."[56]

The prefect changed his attitude somewhat in the months following the events of October, when two pamphlets circulating in his town sought to capitalize on the victory of anticlericalism in Brest, and to offer both the population and the administration as models to be emulated in other struggles against missionaries throughout France. "Three Days of a Mission in Brest," the more inflammatory of the two pamphlets, contained a twenty-five-page account of the events in Brest, inviting its readers to "Let the energetic and sage conduct of the people of Brest serve as an example to all the cities where these men preach intolerance and seek to re-ignite hatreds which had been extinguished, and carry the standard of fanaticism and discord!"[57] Underscoring the liberal principles on which the opposition was organized, the pamphlet (in terms remarkably similar to those used by the prefect) applauds the tactics employed by the people of Brest, both their "orderly" charivaris and their use of the municipal council to organize an official deputation to the bishop of Quimper. The author also publicized the language and terms evoked in the songs and seditious writings circulating during the incident in Brest, in particular the attacks on the priests for their immorality and hypocrisy and their tendency to employ profane tunes and all manner of stagecraft in their apparently "pious" spectacles. The following excerpt beautifully illustrates this way of presenting the missionaries:

> [The precipitous departure of the Jesuits] is surely a great calamity to those who wanted to benefit from their grace, and enjoy the ecstasy of remarrying;

there is especially displeasure among those young virtuosos to whom one had proposed the singing of the Mission canticles to Vaudeville tunes. But it is also a victory for those peaceable people who like neither the scandal which one excites at the expense of religion, nor the exercises of piety which produce nothing but bigotry and ridicule.[58]

The author also emphasized in this regard the performance of *Tartuffe* demanded by the population as soon as the missionaries arrived in town, and which attracted a great number of spectators (principally the women of the town) when it was performed.[59] Interestingly, the prefect alluded to this performance of *Tartuffe* only once in his extensive correspondence with the minister of the interior, acknowledging that in permitting this performance the mayor was perhaps unwise.[60]

While the publicity this pamphlet gave to these events, to a certain way of seeing the missionaries, and to the tactics which could be employed against them in other contexts lent it some importance in the eyes of the authorities, it was its last few pages that were especially worrisome. In these pages the author reproduced four official documents narrating the "Three Days of a Mission in Brest:" 1) a letter from the bishop of Quimper to the mayor of Brest; 2) the account of the deliberations of the municipal council; 3) a telegraphic inquiry from the minister of the interior to the subprefect of Brest; and 4) a response by four police commissioners to the minister's telegraph. Interspersed with editorial comments, this reproduction of the actual correspondence by which local officials worked out their views and policies regarding the struggles over the mission in Brest rendered this official negotiation over the missions public in a way truly exceptional for this period.

The first letter, from the bishop to the mayor, in which the prelate explained his decision to ban the mission, along with his disappointment with the local government for having to do so, offered the author of this pamphlet an opportunity to editorialize about the laws of the realm and the precise role which they should play in matters concerning religion. The bishop of Quimper's letter opens with the following explanation for his decision to disband the mission:

> After the assurance which you have given me . . . that it would be impossible for you to maintain public tranquillity if the mission were to take place; according to the wishes of a certain number of *pères de familles* and notable citizens of Brest meeting at the city hall, who shared the same concern about the agitation which a mission would provoke, I thought it necessary to suspend the mission.[61]

Editorializing with footnotes, the author mocks both the prelate's presentation of the opposition in Brest and the language used to describe his decision to "suspend" the mission. To the depiction of those meeting in the city hall as merely "a certain number" of *pères de familles* and city notables, the author retorts: "This *certain number* was composed of a thousand and some *pères de familles*, all of whom signed the Declaration edited and deposed at the city hall." [62] To the representation of the bishop's decision to "suspend" the mission the author replied, "This suspension is, without a doubt indefinite! There remains a bit of prideful resistance in these phrases." [63] The following section of the bishop's letter, which clearly expresses his regret "to see the religion of the state unable to enjoy, in Brest, the freedom of religion guaranteed by the Charter to all religions," provoked a response which clearly articulated the legal principle at issue in the struggles with the missionaries in Brest. In a lengthy footnote to this point in the bishop's letter the author replies:

> This letter, in general, is not without skill, but this last phrase is a *gaucherie*. How can the religion of the state be seen not to enjoy the freedom guaranteed in the Charter because we don't want to receive a troop of priests without vows, missionaries without a mission? The religion of the state, that some forty priests regularly exercise in six different churches, is not liberally practiced in Brest? Must we accept that for the freedom of religion to be acknowledged that only the Apostolic and Roman religion invade all of France, combating all other dogmas, destroying all other religions? No. The freedom of religious opinion can exist only when we put the brakes on this false proselytism, which we would never tolerate among Jews and Protestants.[64]

Republishing and responding to the telegraphic order in which the minister of the interior asked local authorities to justify their decision not to pursue "the authors of this disorder," the "Three Days of a Mission in Brest" offered the following depiction of events of late October which at once derides the term *disorder* and defends the organized and orderly aspect of the opposition as well as the absolute right of the population to protest.

> The word "disorder" which appears in this communication is improper if it signifies *excess, troubles*. There were considerable assemblies, but *without disorder*. . . . Supposing that we did *commit disorders*, it would be very difficult for His Excellency, without doubt, to identify the guilty parties, to punish those who were the authors. The last public gathering brought together 3,000 individuals who joined in crying: "Down with the Mission!" If this is a crime, there were 3,000 perpetrators; but if one searches for the

instigator of these noisy, but not dangerous reunions, then one has to convict public opinion; and we know that today it is impolitic to punish or outrage public opinion.[65]

As if to prove the justness of the opposition's stance, the pamphlet offers as its final document the report by which the local commissaires de police responded to the minister of the interior's telegraph, a report which clearly defended the population's actions.

> Permit us . . . . to present to you, that from the first day we decided not to use the armed force at our disposal, that we couldn't arrest anyone in *flagrant délit,* that the considerable gathering (of more than 2,000 people) took place at night, making it impossible for us to determine the principal instigators of the assemblage, and that later research proved to us that there were no leaders, but that this represented the general will pronouncing itself against the missionaries, a will which expressed itself a second time, as much by the actions of the Municipal Council and the notables of this city who met with the bishop, as by the numerous signatures attached to the minutes of the deliberation of the Council from the 26th of October, and that in these disorders, both persons and property were respected.[66]

The author of the pamphlet concludes his presentation of the "Three Days of a Mission in Brest" by interpreting the sagacious response of local officials as evidence that, like the citizens of their city, they believed in and were willing to defend the rights inscribed in the Charter.

> I repeat then, that all of our rights were respected; at the very moment when one tried to violate our rights by forcing us to receive, in spite of the will of 30,000 inhabitants, one of these missions that the Charter does not impose upon us, that it cannot impose without ceasing to be a Charter.[67]

In his correspondence with the minister of the interior between November 1819 and January 1820 the prefect expressed his frustration with this particular pamphlet as well as with a second ("To the Inhabitants of Brittany") which clearly "seeks to provoke popular resistance" to authority. He criticized those members of the administration who made the reproduced documents available to the author of the first pamphlet. These were the mayor, who in "weakness" turned over the letter from the bishop and the deliberations of the municipal council, and one of the commissaires de police, whose "indiscretion" led him to offer the telegraph from the minister of police as well as the report of the commissaires which served as a response.[68] Mostly the correspondence from December and January illustrates the frustration of this leading administrator who could apparently do nothing to stem the tide of protest which he feared would spread beyond his department, emboldening other opponents of missions elsewhere to mimic the tactics of the people of Brest. His successive efforts to prosecute the authors and publishers of these pamphlets failed, in spite of his plan to pack the jury in the case of Corbière's pamphlet with "men recommendable by their morality." In fact, the ultimate acquittal of Corbière for his "Three Days of a Mission in Brest" offered an occasion for eighty local "ultraliberals" to honor the author with a banquet.[69]

The case of Brest in 1819 is truly exceptional because of the absolute success of the anticlerical protesters and the extraordinary publicity afforded the public negotiations between civil and ecclesiastical officials, thanks to the pamphlet of Mr. Corbière; but in many ways the events of Brest were quite typical. The tactics employed against the missionaries in this context—the songs, caricatures, charivaris, meetings and deputations of leading citizens, pamphlets publicizing events, a command performance of *Tartuffe*—would become standard fare in confrontations with missionaries all over France. The local administration's willingness to act on behalf of the citizens of Brest would also be imitated elsewhere. The local bishop's depiction of the government and his statement of its obligation to defend the state religion against the outrages of its opponents were also echoed in letters from prelates elsewhere in the context of their own struggles with local officials. Finally, the way of seeing the missionaries, popularized by the songs and pamphlets in this incident, and the way of figuring the struggle between missionaries and the people as a battle over the rights accorded in the Charter, defended by the king himself—these too would be reproduced throughout the nation over the fifteen years of the Restoration. But in other contexts, where the local administration did not favor the protesters but instead used the force of the law against them, or transmitted a more ambiguous message, the denouement would be quite different.

Limoges, 1828: The State in Defense of the Missionaries

The case of Limoges in 1828 is most noteworthy for the severity of the local civil administration vis-à-vis the local opponents of the visiting missionaries. Unlike the civil administrators in Brest, the mayor of Limoges coordinated his actions with the prefect and leading military authorities so as to use the full force of the state against the troublemakers seeking to undermine the tranquillity of the mission in his town. In spite of the repressive efforts of the civil administration, the protesters against

the missions deployed a steady stream of tactics against the missionaries, both before they arrived and especially in order to disrupt and undermine the mission once it was under way. The mere announcement of
the coming mission in Limoges inspired critics of the missionaries to
cover many public edifices with messages intended to garner opposition
to their arrival. Handwritten inscriptions first appeared on the 31st of
January "on the door of the residence of the *Premier President,* on the
door of the post office, and other sites most frequented in public." [70]
Writing on February 4th to the minister of the interior, the prefect of the
Haute-Vienne explained that since the arrival of the missionaries "the
practice of placarding the city with anti-missionary inscriptions had
multiplied, covering the doors and walls of many houses situated on the
marketplace with the words, 'Down with the missionaries, down with
the Jesuits.'" [71] Because they were apparently scribbled under the obscurity of darkness, the authorities were unable to identify the authors
of these anticlerical placards. After the 16th of March, when the revival
actually began in the city of Limoges, opponents of the missions tried to
disrupt religious services by throwing firecrackers and stink bombs inside the churches. The fact that the services were usually held at night,
when the interiors of the churches remained dark, made it impossible,
once again, for the authorities to apprehend the authors of these acts. In
response to these disruptions the mayor of Limoges went on the offensive against those who were opposed to the mission, first, by posting
placards all over town clearly articulating the local administration's determination to support the mission, and second, by conceding to his local bishop's request that he deploy military force to defend the religious
services and outdoor ceremonies of the mission.

The placard posted by the mayor of Limoges is worth citing in full because it beautifully articulates the message propagated here and in other
cities in France where the local administration showed itself willing to
defend the missionaries in the name of the Charter, and even the newly
available Sacrilege Law.

> The Mayor of Limoges to his fellow citizens,
> Inhabitants of the City of Limoges!
>
> The ministers of the religion of the state have come among you to
> preach the truths of the Gospel, to help your pastors in their ministry.
> The believers who have come together to hear them have the right
> to the protection of our laws.
>
> However, some young thoughtless creatures, enthusiasts, no doubt,
> of liberty, but who understand it badly since they want to attack the

> liberty of their fellow citizens, have permitted themselves to spread
> disgusting odors and act disruptively in churches where no one had
> forced them to present themselves.
>
> This conduct injures the legal order; it is anti-social, anti-liberal because
> it tends to undermine the most respectable of all our liberties, that of
> conscience. It is anti-French because it principally insults a feeble sex
> which merits everywhere our respect and protection.
>
> We hope that these disorders will not be reproduced in a city whose
> inhabitants have always distinguished themselves by the peacefulness
> of their habits and the moderation of their opinions.
>
> If this hope is ill-founded, the magistrates charged with enforcing
> the respect due to liberty, security, peace, and the beliefs of its citizens,
> will not hesitate to fulfill their painful but necessary duty.
>
> We feel it necessary to remind you of the following article 13
> of the law of 20 April 1825:
>
> "Will be punished by a fine of 16 to 300 francs and by an imprisonment
> of 6 days to 3 months, those who, by their troubles or disorders
> committed, even outside an edifice consecrated to the religion of the state,
> have postponed, interrupted, or prevented religious ceremonies."
>
> *Limoges, 21 March 1828.*[72]

Clearly this placard issued a very different message to the people of Limoges than did the decision of the prefect ruling in Brest to support his population's desire to block a mission, and his refusal to prosecute troublemakers who had every intention of disrupting and preventing the religious ceremonies associated with the revival. Indeed, the mayor of Limoges's proclamation echoes the logic of the bishop of Quimper, who likewise used the Charter to decry the acts of troublemakers and to defend the freedom of the missionaries to publicly perform ceremonies associated with the state religion. Indeed, the mayor of Limoges did exactly what the prelate serving Brest would have liked his prefect to have done.

Even more than the placards posted throughout the city of Limoges, the decision of the mayor to bring in several military detachments to ensure order during the mission dramatized the local administration's views on the relationship between church and state, and the definition of "freedom of religion" which it was committed to defending. Every night, the prefect recounted, the repeated "demonstrations of force suffice to assure tranquillity in all of the parishes, and as assemblies gathered in protest outside the churches, the presence of the military easily dispersed the troublemakers."[73] Actions against the missionaries continued right through to the end, when some protesters gathered outside the house where the visiting priests were staying. What the troublemakers said was not discussed; rather, this minor incident was evoked by the prefect of the Haute-Vienne to attest to the general success of the local administration in ensuring order during a mission in a context where the local population "was disposed to support the preachers against their turbulent adversaries."[74]

Certainly the administrators of Limoges were not faced with the same clear assertion of a "general will" opposed to the mission that was expressed in the city of Brest. The administrators' interpretation of this population's desire for a mission encouraged them to act on behalf of the missionaries and against their small number of opponents. But the real general opinion of the population of Limoges in 1828 is hard to ascertain. What was clear, however, was that administrators of the town had a completely different view of the stance representatives of the state should take vis-à-vis the missionaries, and by the measures they adopted toward the troublemakers dramatized a completely different conception of the relationship between the church and the state than that implied in the actions and writings of the administrators from Brest.

Dramatizing the Juste Milieu: The Struggles over the Missions, 1815–1830

In most cities where the missionaries orchestrated their revivals, administrators pronounced themselves as favoring neither of the extremes typified by the examples of Brest and Limoges. Rather they navigated a complicated middle ground. Most government officials transmitted complicated, mixed messages regarding the key questions raised by the struggles over the missions: how was the Charter, and the freedom of religion, to be interpreted and defended? What was the proper relationship between the church and state? While demonstrations of total support for the missionaries or the protesters organizing against them were rare, the official correspondence regarding the missions reveals that the civil authorities seemed to acknowledge that the staging of the missions was open for public negotiation. This was made apparent by their responsiveness to popular complaints about the missionaries and by their willingness to intervene in small ways to try to control different aspects of the revival. While Brest in 1819 was the only city where the officials conceded fully to the anticlerical protesters by chasing missionaries from town, officials elsewhere did intervene to control the timing, the content, the physical staging or geography, as well as the personnel or cast who would ultimately appear, particularly in the spectacular outdoor ceremonies of the missions.

The missionaries' desire to conduct regular services at night in order to reach the working population, to stage their revivals in order to supplant carnival celebrations, and to capitalize on the 21st of January for expiatory ceremonies all led civil officials to try to intervene and control the *timing* of the missions. On the matter of the timing of daily spiritual exercises, most civil officials were in agreement about the dangers of allowing missionaries to conduct them under the obscurity of darkness. It was generally assumed that such evening exercises offered easy opportunities for troublemakers to disrupt the mission. Indeed, in the more notorious anticlerical incidents from the period (Brest, Rouen, Strasbourg), the evening exercises became occasions for veritable riots, and as Sevrin has said, "this gave these services the reputation of being very dangerous among the middle class, and served to secure the suspicious and uneasy attention of the government. It led prefects and mayors all over the country to pressure bishops and the parish clergy to hold these reunions earlier in the day, or at least to shorten them, so that they would be over before total darkness set in." [75] All the correspondence regarding the missions evokes the dangers of the evening services. Whether overtly critical of the evening services or not, the correspondence makes it clear that they were perceived as a problem, a potential starting point for anticlerical riots, and as such had to be carefully controlled. Thus this is one case in which the population's use of certain tactics (disrupting church services at night, using the exit from the church as the occasion for an anticlerical riot) turned the question of the timing of the daily exercises into an issue for public negotiation. On this issue, the local administration always failed to get the missionaries to budge, and so local officials were forced to secure the evening ceremonies by deploying police and military personnel in order to prevent public disorder, thereby leaving some with the impression that they supported the missionaries.

The popularity of carnival, and its importance in the material lives of a town's inhabitants, led many local officials to try to convince missionaries to postpone their revival until the end of this lucrative festive season. While they were always unsuccessful in their efforts, the fact that they were trying to persuade prelates and missionaries to concede to the popular will in this matter is clear in the official correspondence, and this fact was often made public at the time by the local press. We saw an example of this in the case of Marseilles, where *Le Phocéen* published both a letter of local merchants requesting a postponement of the mission until after carnival and an article applauding the efforts of the prefect to prevail upon the missionaries on their behalf.[76] In other cases, local officials tried to mediate between the missionaries and the local population, on the one hand, by allowing the revival to go forth during the carnival season, but, on the other hand, by authorizing public carnival celebrations during the mission and thereby condoning festivities which were often subsequently turned against the visiting priests.[77]

The problem of the 21st of January, while occasionally raised by the local population complaining of the missionaries' excesses, was usually raised by the administrators themselves, conscious of the degree to which the missionaries' ceremonies departed from the official orders they were given about how to commemorate the execution of Louis XVI. Different decisions by local administrators—to abstain from the missionaries' ceremonies, to call missionaries in and chastise them for their behavior, or to appear in full regalia in their expiatory processions—reveal a wide range of positions on this issue, more or less clear to the local population. We saw, in the case of Marseilles, civil officials self-consciously absenting themselves from the missionaries' expiatory ceremony on the 21st of January, although they did participate openly in other public processions and ceremonies.[78] In La Rochelle the prefect showed himself to be hostile to the missionaries' exploitation of the 21st of January, and in his report he quoted the critical responses of those who, leaving the church, apparently said, "What charlatanism! What monkey business!"[79] Most civil officials mimicked the actions of this prefect of the Charente-Inférieure; carefully listening for and reporting on the reception of the expiatory ceremonies on the 21st of January, they usually did little to block them. On the other hand, while reports of civil officials participating in outdoor ceremonies and mission cross processions are common in this period, reports of uniformed civil servants in the context of the missionaries' special ceremonies on the 21st of January are quite rare.

The *content* of the missions was consistently subjected to surveillance and disciplinary action by local civil officials. Responding to direct complaints about attacks on the Charter, the *biens nationaux,* and civil marriage in their sermons, or anticipating such complaints based on knowledge of the missionaries' reception elsewhere, civil officials consistently sought to censor the content of the missionaries' public sermons. Their first concern was to gather information. In advance of the mission, local administrators would consult with the local prelate, or the missionaries as soon as they came to town, and interrogate the priests about the intended content of their sermons; once they began preaching, administrators gathered intelligence about their sermons from police officers who were placed in churches, either clandestinely or openly, and from inhabitants known to have participated in the mission.[80] In cases of clear infractions, missionaries were called in and reprimanded by civil officials. While many local administrators toyed with the idea of prosecuting priests, no one appeared to have done so.[81] However, many officials reported that their negotiations with the missionaries and the presence of visible police spies inside churches had good effects, and tended to temper the oratory of the priests.[82] How visible were these efforts of local officials to the population at large? Clearly some public discussion usually prompted surveillance; consultation with participants in the missions made these people aware of the administrator's efforts, the spies themselves were often visible within the churches, and certainly the liberal press regularly publicized cases in which infractions were committed and in which civil administrators reprimanded the missionaries. But the ability of the missionaries to evade this surveillance and censorship was equally evident, publicized at once by the sermons of the missionaries, defending their right to preach as they saw fit, as well as by the liberal press, which regularly exposed the missionaries' tendency to flout local administrators' efforts.

Officials were marginally more successful in controlling *where* the missionaries conducted their revival. Occasionally there were efforts to block the infamous ceremonies in cemeteries.[83] Many disputes erupted regarding the controversial placement of mission crosses. Occasionally the reason for the disputes was revealed in official correspondence, as in Ferté-sous-Jouarre, where the priests' determination to erect a cross on the site of a dancing hall provoked protest, or in Tarascon, where the demolition of a liberty tree and its replacement by a mission cross led local inhabitants to object.[84] More often the records are silent on the cause of the dispute, and demonstrate that because these were sites which were expected to draw large assemblies even after the missionaries had departed, the police seemed most interested in choosing public squares which allowed for easy surveillance. In general, the local civil authorities conceded to the missionaries, and offered their support in securing tranquillity during the erection of their crosses on the sites the priests had chosen. Yet even in these instances, the correspondence regularly alludes to extensive negotiations between prelates, missionaries, and local civil officials regarding the choice of sites; the degree to which such discussions were public is hard to ascertain.[85] However, since the funding for the huge crosses usually came from individual donations, and since the local population was usually engaged in the fund-raising process, it is very likely that discussions of the ultimate ceremony when they would be erected would have been a subject of public debate. It was by their responses to the increasingly frequent attacks on these mission crosses that civil officials expressed most clearly their willingness to negotiate with their communities about the public erection of these symbols of the missions. For in their relative laxity toward those who committed sacrilegious acts against these crosses during the Restoration, and in their decision to move them from public squares to the interiors of churches after the Revolution of 1830, the representatives of the state clearly responded to the growing anticlerical sentiment engendered by these symbols of the missionaries.

Civil officials most effectively controlled the staging or geography of the mission in their repeated efforts to consign the missionaries to the interiors of their churches. In every case in which the mission was prevented from taking to the streets and transforming the town into a stage for its expiatory spectacles it was because of anticlerical protest. In Dijon the prefect explained his decision to restrict the missionaries to the interiors of churches by simply evoking the specter of disorder such preachers *might* excite, whether among the acquirers of *biens nationaux* or even the pious inhabitants of his region, "who distrust the influence of these outsider priests."[86] In Arles it was the controversial denial of the last rites to an ex-Jacobin that led authorities to prohibit outdoor ceremonies in 1817.[87] In Nîmes, after the passage of the Sacrilege Law, the simultaneous arrival of a flood of cheap copies of *Tartuffe* and two command performances of the comedy during the missionaries' stay convinced the archbishop to ban all outdoor ceremonies.[88] In Nantes in 1829 it was the potential disorder of the missionaries in the context of the heated discussion in the Chambers of Deputies which led the prefect to limit all the spectacles of the missionaries to the interiors of churches.[89] However, as with all their efforts to control the physical staging of the missions, civil administrators were not always successful in blocking the outdoor ceremonies and processions. Missionaries overtly disobeyed orders to remain inside the churches and used their pulpits to denounce the efforts of government officials, evoking an image of a persecuting state, which their superiors in the ecclesiastic hierarchy repeated in vociferous, often public defenses of the revival and its ceremonies. But civil administrators also allowed the outdoor ceremonies in many contexts, and made their support for the missions clear by actively deploying the police to protect the followers of the mission or by themselves participating in their spectacles.

Indeed it was by their decision to participate or not to participate in the public ceremonies of the missionaries that civil officials most clearly demonstrated their attitude toward the revival. In some cases the missionaries' efforts to actively engage the official representatives of the state in the outdoor ceremonies produced extensive controversies. In the case of Tarascon in 1819, a controversy erupted because of the subprefect's efforts not only to force members of the National Guard to appear in the missionaries' processions but to get those who had participated in the mission's spiritual exercises to wear the cross symbolizing the mission on their lapels. In fact, the prefect followed advice from the minister of the interior when he criticized the subprefect for trying to force the National Guard to appear in public processions, and explicitly forbade communicants within its corps from wearing the symbol of the mission on their uniforms; he did not prevent them, however, from taking part in the procession around the erection of the mission cross.[90] In other cases, administrators directly banned official participation in any of the outdoor processions, citing the law of 24 messidor year 12 which explicitly forbade civil officials from appearing in any public spectacles not orchestrated by the government.[91] Sometimes prefects made this decision preventively, before actual disorders forced their hand, but usually it was in direct response to anticlerical protest; the minor incident in Tain, where the population performed a farandole outside the church on the *dimanche des brandons,* was enough to convince the leading local official to prohibit civil officials from participating in uniform in the missionaries' spectacles.[92] Quite often local officials seemed to have compromised on the problem of participating in these spectacles by allowing members of the military and the civil administration to take part in the processions, but not in uniform.[93] By and large, however, officials did participate in the missions, often earning the official censure of their superiors in Paris. The examples of large processions, protected and swelled in size by the presence of uniformed National Guardsmen and military personnel, are easy to find. Indeed they constitute the evidence that historians have so often cited to capture the clerical, reactionary bias of this regime, and its willingness to give the missionaries its public, official sanction.[94] Clearly the evidence presented thus far complicates this image somewhat; civil authorities were very cautious about giving the missionaries their unequivocal and overt support. Yet, in the majority of cases, local civil officials did give the appearance of supporting the religious revival. In most of the missions between 1815 and 1830, civil officials either lent their material support to protect the security of the missionaries or participated themselves in their spectacular expiatory ceremonies.

Yet the mission, as actually performed in any given locality, was always a subject of public discussion. All its details, from its timing to its setting to its personnel, were open to negotiation. The liberal press played a key role in publicizing the degree to which this was a negotiation, one in which it actively encouraged its readers to participate by pressuring their local officials to censor and discipline and, best of all, to chase the missionaries from town. But the missionaries publicized this fact as well: in their sermons they directly assailed those protesters disrupting the missions, as well as the civil officials who appeared to be conceding to them by trying to block outdoor ceremonies, reschedule evening services, or prevent the erection of a mission cross on a particular site. Prefects, subprefects, and mayors responded to the efforts of their local populations against and on behalf of the missionaries as they made their decisions, but they also were aware of controversies elsewhere, and made decisions about the area under their own jurisdiction with a sense of participating in larger, nationwide controversy. If local officials' behavior toward the missionaries provided one way for the regime to register its position on this public negotiation, their behavior toward the protesters offered another.

Over the course of the Restoration the anticlerical protest against the missionaries swelled, reaching riotous proportions especially after 1825. As we shall see at length in chapter 5, the spate of sacrilegious crimes committed against the missionaries, their crosses, and their ceremonies offered ample opportunity for the regime to weigh in against or in favor of the protesters. But as with the approach civil officials adopted toward the missionaries, prefects, subprefects, and mayors ineffectively and inconsistently applied the police measures at their disposal against the troublemakers. Like the missionaries, their opponents were, more often than not, given free rein. Indeed, many in the civil administration were sympathetic to the protesters, or at least receptive to their way of conceiving of the missionaries.

While the critics of the missionaries denounced and publicized spectacular examples of the government's support for the religious revival and the political message at its core, the missionaries and their supporters in the church hierarchy continuously complained about the regime's apparent willingness to turn the full force of the law against the Catholic church as opposed to the "troublemakers" undermining the tranquillity of the missions. If the regime was not always successful in controlling the missionaries, its persistent efforts to do so were interpreted by the church hierarchy as signs of a growing persecution. In their direct pleas to government officials, these men of the collar beautifully expressed the very real threat which these disciplinary measures represented in terms of the long-term relationship between church and state in France.

One churchman from Provence relied upon historical precedent and religious necessity in the specific context of a depleted ministry as he asked the minister of the interior to consider the appropriate jurisdiction of mayors and prefects in the matter of the missions.

> Missions have always taken place in this diocese since the Corcordat, even when the Emperor banned priests from outside from performing them, and they have always had a salutary effect. Curés are rare, those who exist are old and infirm. What would we become if in order to instruct the people to whom we must minister, we need to get the consent of mayors? Because, it's the mayors, as we all know, who report to the prefects. Our ministry is impossible if we are to be at the mercy of a few accusers. We certainly don't want to cause disorder; but missions have never caused disorder in this diocese.[95]

In response to specific accusations regarding the inflammatory content of their sermons, this prelate defended the missionaries in even more heated terms, invoking the laws of the realm and all of the arguments we saw deployed by the archbishop of Aix in 1820, the bishop of Quimper in 1819, and the bishop of Strasbourg in 1826: the missions were legal, authorized by the king, and protected by the Charter's freedom of religion; missions (and religion in general) have always served to stave off, not cause, disorder; and if disorder were a problem, it was because of the opposition, not the missionaries. Like so many of his colleagues in the church, this clergyman enjoined his superiors in the state to turn the efforts of the police against "the small handful of troublemakers":

> If we knew that the missionaries were guilty [of producing disorder] we would ban them. If you judge them to be so, pursue them. But we cannot, no matter what happens, submit the freedom of religion and the preaching of God's words either to the malice of some, or to the demands of prefects, solely informed by mayors. The missions are legal; we know that the king himself regards them as the only means of regenerating public morality. Your Excellency can certainly not wish that we be deprived of their good effects.[96]

If the prelates' letters often express incredulity about the disorder the missions purportedly produced, others acknowledge the opposition they would inspire given the painful but necessary nature of their message. Casting themselves as heirs to the apostles, prepared to be humiliated and to suffer in the name of Christ, they depicted the decision to censor the missions as a struggle between good and evil, leaving it for the administrators to determine with whom they would cast their lot. Such were the terms of the bishop of Dignes's defense of the missionaries inspired by a prefectorial denunciation and a ministerial investigation which led to the cancellation of a mission in Manosque in Provence.

> Those clamoring against the missionaries are society types, usurers, bad citizens, unworthy subjects of his majesty, libertines, unbelievers, and troublemakers. This whole race of people, thanks to our liberals, are ever becoming more numerous, bringing misfortune to France. . . . When infernal plots conspire to oppose us and our fellow-workers in the orchestration of a mission, . . . we will retreat if it is necessary, shaking the dust off of our feet.[97]

This quotation reminds us of Sevrin's depiction of the Restoration as a period when only extreme interpretations made sense; the contradictory "*juste milieu* was difficult and easily suspect."[98] For many prelates of the Restoration the disciplinary efforts of the state could be seen only as a return to the worst persecution of the Revolutionary era.

In their depiction of the "persecution" which the church was suffering at the hands of the Restoration's civil officials, these prelates were not entirely wrong; for if the regime failed in most cases to control the staging of individual missions, there is no question that the government's persistent efforts to curtail their message and control every aspect of their revival had serious, long-term consequences in terms of the relationship between the state and the church in the nineteenth century. The full extent of these consequences would not become clear until after 1830, when the July Monarchy quietly but firmly transferred mission crosses to the interiors of churches, forced priests to say prayers for the new king, and progressively replaced the intransigent noble prelates with more easily controlled "bourgeois-priests." But the groundwork for these shifts was prepared as a result of struggles with the missionaries throughout the fifteen years of the Restoration.

It was the opposite extreme message which mobilized popular anti-clerical protest against the missionaries. Rather than seeing the disciplinary state as trying to subjugate the church and revive the worst persecution of the revolutionary era, critics of the missionaries saw in the regime's apparent public support for them so many signs that a clerical plot was afoot to revive the evils of the Old Regime, defined by a theocracy not known for 300 years. Because of this fear, and in defense of the secular, liberal values born of the Revolution, the people of France rose up in ever greater numbers against the missionaries and, ultimately, against the regime. The differences which separated the missionaries from the civil officials representing the regime and the willingness of these officials to respond favorably, or at least not punitively, to those organizing against the missions opened an enormous space in which the central political issues of the period could be worked out. In many ways the expiatory missions of this period defined the terms of public negotiations about the legitimacy of the regime, the principles on which the social and political order should be founded, and the role which the population should play as the "arbiters" of France's future. But to understand all this we must step beyond the official theatrics of the church and state and turn to the array of practices by which the population demonstrated the impossibility of the politics of *oubli*, the unacceptability of monarchy organized around the model of the Eucharist, and, most important, turned the theater itself into the perfect vehicle for exposing and resolving the crisis of representation which the "competing commemorations" of this period made manifest.

PART II

Theater as Politics

T he preceding chapters integrate the Restoration into the long history in which the church and state conspired and competed to represent authority in a monarchical mode, particularly in light of the challenges posed by the revolutionary events of 1789–1815. Although the missionaries and the regime responded differently to the dilemmas presented by the twenty-five-year "ceremonial interregnum," when monarchy did not rule in France, both were guided by the imperative of counterrevolution; in both cases this imperative produced large-scale national campaigns and spectacles which directly transposed the struggles of the revolutionary period to the "counterrevolutionary" Restoration. The next three chapters consider the corresponding set of cultural practices by which the population at large participated in the negotiation over legitimate authority. Like the competing spectacles of the church and state, the repertoire of practices now demanding our attention have a long history which spans the Old Regime, the Revolution, and the Empire, and goes beyond the Restoration into later decades of the nineteenth century. As in Part I, the main purpose of studying the cultural practices of the audiences for whom these spectacles were intended is to understand the legacy of the French Revolution in the early nineteenth century, particularly in light of the counterrevolutionary cultural politics of the church and state between 1815 and 1830.

In recent years, historians have recast the Revolution of 1789 in cultural terms, focusing on the array of festivals, symbols, and gestures by which the revolutionaries tried to "remake every nook and cranny of everyday life" in a republican mold. They have emphasized the fact that during the revolutionary decade one could not go about one's daily life without participating in politics, when the slightest gesture could be read as a sign of political affiliation. Did one wear the tricolor hat, the red liberty cap, or the white (monarchical) cockade? What language did one use? Did one address one's fellow citizens with the informal "tu" and say "citoyen/ne" or the more formal and "aristocratic" "vous"? Did one continue to live by the Christian calendar, or did one organize one's life around republican festivals? By their decisions on such everyday matters, the men and women in France participated in and helped to constitute the political order during the French Revolution. In the words of Lynn Hunt:

> Even the most ordinary objects and customs became political emblems and potential sources of political and social conflict. Colors, adornments, clothing, plateware, money, calendars, and playing cards became "signs of rallying" to one side or another. Such symbols did not simply express political positions; they were the means by which people became aware of their positions. By making a political position manifest, they made adherence, opposition, and indifference possible. In this way they constituted a field of political struggle.[1]

Recent works on festivals and struggles over religion during the French Revolution have emphasized the same politicization of everyday life, and the need to attend to cultural practices both in order to understand the ways in which the political field was constituted in this period and to make sense of the legacy of the Revolution in the nineteenth century. Mona Ozouf's *Festivals and the French Revolution* argues that as a result of the revolutionaries' efforts to impose a rational, national organization of time and space, and a set of rituals and symbols which could wean French citizens from their attachment to Catholicism and monarchy, a transfer of sacrality was effected in favor of the secular, liberal principles of the nation.[2] While her own work focuses primarily on the prescriptive directives for this festival project issued in Paris, her reading of police reports regarding its reception throughout the country gives us a portrait of the terrain and practices in and through which the struggles over the sacred were played out in this period. In fact she argues that the festival project was largely a failure during the revolutionary decade itself, if one measures success in terms of the degree to which French men and women came to organize their lives around the invented republican calendar and the rites and rituals of the new secular religion of the nation. But the project was an unqualified success, in her view, in the long term; for it left a legacy of secular and liberal values which the French would ultimately embrace over the course of the nineteenth century. Suzanne Desan's even more recent work, *Reclaiming the Sacred: Lay Religion and Popular Politics in Revolutionary France,* inspired by the work of both Hunt and Ozouf, examines the struggles over religion which emerged during the revolutionary decade precisely in order to understand how the new practices and discourse associated with the Revolution could be used to defend ancient religious rights in ways which enabled Catholic republicans of the Yonne to produce their own conception of the sacred.[3] In other words, by attending to the specific cultural practices of the men and women in the department of the Yonne, Desan is able to demonstrate precisely how the "transferal of sacrality" suggested by Ozouf was actually accomplished, in a particular context in which republicanism was not necessarily seen as opposed to Catholicism.

This recent work on the revolutionary period suggests a certain approach for understanding the legacy of the French Revolution in the nineteenth century which is particularly valuable in the context of the Restoration. Some historians have already begun to move in this direction. Maurice Agulhon's earlier research on the republican tradition in the nineteenth century, for example, takes seriously the cultural practices around which the political struggles of the Revolution were played out; in his words they left the following legacy for the nineteenth century:

> By replacing statues of kings with statues of liberty, and ceremonies ordained and blessed by the Church with civic and civilian festivals, the Republic had demonstrated its ambition to introduce change not only in the major political ideas and institutions, but also in rituals, within the framework of everyday life and, in a word, folklore (using the term in its broadest sense). Following the gigantic Republican experiment, France approached the nineteenth century with two folklores. Not only did it have two political movements (Revolution and counterrevolution) and two systems of thought, but also, and consequently, two symbolic systems.[4]

If Desan's emphasis on the amalgamation of republicanism and Catholicism in the Yonne already complicates this depiction of "two" opposing symbolic systems and practices, Agulhon's basic assertion that understanding the legacy of the Revolution requires attending to the cultural struggles within the framework of everyday life is absolutely right. This perspective governs my effort to make sense of the political culture of the Restoration.

I take seriously the expansion of the political into the practices of everyday life portrayed by Hunt, the problem of the transferral of sacrality to the secular, liberal principles proposed by Ozouf, and the complex manner in which political struggles were played out, as depicted in the work of Desan, and think all of this through in the light of the counterrevolutionary cultural politics of the church and state during the Restoration. As Part I has already shown, when the Bourbons were restored to the throne in 1815, both the regime and its supporters in the church reacted to, and in many ways were responsible for transforming, but also consolidating, many legacies of the French Revolution. The politics of *oubli* and the politics of expiation furthered the politicization of everyday life which characterized the revolutionary decade, even as they inscribed the emblems and practices of revolution and counterrevolution with new layers of meaning and significance; they also inspired a whole new set of practices by which the population could and did engage in the "struggles over the sacred" or the efforts to determine the foundations on which the postrevolutionary political order should rest. During the Restoration, as during the revolutionary decade, a multitude of minor practices offered the opportunity to participate in and thereby help to constitute the national political order. Did one attend *mise-en-place* ceremonies in the first year of the Second Restoration? Did one hand over personal possessions bearing the now proscribed emblems of the Revolution and Empire, stay at home and simply continue to use them, or actively traffic in them over the course of the Restoration? Did one respectfully and enthusiastically participate in the religious revival, organize charivaris or theater riots against them, or appeal to local civil authorities to discipline them? Did one actively disfigure the coins of the realm to make the king appear to be a Jesuit, or hang the king in effigy, or laugh at the famous lines of Molière's *Tartuffe*? It was by their decisions on such everyday matters that the men and women of France involved themselves in national politics, and played a critical role in consolidating the various legacies of the French Revolution.

CHAPTER FOUR

"Practicing" Politics in an Age of Counterrevolution

According to the terms laid out in the Charter, the vast majority of French citizens were officially excluded from the practice of politics during the Restoration. Suffrage was limited to one in 360 men; the right to hold office was even more restricted. Even the municipal councils, which had existed before the Revolution as institutions that gave a broader range of citizens some say in local politics, were between 1815 and 1830 replaced by appointed councils whose power was greatly curtailed.[1] Freedom of expression, freedom to meet in public, and to express one's views were all officially restricted during the Restoration. The purpose of this chapter and the next two is to portray the many practices by which French citizens made themselves active participants in politics in spite of these official strictures.

If we know anything at all about how, when, and where this complex repertoire of practices was deployed, it is because the police kept careful records of them in their rich dossiers on what they called "seditious" activities. At the National Archives the police bulletins are full of brief reports which hint at this world of unofficial politics, without giving very many details. A report from Grenoble, for example, cryptically directs our attention to public meeting places, and makes us take seriously the importance of songs and different kinds of printed matter in spreading certain ideas: "Public opinion and the political situation deteriorates every day in the Department of Isère . . . nothing is neglected in the effort to foment passions. Discussions in cafés in the cities, songs, prints, extracts of newspapers in the country. In all of the arrondissements of this department the same system is followed." [2] But such a report gives us none of the details we would need to understand how this really worked, who was involved, and what was the content of the "sedition" to which its author alluded. But, fortunately for us, the local police also seized and preserved "seditious" writings, songs, and objects and supplied their superiors with lengthy and detailed reports which help us to understand how and by whom and in what contexts these types of sedition were deployed. Their reports also point to a world of more ephemeral forms of expression—seditious cries and gestures, for example— practices which leave no "collectible" evidence, but which have been preserved for us by detailed narratives of local police officials. The police of the Restoration may not have been very effective at stopping or punishing people for their seditious activities, but, thanks to their careful surveillance, we have the means of portraying this world of unofficial politics. [3]

The emphasis in this portrait is on the "practices" by which this unofficial politics was constituted. In a political context in which official participation was so limited, our first task is to understand how the people carved out a space within which they could express themselves. What forms of expression were available? Was there a particular calendar which defined seditious practices? Were there certain privileged venues for political expression? Is there a coherence to the message articulated through this wide range of practices—both in the content and the form which they took? Is this coherence ideological—can we call it "Bonapartist," or "liberal," or "anticlerical," or "antimonarchical"? Who was involved in this wide range of practices? To what degree were the practices that the people of the Restoration relied upon drawn from a repertoire used in the Old Regime? To what degree were they refashioned, or new and specific to this postrevolutionary, "counterrevolutionary" moment? We will answer all these complicated questions slowly, in this as well as the next two chapters. Attending first to *when* and then to *where* French men and women were most likely to practice politics in this period, we then pause at great length to analyze *how* they did so, enumerating the full range of written, oral, gestural, and symbolic practices deployed in this period. Finally, we will look at *who* it was that participated in politics in these diverse ways.

The Setting: When?

Most historians have depicted the early nineteenth century as a period whose calendar was determined by the folkloric traditions usually ascribed to the early modern period.[4] They have stressed the importance of such events as Carnival, Easter, the 1st of May, and the cycle of twelve days stretching from Christmas, on the 25th of December, to the Epiphany, on the 6th of January. The role of the seasons, which organized the people's work lives, has also been emphasized. The special events in a given town might have included the celebration of the town's patron saint day or of private events such as weddings, births, or deaths (since funerals were also occasions for feasts in this period). In addition to witnessing or participating in the special moments in the "folkloric" calendar, French citizens—even those living outside urban centers—were also involved in explicitly political ceremonies orchestrated from Paris, as well as religious spectacles which underscored a particular national, political calendar.[5] As we have seen in previous chapters, regular annual celebrations were orchestrated for the days commemorating the executions of Louis XVI and Marie Antoinette (the 21st of January and the 16th of October); the kings' days—Saint Louis (August 25th) and Saint Charles (November 4)—were occasions for feasts, games, and free theater performances. A number of Catholic holidays were also singled out by the regime for special celebration, usually in the form of a procession organized by local churchmen with the participation of local civil officials. Major national political events were represented in the local arena in the form of exceptional celebrations. The birth of the Second Restoration was celebrated all over the country, as we have seen, in the context of locally organized *mise-en-place* ceremonies. When the duc de Berry was assassinated in 1820 and when Louis XVIII died in 1824, exceptional periods of mourning were enforced and local funeral ceremonies were organized. Charles X's coronation in 1825 was celebrated with pomp not only at Reims; local officials organized festivities to mark this occasion all over France. The Papal Jubilee was given special publicity by the missionaries who reproduced the kind of expiatory ceremonies in which the king participated in Paris wherever they traveled and preached in 1826. Other minor events which erupted into the lives of people living all over France were political discussions taking place in Paris, but publicized locally; laws, announced by official placards and read in markets and churches; or the publication of pastoral letters, posted in public or circulating in various forms. The royal family also traveled throughout the kingdom, gracing even the smallest towns with official visits. Even the king himself made appearances of the sort depicted in *The Red and the Black,* providing local notables with the opportunity to jockey for position in competing for the king's attention.[6]

The precise way in which these external events were represented in the local arena was dependent on local officials and on local circumstances; because of the degree of improvisation officially encouraged there was not absolute uniformity in the national calendar in the lives of most French men and women. However, there were national points of reference, a set of specific dates which came to represent the government, and/or the religious revival, and which offered a framework for expressing opposition. There is no question that the "folkloric" calendar also governed certain types of political expression. Carnival offered opportunities for drawing upon old and accepted forms of inverting and mocking authority, and these were seized in this period, particularly because the carnival season also often brought missionaries to town. Patron saint days likewise offered people living in a particular locality the opportunity to express themselves. Exceptional local events, such as the visit of a national dignitary, the campaigns of the missionaries, or the publication of a local archbishop's pastoral letter, provoked seditious acts according to a "local" calendar. But the police records from this period demonstrate that a wide range of seditious practices also obeyed a national calendar, a political calendar whose reference points date from the Revolution, the Empire, and the competing spectacles of the state and the church of the Restoration.

Although very rarely, some opponents of the regime chose key dates from the Revolution and the Empire to express their discontent with the reigning monarchy. In the Ardèche some merchants held a feast on the 14th of July in 1827 at which they audibly toasted liberty.[7] The prefect of the Lot announced in his report from 1829 that although no reunions were organized to celebrate the 14th of July, "it is with pain that I learned that in some localities this deplorable day was remembered with a sort of solemnity."[8] August 15th, celebrated during the Empire as Saint Napoleon's Day and during the Restoration as the day commemorating the Vow of Louis XIII, was more commonly seized on as an opportunity to remember Napoleon and criticize the reigning monarchy. In Toulouse in 1815 it was the supporters of the king, the fervent *verdets,* who took advantage of this day to brutally murder a local general known to be a supporter of Bonaparte. After having attended the procession in honor of the Vow of Louis XIII, the general was attacked and stabbed more than fifty times for his apparently insincere royalism.[9] In the same year, supporters of Napoleon in a small town near Dieppe in the Seine-Inférieure seized the occasion of the 15th of August to go to their local church and worship before an altar where a statue representing Saint Napoleon had been destroyed.[10] A few years later in the same department an inhabitant of Rouen placed a placard outside the church of Saint Vivien, announcing local festivities in honor of Saint Napoleon, in an *affiche* which borrowed the formula for announcing official events.[11] Publicly acknowledging official celebrations from the Revolution and the Empire was clearly difficult, and the police reports are relatively silent on the wide range of practices which might have been deployed on such days in private, or in public, but which went undiscovered. More common than using these forbidden dates was the practice of orchestrating a kind of "anti-fête" to the regime's and the missionaries' official celebrations.[12]

The 21st of January, celebrated as a festival between 1794 and 1799, and commemorated as a day of mourning by the regime, and of expiation by the missionaries between 1815 and 1830, became an occasion for many seditious acts during the Restoration. Nonparticipation by local officials or the general population in the commemorations was one way of expressing opposition to the official celebration, but some French citizens went further and even organized reunions and balls on the eve of the day of mourning. In some cases the festivities were written off as nonpolitical; music and merrymaking on such a day were considered scandalous, but not dangerous. But other cases worried the authorities more. For example, one prefect wrote of a ball in the Lot-et-Garonne, organized on the 20th of January by a veteran of Napoleon's army, which was attended by "all of the best-known local enemies of the government."[13] The most serious case of sedition carried out on the 21st of January took place in the Seine-Inférieure, where a man from a small commune described as "one of the hottest partisans of the Terror" reproduced the same ritual annually: he walked through his town with a mannequin of Louis XVI, held a mock trial, and then killed the king in effigy. There were no details in the archives regarding what became of this man, but it does seem that he was permitted to do this more than once, so the authorities could not have treated him too harshly.[14] In the Dordogne, in 1822, a similarly revolutionary message was expressed when someone posted a placard that called for the head of Louis XVIII, "so that his blood can wash the stain he dares to impute to the French nation," and concluded with "Long Live Napoleon II."[15] In Toulouse the critics of the government were more menacing still. David Higgs's study of Restoration Toulouse describes an incident "on the 21st of January, 1830, [when] the Toulouse theater performed 'A-Propos patriotique' and a rendition of 'The Marseillaise.' The Garde nationale formed up, and together with the Law Students noisily paraded around the town singing the national anthem." Royalists in town apparently did not respond, but, in Higgs's words, "they doubtless appreciated to the full the symbolism of armed men and youth swaggering across the public space of the city singing the song of the Revolution," and, I would add, particularly on the 21st of January.[16]

Of all the national festivals orchestrated annually to celebrate the monarchy, it was the saint days of the two kings that became the most favored occasions for a wide range of seditious acts. If all of the regime's national holidays were meant to be improvised at the local level, it was the kings' saint days which were meant to approximate most closely the kind of popular festival organized by the towns themselves in honor of their local patron saint. Feasts, games, and free theater performances were among the forms of entertainment offered. Yet local officials still seemed to have trouble getting the residents of their towns to participate. And when they did participate, their festivals often turned into occasions to laugh at and criticize, rather than to honor, the king.

The prefect of the Puy-de-Dôme complained about nonparticipation in the festivities associated with Saint Louis in the two cities of Clermont-Ferrand and Issoire, where large numbers of people "made an effort to ostentatiously avoid appearing at the solemn mass on that day."[17] In the Haut-Rhin the day of Saint Charles was similarly unpopular. The prefect noted, "the inhabitants [of Mulhausen] have demonstrated, on this beautiful day, a shocking indifference. All of the factories were operating as if it were an ordinary day." The white flag could be seen only on the city hall, outside the residences of a few city officials, and outside the homes of perhaps four or five citizens.[18] In one town in the Ardèche the people used the occasion of Saint Charles in 1825 to demonstrate their disfavor with the new king, as opposed to his predecessor. Describing the festivities of Saint Charles, the prefect explained, "the families known for their estrangement from the government (and who had, however, enthusiastically attended such festivities in previous years) did not come back this year."[19]

In Grenoble the festival of Saint Louis turned into a struggle between the local supporters of the king and the larger number of critics, who dissuaded the majority of the inhabitants of the town from taking part in the day's festivities. The prefect wrote that great support for the king was expressed in the participation of a large number of inhabitants of the city, in the mass and a ball held on the eve of the festival. But he added that these signs of attachment to the royal family by one part of the population brought out "the extreme coolness" of an even greater part of the population. On the day of the festival itself, "Almost all the shops in town were open. Work was not in the least interrupted. Public edifices and the homes of functionaries and a few royalists were the only buildings lit up. Finally, the people were dissuaded from taking part in the dancing and other diversions which were usually very popular. The night, in the garden of the city hall, beautifully illuminated for the occasion, saw a reunion of but a very small group." [20] In Toulouse, the celebration of Saint Louis went off quite well, with "the inhabitants giving themselves over to gaiety." But at night, after the participants had gone home, the musicians hired for the festivities began stopping in front of the homes of different local officials and playing seditious songs which included such refrains as "Down with Louis, Down with Louis." People drinking in a neighboring café joined in chorus with the musicians. The café had to be evacuated.[21]

More often than singing their opposition to the king on his saint day, critics expressed themselves with seditious cries. In Rouen, on the day of Saint Louis in 1820, the local liberals organized themselves to shout "Long live the Charter!" as the procession passed before the local authorities, and as the rest of the people assembled shouted "Long live the king!"[22] In Grenoble, two years earlier, a group of veterans similarly timed their "Long Live the Emperor! Shit for the King!" to coincide with the firing of the cannon and the shouts of "Long Live the King" which marked the opening of the festivities in their town.[23] Even republicans could be heard shouting amidst the "Long live the King's" of their fellow citizens. In Nantes one man was heard shouting "Long live the Republic" and was quickly carted off to jail.[24] Cafés were often the sites of seditious cries and toasts. In the same year one rather drunken offender said, "Poor Napoleon II! My heart is with you right to the very last drop of my blood."[25] In 1825, during the festival of Saint Charles a group of old soldiers proposed a toast to the health of the Emperor Napoleon and "expressed out loud the most seditious of sentiments."[26]

Voices of discontent could also be expressed in print. In Marseilles, where according to the authorities the festivities in honor of Saint Charles were quite exemplary, the local newspapers seized the opportunity to mock the event and offer an alternative interpretation of the celebration for their readers. In the prefect's words:

> Only one painful sentiment could sadden me in the wake of the grand solemnity, and that is provided by reading the newspapers of Marseilles. Only one . . . *The Journal of the Mediterranean,* offered a description of the festivities in a manner worthy of its object. All the others, a veritable public plague, born of the revolutionary disease, took advantage of the occasion to make their discordant voices heard, by criticizing in the most impudent fashion the organization of the festival, and by insinuating false and absurd accusations against the public authorities.[27]

Placards were often erected on these days, saying simply either "Long live the great Napoleon!" as in Dieppe in 1816, or specifically attacking the current monarch, as the placard in Saint-Germain-en-Laye which read "Mort à Charles X! Vive Napoléon II!"[28] In one case in Angers, protesters simply tore down the poster announcing the day's festivities, and stomped on it until it was completely destroyed.[29]

Free theater performances, which featured royal themes, often contained key lines that offered opportunities for the audience to demonstrate its support or criticism of the monarchy. In Rouen the boos outweighed the applause in 1823 as the actor pronounced, "And to follow the Bourbons, that's to fly toward glory."[30] Three years later, in the same city, the festival of Saint Charles was the occasion for booing and hissing to the lines "Long live the King, Live Forever the King," from *La Partie de Chasse.*[31] In St-Quentin in 1825, the audience expressed its displeasure with its monarch by standing up and walking out together as soon as the curtain was raised on the play chosen for the celebration of Saint Charles. The following day the local newspaper contained an article which made fun of the poor showing at the ultimate performance, ironically speaking of the thirty to forty spectators who "filled" the room.[32] Members of another audience, in Brest in 1827, took a slightly different tack. Rather than walking out as the curtain went up on *La Croix d'Honneur,* they simply whistled and prevented the play from beginning.[33]

Protests in the context of king's day celebrations also took the form of attacks on the symbols of the monarchy erected early in the regime. In the Landes, for example, a ball was given on the eve of the festival of Saint Louis, and several young men used this occasion to deface the bust of Louis XVIII standing in the central dance hall while shouting insults at the king.[34] A similar case took place in Besançon, where one man attacked not a bust of the monarch but the white cockade which represented the Bourbons. For squashing the cockade under his shoe while shouting insults at the king on the day of Saint Louis, this man was sentenced in 1816 to five years in prison. In 1819, in honor of precisely the same festival, the king granted the offender a pardon.[35]

The festival of Saint Louis was also an occasion for critics of the regime to flaunt the prohibited emblems of the revolutionary and imperial periods. In Bordeaux, for example, a small tricolor flag was put up during the night before this festival in 1824. In Dieppe the protesters were bolder. On the day of Saint Louis in 1816 a group of young men came out wearing red carnations on their lapels.[36]

Special events which celebrated the monarchy at the local level offered many the opportunity to express their opposition. Visits from members of the royal family, usually accompanied by processions, were often occasions for seditious cries.[37] Popular protest was also expressed on days marking important events in the lives of the reigning Bourbon family, such as the death by assassination of the duc de Berry.

The extravagant coronation at Reims in 1825 became the target of criticism for songwriters, journalists, caricaturists, and novelists.[38] In some cases, local authorities merely complained of seditious speech, or reported on the "plot" of liberals to stir up trouble on the eve of this important national event.[39] But in some towns the local festivities for the coronation were sabotaged, as in the Gers, where the candles intended to be used to light a bonfire were thrown into the river, and where the "Long live the king! Long live the Bourbons!" on the placard announcing the day's festivities were defaced to read "Long Live his Majesty Napoleon II."[40] It was by placards posted in the middle of the night that critics of the government most clearly articulated their concerns regarding this particular event; in the Lot a series of placards found in May and then again in June of 1825 illustrate that for many the coronation augured a return to the worst tyrannies of the Old Regime, and seemed to demand outspoken support for the Charter, the rule of law, and the secular foundations of monarchy. Expressing the fears of the authors were placards reading "No more lords," "War against tyrants and despots," "Down with serfdom," while other placards clearly pointed to the political principles, groups, and institutions that would protect the French: "Long live the liberals, the Charter, and the King," simply "Liberty," "Honor to the deputies of the left," "Union of liberals, radicals and Carbonari," and "The Law, the Nation, and the King."[41] In Paris, on the side of a bridge, written in large letters in chalk were the words "En t'ait fait sacré, tu sera massacré." The English translation doesn't capture either the rhyme or the insult implied in threatening the king with the familiar *tu:* "Because you have had yourself anointed, you will be massacred."[42]

Most festivals orchestrated by the regime did not excite active protest; then again, most royal festivals were also not terribly popular. Administrative reports show that members of the National Guard, the army, and officials of the local administration regularly took part in the ceremonies of state, but most people seemed content to stay home or to remain on the sidelines and not respond in one way or the other to the regime's ceremonial efforts. Yet the evidence considered thus far makes it clear that certain national dates became occasions for similar sorts of seditious practices all over France, a fact which is itself important in trying to understand how and when certain practices assumed "national" dimensions. However, as much as the regime's regular annual festivals and its exceptional visits and celebrations offered a national framework within which French citizens could and did express opposition in various ways, the evidence provided thus far demonstrates that this calendar did not provoke sustained opposition of a sort that was truly dangerous for the regime.

The Setting: Where?

Certain venues seemed to emerge repeatedly among the police files as particularly fertile ground for unofficial politics. Most important among them were natural gathering places: cafés, cabarets, the marketplace, and the theater. Within a given town there seemed to be a general understanding among the inhabitants as well as the authorities that certain public spaces—whether cafés, bookstores, or pharmacies—were frequented by people sharing a particular political perspective. Residential patterns also followed political lines.[43] Thus a seditious cry emitted in one neighborhood as opposed to another, or a tricolor ribbon affixed to the door of an official's home, or the singing of a Bonapartist song outside a royalist café had specific, easily decipherable meaning for the inhabitants of a given town.

Certain venues, such as the town marketplace or the regional fair, were critical in the unofficial politics of the Restoration because of convenience or tradition. The local marketplace was a place frequented by most French citizens, even those living in remote villages. Local news was exchanged here, either by formal announcements and placards or, informally, through gossip. Because everyone was present here at a certain time in the week it was a convenient site at which to erect placards or leave seditious symbols for people to find.[44] The regional fair was an important place in popular festive culture. Because the fair was often a host to street theater, dancing, and drinking, the fair provided a space similar to the café and the theater, and an event similar to a local festival. But as a link to a national market and to urban values the fair played an especially important role.[45] News from outside the community arrived through contact with such fairs; traveling salesmen were thus often blamed for the organization of certain forms of protest which began to appear in different parts of France. Traffic in seditious objects, such as silks embroidered with Napoleonic busts from Lyons or tobacco cases mocking Charles X from Strasbourg, took place at these fairs. Objects representing national political ideologies were thus made available for merchants (and private individuals) to buy and bring back to the local arena.

Police reports and circulars addressing the problem of traveling salesmen offer the government's vision of the geography of unofficial politics, highlighting the key role which the fair and, in particular, its peddlers play. According to the authorities, "France [was] covered with peddlers" who travel "into the tiniest hamlets, and reach even the most isolated habitations." Taking advantage of local fairs to sell their wares and "spread their alarming news," these peddlers were deemed particularly dangerous because of the exaggerated influence they could have on "the peasant who has never lost sight of the bell tower of his village, [to whom] these peddlers seem to be a kind of oracle, the more believable the more readily they approach him in their language and their customs." This was the language of the minister of police, who in a circular from 1815 enjoined his prefects to do everything in their power to control these traveling salesmen, who so easily played the part of "agents spreading lies and intrigue."[46] In a circular from 1823 the minister of police reminded his prefects of the laws on *colportage*, at the same time as he offered the following depiction of the network of public places in which the peddlers exerted their insidious influence:

Mr. Prefect, I have drawn your attention several times to the problem of these travelers, who under the pretext of commercial interests, traverse France, and seem to have no object other than to plant wherever they go the seeds of sedition.

The reports which come to me from different points of the realm prove that the same maneuvers are being carried out today, only more actively than ever. Alarming news, declamations against the government, nothing is spared; and these phrases, repeated in inns and cafés, and other public places will spread through the population of the cities and the country, and produce the most unfortunate consequences.[47]

A large proportion of the seditious offenses committed during the Restoration took place in cafés and cabarets.[48] Newspapers of various parties were available there, and so it was a natural site for political discussion.[49] From a letter from the prefect of the Mayenne to the minister of the interior in 1823, asking for advice on how to handle people who read extracts from newspapers aloud in public places, we get a nice portrait of the role of cafés and cabarets in the propagation of the printed word, particularly, in his mind, in the rural context.

> In the cities, this tactic [of reading extracts from newspapers aloud] produces very little effect, because even in the cabarets there are men who can themselves read, and therefore have no need to listen. But in countryside such as one finds in Mayenne, where for every one hundred people there are hardly ten who can read their church books, when a traveler or a local reads, in his own fashion, the newspaper in a cabaret, he is sure to draw a large number of auditors who can't appreciate what it is he's trying to convince them of.[50]

Some café owners provided a space for people who shared their political perspective in which to congregate, while others tried to protect themselves from police scrutiny by avoiding politics or even by denouncing people who sang or spoke against the government in their establishments.[51] Whether explicitly encouraged by the owners or not, it was here that the people met, drank, talked, and found occasions to scream, sing, and act out their opinions. Despite well-placed informers, it was difficult to prosecute people arrested for crimes in cafés, either because witnesses refused to testify or because drunkenness was an easy and acceptable excuse.[52]

The theater was a public space which offered particularly fertile ground for political expression during the Restoration. The *parterre* (pit) has a long history in France as a place from which people could voice their opinions.[53] But in the Restoration this arena became peculiarly important. Throughout the Restoration the police tried to get the theater under control, and the many ordinances penned in these years defining proper conduct for the theater offer a guide to the many ways in which the people expressed themselves in this particular venue. One ordinance enacted by the mayor of Rouen in 1821 was typical.[54] It contained provisions which prohibited the audience from demanding a play that had not been announced in advance (Article III), from walking or talking in the corridors during a performance (Article XXVII), or from otherwise troubling the tranquillity of the spectators by clamors or signs of disapproval of any kind, before, during, or after the performance (Article XXVIII). Actors were not allowed to add anything to a previously accepted script, to respond or speak directly to the audience (Article XIX), or to read notes thrown onto the stage by members of the audience (Article XVI). The director of the theater could not be called to the stage by the audience (Article XV) or go on stage without the direct permission of the police, who were to be given a full account of what he would say in advance (Article XVII). Intermission was limited to between five and twenty minutes (Article XVI); the auditorium was to be vacated and closed immediately following performances (Article XII). The police files describing theater incidents bear testimony to the fact that each of these provisions was repeatedly violated at one point or another during the Restoration.

All over France, men and women went to the theater and whistled, booed, and hissed. They distributed flyers, posted placards, and read one play in the *parterre* while another was performed on stage. They demanded the performance of plays other than the ones announced, requested the appearance of the director of the theater, and clamored for (and were often granted) the repetition of particular lines that had some bearing on a local or national political issue. The regime used the theater to celebrate the king's days, and spectators expressed their support for or criticism of their king by applauding or booing when he was represented on stage.[55] Sometimes the king and his family were attacked even when a play had no obvious connection to royal themes at all. In one case reported from Elbeuf, an incident took place during a "fantasmagoric" spectacle; as a series of monstrous figures were featured on stage, someone in the audience screamed, "Voilà Louis XVIII," "Voilà la Duchesse d'Angoulême," "Voilà le Duc de Bordeaux," and "Voilà le Duc d'Angoulême" to the great amusement of the spectators.[56] While political expression in the theater never became dangerously violent, it was persistent and on some occasions achieved a national level of organization, and so seemed quite alarming to the authorities.[57]

In an article about the theater incidents from the Restoration period, Alain Corbin argues that disturbances in this particular venue were important for a range of social and political reasons. He argues that in this period different groups used the theater to establish and to maintain their social identity.[58] But Corbin also points to explicitly political divisions that provoked theater incidents. Liberals and royalists sat on opposite sides of the theater, or in the *parterre* as opposed to the *loges,* and responses to plays turned into screaming matches between sections of the audience.[59] According to Corbin, the inside of the theater—split between a left and right—symbolically reproduced the Chamber of Deputies, even in theaters in small towns. In the town of Bernay, in the Eure, the following scene took place in the theater: "On one side all the spectators had white bouquets, while on the other everyone had red. The faction with the white rose had announced that they would demand the favorite tunes of Henry IV." [60] Evoking the deeper political meaning of such incidents, Corbin offers the following portrait of the theater:

> The playful character of the place, devoted as it was to fantasy, authorized each person to take himself for a parliamentary orator. To the censorship exercised against the plays, to the surveillance which meddles in the audience's affairs, opponents reply by adapting the theatrical venue through astonishing practices. This subverts the very representation at the center of the theater; it abolishes the temporal distance separating the dramatic action from the great political debates of the moment. The continuous switching between past and present, real and imaginary allows for a confusion of roles, among the actors as well as the audience. The applause, the whistles, the cries, the boos, a cough can, depending upon the circumstance, sanction the play of the actors, the text to be applied, the comportment of the adversaries seated in the auditorium or the intervention of the gendarmerie.[61]

In his depiction of the theater, Corbin comes closest to evoking the argument I will make in chapter 6 regarding why the theater became a favored venue for protesting against the missionaries and the regime during the Restoration. It was precisely because of the carnivalesque character of this site, the fact that by their actions the audience could subvert "the very representation at the center of the theater," that the theater became the perfect place for exposing and criticizing the crisis of representation suffered by the regime; but it was also why it was turned so easily against the spectacles of the missionaries. In a side comment, Corbin suggests that the perspective of the missions might help to explain the popularity of the theater in the unofficial politics of the Restoration.[62] Corbin's intuition is correct; again and again, in city after city, protesters demonstrated that the theater was the perfect venue in which to organize an *anti-fête* against the spectacular ceremonies of the missionaries. The theater in the Restoration enabled protesters to offer a response to, a reproduction and a carnivalesque reiteration of the religious revival of the missionaries more than of the Parliament.

The activities in cafés, cabarets, and the theater often spilled into the streets. People leaving cafés continued to sing seditious verses or shout "Vive l'Empereur" as they passed by the homes of local officials or statues of their ex-emperor.[63] Despite efforts by the police to disperse audiences after incidents in the theater, they often congregated in the square in front of the theater, continuing to disturb the authorities for hours after the performance.[64] The streets became a favored venue for criticizing the missionaries, who were themselves turning the main thoroughfares of towns into theaters for their expiatory spectacles. Likewise, key sites in town which were highlighted by the missionaries' processions—sites where guillotines or liberty trees had been replaced by mission crosses—became the focus of protests, sacrilegious mockeries, and even violence. In towns where missionaries were unwelcome, protesters assembled in the squares in front of the homes of ecclesiastical and civil officials who had invited and were offering support to the visiting priests; these assemblies became very large, as we saw in the case of Brest, where two to three thousand citizens joined together in the traditional, oft-deployed practice of the charivari. The church itself, the venue to which the mission was often restricted, became the focus of a wide range of seditious and sacrilegious acts.

Because the laws defining seditious activities explicitly excluded from prosecution those acts which took place in private, the police records are often silent on the oppositional practices exercised in people's homes. However, the numerous police reports which acknowledge the need to abandon efforts to prosecute offenders because their seditious speech was uttered not in public but in the privacy of their own homes invite us to imagine the kinds of seditious acts which may have gone unpunished in this context. As we ponder the many forms of symbolic sedition practiced in this period, and in particular the traffic in objects bearing illegal images and emblems, we are forced to imagine what French citizens did in the privacy of their own homes as they integrated such objects into their everyday lives.

The Action: How?

Written forms of protest, and particularly the placard, occupy a privileged place in the police files because, to a greater extent than some of the oral, gestural, or symbolic forms that will be considered, they were thrust into public view, and therefore relatively easy for the authorities to collect. The official placard, publicizing a recent law passed by the government, spreading the news of a local prelate's pastoral letter, or announcing a coming state ceremony or mission, played a critical role in spreading local and national news. The practice of reading these aloud as they were posted at key points in town—near the city hall (if there was one), on the church wall, or in the marketplace—made these critical purveyors of information intelligible to a largely illiterate population.[65] The *un*official placard often constituted a direct response to this official use of print during the Restoration. Official *arrêtés* (orders) and announcements were destroyed and replaced, or merely defaced; or seditious placards parodied the form of the official placard, either trying to grant the authors and their message the status afforded by an official pronouncement, or mocking local authorities by using their language and their forms. But the seditious placard also mimicked the official placard in its ability to spread information, to provoke public discussion, and even to inspire and organize other forms of protest.

Seditious placards written as a form of protest appeared in different shapes and sizes in this period. They could be as small as an index card, and thus be easily concealed in one's pocket until they were posted for others to read. In such a case it is likely that the author showed it around before posting it, since it would hardly have attracted much attention, nor would it have been very easy to read once it was displayed.[66] Or one could transform a public edifice into a placard by writing on it a message using coal; this made it harder for the police to take it down, and it allowed for a somewhat less ephemeral effect.[67] Most often, placards were medium-size, readable from a distance, but most appreciated up close, where the details of an icon or smaller words placed around the edges could be seen.[68] They were hung most often on public edifices outdoors—on church walls, the wall near the marketplace, or the doors of residences of important officials. But they were also hung inside, especially inside theaters. To avoid being caught, people hung their placards in the middle of the night. Sometimes only one placard was posted, while other copies were mailed directly to the local officials whom they criticized.[69] Another tactic was to plaster a town with lots of copies of the same placard.[70] Because the handwriting was the only clue the authorities had to track down culprits, authors of placards tended to write them in a disguised hand.[71]

The meaning of the placard was as often inscribed in its placement as in its contents. For example, in order to evoke the specter of the clerical plot, and the threat that the priests would soon control the government, one protester turned the door of the home of the minister of ecclesiastical affairs and education into a placard by writing, "Here will reign the priests (*la calotte*); the French are all in the dung (*la crotte*)." This particular act apparently drew the attention of passersby, who stopped, commented, and caused what the police official described as a "public scandal."[72] Another carefully placed placard protesting against the "clerical plot" appeared in Rouen, where the local churchmen were suspected of controlling the civil authorities. Here the site chosen was the courthouse, and in this case one did not have to read to clearly appreciate the message, since next to the text which read "Young people, it is here then, in our city, that this sordid race would like to dictate our laws," was a drawing of a man in clerical garb hanging from a gallows.[73]

Appropriating the form of the official placard, protesters directly responded to their local authorities, their laws, their religious pronouncements, and their ceremonies. One Bonapartist placard, which announced the celebration of the 15th of August as Saint Napoleon's Day, borrowed the formula of the official festival *arrêté* to do so. The placard, which read "Festival of St. Napoleon / According to the Ordinance of the Mayor of Rouen / In light of the deliberation of . . . . / 1806 concerning the . . . ," was posted on the door of the church in the middle of the night before the 15th of August in 1818 so that local officials arriving in the morning to celebrate the regime's Vow of Louis XIII would have found themselves confronted with the fact that the festival which this new religious holiday was designed to replace was hardly forgotten.[74] Similarly, a placard posted during the night before the 24th of January responded directly to the official *arrêté* announcing the day of mourning for Louis XVI, posted and celebrated but a few days before. This poster adopted the general form of a festival announcement, but in its message it rejected the efforts of the regime to "force us to hold a funereal and expiatory service for the death of Louis XVI. What an excess of villainy! Instead of imposing this humiliating tribute to the innocent and generous people of France . . . let the odious head of Louis XVIII fall, so that his blood can wash the stain that he dares to impute to the French nation. Vive Napoleon II!"[75] Protesters could merely borrow certain features of the official placard without parodying the whole; one Bonapartist placard, for example, which began by mocking the physical attributes of Louis XVIII concluded with the following phrase, typical of official pronouncements: "It is forbidden for anyone to remove this *affiche*."[76] Official placards were themselves destroyed or defaced.[77] In one particularly funny incident, the placard describing the planned festivities for

Saint Charles's Day offered the occasion for some to imply the functioning of a clerical plot in their town, when they added the following note
to the bottom of the official placard:

> To end the festivities in such a way as to give unequivocal proof of their com-
> plete submission, the civil and military authorities will kiss the asses of the
> ecclesiastical authorities.[78]

Just as playing with the official placard allowed protesters to convey
several messages at once, other standard printed forms were adopted to
convey complex messages quite economically. In Besançon, the author/s
of one placard used the form of the theater *affiche* (bill) to mock local
church officials in the context of the local celebration of the Papal Jubilee. Announcing a performance of *Tartuffe* with a special intermission
featuring the local "hypocritical [churchmen] dancing a *pas de deux*
with nuns [from a local convent]," this particular *affiche* raised the specter of the church's hypocrisy and problematic theatricality both in its
content and its form.[79] Likewise, a "For Sale" sign posted outside the
archbishop's palace in Rouen at the height of the controversy over his
unpopular pastoral letter in the spring of 1825 allowed the sign's author
to invoke the widespread rumor that he, his subordinates, and their spiritual services could be "bought" at the same time that it asked him to
leave.[80] Exactly the same message was repeated in another version which
appeared the following year on the occasion of the mission in Rouen;
now the message read "Church to rent, missionaries to chase, a curé to
reform for having invited them." (In French this rhymes: "*Eglise à louer;
missionaires à chasser; curé à reformer pour les avoir demandés.*")[81]
This second formulation was repeated, word for word, in a placard
which appeared on the church door in the Moselle in response to a mission in Metz.[82]

Most frequently, placards contained the time-honored formula
"Down with this" or "Long live that," usually filled in with "Down with
Louis XVIII" or "Down with Charles X" and "Long live Napoleon" or
"Long live Napoleon II" in this period. These were often attached to
specific concerns. In the small town of Baqueville in the Seine-Inférieure,
a "Long live the Emperor" followed a complaint that Louis XVIII was
not fulfilling his ancient obligation to provide bread at a reasonable
price. Quite explicitly stating that "if Louis XVIII doesn't give us our
bread at a just price, our Emperor surely will," this particular placard
ends by evoking the symbolic representations of the two regimes: "Down
with the white flag, Long live the tricolor and liberty, Long live the Em-

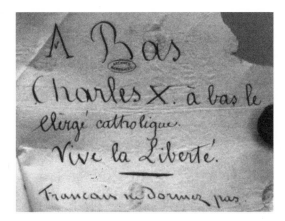

Figure 1. "Down with Charles X, down with the
Catholic clergy, Long live liberty, People of
France, don't sleep!" National Archives, Paris.
Photograph by Sheryl Kroen.

peror, because the Bourbons make us sick to our stomachs." [83] Placards
against Louis XVIII featured stock insults about his obesity, whereas,
under Charles X, placards most commonly attacked his ecclesiastical
policies or his or his ministers' overzealous support for the priests and
the émigrés who together represented the feudal yoke of the Old Regime. In Strasbourg, in the wake of the mission in 1825, someone posted
a placard which announced, "Down with Charles X, down with the
Catholic clergy, Long live liberty, People of France, don't sleep!" [84] This
basic message found its way onto walls and public places all over
France, merged with an iconography which associated the priests and
the king with the Jesuits and which featured the king himself as a cleric
(see fig. 1).

Placards played several critical roles in the unofficial politics of the
Restoration. As ephemeral as they were, they offered occasions for people
to publicly express an opinion, to respond directly or indirectly to official authorities, to popularize stock insults as well as phrases and icons
which were used to mock the king, his ministers, and the priests, and to
adulate Napoleon, his son, or even the republic. Quite complex and
wordy placards summarized and publicized some of the pamphlet literature of the period. Placards often directly inspired other kinds of practices: seditious cries were often emitted directly in response to a provoc-
ative placard; by posting placards mimicking official placards, or merely
defacing existing ones, authors could inspire spectators to disturb a royal

festival or a mission or at least to remember other holidays which they were not able to celebrate (such as Saint Napoleon's Day). Placards were also used to spread information and, especially, to organize protest. We will see this most clearly when we look closely at theater incidents of this period, in which placards played a critical role, not only in individual incidents but in spreading word of such incidents all over the country. Like the seditious cries to which we will now turn our attention, placards were inscribed in specific times and places, were available to a limited, local audience, and even that, for a very short period of time; yet, like many oral and gestural practices which people developed to express themselves in this period, there is an extraordinary coherence to the themes and the images and even the specific texts which appeared on placards throughout France.

Seditious cries, usually brief, insulting, and carefully inscribed in time and place, offered even the least educated peasant a means for expressing him- or herself in this period. In his study of political culture in Toulouse during the Restoration, David Higgs argues that seditious cries "beg for a reading as part of a popular, oral, and contestatory discourse . . . ."[85] He finds the cries issued in Toulouse to be "stylized, repetitive, and vague," identical to the kinds of one-liners found in other parts of France at the same time.[86] Susanna Barrows, studying the same practice, but under the authoritarian Second Empire, sees seditious cries as a way of "understanding the *imaginaire* of ordinary citizens in a period of harsh repression." She stresses the complexity of what she calls not mere seditious cries, but "speech acts," "texts to be decoded in their totality," "a public multimedia and often iconographic set of actions."[87] Her way of thinking about seditious cries is useful for the early nineteenth century, for, as in the 1850s, seditious cries in the Restoration obeyed a certain rhythm and geography. They were often provoked and given meaning by exceptional events, celebrations, or objects. Every time a local civil official or missionary invited the crowd to join him in saying "Long live the King" or "Long live Jesus and the Catholic Church," it became an opportunity which many seized to express their support for the exiled emperor or to shout "Death to the Jesuits."[88] The assassination of the duc de Berry was the occasion for several cries from "Long live Napoleon" to "The duc de Berry is dead, so much the better."[89] While insults to members of the royal family were occasionally spontaneous, they were more often prompted by a visit of one of them.[90] Usually people shouted and screamed in a crowd—on the sidelines of a procession, in the *parterre* of a theater, in a market-

place, or in the middle of a church ceremony; this served the double purpose of making their message heard by a large number of people at the
same time as it made it difficult for the police to identify the culprit or
culprits. Punishment required a direct denunciation, which was quite
rare.[91] Where people were most often apprehended was in cafés, where
they quite audibly toasted Napoleon or his family, or insulted some
member of the royal family.

Even more troublesome for the authorities than seditious cries were
songs with problematic lyrics or songs which merely evoked memories
of problematic events by their tunes. Songs played a particularly important and interesting role in the unofficial politics of the Restoration. On
the one hand, they constituted part of a rich oral culture, available to the
entire population. Songs were used by civil authorities and the missionaries in the context of their public celebrations; they were a key feature
of popular festive culture, and the world of the café, the cabaret, and the
fair.[92] But songs also occupied a privileged place in the print culture of
this period.[93] They circulated in manuscript and in printed collections
and thus played a key role in constituting a truly national print culture;
but because they could also be easily performed and improvised, songs
offered this national repertoire of images, lyrics, and tunes for local consumption by the entire population, not merely the literate few.[94]

Like placards, songs were used as a means of spreading information
and organizing protest. In the Seine-Inférieure two different songs circulated in the wake of the local archbishop's unpopular pastoral letter
in the spring of 1825; one contained twenty-two verses, the other forty-
four verses, which carefully and derisively explained the entire contents
of the prelate's recent decree.[95] These songs, which played an important
role in gathering opposition against the archbishop also found their way
beyond Rouen; the prefect of the neighboring department of the Eure
complained that he saw people exchanging these and other songs and
writings "against the Jesuits" in the town square in Evreux.[96] National
news was disseminated by way of "seditious" songs. One police report
from Lyons in 1824 complained that the recent protests of the left in the
Chamber of Deputies against the expulsion of the opposition deputy
Jacques-Antoine Manuel found their way into songs which were being
distributed in Lyons.[97]

Protestors rewrote explicitly revolutionary songs, like the "Marseillaise," but they also mimicked the revolutionaries' practice of adapting
popular drinking songs to political ends.[98] Even if the people singing
them did use unproblematic lyrics, if the song was well known in its

revolutionary or Bonapartist rendition it could still evoke memories and hopes attached to those events. One prefect complained about precisely such a problem in the context of a letter to the minister of the interior about the missionaries' practice of writing canticles to well-known revolutionary tunes; in the recent mission in Le Puy in 1822 it was the "Marseillaise" and the "Reveil du Peuple" which had been adapted by the missionaries, and the prefect was quick to point out how easily such tunes could serve to evoke memories and even spawn revolt: "it is important to ban from Catholic temples such tunes, already happily forgotten, and to which those seeking to lead a revolt or spread sedition need only add their old lyrics to carry away the masses." [99]

That songs from the Revolution and the Empire, or recounting and evoking events from those periods, were both circulating and sung in public we know from the police records. This was a source of great frustration to the authorities, who had a lot of trouble controlling either the traffic in the printed song or the public singing of seditious verses. One report from Paris, which evokes the scene for the singing of a Bonapartist song, is particularly enlightening both for its portrait of the crowd, attentively listening, and for the image it offers of the frustrated police official, impotent to stop such activities, and aware of the danger they could represent: "All of the windows and doors in the neighborhood [of the Faubourg St. Antoine] were full of people. The civil guard formed around them. It was between 9 and 10 A.M., when all the workers eat lunch. I was curious to listen to their song, which was making a huge racket." The official then revealed the content of the song, which spoke ruefully of Napoleon's death, but offered his son as the hope for France's future. The official made the dangers of such singing clear when he wrote to his superior, "You know that the unhappy Hundred Days were announced by such songs." He concluded with a long description of the state this scene had produced in him: "I was in a fit of convulsive trembling for more than an hour . . . may God watch over France and over us; I feel death in my soul after hearing this cursed song." [100] Another official, this time a member of the Royal Gendarmerie from the Dordogne, tells a similar story. While walking along the left bank of a river, he found himself attracted by some songs coming from the right; once he finally got close enough to see and to hear, he made out that about fifteen young men were together, some standing, some seated, just outside an inn, singing a song expressing republican ideals. The key lines went: "The sovereign people are advancing / Tyrants will

die / The Republic calls us . . . A Frenchman must live for her / For her
a Frenchman must die." The report makes clear that the men were singing very loudly, since, although he wasn't close to the singers, this official
heard every word quite clearly. He also noted "that the singers appeared
to go out of their way to stress certain words, giving more force to their
voices as if these words inspired in them sentiments of hatred and of
hope, words like *tremble*, ... *Tyrants, the sovereign people, the Republic, for her a Frenchman must die.*" Interestingly, this official found
himself vacillating between feelings of indignation and pity, "thinking
about young men who were clearly strangers to the passions and memories of the revolution, who were at this moment unthinkingly repeating
the words of those incorrigible sedition-mongers, deaf to the voice of
reason and experience, to the cries of the homeland so long torn apart."
Angry with the "sedition-mongers" (*factieux*), but perplexed and moved
by the naive singing of the next generation, the officer found himself
"plunged into sad thoughts, which made [him] tremble for the future of
France." [101]

Police reports from all over France attest to the government's frustrating efforts to control the widespread practice of singing. It was when
people sang in public—in cafés, in workshops, in the streets—that the
police took action; they tried to get copies of the songs, identify the authors and propagators of injurious verses, and arrest the individuals doing the singing. By their own admission, the police gathered but a tiny
fraction of the seditious songs which circulated and were sung in this period. [102] On the rare occasions when they did catch offenders in the act
of singing seditious songs, the authorities doled out stiff penalties. [103] But
more often, the authorities expressed frustration over the inability to
identify the authors of songs or to get witnesses to testify against their
friends or neighbors caught singing them. [104] Much more common than
reports of prosecution for such public singing are accounts of incidents
which had no consequences for their authors: either indulgent authorities chose to look the other way, or there was insufficient evidence, or a
generous jury acquitted alleged perpetrators of seditious singing. [105]

As was true for most seditious practices in this period, government
officials tended to see singing as part of an organized effort to gather opposition to the government; at the center of this particular plot were
traveling singers and peddlers, spreading the same problematic verses all
over the country, and it was thus on these key troublemakers that police
officials focused their attention. One police officer writing from Paris in

1829 explained his efforts to track down and punish traveling singers in the following terms:

> One of the tactics which the secret agents of the government's enemies use to remind the people of the times of glory . . . is to get them to sing in cabarets and other public places, verses which recall the memory of Bonaparte. The *Souvenirs* of Béranger are sung in workshops, in the courtyards of factories, where traveling singers arrive and lead the crowd.[106]

A report from the Jura in 1818 focused on the traffic in seditious songs, arguing that where the government had to crack down was on the clandestine peddling of Bonapartist verses. Having himself brought in one peddler for selling copies of "Le Champ d'Asile," a song honoring Napoleon, this police officer was shocked to hear this *colporteur* declare that "nowhere had anyone told him he could not distribute this song." He wrote to this superior in Paris for support in carefully surveying this clandestine literature, arguing in the following terms:

> The leniency of the government, the advantages of freedom of the press, are not incompatible with a wise surveillance. I thought it necessary to prevent the clandestine distribution of this song, of little danger in and of itself, but which none the less makes a certain impression on the multitude, attracts the crowd, brings back memories that time has forced to fade, and that reason has made us forget. . . ."[107]

Superiors in Paris always encouraged local police officials to pursue traveling singers and salesmen and to prosecute these key figures in the national traffic in seditious songs to the full extent of the law; but neither, was, in fact, very easy to control. Like the circulation of printed matter more generally, the little pamphlets of verses tended to fall between the cracks of police surveillance and public prosecution. Indeed the complaints of police officers allow us to appreciate what they knew everyone around them appreciated: that a certain amount of sedition was tolerated, and certain practices were easier than others to get away with. The widespread traffic in songs was one such area.[108]

Periodical literature was the form of print culture most subject to surveillance and prosecution under the Restoration's press laws, and yet by all accounts, even newspapers regularly tested the limits of the regime's toleration and only rarely suffered the consequences. Between 1815 and 1830 the opposition press issued a continuous stream of criticism of the government and its policies. Publicizing key political disputes, maintaining public pressure in favor of the freedoms promised by the Charter (particularly freedom of the press), and consistently attacking the religious revival of the missionaries, the periodical press played a key role in shaping the unofficial politics of this period.[109]

One crucial role played by the opposition press was to publicize other types of publications which joined it in its assault on the missionaries and the monarchy. From the very beginning of the Restoration, for example, publishers began to reprint writings from the Enlightenment, and the periodical press reported generously on each new edition, explaining that by making such works available "to the mass of the nation" these publishers were rendering "a veritable service" to France.[110] Between 1815 and 1824, multivolume sets of the writings of Voltaire and Rousseau were issued with increasing frequency. According to one estimate from the period, more than two million copies of these two authors' works appeared in this short time.[111] Like the prefaces which accompanied such volumes, newspaper articles explained the critical role such works played in fortifying "the good spirit of the century," particularly in light of the Catholic church's overt assault on the Enlightenment, announced in a *mandement* of 1817, and publicized by the missionaries' sermons and autos-da-fé all over France throughout the Restoration.[112]

If articles in the press and these early new editions of Rousseau and Voltaire were signs of a kind of "war of books" of the Restoration, the explosion of pamphlet literature after 1825 attests to the increasing importance of the printed word in extending this battle to a broader segment of the population.[113] Police bulletins from 1825 and 1826 are dominated by reports that increasing numbers of pamphlets in 32 format, costing as little as 5 to 10 sous, were showing up all over France.[114] At a time when the average Parisian worker earned 20 to 100 sous a day, and when a four-pound loaf of bread cost 13 sous, such little books were clearly accessible to a broad population.[115] The police saw this surge of cheap editions as yet another means by which a small group of troublemakers was trying to agitate the population against the government. As one report explained:

This is something which merits serious attention, this new tactic which the troublemakers employ with perseverance, of producing a mass of these small impious and seditious works, and then distributing them in public places at very low prices or even giving them out for nothing. One can see here not only the intention to pervert public opinion, but especially to agitate the population.[116]

Another report stresses the content and the style of these new publications in order to underscore the effort made to reach the broadest possible public.

> The little brochures in 32 continue. Baskets placed before booksellers are full of them. Not only does one reprint separately, with notes and prefaces, anything which would serve to incite passions, but one publishes a mass of these little pamphlets in a popular style, evidently destined for the people.[117]

This "mass of pamphlets" included a broad range of titles. Most commonly reported were reprints of Voltaire's *Philosophical Dictionary, Candide,* and *La Pucelle.*[118] Generally anticlerical titles, such as a *Brief History of the Inquisition, The Secret Education of the Jesuits, The Civil Constitution of the Clergy,* or *The Liberties of the Gallican Church,* as well as Moliére's *Tartuffe,* comprised a large proportion of the titles.[119] Attacks on the nobility or anything that evoked the specter of feudalism were common: *The Feudal Dictionary* instructed its readers on how to see evidence of feudalism returning all around them; Old Regime titles which were relevant were reprinted, including Mirabeau's "Discourse on the Birthright" and the scurrilous *Biography of the Women of the Court* and the *Adventures of the Duc de Roquelaure.*[120] General histories of France were featured in the list of pamphlets in 32, as were histories of the French Revolution, which, much to the chagrin of the police reporting, "enthusiastically described Danton, but covered royalists, Vendéens, and even Louis XVI and Marie-Antoinette with insults."[121] Béranger's songs were also reprinted and distributed in this cheaper format.[122] Pamphlets of this sort also publicized important speeches or essays regarding debates in the Chamber of Deputies, or trials involving liberal newspapers and, as we shall see, troublemakers prosecuted for their part in theater riots.[123]

The police bulletins report on only those writings which clearly criticized the regime, or directly assaulted the church and especially the missionaries, and which apparently sought to lead the population to oppose the status quo; but other sources reveal that such publications participated in a veritable pamphlet war in which royalist and Catholic publishers actively participated. The missionaries, of course, publicized this public struggle from their pulpits and in their autos-da-fé, but supporting the religious revival were Catholic publishers who issued their own reading materials at equally low prices. To counter the flood of anticlerical titles assailing the missionaries' revival were countless positive accounts of individual missions, as well as a widely circulating prophetic literature which dovetailed with the missionaries' central message.[124] Organizations emerged to provide the public with alternative reading material; the most significant of these were the "oeuvre" of Good Books in Bordeaux, which established a vast lending library, and the Catholic Good Book Society, which distributed more than 800,000 cheap editions of its own between 1824 and 1826.[125] Bailly de Sarcy, the publisher of *The Catholic Tribune*, organized "The Society for Good Studies" in 1828 in the Latin Quarter, where it provided meeting rooms, libraries, and lectures on moral and religious subjects to counter the influence of analogous reading clubs and lectures supported by competing liberal groups.[126]

The periodical press continuously reported on the battle of the books, with the liberal press deriding the missionaries' autos-da-fé, advertising the availability of cheap copies of Voltaire and Rousseau, and directly attacking the Catholic and royalist press. The *Ami de la Religion* popularized the missionaries' tendency to cast the writings of the philosophes as poison and directly accused the liberal press of spreading it among the population: "This poison, doesn't it circulate enough, and must one really augment the dosage?"[127] The *Constitutionnel* led the attack on the missionaries and depicted the public battle over the Enlightenment literature as a race, one that the missionaries and their supporters were clearly losing. As one article put it: "The more of Voltaire the missionaries obtain for their autos-da-fé, the more [his] works . . . are sought after. The number of publications surpasses the number of burnings."[128] Or another: "It's a remarkable thing, the surge of public opinion in favor of Voltaire. Never has the author of *La Henriade* enjoyed such widespread popularity in France. From the instant that he was attacked, the public pronounced itself against the aggressors! . . . To each insult, the publishing industry responded with a new edition . . . "[129] Such articles always concluded with an announcement of a new edition and information about where and at what price it could be purchased.

The very fact of this huge reproduction of Voltaire and Rousseau, and the apparently massive traffic in pamphlets which it precipitated, itself stood as a reproach, a retort to the efforts of the missionaries to denounce these authors and the rational spirit they represented. Efforts were made to block this traffic, which the police recognized was beyond the reach of existing censorship laws, but these failed. In the course of the debates on potential laws to control this commerce the deputy Pierre-Paul Royer-Collard posed the following critical question: "The books of the booksellers have made their way into people's minds. It is

from there that we must chase them. Do you have a law which can accomplish this?" [130] Royer-Collard's assertion is tantalizing and leaves us
with an interesting question. Just how widespread were the ideas of the
philosophes? Were they now "entering the minds of the people" because
of the public battles with the missionaries? Among members of the literate public who were opposed to the missionaries and the government,
there is no question that the ideas, especially of Voltaire, had become
better known. Lawyers defending people arrested for "sacrilegious"
crimes often cited Voltaire; liberal newspapers and anticlerical pamphlets consistently evoked and popularized the ideas of the philosophes. [131] The language of Voltaire also crept into police reports, as in
the following report on the missionaries in the largely Protestant town
of La Rochelle: "Mr. Guyon distinguished himself in a sermon wherein,
after having reviewed all of the religions of Europe, he tried to prove that
ours is superior to all the others. The numerous assembly which this service attracted withdrew terribly unhappy with his sophisms, and each
asked, 'What has he proven? Nothing,' and everyone must have repeated
the beautiful verse of Voltaire: 'I don't damn you, why do you damn
me?'" [132] But whether or not the philosophies of Voltaire and Rousseau
or the mass of "impious and seditious" pamphlets had "made their way
into the minds of the people" is a bit harder to assess. That the names of
the key Enlightenment figures became common currency among the
population at large and that certain key ideas achieved the status of political slogans, however, is completely clear. As we will see later when we
consider the traffic in seditious objects more generally, the combined effect of the opposition press and this mass of cheap pamphlets was to
popularize a set of references from the Enlightenment and to transform
them into a common critical vocabulary for protesting against the
church and state during the Restoration.

One version of Voltaire, advertised in the pages of *Le Constitutionnel* in 1826, beautifully expresses the significance of this traffic in the
Enlightenment in the context of the Restoration. Announcing a new
pamphlet version in 32, the publishers (Badouin Frères) had the particularly ingenious idea of "reassuring the subscribers regarding the fate of
their charming edition" by making it fireproof! As the advertisement explains, "At a time when one so charitably burns so many of our most
useful and philosophical works, the precaution is not without use." Ending the announcement with a description of the illustration that adorns
the cover, the journalist transposes the kind of language and imagery
long used to depict the sovereignty and *magnitus* of kings to the phi-

losophy of the Enlightenment: "It is exciting to see on the cover of the book . . . the Phoenix . . . the bird which is the emblem of imperishable existence."[133] While this particular version of Voltaire's works, humorously marketed as "inflammable," makes the point most boldly, clearly the whole campaign of the publishers, working with the assistance of the liberal press, functioned to ensure the imperishability of Enlightenment ideas and their continued importance in constituting the foundation of modern society and politics.

An even better example of the role the periodical press could play in combination with this widely circulating pamphlet literature can be found in the spate of *Tartuffe* incidents which shook the nation, and in which these two forms of print played a critical role. The liberal publications *Le Constitutionnel* and *l'Ami de la Charte* reported generously and supportively on theater incidents taking place all over the country. These newspapers spread the idea of demanding a performance of *Tartuffe*, or applying the themes and images of the play to a local event, and identifying the lines to which they ought to respond once the play was performed. Newspapers also publicized the pamphlet version of *Tartuffe* available in 32 format. One police report from Paris in 1826 cites the *Mercure*, which announced: "The conspiracy of the 32 format continues . . . Messieurs Badouins gave the signal with their little *Tartuffe*."[134]

Given the contents of the broad range of seditious pamphlets, of which *Tartuffe* was but one example, and the fact that this widely circulating literature conspired with the opposition press to provoke other seditious practices, it is not surprising that government officials continually expressed frustration about their inability to control this traffic. One police report from May of 1826 beautifully summarizes the impotence of the administration to control these forms of print, which simply eluded the censorship laws of the realm.

> Pamphlets in small format for 5 sous augment in number every day. The Publisher Touquet printed a catalogue today of all the pamphlets which he has published since the 1st of January. There are 52, and he announced an additional 12 which were in press. The perseverance with which he pursues this enterprise beautifully demonstrates the intention to organize a new way of eluding current censorship laws, which, in fact, can only be exercised against the periodic press.[135]

If pamphlet literature slipped through the cracks of the Restoration's censorship laws, the traffic in prints, individual song sheets, and single-page seditious writings was even harder to control.[136]

The cases in which peddlers were arrested for selling seditious prints give us a peek at the wide range of seditious print material circulating in this period. Arrests of individual peddlers often led to searches in the storerooms of their suppliers. Boxes and boxes of prints from the Revolution and the Empire come into view: reports regularly allude to the efforts early on in the regime to destroy such objects, but also to the broad range of tactics local officials actually adopted in the context of their *mise-en-place*. Rather than simply destroy their stock, officials were content with the promise that problematic images would be hidden from view and not sold; or occasionally they report on cases in which problematic prints were transformed, with slogans being effaced, and even heads of famous figures being replaced. We see a world of peddlers feigning illiteracy and ignorance of the content of their wares, even when the prints in question were illustrations clearly depicting Bonaparte or his wife and the symbols of the empire. We see juries regularly acquitting offenders on the grounds of ignorance, or because such articles portrayed "historical subjects," rather than provocations to seditious acts, and thus did not constitute grounds for incrimination.[137]

The vast majority of prints of this sort were Bonapartist, featuring Bonaparte himself, or great battle scenes, or famous generals serving the emperor, or his wife, or, later in the regime, his son. But a large number of these images were not merely "historical" and unproblematic representations dating from previous periods. One caricature circulating in Le Mans featured Napoleon taking the throne back from Louis XVIII.[138] One particular one-page publication which appeared in several different departments, and which clearly communicated a seditious message, was a print featuring various imperial accoutrements (including Napoleon wearing a crown) which, when folded, had the appearance of a fleur-de-lis. Thus having the outward appearance of support for the monarchy, these images propagated the clear message that underneath the façade of legitimism was an avid Bonapartism.[139] (See fig. 2.)

Alongside this traffic in seditious prints was an even broader commerce in everyday objects bearing political insignia and slogans. With the return of Louis XVIII and his successor, Charles X, came the images of Bourbon kings, the white flag, the fleur-de-lis, all of which found their way onto public buildings, but also onto everyday objects like card games and plateware. Furthermore, the public assault on seditious images of Napoleonic and revolutionary emblems in the first year of the regime, which involved requisitions of merchants' stock as well as the removal of such emblems from public edifices, delineated a clear symbolic battleground in which people could and did participate. Accompanying missionaries were peddlers making available the symbols of their revival: the little cross symbolizing participation in the mission that one could wear on one's lapel, but also booklets of canticles, images of Christ and the king, and, of course, mission crosses. But for those who opposed the monarchy or the missionaries, a wide array of objects that featured a spectrum of alternative emblems and slogans was available for purchase.

Absolutely all the battles which were played out in the pages of the pamphlets and broadsheets of this period were replayed in the host of everyday objects circulating at the same time throughout the realm. To counter the anti-Enlightenment message of the missionaries or certain laws of the regime, one could purchase not only cheap copies of Voltaire but also razors bearing the likeness of the author of *Candide*, or of Montesquieu.[140] One could buy or sport scarves, umbrellas, or ties which made manifest one's support for the Charter, freedom of the press, specific deputies such as Benjamin Constant and Cassier Perrier, or the famous songwriter Béranger. These objects read like a narrative of the key struggles of the Restoration period: ties with "Sacrilege" or "The Jesuits" attest to the controversy over the Sacrilege Law of 1825; scarves with the slogan "The Project of the Law on the Freedom of the Press" attest to the battle over the press law in 1827.[141] To oppose the Bourbons and royalists, or show one's support for Napoleon, one could buy playing cards with slogans such as "Down with the Bourbons," or "Long live Napoleon," or "Down with the Bourbons, Death to the royalists," or cards figuring little eagles.[142] (See figs. 3 and 4.)

Bonapartist objects appeared in many forms. One could buy little busts of the past emperor or plateware representing different scenes in his political and military career.[143] Silks featuring Napoleon in various poses and assorted imperial accoutrements were made into jackets which were sold and worn in different parts of France.[144] Bonapartist pipes "in white porcelain, with a blue effigy of Bonaparte" were sold publicly in Besançon.[145] Napoleonic images could be carefully concealed in different kinds of objects. In 1822 the police in the Marne confiscated hats which had a pro-Bonapartist engraving hidden at their base under a piece of taffeta.[146] Likewise, in 1820, in Allier, tobacco cases were seized which had portraits of Napoleon, Marie-Louise, and their son covered with pieces of cloth.[147] In Toulon it was boxes of candy which were sold with images of Napoleon hidden under their covers.[148]

Figure 2. *a*, "Innocent fleur-de-lys"; *b*, "Bonapartism
under a facade of royalism"; *c*, "Bonapartism revealed."
National Archives, Paris. Photographs by Sheryl Kroen.

The tricolor was extremely popular and took a variety of forms in
this period. In 1819, men were seen wearing tricolor ribbons as watchbands in Rouen; in 1821 tricolor swimsuits were being sold; in 1823 it
was neckties that appeared in blue, white, and red.[149] Tricolors were
found embroidered on chairs, printed on labels for wine bottles, and
painted on the insides of tobacco cases.[150] In St-Quentin in 1829, some
travelers from Paris were said to be wearing tricolor hats.[151] Occasionally people simply combined the colors "innocently" (or so they told the
juries), as in 1817, when two flower merchants used three different ribbons in the proscribed colors to tie up the bouquets of flowers they sold
(the only other color they possessed being black!); in Rouen in July of

c

1822, the mayor ruefully reported that one citizen "continues to swim at the swimming school with his blue bathing trunks, his red belt, and a white bathing cap." [152] Occasionally, tricolor emblems were explicitly tied to republican emblems and ideals, as in the tricolor suspenders sold in Rennes in 1825 which also featured liberty caps and such slogans as "the sun to free men" and "Liberty to Haiti." [153]

Not only did people buy and sell and wear the proscribed emblems in public; they also used them, much as they used the placard, to attract attention and to disrupt official ceremonies. Occasionally such objects were thrust into public view, and were clearly intended to attract attention. In Digne, in 1826, tricolor cockades appeared in the central town

Figure 3. Bonapartist
suspenders. Museum of
the National Archives,
Paris. Photograph by
Sheryl Kroen.

square repeatedly over the course of two months.[154] The same thing happened in two different cities in the Seine-Inférieure in 1819 and 1821.[155] During the period of the *mise-en-place,* someone in the same department responded to the official destruction of republican and imperial emblems by carefully placing a red bonnet on the top of a church bell tower for the inhabitants of the town to discover on Sunday morning on their way to church.[156]

Protests aimed at the monarch were expressed through attacks on the artifacts and symbols representing him. Busts of the kings and of Henri IV, erected throughout the Restoration, were often vandalized.[157] In one case, the king's crown and scepter were defaced on one statue, and a crown and a cross bearing the Bourbon fleur-de-lis were defaced on others.[158] As we saw in the discussion of protests on the occasion of the king's saint day, the white cockade also became the focus of attacks.[159] The coinage of the realm became a regular object of symbolic sedition during the Restoration. Disfiguring the bust of the king to give him the appearance of being a Jesuit was a repeated and particularly widespread

Figure 4. "Liqueur de Béranger." Seditious wine label. Museum of the National Archives, Paris. Photograph by Sheryl Kroen.

practice that constituted a critical tool in the anticlerical arsenal of the period. While symbolic attacks on the king and the symbols of the Bourbons occupied an important place in the political sedition of the period, it was the attacks on the symbols of the church and especially the missions which were especially widespread. Sacred hosts and vessels inside churches, and especially the mission cross itself, became the focus of repeated attacks throughout the Restoration. Like the image of the Jesuit-king, this repertoire of anticlerical symbolic sedition will be considered separately in chapter 5.

Whatever their form, a certain humor predominated in the seditious practices we have presented. During this period people protested less often with violence than with derision and wit.[160] Puns were common. One song called, "C'est sur," was used to mock a local clerical figure named Le Sur; each stanza, which was full of insults aimed at the churchman, would end with a rousing, "C'est sur," meaning at once "that's for sure" and "it's Le Sur."[161] Insults were a common way to attack the powerful: if the king was often called a fat pig, high clerical officials were referred to as fools, bigots, and even contemptible insects.[162] By using rhymes or clever forms, some writers made a barrage of insults seem even funnier.[163] The humor was often earthy—full of curses and references to food and defecation.[164] But the humor could also be quite sophisticated, as in the writings which borrowed forms of beatitudes or confessions, or jokes written in Latin.[165] In the many *Tartuffe* incidents all over France after 1825, allusions to Molière's comedy provided the basis for one big joke about the men of the collar and the civil authorities thought to be in their power.

The Setting: Who?

Who was it that perpetrated these seditious crimes? Who wrote the placards? Who sang the songs? Who went to the theater? Who wore tricolor bathing suits? Who sold them? Who spread rumors that Napoleon was coming back to France? These questions are best answered in two steps. First, I will look at how the authorities saw the problem. Then, by looking closely at the reports of incidents where the perpetrators were actually caught, and by extrapolating from them what we know about the forms which popular expression took, I will put together a collage of possible participants in the unofficial politics of the Restoration period.

In reading the police files from these years, certain figures emerge repeatedly as being particularly worrisome to the authorities. Some which I have already discussed include the café or cabaret owner, the merchant at the regional fair, and local officials such as mayors, subprefects, and prosecutors who were uncooperative in organizing public ceremonies or enforcing the law. The theater director was often singled out for attention in cities where the theater became the site of serious political agitation. One figure who emerges again and again as particularly dangerous and influential in these years, both in police reports and in popular fiction, was the *colporteur*.[166]

While the police reports occasionally indicate the names and professions of the perpetrators of seditious crimes, more often—whether they knew the authors of the crimes or not—they saw individual acts within the context of a general plot orchestrated by liberals and "revolutionaries" in Paris. Even when the evidence contradicted their assumptions, the police persisted in portraying politics as something which arrived from Paris and was organized from the top (that is, by the middle class) down. On the one hand, this can be explained as a useful tactic for the local official, who always had a personal interest in deflecting responsibility or blame for seditious activities from the residents of his town. He could argue that he had his population under control, but that they were being "agitated" by outsiders. On the other hand, this way of interpreting political protest also seemed to stem from the inability of most public officials to imagine that popular protest *could* spring from the lower classes or from the provinces *without* direction from outside or above. That this notion of a liberal, middle-class plot was an assumption of the police which bordered on obsession is made particularly apparent both by its ubiquity and its use as an explanation even when the police's own evidence contradicted their notion of such a plot. In chapters 5 and 6, when I discuss popular anticlericalism and the widespread use of *Tartuffe* after 1825, I will show that liberals from Paris *were* often involved in spreading certain ideas and forms of protest. But the "liberal plot" theory, so popular among state officials, was simply inadequate to explain the widespread participation in certain forms of protest; in fact, it often concealed much more that it explained.[167] So, for the moment I will put aside the complicated question of who, if anyone, *orchestrated* popular political protest in this period, and try instead to assemble a portrait of the population involved in seditious activities by looking at the raw material available in police reports.

Most of the examples of popular protest assembled in this chapter went unpunished, either because the perpetrators of the crimes were never identified or because they were exonerated for lack of proof. However, the few cases which did involve arrests demonstrate that a wide range of social groups was involved in seditious activities in this period. Of the forms of popular expression discussed, it was singing and seditious speech in cafés which most often led to arrest; and in the examples discussed in this chapter, students, officers, merchants, artisans, and workers were among those identified in police reports.[168] None of these were women. In situations where large groups were involved in incidents—in the theater, or in the disruption of a mission, or along the route of a procession—we rarely learn about the people who actually caused the disturbance simply because they were able to get lost in the crowd. But police reports, especially on theater incidents, allow us to see which groups were most likely to be involved in such disruptions. Most active in the theater incidents were students (of law and medicine), military officers, journalists, lawyers, artisans, and, somewhat less often, factory workers.[169] Women were present in the theater, although none were arrested in any of the incidents in the Restoration; in fact, the organizers of incidents often suggested that they stay at home for their own safety.[170]

In none of the cases of placards or seditious writings included here were the authors discovered. In one case, a wigmaker was suspected of writing a placard, but he was never prosecuted for lack of evidence.[171] In another case, a bookstore owner was suspected of being the author of seditious songs circulating in Rouen, but he also was not pursued.[172] The majority of French citizens in this period were illiterate. Therefore, these written forms of expression could only have been penned by the small fraction of the population that was educated. However, the illiterate majority could have the placards read to them, or they could decipher the icon which often accompanied and represented the text, or they could have their literate neighbor write their ideas down for them. So they were not *necessarily* excluded from forms of sedition which seemed to require the ability to read.[173] Nevertheless, certain texts were clearly the product of the well-educated—such as the placard circulating in Rouen in 1825 which mocked the men of the collar in Latin.[174] But most placards were written in rhyme, and the songs were adapted from popular tunes and so were easy for men and women to remember and repeat even if they were not their original authors.

From the police reports one gets the impression that the majority of French citizens did *not* commit seditious crimes in public during the Restoration. Some incidents took place in public when large numbers of French men and women were present. The police usually emphasized the fact that those "troubling the tranquillity of the event" were small in number. The Jubilee celebration in Lyons, for example, which attracted 40,000 spectators, was disrupted by a performance of *Tartuffe*. But the local officials reported that only a dozen or so individuals used the two performances of this play to criticize the proceedings, as compared with the mass of spectators who seemed to support the celebration.[175] In two different theater incidents in Rouen in 1821 and in Angoulême in 1826, the authorities spoke of over 2,000 spectators. In the case of Rouen, the police estimated that only 100 of the people in the audience actively disrupted the play, and emphasized the good behavior of the other 1,900.[176] In the case of Angoulême, only four people were actually taken into custody for disturbing a performance in 1826. But this was because the assembled crowd, while not actively participating in the theater incident, prevented the authorities from apprehending the troublemakers.

In this way they showed at least tacit support for them as opposed to the police.[177]

In the anticlerical protests which became increasingly common over the course of the Restoration, the numbers of men and women willing to commit seditious and even "sacrilegious" acts grew. In the previous chapter, in the context of the anticlerical incident which broke out in Brest in 1819, we saw that the police described crowds of 2,000 to 3,000 citizens; they explained that it was impossible to distinguish leaders or instigators within the crowd and acknowledged that the general will of the city was expressed by the "orderly" charivaris outside the bishop's palace. But police reports which acknowledge that whole populations offered their participation and consent in such outward opposition were quite rare. However, in town after town, as protesters organized against the missions, attacked their crosses, or turned to the theater to demand a command performance of *Tartuffe*, very large crowds became involved, either explicitly supporting those opposed to the missions or actively participating in demonstrations in favor of the visiting priests. In towns where missionaries orchestrated their expiatory spectacles, and protesters made their opposition manifest in large-scale organized opposition, it was simply impossible not to be aware of, or in some way to participate in, the struggles which erupted over them. In the anticlerical incident which shook Rouen in the spring of 1825 the streets were plastered with placards; people talked about politics at the market; songs and seditious writings were exchanged and sung in cafés; at night the streets were flooded with people as thousands of spectators were forced out of the theater by the police trying to maintain some control over the situation. It would have been difficult, if not impossible, to live in Rouen in the spring of 1825 and not be aware of and affected by the political controversy concerning the archbishop and the banning of *Tartuffe*. But even minor incidents exposed large numbers of people to forms of protest. They might have been at a religious revival enjoying a sermon when a stink bomb went off and forced them to leave the church. Or they might have gone to the market to do their weekly shopping and come across a pile of tricolor cockades which someone had planted there the night before. It is hard to say how people responded to such acts. But they could not have remained completely unaware or unaffected by them.

We have access only to information about forms of popular protest that were committed in public. Yet what took place in public gives us some indication of what might have taken place in private. Talking and singing against the regime, or in memory of previous regimes, surely went on behind closed doors, where the people knew they were safe from prosecution. We know that seditious objects—objects bearing insignia from the Revolution and the Empire which had been declared illegal in 1815—were circulating in France in these years because merchants and *colporteurs* were often arrested for trying to sell them. But it is difficult to assess how many people had such objects among their private possessions and thus participated in this form of sedition in the privacy of their own homes.

The portrait of the participants in the unofficial politics of the Restoration will be amended and clarified as we turn in the next two chapters to the anticlerical practices deployed against the symbols and ceremonies of the missionaries between 1815 and 1830, and the incidents that erupted around *Tartuffe* in the theaters of France after 1825. Police reports on this range of seditious and "sacrilegious" practices are extremely clear on the social and political complexion of their perpetrators, and will serve to bring home the point only tentatively argued here, namely that there was far broader participation in the constitution of national politics during the Restoration than has been hitherto appreciated.

Nevertheless, there are several conclusions which can be drawn from what has been presented thus far. First, although most men and women who posted their placards, sang their songs, and trafficked in seditious emblems and prints did so in the local contexts in which they lived, one can discern commonalities in the timing, themes, and emblems which were national in scope. To some degree this was because French men and women everywhere were presented with the same frame of reference wherever they lived, by the national revival orchestrated by the missionaries and by the national ceremonies orchestrated by the state, both of which were inspired by the similarly national cultural campaign which so transformed and politicized daily life during the revolutionary decade. Second, the ideological content of the manifold practices we have considered is complicated. While the great majority of seditious cries, placards, songs, images, and objects were Bonapartist, they evoked and proclaimed ideals as well as emblems which were also republican, or sometimes merely antimonarchical. The blurring between oppositional ideologies in this period, which other historians have noted when studying the growing amorphous coalition of "liberals" in high politics, is a critical legacy of the Restoration which affected not only the narrow range of men actively engaged in electoral politics but also the broad population engaged in the world of "unofficial politics." [178] The long-term significance of this blurring, especially of republicanism and Bonapartism, would become clearest after the Revolution of 1848, when the population turned so easily, it would seem, from republicanism to Bonapartism by 1851. Third, the content of the practices which have been considered thus far demonstrates the absolute impossibility of the regime's politics of forgetting. Every Bonapartist slogan, every effort to remember and mark the 14 juillet or 15th of August, every tricolor watchband and revolutionary song defied the regime's efforts to "purify" the landscape of all "corrupting" reminders of the previous twenty-five years. The impossible effort of the government to return its population to a world where alternative ideologies did not exist, when legitimate monarchy could be conceived of as the only "natural" alternative, was thus continuously asserted in the everyday acts by which the men and women of France remembered and drew upon the repertoire of symbols and ideals and practices from the past. The ideological reality expressed most economically by the fleur-de-lis which could be unfolded to become a Napoleonic eagle, or a seemingly innocent top hat or tobacco case which concealed Bonapartist emblems, was continually made manifest: the legitimacy of monarchy was fragile indeed, and rested only on the apparent, but quite questionable, ability of the white flag and the fleur-de-lis to remain "the only signs of rallying." [179]

CHAPTER FIVE

Popular Anticlericalism

Defining the Sacred in
Postrevolutionary France

It is no doubt true, as Mona Ozouf has argued, that the Revolution of 1789 marked the dawn of a new era, when the "transfer of sacrality onto political and social values was accomplished," binding together rights, liberty, and the fatherland as the foundation for "a new legitimacy and a hitherto inviolate patrimony."[1] Yet it is also true that the cultural revolution of this period, epitomized by the festivals of the French Revolution and the symbols and rites of the new secular nation, was not an unqualified success; for as Ozouf has also argued, the continued commitment of the French to their own festive traditions and to the Catholic church and the rites and rituals associated with it set many men and women against the innovations of these years. This chapter demonstrates that it was during the "counterrevolutionary" Restoration that the ultimate success of the revolutionary project was achieved, largely because of the reaction precipitated by the national religious revival of the missionaries. The missionaries' assault on the legacy of the Revolution, and their effort to resurrect the spiritual and political foundations of the Old Regime, provoked a wave of anticlerical protest which showed the population to be willing and determined to defend the transfer of sacrality to secular and liberal values in a way that was not yet true during the revolutionary decade.

All the anticlerical practices discussed here can and will be interpreted on many different registers: they were inspired by local struggles over unpopular clerics, or they related to long-term disputes between Protestants and Catholics in particular regions, or they were provoked by specifically national events, whether related to the religious revival or to the clerical policies of the regime. Many of the anticlerical practices of the Restoration period can be interpreted in strictly religious terms. As the missionaries spearheaded their revival of a "new Catholicism" with the support of the church establishment, men and women reacted and protested in narrow terms, against specific innovations and in defense of ancient religious and festive practices. With songs and placards criticizing pastoral letters, with disruptive tactics which interfered with missionaries' sermons and ceremonies, and with carnivalesque practices which mocked the priests' determination to block access to the sacraments, various French men and women developed a trenchant critique of the "new Catholicism." But in the process of defending their religious and festive "rights," these opponents also produced a more explicitly political critique. As they turned to the state to intervene on their behalf against unpopular clerics, as they demanded a role in determining the fate of the missionaries in their towns, and as they developed a critical repertoire of practices which cast the clerics as illegitimate on the basis of their questionable morality and, more specifically, on the basis of their "theatricality" or "hypocrisy," they produced a way of seeing and interpreting the world that cut right to the heart of the crisis of legitimacy which beset the regime throughout its fifteen years. At once undermining the authority of such priests, and clearly demarcating the line which should separate secular from religious power in their lives, the critics of the missionaries gradually turned their repertoire of seditious practices against the regime itself. Initially accused of being the mere victims of a clerical plot, the regime itself and particularly King Charles X came to embody all that was impossible about the social and political order of the Old Regime; in the process of articulating and criticizing the illegitimacy of a monarchy defined upon such a foundation, anticlerical protesters expressed and cemented their commitment to the secular and liberal values which should determine the nature of their social and political order. While the events of 1830 and subsequent revolutions would translate this commitment into institutions and laws, it was during the Restoration that popular support in favor of such a denouement was achieved.

Religious Disputes: Opposition
to the "New Catholicism"

One did not have to be irreligious or an active member of the liberal opposition to object to the harsh measures suggested by some of the pastoral letters issued by the church hierarchy and popularized by the missionaries in these years. Even the *mandements* which simply called for a
return to a strict adherence to Catholic ritual seemed extremely harsh to
people who had for many decades developed their own way of practicing Catholicism in the absence of priests. We have already seen evidence
of this fact indirectly, in chapter 3, in the many letters by which local
state officials expressed concern over the unpopular rigorism of the
missionaries and the measures they adopted to temper the pernicious
consequences of their revivals. In fact, the police files are frustratingly
opaque on the specific nature of popular forms of expression which led
their authors to these conclusions; they often speak only vaguely of rumors, of outrageous placards and cries proffered against visiting missionaries and intolerant local priests. They speak critically of the missionaries' refusal of the sacraments on the basis of "political" crimes,
such as the possession of *biens nationaux,* or the general unpopularity of the clerics' threats of damnation for innocent pleasures such as
dancing or theatergoing. But such reports actually give us little insight
into the specific religious innovations which were most troublesome to
French men and women. We do, however, have some scattered evidence
to help us understand this.

In some instances we have examples of French citizens appealing to
local civil officials and higher church authorities to intervene in specifically religious matters. In May of 1825, for example, *Le Constitutionnel* and *L'Ami de la Charte* published articles about three particularly intolerant curés who were refusing to give their parishioners the
right to be godparents. A police report from October of 1825 confirmed
these allegations and noted that important people within the towns concerned appealed to mayors and to bishops and eventually got their way.[2]
There was a similar case in Arles, where a mayor repeatedly appealed to
a local bishop and curé to intervene against the missionaries who were
pressuring local churchmen to deny the last rites to an old Jacobin.[3] In
other instances, people resisted the clergy's efforts to deny the sacraments by conducting them themselves, without the official sanction of
the religious authorities. In a case in Niort, where a local judge had committed suicide, an extravagant funeral was organized, even though the

local ecclesiastical official refused to participate. The ceremony took place in broad daylight; the casket was decorated with the insignia of the magistrature, and was followed by a numerous cortège. Local civil officials took part in the ceremony, and as the disapproving prefect who reported on the incident noted, "what is even more inconceivable, the Acting Prosecutor of the King gave a eulogy at the tomb of the deceased."[4]

In the rich dossier on the anticlerical incidents in Rouen from 1825, we have more concrete evidence of the very specific kinds of religious innovations which were most offensive to French men and women. The songs circulating in the wake of Archbishop Le Croy's *mandement* of that year, and the placards and seditious writings posted and passed from hand to hand in the weeks after its publication, allow us to imagine how similar religious proclamations were received elsewhere, where the police were less successful at seizing such documents, or more vague about their contents if they did. This wide range of documents underscores the unpopularity of the insistence of the "new Catholicism" on a strict adherence to the sacraments and the requirement of regular confession; they also point to the kinds of "rights" which the priests were denying to the people on these grounds: the right to be godparents, the right to baptismal and mortuary rites, the right to have one's children declared legitimate and within the bounds of the church. It is by the juxtaposition of verses which describe the new rules and regulations within Catholicism with others which question the sincerity and morality of the priests propagating them that the songs most effectively cast the "new Catholicism" as unjust, and their own access to the practices and sacraments of their religion as "rights."

One apparently popular song entitled "The Mandement" evokes the struggle over the "new Catholicism" most elaborately in its thirty-three verses which both lay out the most troubling content of the local archbishop's recent pastoral letter and mockingly criticize its author and the priests of his ilk. Opening with the couplet "To be a good Catholic / listen to the mandement / of the Archbishop of Rouen / you will see how he explains himself / as a man of quality / who has humanity," the song quickly turns to derision, presenting the archbishop as the head of a greedy troop of priests who, while presenting himself as Christ's equal, capable of offering grace, in fact only worries about his grandiose titles and the quality of his clothing, just as the curés serving him are concerned that they and their nieces are furnished with beautiful adornments.[5] Only after this mocking prelude does the song present some of the specific religious innovations of the pastoral letter. The following three stanzas treat in turn the prohibition against baptizing one's own children at home; the threat of excommunication (*dit le concile*) for parents who fail to get proper godparents for their newborns within eight days (even though this is sometimes *difficile*); and the new requirements that prospective godparents should have taken communion within the past year and that they know (*c'est de rigueur*) their catechism by heart (*par coeur*)."[6] Five stanzas which attack the cupidity and hypocrisy of this new breed of priests, explicitly (and inaccurately in this case) depicted as Jesuits, follow, after which the song returns to an even more derisive portrait of religious rigorism as bordering on social and political persecution.[7] The fourteenth verse opens with the threat "Christian, go to mass / or you will be denounced / by your curé; without even knowing it / he will have you watched / by some kind of spy"; and the next verses lay out the range of religious offenses, from playing games, working, drinking, or dancing on Sunday, to going to a café or a restaurant during church services, to not taking communion once a year, all of which would result in denunciations, excommunications, refusals of sacred burial, and public chastisement.[8] Quickly, the range of offenses which the priests intend to control expands beyond the religious (*religieux*) to the political (*bien mieux*).[9] Before continuing the list of unreasonable religious demands contained in the *mandement,* the song offers three verses accusing the priests of particularly horrific crimes: rape, incest, false testimony, and bestiality, sexual acts which a pastor might perform "with a man or a woman." While the priests must merely confess for such outrageously sinful acts, the next stanzas go on to lay out the range of more minor offenses for which they threaten their flocks with excommunication: civil marriage, marriage between cousins or between a godchild and a godparent, registration of births and/or deaths with civil versus ecclesiastical authorities, not taking communion every year, singing or drinking in a cabaret.[10] Ending, as it began, with information about the *mandement*'s official character, its author, date of publication, as well as the subordinates of the archbishop who signed it, the song leaves the final image of a persecuting alliance between the priests defending this horrible new regime and the police willing to enforce it: "the gendarmes of *France* . . . . / have with our pastors / made a sacred *alliance*. / The priests will bless us (*nous béniront*) / the gendarmes will seize us (*nous empoigneront*)."[11]

This juxtaposition of mockery and derision regarding the priests, on the one hand, with the portrait of their new religious system, on the other, was a consistent feature of popular anticlericalism. In the particular context of Rouen, this song was representative of the numerous songs and placards deployed against the church establishment in the context of the theater troubles in the spring of 1825. The corruption and hypocrisy of Archbishop Le Croy and his vicar-general (Le Sur) were underscored in the "For Sale" posters hung outside the archbishop's residence and in another song which explicitly explains the archbishop's rigorism as an effort to make himself famous: the second verse which proclaims "Le Croy, wanting people to talk of him / produced this *mandement* . . . " is followed by twenty more verses which switch back and forth between presenting the new rules and regulations of the recent *mandement* and depicting a delighted archbishop, enjoying the upheaval he has caused in Rouen, and expecting recompense that will come as word spreads from Rouen, through France, all the way to Rome.[12]

If songs and placards of this sort explicitly challenged the rigorism of the "new Catholicism" by identifying its particularly onerous aspects and questioning the morality and justness of its authors, other practices were deployed which dramatized these points even more poignantly. In the context of a national religious revival which, on the one hand, placed enormous emphasis on the taking of the sacraments, but, on the other hand, restricted access to holy rites on the basis of all manner of political and social as well as religious failings, anticlerical critics attacked the religious innovations of the revival by parodying these contentious sacraments.

Some people turned the church itself into a theater for such sacrilegious mockery, as in Blois in 1825, where a group of six men entered a church dressed in priestly vestments, with two of them then pretending to offer confession and baptize one another as they made stops at the confessional and the baptismal font.[13] Others widened their critique by performing such mockeries in cafés and cabarets, the kinds of sinful venues the missionaries were also attacking. In Tarbes, in 1826, a parody of a funeral was conducted in a cabaret.[14] In the commune of Parois in the arrondissement of Verdun, the last rites were administered in a cabaret to an extremely inebriated deputy mayor by five inhabitants of that town, including the mayor.[15] In Le Puy, there were rumors that some inhabitants gathered in an *auberge* during midnight mass where they "parodied the sacred mysteries by a sacrilegious imitation of the most disgustingly derisive nature."[16]

Just as the missionaries carried the "new Catholicism" into the streets, so did its critics use the streets as the venue for their expressions of disapproval. In Epinal, ten young men marched around the town, parodying the ceremonies and benedictions of the procession of the *Saint Sacrement,* in a manner which the prefect deemed completely ridiculous.[17] In Moncourt, near Verdun, a retired teacher, accompanied by several woodcutters, promenaded through their village screaming impious things after a drunken orgy. They then went to the home of one of their friends where they proceeded to parody the administration of the sacraments.[18] In a small village in the Meurthe, the celebration of a local patron saint day provided an opportunity to mock the churchmen. Here a farmer and a butcher, dressed like priests, went through the streets and into local inns, the public festival hall, and many private homes where, pretending to be clergymen, they offered their religious services to everyone they encountered.[19]

This apparently widespread practice of masquerading as one's superiors and mockingly performing official acts reserved for them, particularly in the context of a carnival or a patron saint day celebration (or in the carnivalesque setting of the cabaret), fits squarely within an old and accepted popular repertoire of practices deployed for centuries against authority figures or what were perceived as unjust changes in the social or political order.[20] In the context of the Restoration it was particularly à propos that anticlerics turned to such practices to challenge the missionaries; for not only did such carnivalesque mockeries cut right to the heart of the religious innovations to which they were opposed, they simultaneously served as a response to the broader assault which the missionaries were waging on the practices associated with popular festive culture. This whole repertoire of practices had, in fact, been under assault in France since the Revolution. During the revolutionary decade it was the state that took on and tried to discipline the "savage," "irrational," and "particular" practices associated with popular local festive culture, in favor of the more orderly, rational celebrations of the republic government.[21] This largely unsuccessful effort to impose a new calendar, with such innovations as the *décadi,* and to prevent the popular celebrations of carnival and local patron saint days was abandoned by Napoleon as one of many efforts to restore normalcy to the lives of the French in the wake of the Revolution.[22] However, Napoleon did try to restrict popular religious celebrations, too often the occasions for sanctioned unruliness and sedition, by legally limiting the number of permissible religious festivities to four: the birth of Christ, the Ascension, the Assumption of the Holy Virgin, and All Saints' Day.[23] During the Restoration a new assault on such traditions was mounted, not by the state but by the churchmen associated with the religious revival.[24] It is not surprising, therefore, that like the mockeries of the sacraments which we have already discussed, a broad repertoire of practices associated with carnival and popular festival culture was turned against the men of the collar in these years.

In Defense of Carnival and Popular Festive Culture, and the Many Uses of the Carnivalesque

The missionaries engaged in an active campaign to assail popular festive culture, whether by timing their missions to interrupt "sacrilegious" carnival celebrations or by inveighing from their pulpits against dancing, the theater, and drinking. All over the country, French men and women responded to this assault by defending their ancient practices, and the civil authorities repeatedly showed themselves to be sympathetic to their claims. In defense of carnival, and by the deployment of many practices which can be characterized as "carnivalesque," the opponents of this particular aspect of the missionaries' revival vociferously defended their right to their ancient customs at the same time as they asserted their right to determine the nature of the sacred, and thereby their role in defining the foundations of the social and political order which should govern their world.

The missionaries' practice of timing their revivals to interrupt the celebration of carnival provoked widespread protest and sympathy from state officials on purely material grounds. As we saw briefly in the episode in Marseilles with which chapter 2 opened, the mission there in 1820 involved a struggle regarding carnival. Even before active protests were articulated to this effect, the prefect of the Bouches-du-Rhône anticipated the problems the proposed timing of the mission would pose for local merchants, and he tried to intervene and convince the missionaries to postpone their arrival in Marseilles until after this lucrative festive period.[25] His concerns were well-founded, as the petition from local bakers from 11 February 1820 makes clear. Published in the local liberal paper, this petition beautifully evokes the kinds of arguments other merchants across France made in response to the missionaries' efforts to undermine the festivities which often provided their livelihood for the whole year. The bakers' petition opens with the sarcastic contrast between the "spiritual food" the missionaries were spreading so prodigiously and the very real food the clerics were denying the merchants of Marseilles for whom the feast day associated with carnival, "a day of gastronomic memory," was a veritable "Saint Friday." After providing a mouth-watering list of the kinds of delicacies they would not be able to sell during this traditionally profitable season, the bakers appeal to the clerics for charity on behalf of their community of devout merchants, already supporting their local priests, and whose wives and children were themselves participating in the mission.

> You must be charitable since you preach charity. Cast a sympathetic glance at our young boys whose sales for the carnival season represent their annual salary, at our wives and our children who say from morning to night, "Bless forever," and "the Tyranny of Hell. . . ."
> Would you please entertain our humble request?[26]

The prefect of the Bouches-du-Rhône was hardly the only local official to respond sympathetically to the material complaints of his resident merchants. All over France, civil officials tried to temper the effects of the missionaries, encouraging the visiting clerics to change the timing of their revival, or trying to mitigate its effect by condoning and defending popular festivities in spite of the presence of the missionaries. The following report of the police commissioner from La Rochelle illustrates beautifully the sympathetic perspective of such state officials.

> I must not hide from Your Excellence [the minister of the interior] the fact that the city of La Rochelle is in a state of misery during this period of carnival, when its workers are deprived of the means of their existence. The café keepers, restaurant owners, bakers, ice-cream vendors, carpenters, musicians and all sorts of others who depend on carnival to compensate for the horrible winter we have just had, have reason to complain, for they will surely suffer.[27]

People not only protested against the missionaries on material grounds; they also acted in defense of their pleasures and their rights to their ancient customs. Again, this was an argument to which the civil officials were sympathetic. We have examples of local officials writing to the minister of the interior and complaining that intolerant clergymen were disrupting social peace by their inappropriate and ill-timed attacks on popular festive practices. The prefect of the Creuse, for example, complained in 1818 about an incident in which an overly zealous priest chose the local celebration of Saint Louis as an occasion to give a fire and brimstone sermon about the sins of the people assembled, putting a significant damper on the festivities; in his letter he noted that he was sure that prefects from other departments were confronting the same problem.[28] In May of 1829 in the Côtes du Nord, the inhabitants of a village were successful in their appeal to the civil authorities against a priest assaulting their festive practices. In the small town of Monstoir, a curé tried to stop dancing at a patron saint day celebration by breaking the instrument which provided the music for the dancing. After a brawl it was decided by a number of people present to bring a civil suit against the priest.[29] A later report acknowledged that the curé was, in fact, cited before a tribunal in Guincamp for his offense.[30]

Most often, local officials tried to mediate between their citizens' desire to defend and practice popular customs and traditions and the visiting missionaries' determination to undermine them. Quite typical in this regard was the incident from the Drôme in 1817, where the mayor found himself acceding to the local population's requests to celebrate the *Dimanche des Brandons,* celebrated in his area "since time immemorial" with dancing and music, in spite of the presence of missionaries who carefully timed their arrival to interrupt this local culmination of carnival.[31] In this context the customs associated with carnival were used to protest against the unpopular curé who had brought the missionaries to town, to defend a second priest whose right to give the sacraments was threatened by these missionaries, and finally to disrupt the services of the missionaries. On the Sunday in question (23 February 1817) there were two organized actions. First, in the morning, "a great number of women and children (there were no men), who had not so long ago desired the departure of the vicar [rumored to have had his rights to administer the sacraments taken away], came together outside the presbytery and began to scream that they wanted him to stay." The official in question interpreted this act as a clear attack on the curé supporting the visiting mission, "even though his name was never pronounced." Later in the day a second incident took place, this time outside the church where the missionaries were preaching. Early that morning the people from the town had requested permission from the mayor to celebrate the *Dimanche des Brandons* according to local custom, a request that was accorded on the condition that they wait to begin their festivities until the conclusion of Sunday's church service. "These orders were apparently not followed, since the farandole arrived in the town square while the service was still under way, and the noise of the drums interrupted the preaching." The doors to the church were shut tight and the dancers and the musicians were dispersed. No punitive action was taken against the revelers. In fact, by their display of opposition to the missionaries the men, women, and children of Tain convinced the local authorities to abstain from participating in the erection of the mission cross at the end of the missionaries' stay.[32]

This example from the Drôme points in the direction of a broad spectrum of practices by which opponents of the missionaries relied upon customs and traditions associated with carnival and popular festive traditions to disrupt church services and, more generally, to mock the missionaries and their message. Sometimes carnival revelry simply seemed to spill over into the churches and ceremonies of the missionaries. People often interrupted church services after having a few drinks or after attending a masquerade (and therefore dressed in costume).[33] In Draguignon some young men organized a masquerade around the symbol of the *éteignoir*, or candle-extinguisher, often used in this period to refer to the priests' determination to return France to the Dark Ages.[34] All over the country, critics of the missionaries interrupted church services by tossing through the windows the kinds of noisemakers and firecrackers they would normally set off in the context of carnival festivities.[35]

More often, French men and women simply deployed the kinds of practices associated with and condoned during the carnival season to publicly criticize and undermine the authority of the missionaries. The practice of disguising oneself in order to criticize visiting missionaries, for example, was quite widespread. We have already discussed the many instances in which men donned the garb of clerics to challenge the missionaries' determination to block access to the sacraments. While most officials criticized this behavior and even tried to identify and punish the offenders, it is clear that such masquerading in the context of the carnival season was tolerated, if not directly authorized. Sevrin cites an example in Villeneuve-le-Roi which is perfectly analogous to the incident just described in the Drôme. In his words, "In 1819 carnival became a sort of public manifestation against the missionaries. . . . With the explicit authorization of the mayor, the population represented the missionaries by using masks; and the same farce was repeated the following Sunday."[36] Men disguised themselves as women and, seating themselves in the women's section of the church, disrupted religious ceremonies by singing or shouting impieties; in so doing, such men adopted an old practice of using sexual inversion, which held particular meaning in the context of a religious revival that segregated the sexes, inveighed against innocent pleasures between men and women, and focused its attacks and appeals on the female half of the population.[37] Other critics of the missionaries disguised themselves in blackface in order to conceal their identity while posting placards or destroying religious symbols under the

cover of darkness; however, by relying upon yet another ancient carnivalesque custom, such protesters evoked a broader tradition of challenging unpopular official acts in the name of a popular, moral economy.[38]

The charivari, long used by French men and women to draw attention to irregularities or innovations in the social order, was often deployed against the missionaries. In Brest in 1819, opponents of the missionaries relied upon repeated noisy congregations outside the bishop of
Quimper's residence and a smaller charivari outside the mayor's residence. In the charivaris aimed at the archbishop, the crowd pronounced
"our pastors are sufficient!" and clearly articulated the desire to maintain the status quo; but the special charivari orchestrated for the mayor
was intended to get him to join the opposition and help enforce the
"general will."[39] Successful in this case in convincing the authorities to
ban the mission from their town, protesters adopted the same tactic
in 1827, when the missionaries finally did manage to stage a mission in
Brest.

Representing authority figures in effigy and then committing acts of
violence against them constituted another ancient tradition that was effectively deployed against the missionaries. Most common was the tactic of hanging the hated clerics in effigy, particularly in public places
where real-life missionaries would be conducting outdoor ceremonies.
In Brest in 1826, critics of the missions hung such a mannequin, "artis-
tically rendered, figuring a Jesuit," from trees lining the street where the
procession was to be held.[40] Similarly, in Quimper, Jesuit mannequins
and injurious placards were hung along the procession route planned by
the missionaries in celebration of the Jubilee.[41] Images of such priests
hanging from scaffolds were common fare in the caricatures circulating
in the context of anticlerical incidents. Songs featured these as well. Occasionally protesters went beyond symbolic violence against the missionaries, as in Besançon in 1825 and in Rouen in 1826. In the latter
case one missionary was stripped naked and thrown into a small bou-
tique set up in the streets during the mission. This priest had to be disguised and accompanied by gendarmes and the Royal Guard in order to
leave town safely.[42]

In the largest anticlerical incidents, in Rouen in 1825 and 1826, in
Strasbourg in 1826, in Brest in 1819 and 1827, and in smaller incidents
such as that in Limoges in 1828, the whole range of carnivalesque practices which have been enumerated here were deployed in tandem. They
were encouraged and inspired by pamphlets and newspaper accounts
which reported incidents of such practices elsewhere.

All the practices which have been described thus far in this chapter had very real, practical consequences. They gave French men and women a way of participating in the public negotiation over the staging of the missions: whether they should take place or not, and if so, when; what aspects of their message (religious and political) had to be censored; and how or whether the public space should be remade to dramatize the missionaries' particular narrative of France's past, present, and future. But by their reliance upon the range of carnivalesque practices presented here, the critics of the missionaries accomplished much more, for in addition to securing practical concessions regarding the missions in their towns, they popularized a way of perceiving the missionaries in relation to their communities and their political authorities which would have important long-term consequences. By employing the carnivalesque, they encouraged those around them to consider the legitimacy of the missionaries based on an analysis of their tactics. Condemning the missionaries themselves for their stagecraft, for the vast gulf which separated their supposed austerity and piety from their elaborate spectacles and real immorality, such critics exposed the clerics to a two-pronged critique: first, they challenged their religious agenda by drawing attention to the priests' immorality and hypocrisy; and second, they undermined their authority and questioned their legitimacy by criticizing their theatricality.

As the song deriding the *mandement* of the archbishop of Rouen made clear, a standard tactic employed to criticize the religious agenda of the missionaries was to draw attention to the priests' questionable morality. A stock feature of anticlericalism for centuries, this charge that austerity and religiosity were merely self-serving ruses was particularly germane in the context of the Restoration, when the severe message of the missionaries coincided with the material improvement in the lives of the clergy. Rumors of scandals involving priests were generously reproduced in the liberal press; images of missionaries as hypocritical Tartuffes, espousing one set of values and ideals for their followers, but living by an entirely different set of rules themselves, proliferated in the songs and placards and theater riots of these years.

Related to these repeated charges of immorality and hypocrisy were the many anticlerical practices which explicitly challenged the theatrical tactics of the missionaries. Protesters could orchestrate their own festive processions within the context of mission processions, managing at once to disrupt the ceremony of the missionaries and draw attention to its carnivalesque quality.[43] Or they could orchestrate their protests in theaters, as they did across the nation in these years, to accomplish the same dual goal. Newspaper articles in the liberal press articulated this critique repeatedly over the course of the Restoration. In Marseilles in 1820, the *Phocéen* accused the missionaries of "seducing the population" and "abusing [their ignorance] by their imposture and hypocrisy," and challenged these so-called "sacred jugglers" to relinquish the "profane pomp of their spectacles."[44] An article which appeared in 1825 in the *Constitutionnel* combined an assault on the theatricality and sumptuousness of the missions with a damning portrait of immoral clerics enjoying the "adventurous" and "jolly" life on the road. "In general," opens the article, "these sumptuous affairs, which compromise a religion that makes a duty of simplicity, begin to weary all men with reasonable religious views." Characterizing their declamations as "more theatrical than Christian," attacking the "phantasmagoria aimed more at striking people's imaginations than at saving their souls," the article goes on to condemn the traveling priests for enjoying "the continual changes of scene, . . . whole towns raised and garrisons dominated," "the boisterous welcome of young girls to whom one distributes and teaches hymns," "the sumptuous dinners or at least dainty meals which consist of a succession of local dishes from all the regions visited." "Here," the article concludes, "is more enjoyment for a priest who likes to get about and who fears boredom offered by the simple and poverty-stricken life of a country parson."[45] Longer pamphlets circulating in this period made the same point; one in particular, which was inspired by the pastoral letter of Archbishop Le Croy of Rouen, casts the missionaries as "actors" in the context of a long and ironic critique of the clergy's historical antipathy to the theater. About the missionaries and their sacred ceremonies the author declared, "Certain processions and other religious ceremonies practiced by the clergy, are infinitely more obscene, more guilty, more destructive of the majesty of our sacred religion than that which happens in the theater."[46]

Administrative reports on anticlerical protests demonstrate that the critical perspective offered by such portrayals was gaining popularity. The prefect of the Bouches-du-Rhône argued that for some people in the town of Marseilles in 1820 "the liberal press and the protests in the theater" constituted "the counterweight to the mission."[47] As we shall see at length in chapter 6, the theatrical metaphor became so useful for understanding the missionaries that it defined the very structure and content of the local administrator's lengthy analysis of the events in his town of Brest in 1827, which he portrayed as a face-off of "theaters."[48]

Prefects who were themselves opposed to the missions easily adopted the language of critics who attacked the priests for their spectacularity and theatricality; the prefect of the Charente-Inférieure accused the missionaries in La Rochelle of the *jonglerie* (trickery) which defined their extravagant expiatory ceremony of the 21st of January.[49]

Offering a critique which undermined the religious authority of the purveyors of the "new Catholicism," the carnivalesque tactics of the anticlerical protesters also popularized a way of seeing the missionaries in relation to the regime that exposed the political authorities to ridicule as well. Increasingly popular over the course of the Restoration was the view that, like the new religious order of the hypocritical missionaries, the political order was not what it appeared to be. While ostensibly committed to the Charter and the secular legacy of the Revolution, the regime was really falling progressively under the pernicious and duplicitous influence of such clerics. In other words, the social and political order was threatened by outsiders, "Jesuits" who, relying upon their special talent for ruse and duplicity, were gradually gaining control over the whole range of religious and political authority figures, from the local curé and mayor right up to bishops, archbishops, ministers, and the king. While quite apparent in the continuous negotiations over the staging of missions throughout the fifteen years of the Restoration, the fear of a clerical plot reached new dimensions after 1825, giving rise to a wave of anticlerical protest through which the population asserted its obligation and right to defend and define its relation to the sacred.

The Obsession With the Clerical Plot: Struggles Over the Sacred

All historians who have written about the anticlericalism of the Restoration concur that 1825 was a critical turning point in the growing obsession with and fears of a clerical plot. Whether attributing such fears to the apparent machinations of organizations such as the Congregation in the passage of the controversial Sacrilege Law, or to the concerted efforts by the liberal press to propagate rumors of priestly influence over ministers and even the king in the wake of the coronation, the Sacrilege Law, and the Papal Jubilee, all agree that these events conspired to make the clerical plot the only way for French citizens to make sense of local and national events.[50] The difference in the tone and content of police reports presenting anticlerical protests before and after 1825 is pal-

pable. While many prefects and local officials complained of the pernicious consequences of the missionaries' religious intolerance, and even
the political ramifications of their expiatory assaults on the revolutionary past, or their condemnations of such controversial revolutionary
legacies as that represented by the *biens nationaux*, after 1825 such officials focused more and more on the ways in which the regime itself was
coming to be perceived as in the grip of such churchmen. Administrators
had expressed such fears before, as in the report of the prefect of the
Vosges, who wrote to the minister of the interior in 1820 to explain that
while the ardor and the devotion of the clergy "could be of immense utility for the royal government," the overly zealous priests "merely justify
fear among the population that the priests are trying to usurp political
power." [51] But after 1825, administrators all over the country began to
use the language of the clerical plot, echoing the impressions of the prefect from Allier who tried to explain the "uneasiness" which prevailed
about him, in spite of the recent prosperity of France, as a result of the
"fear of seeing public liberties give way under the reign of theocracy." [52]

In so doing, administrators merely reiterated the message which prevailed in anticlerical placards and songs after 1825. Placards from
Strasbourg in 1826 linking "Down with Charles X" to "Down with the
Catholic Clergy" and "Long live liberty" implied that it was the connection between church and state which boded ill for the future; the
warning "French citizens, Don't Sleep" left no doubt as to whose responsibility it was to prevent the loss of liberty which such a theocracy
would bring to pass.[53] In Toulouse the same theme emerged in placards
posted in three different points in town, and was extended beyond the
person of Charles X to the Bourbons more generally, whose power and
ultimate downfall were related to the backing of the Jesuits:

> The Bourbon in their politics (*politique*)
> Approve nothing but Jesuitism (*Jesuitique*)
> They are right, for this is their only support
> As a result of which, all for them is lost.[54]

If Charles X was seen to be linked to the return to power of the hated
Jesuits, his counterrevolutionary clerical politics were also perceived to
be responsible for the actions of unpopular local clerics. In Evreux in
1825, a priest who was restricting access to the sacraments was attacked
in an *affiche* posted in two different communes within his parish:

> Down with Charles X, and the clergy, already the curé of Soulbec is refusing
> absolution to the acquirers of *biens d'émigrés*.[55]

While I would agree with other historians in identifying 1825 as a key turning point as regards the growing obsession with a clerical plot, I would propose a broader framework for making sense of this and for interpreting the range of protests it inspired. I do not see the fear of a clerical plot as linked to any specific event (such as the Sacrilege Law) or to the anticlerical campaign of a particular group (middle-class liberals). Rather, I would first follow Geoffrey Cubitt's lead, and argue that such conspiracy theories generally found fertile ground in the nineteenth century because the Revolution produced a century of "unprecedented political and social turmoil" after "long centuries of monarchy and hierarchy." [56] But I would be more precise and argue that what made this particular conspiracy theory potent and believable during the Restoration was not the general trauma of the Revolution but rather the revival of the missionaries which directly challenged one critical legacy of the Revolution, namely the transferal of sacrality to the secular and liberal nation. If 1825 marked a turning point, it was because the regime appeared to change course, and both in legislative and ceremonial terms began to express its clear support for the missionaries' conception of monarchy and the social and political order on which it should be founded. It is the specific nature of anticlerical protest after 1825 which makes it clear that the obsession with the clerical plot in these years was born out of a profound struggle over the definition of the sacred in postrevolutionary France.

In their religious revival the missionaries offered an older model of legitimate political authority, organized around the symbols and narrative of the Eucharist. If the missionaries emphasized the connection between the sacred Host, the calvary, and the body of the king in the context of their expiatory spectacles, it was the Sacrilege Law of 1825 which, for the first time, showed the regime's willingness to go against the secular legacy of the Revolution and to enact legislation which rested upon the same conception of kingship, since it equated attacks on the sacred Host with attacks on the body of the living monarch. The coronation of 1825 and the king's participation in the expiatory ceremonies associated with the Jubilee of 1826 further dramatized ceremonially the regime's apparent commitment to a vision of monarchy that relied upon the grace of God and the citizenry's renewed commitment to the king by way of religious vows and rites which explicitly assailed the legacy of the Revolution. After 1826 the missionaries' revival conspired with the legislative and ceremonial innovations of the regime to identify certain kinds of practices by which the people could at once protest against the churchmen, their monarch, and, most important, the way in which the two appeared to be working to reconstitute the social and political order according to the now impossible and inappropriate model of the Eucharist.

The full range of anticlerical practices deployed during the Restoration functioned in much the same way that the religious riot functioned during the period of the religious wars. Much as Catholics and Protestants in the sixteenth century used the riot "to bring their zeal to bear upon the state of men's relation to the sacred," and to act on behalf of the political authorities when they did not appropriately "use [their] sword to defend the faith" of the people, so did the anticlerical protesters of the Restoration use sacrilegious acts to define and defend their conception of the sacred in postrevolutionary France, precisely because their political authorities were failing the citizenry by their apparent commitment to reconstituting society and politics on the basis of a sacrality which was no longer acceptable to them.[57]

As in the religious riots of the sixteenth century, anticlerical protests during the Restoration were aimed at the sacred objects by which the missionaries, and increasingly the state, defined their vision of the religious and political order. After the passage of the Sacrilege Law in 1825, civil officials reported an increase in the kinds of robberies and profanations in churches which the new legislation was designed to curtail. Between 1825 and 1829, seventy-five serious incidents involving church robberies and vandalism were reported in the police bulletins coming in from all over the country.[58] Some of the robberies in churches might have been for material gain, although the frequency with which the offenders also committed other sacrilegious acts in the process of their burglaries suggests that they had other motives. In almost all of the cases reported, the vases containing the sacred hosts were stolen. If not stolen, they were often turned upside down, their sacred contents strewn all over the altar, the stairs leading to the altar, and occasionally the whole church.[59] In Laval, in March of 1826 in the Church of Saint Vénérend, sacred hosts were thrown on the floor and intentionally crushed under the feet of the offenders.[60] A report from April of the same year spoke of an incident in St-Malo involving the general destruction of all religious objects on the altar. "During the night of the eighth of this month, robbers entered the Church of St. Sevran (Ille-et-Vilaine), forcibly opened the tabernacles of the high altar, carried off the sacred vases and spilt the sacred hosts, smashed the crosses, the locks and the doors, and many trunks and cupboards."[61]

Attacks on the massive calvaries which symbolized the mission and its message were rife throughout the Restoration, but increased after 1825 to reach their apogee during and for four years after the Revolution of 1830. Such attacks could have many meanings. In some cases they could be used to defend ancient festive practices, as in Ferté-sous-Jouarre, where attacks on a mission cross were provoked by the missionaries' decision to place it on the site where a dance hall was supposed to be erected. But even in this case, where a new cross was erected to replace the one attacked, the Revolution of 1830 precipitated a new assault on the cross, no longer directly identified with the attack on dancing, but because of its political significance.[62] Protestants attacked mission crosses to assert their own sense of the sacred, as was clear in a small town in the Drôme where several young men not only destroyed the base of a mission cross right outside a church where missionaries were preaching but also urinated and defecated on the cross and the doors of the church.[63]

All the sacrilegious acts discussed in the previous section—disrupting sacred ceremonies, mocking the administration of the sacraments—can clearly be seen as part of the same spectrum of practices as sacrilegious attacks on hosts and crosses, which taken together represented a clear challenge to the right of the priests (and their supporters in the state) to define the sacred in ways that did not meet the approval of the population. If the very nature of the anticlerical acts does not prove this fact, the response of priests, local officials, and local supporters of the missions demonstrated that they were certainly interpreted that way.

Just as missionaries often took advantage of anticlerical protests to bring home their message as to the need for a religious revival, so did local ecclesiastical and civil officials seize upon attacks on sacred vessels, the Host, and calvaries to demonstrate the respect of the larger majority of the population for the sacred symbols of Catholicism. In Marseilles the religious authorities turned the sacrilegious spilling of the sacred Host into such an occasion when they organized a special ceremony around its reconsecration: "The clergymen of the parish where the hosts were found, gathered them up, and the number of believers who gathered around to witness this ceremony proved the respect which the inhabitants have for sacred objects, and their indignation regarding the crime which was committed."[64] Likewise in the commune of Montargis, the replacement of a cross which had been intentionally destroyed served as the occasion for an elaborate ceremony, which "a considerable number of people witnessed in a spirit of edifying meditation."[65]

Attacks on crosses—whether real physical attacks or merely efforts to prevent their being erected at all—became occasions for protracted struggles between supporters of and protesters against the missionaries. The extraordinary amounts of money spent on elaborate crosses, usually collected from local populations, the willingness of various groups of followers to protect a mission cross and to participate in ceremonies denouncing those who attacked the crosses were all evidence that this period was defined by a struggle over the meaning of the sacred in post-revolutionary France, with significant numbers of French citizens on both sides.

By 1830 the scales had clearly tipped in favor of the anticlerical determination to constitute the social and political order on a purely secular basis. In the context of this new revolution and the four following years, struggles erupted throughout France over these contentious symbols of Catholicism and political legitimism tied to the expiatory narrative of the missionaries. As one historian of these incidents has argued, it was the political significance of these crosses which made them the focus of intense struggle after 1830.[66] For this historian the political significance related to the resurrected alliance of church and state, the terrifying theocracy which was at the heart of the fear of a clerical plot. I would go further and argue that by attacking the mission crosses, anticlerical protesters were articulating the impossibility of constituting legitimate political authority through the symbols and rites of Catholicism according to the newly revived model of the Eucharist. If the type of anticlerical practices considered here implies this, particularly those involving "sacrilegious" disruptions of services, mockeries of the sacraments, and attacks on hosts and crosses, the political significance of this range of acts becomes ever more obvious when one includes in this repertoire the increasing tendency after 1825 to turn "sacrilegious" attacks against the very "portrait of the king."

Charles X (dit) Jesuit: The Impossible Portrait of the King

The introduction to Part I, "Politics as Theater," emphasized the ceremonial and institutional foundations which made it possible for the "portrait of the king" to function at the height of absolutism as the symbolic center of monarchy, in exactly the way in which the Host invokes the history, perfect legitimacy, and presence of Christ in the Christian kingdom. If a painting or a medal featuring the monarch, or reproductions of his image on marriage contracts, or the ceremonial invocation of the king in regular *Te Deums* could evoke the "sacramental body that would at once operate the political body of the prince, and lift the historical body up into the political body," it was because in the late seventeenth century religious practices and beliefs and the institutional cooperation of the church and state all conspired to allow the portrait of the king to occupy this sacred place.[67] If repeated struggles regarding the relationship between church and state, and religion and politics, undermined the ability of absolute monarchy to be so construed by the end of the eighteenth century, the missionaries' effort to restore this eucharistic conception of monarchy during the Restoration precipitated a reaction which explicitly demonstrated the impossibility of relying upon the symbols and rites of Catholicism to constitute legitimate public authority. The widespread practice of disfiguring the portrait of King Charles X after 1825, and in particular to represent him as a priest, makes this point quite dramatically.

Representing the most perfect expression of the obsession with a clerical plot, the wide range of practices which figured the king as a Jesuit made the point that the head of the realm was no longer merely controlled by the priests in a deceptive manner but rather that he himself *embodied* this hated species of priest. Charles X as a priest became standard fare after 1825; this image was evoked in songs and featured in caricatures and seditious placards.[68] Its most unusual form appeared in Metz in April of 1827, when, as a result of a particularly irreverent seditious act, a baker and his apprentices were brought up on charges of baking and selling gingerbread cookies in the form of Charles X's head, wearing what appeared to be a priest's cap, or *calotte,* and clearly marked "Charles X" on the bottom. The cookies themselves, as well as the mold by which they were made, were seized by the local police. In his report the prefect expressed his indignation at the seditious cookie: "I cannot express how deplorable it is to see proof of such disorderly flights of imagination, which could lead people to relinquish to such an extent the respect due to his royal majesty . . . these gingerbread cookies and the molds which served to produce them were seized by the police, and the baker, Billy-Baidar, has been turned over the judicial authorities."[69] As in most cases of sedition in this period, the offender was ultimately acquitted. In this case the acquittal was due to the testimony of three tinmen (mold-makers) who claimed that they had "placed the litigious little band on the bust of Louis XVIII as well as that of His Majesty

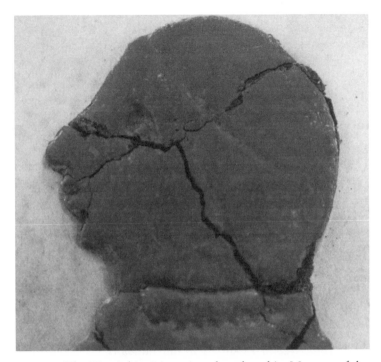

Figure 5. The "Jesuit-king" in a gingerbread cookie. Museum of the National Archives, Paris. Photograph by Sheryl Kroen.

Charles X, and always with the intention of representing hair." The prefect of the Moselle bemoaned the acquittal and sent the cookie itself on to the minister of the interior to demonstrate how difficult it was to believe "that Billy-Baidar could possibly be innocent once one inspected the effigy."[70] The cookie, which one can still inspect in the Museum of the National Archives at the Hôtel Soubise in Paris, has a clear line across the top of Charles X's head which could never be mistaken for hair (see fig. 5).

The seditious image of the Jesuit-king expressed many things at once, all of which articulated the particular crisis of representation facing the regime in the Restoration, especially after the accession to power of Charles X. First, in a particularly economical way, authors of the image of the Jesuit-king brought home the impossibility of constituting legitimate authority on anything but a secular basis. In other words, to portray the king as a Jesuit was to demonstrate how incapable Charles X was of representing his kingdom at the point that his identity or way of conceiving himself was suspected of being primarily religious. The

Jesuit-king became, in short, a kind of oxymoron, which expressed with extraordinary simplicity the distance the French nation had come between the late seventeenth and the early nineteenth centuries. Second, the image of the Jesuit-king exposed the monarchy to assault on an entirely different register, by making the primary question of the day: in spite of appearance, in spite of the whole repertoire of laws and symbols and ceremonies which conspire to give a certain image of the king, what or who is he really?

Two particular ways of figuring the king as Jesuit made this second point most poignantly. The first was an etching, carved into tree trunks lining the main avenue of Troyes in 1826, which read "Charles-dix (*dit*) jesuit."[71] The pun, which at once means Charles X (the tenth) and Charles *dit* ("so-called") Jesuit, reiterates the message of the Metz baker's cookie, but by its form also asks those who come into contact with it to ponder the whole problem of appearance versus reality, just as they had to think twice merely to make sense of the pun before them. In other words, by putting his seditious figuring of the king in the form of a pun, the author of the etching in Troyes identifies the illegitimacy of the king as a function of his theatricality: it is because he is not what he appears to be that the whole system organized around him falls. If this pun made this critical point for the people of Troyes who happened to pass by these tree trunks, seditious coins circulating around the kingdom reiterated the message all the more forcefully and for a much broader audience.

After 1826, coins disfigured to make Charles X appear to be a Jesuit appeared all over France. The prefect in Nancy was quick to blame local liberals for the appearance of such coins in his town. Whether or not they were in fact responsible, the prefect offered a nice portrait of the effect such coins were likely to have had, as well as how effective a means of propaganda they were, given the ubiquity of money.

> Your Excellence is surely aware that the epithet of jesuit has, for several years, been ingeniously used by the liberal party to turn people against anything and everything which does not correspond to their doctrines. To be attached to religion or to the monarchy is to be a jesuit. It follows that the prefect of the Meurthe is a jesuit, that the ministers are jesuits, that the King, himself, is the jesuit par excellence. In an effort to make this idea familiar to all the classes, our liberals of Nancy put into circulation, in the markets, in shops, in cafés, . . . coins bearing the image of the king, with his hair disfigured [to represent a *calotte*].[72]

This image of the king as Jesuit was therefore being spread everywhere. When one paid for one's coffee or bought flour one was reminded of the

Figure 6. The "Jesuit-king" in a defaced coin of the
realm. Museum of the National Archives, Paris.
Photograph by Sheryl Kroen.

duplicitous clericalism of the king, and was encouraged to question the
whole system of kingship orchestrated around his image. (See fig. 6.)

Nancy was hardly the only city where coins of this nature were circulating. According to police reports, such coins were spotted in fifteen
different cities in fifteen different departments between January of 1826
and October of 1827.[73] There were different styles. In Rouen in 1827,
two models appeared: one featured Charles X with a "square cap, of
a jesuit style," while the other had Charles X wearing a *calotte* with a
cross.[74] Occasionally the flip side of the coin was also defaced, as in
Cheymont, where "The seal of France was covered with a candle extin-
guisher, under which were two martins in the shape of a cross."[75] The
methods of altering the coins varied: on some coins the priestly garb was
added with ink, on others by a form of acid, and on still others by either
wax or a sort of black putty.[76]

One could argue that all the attacks on the king's image described
here can be seen as seditious acts which challenged the monarch's authority; but I would argue that these symbolic assaults on the coinage of
the realm must be singled out as more serious crimes which cut right
to the heart of the struggles over the sacred during the Restoration.
According to Louis Marin, nothing captures the eucharistic model of

kingship inherent in the "portrait of the king" better than medal money. In his words,

> In the manner of Eucharistic symbols . . . medal money is the body of the king and of the state really in their imaginary and symbolic representation, their portrait and name, just as the sacramental Host also is, at the moment of consecration, a "narrative" reiteration of the historical sacrifice of Jesus Christ and, by virtue of that, the memorial of a history reproduced in presence just as the imprinted cross marks it in the bread of the ritual.[77]

Likewise, I would argue that repeated attacks on the coinage of the realm, particularly when placed alongside sacrilegious attacks on hosts, sacred vessels, and mission crosses, constituted a direct challenge to the effort to resuscitate the impossible eucharistic conception of monarchy in the postrevolutionary world.

Attacks on the coins of the realm are significant for another related reason, which takes us back to Marin's analysis. According to Marin, nothing epitomizes the functioning of the "portrait of the king," and the whole social and political order which it orchestrated, better than coins. "[F]or they alone are capable of eternally carrying a double authority, that of the prince, on the one hand, and that of public usage on the other, which medal money alone unifies perfectly as index, icon, symbol and thing. Medal money carries in effect, the prince's mark, the figure of his effigy, or emblem, and the sign of his name and titles and it is this mark that, because it attests to the unalterable value, truth and authenticity, founds the universal acceptance of medal money in usage."[78] Marin, describing the function of the image and medal money at the height of absolute monarchy, makes the following contention, which clearly no longer held true by the time of the Restoration. In the late seventeenth century, "the inscription is for always an index of an unimpeachable presence. With the medal, in it, an origin is engraved, an original is traced that cannot be contested. And with it, at the same time, all vices contrary to the history disappear . . ."[79]

By disfiguring the image of Charles X on the coinage of the realm, critics not only invoked the whole discourse of Charles as priest which was accomplished by the pun in Troyes as well as by cookies and caricatures; they precisely demonstrated how "impeachable" the king was, how questionable and alterable his value and authenticity. These acts of sedition challenged the very worth of the monarch by disfiguring the coins of the realm and by dramatizing the very problem of fraudulence which so many acts of sedition considered here evoked in other ways.

Such seditious acts also invited witnesses of the disfigured coins to imagine alternative narratives for legitimate authority: if this king should not be king because he is a Jesuit, because he is not what he appears to be, then who should be king, and on what basis?

"Politics as Theater" versus "Theater as Politics"

The obsession with the clerical plot, expressed most poignantly and economically by the image of the Jesuit-king circulating throughout the realm after 1825, expressed anxiety about the profound crisis of representation besetting the regime during the Restoration; it also inspired organized protest which addressed this crisis both in its content and its form. The fact that politics had been reduced to mere theater was illustrated by the competing spectacles of the church and state and by the manifold local and national events which gave the people of France reason to assume that a clerical plot was afoot, that nothing was as it appeared. In this context, what could be a more apt response than to turn the theater itself into a site of protest, especially around Molière's eminently germane *Tartuffe*?

Alain Corbin was correct when he suggested that to understand fully the theater riots of the Restoration, one has to place them within the context of the missions against which they were so often staged. Like other anticlerical practices which exposed and denounced the theatricality and therefore illegitimacy of the missionaries, the widespread use of *Tartuffe* in the theater served as the perfect riposte to the missionaries' expiatory spectacles. But the theater incidents after 1825 were not only a reproduction of or response to the mission; they were also, and more significantly, a carnivalesque reiteration of what politics itself had become.

In town after town, men and women used their theaters and their repeated demands for *Tartuffe* to expose and denounce this deplorable state of affairs. They popularized this way of seeing and making sense of local and national political events. But in the context of their disorders in the theater they also developed practices and articulated ideas which would enable them to move beyond a simple rejection of "politics as theater." Just as they had engaged in extensive negotiations with their local civil officials about the staging of the missions, so would they use their local theaters to negotiate publicly about the rights of the people, the proper relation which should reign between the church and the state, and the very laws and principles which should constitute the political order. The secular and liberal principles articulated in their placards and songs and symbolic sedition were deployed anew inside theaters. But most important, protesters took over the theaters, they negotiated with and won extraordinary concessions from their civil and ecclesiastical officials, and, as a result, they tentatively moved in the direction of embracing, or at least accepting, the theatricality which was at the heart of postrevolutionary politics. But to understand all this we must finally turn to the theaters, and examine carefully just how *Tartuffe* was used to expose and ultimately to resolve the crisis of representation plaguing this regime.

CHAPTER SIX

Tartufferie

Rouen and Archbishop Le Croy, "Tartuffe" of the Seine-Inférieure

On the 18th of April 1825, the theatergoers of Rouen thronged to the Theater of the Arts to see *Tartuffe*. Upon arrival at the theater they learned—from a banner stretched across the original publicity poster for *Tartuffe*—that another play would be performed due to the indisposition of one of the actors. Inside the theater, rumors began to circulate that none of the actors was "indisposed," but that the play had been banned directly by either the local archbishop, Le Croy, or his vicar-general, Le Sur. Unpopular for their recent pastoral letter, instituting a severe religious regime in the diocese of Rouen, the churchmen seemed the likely suspects in the deceptive banning of this anticlerical play. When the curtain went up on the substituted play the audience began screaming, "*Tartuffe,* we want *Tartuffe.*" This continued for several minutes until the police commissioner intervened and tried to calm the audience by reiterating the official explanation for the substitution. Once he sat down and the curtain rose for a second time, the same screams could be heard, only louder, "*Tartuffe! Tartuffe!* We want *Tartuffe!*" Objects were thrown at the actors trying to begin the substitute play, and insults to the archbishop and the vicar-general were interspersed with increasingly loud demands for Molière's comedy. Finally, having no other recourse, the police commissioner evacuated the theater. But the disturbance did not end. Once in the streets, the audience continued to harass the officials, demanding *Tartuffe* and verbally attacking the church official thought to be responsible for this outrageous censorship. It took hours for the gendarmes to clear the streets.[1]

The following night another play was to be performed. But, from the moment the curtain rose, cries of "We want *Tartuffe,* nothing but *Tartuffe!*" were heard from all corners of the theater. Twice the curtain was brought down. Twice the director of the theater tried to explain that *Tartuffe* was not announced for that night and that it was contrary to regulations to perform a play which had not been announced. But his pleas for order seemed only to aggravate the audience further. The police commissioner was forced, once again, to evacuate the theater. This proved to be a difficult proposition. Many members of the audience resisted and verbally insulted the gendarmes as well as the church officials still thought to be behind this outrage. Ten "instigators" were arrested. But once out of doors, the protests in the street were even louder and the crowd was even harder to control than it had been the previous night. The police spent three and a half hours trying to clear the streets.

These two nights of theater disturbances were but the beginning of a month-long outburst of popular anticlericalism in Rouen. Within days of the initial incident the prefect of the Seine-Inférieure was communicating with the minister of the interior in Paris on a regular basis, sending almost daily reports stressing the growing breadth of the anticlerical movement in Rouen and the surrounding areas. By May of 1825 the prefect wrote with alarm of the extent of the criticism he faced in his decision to prevent the performance of *Tartuffe.* The opposition to his censorship of *Tartuffe* was hardly restricted to the committed liberals of Rouen. In the following report he explained, "I saw, not without terror, the responsibility which weighed on my shoulders once I realized that royalists of all classes overtly pronounced themselves against the course of action which I chose to pursue, and when I became certain that it was likewise disapproved by the magistrates and even by the public functionaries within my jurisdiction."[2] He concluded on the following histrionic note: ". . . I will find myself alone, armed with bayonets, face to face with the entire population of this big city without any recourse other than military force."[3]

The prefect was also aware of the problems associated with the timing of these disturbances. Not only was the entire town—royalists as well as liberals and "revolutionaries," "persons of the upper class" as well as workers from neighboring textile towns—involved in these scandalous scenes, but all this was taking place on the eve of Charles X's coronation. He asked the minister of the interior to imagine in horror as he confronted "the unanimity of these opinions contrary to my own, the perspective of bearing the terrifying responsibility should this big city become the theater of serious troubles on the eve of the coronation, at a moment when such disorders would offend the heart of the King and his august family, and produce a painful sensation in all of France."[4] The coronation was not, however, the only national event which concerned the prefect. He immediately made the connection between the incident in Rouen and the recent Sacrilege Law promulgated in Paris. His analysis of the situation laid the blame for the events in Rouen on the local liberals (the "party"), who he claimed were taking measures to provoke disorder at a time when the discussion in the Chambers held great interest. In a letter dated 20 April 1825, the prefect of the Seine-Inférieure explained to the minister of the interior:

> I am led to believe, Your Excellency, that at a moment when discussions in the Chambers which preoccupy the population, which are here embittered by circumstances particular to this locality, . . . the [liberal] party, . . . will try to profit from a moment of rumor, and try to provoke disorders, and to present this city, like Paris, like France as a whole, as possessed of a violent discontent, and the population as on the verge of an uprising.[5]

The link between the theater disturbances in April of 1825 and the controversial Sacrilege Law in Paris or the coming coronation at Reims was made only by this official. None of the seditious material collected by the prefect or his subordinates substantiates his view that such a liberal plot was afoot or that these national events held any particular importance for the people of Rouen.

To the people of Rouen, the year 1825 did seem a turning point as regarded the clerical plot of the Restoration, but because of distinctly *local*, not national, events. Surely the Sacrilege Law interested the local liberal readers of *Le Constitutionnel*, and perhaps this explains their avid participation in the *Tartuffe* incidents. But the event which explains the large-scale participation of the local population took place not in Paris but in Rouen. Less than one month before the banning of *Tartuffe*, Archbishop Le Croy issued his pastoral letter, signaling the dawn of a new religious regime in the diocese of Rouen.[6] Unlike the Sacrilege Law (under which no one, ultimately, was ever punished), the pastoral letter, and the severe religious regime it instituted, touched the life of each Catholic in the region. For while the Sacrilege Law only threatened with capital punishment those offenders who stole or destroyed sacred objects housed in churches, the pastoral letter threatened parishioners who had not recently taken the sacraments with excommunication. It prevented noncommunicants from acting as godparents; children of civil, but not religious, marriages were declared bastards; and local curés were encouraged to post on the church wall the names of noncommunicants and those living in sin. Prior to the pastoral letter, the archbishop and the vicar-general, Le Sur, had participated in France's religious revival by making changes in the local seminary, affecting the population only indirectly through the training of its clergymen.[7] But the pastoral letter, also known as the *mandement,* criticized *not* the practice of the clergy but the practice (or lack thereof) of the parishioners, and set up a regime which would make them suffer greatly for their lack of devotion. Given that this was a diocese in which participation in the sacraments had fallen off sharply since the Revolution, it is not surprising that the pastoral letter was unpopular.[8]

The severe regime instituted by the archbishop was considered particularly onerous, coming as it did from a churchman who lived in the most sumptuous style. One historian noted this contradiction in his description of Archbishop Le Croy, ". . . the people of Rouen—the parsimonious Normans of Maupassant—would speak sarcastically for a long time of the Prince de Croy, their Archbishop between 1825 and 1844, of his sumptuous manor, of his wasteful style of life, in combination with his grand spiritual rigorism."[9] The vicar-general who assisted the archbishop was unpopular in his own right, for he was known as a Jesuit and an ultramontane.[10]

Word of the new *mandement* spread quickly in the region surrounding Rouen. A prefect from the neighboring department of Eure informed the minister of the interior in April of 1825 that "the *mandement* circulates in manuscript form in many cities. . . ." and that "Monseigneur the Archbishop of Rouen was the object of many discussions in markets and public places in the area surrounding Evreux."[11] If the original pastoral letter was circulating in manuscript, and people were passing word of it in the marketplace and other public meeting places, an even more common means of communicating *and* criticizing its contents was via songs. Two such songs were sent by the prefect in Rouen to the minister of the interior in late April–early May. In a letter of 30 April 1825, the prefect described the first song, "Le Mandement," as "already quite old;" "it was well known before the troubles which took place in the theater."[12]

It was through such songs that popular opinion about the *mandement* was formed during the weeks before the theater incident.

The unpopularity of the local archbishop because of this *mandement* was the reason for the banning of *Tartuffe*—but by the *civil* authorities, not by the churchmen. In a report to the minister of the interior from the 20th of April, the prefect explained that his decision to censor *Tartuffe* was based on his fear that its performance might have been seen by the inhabitants of Rouen as a sign that the authorities supported the popular anticlerical sentiment provoked by the recent pastoral letter. The prefect explained:

> The coinciding of the reading of extracts of the pastoral letter with the rude and disgusting allusions to which the performance would have given rise, and which it would have been impossible to anticipate, seemed deplorable to me; and who knows if the troublemakers wouldn't have interpreted on the part of the authorities who would have allowed this play, a tacit approval of the odious invective to which it would lead, against this act of the Archbishop? It was essential that we avoid such a scandal.[13]

The decision to ban *Tartuffe* represented a curious change of opinion for this prefect. Just four months earlier, when faced with a minor incident in the same theater on the occasion of a performance of *Tartuffe,* he had concluded that it was extremely important *not* to censor plays. In January the issue was not the reputation of the clergy which concerned the prefect, however, but the image of the king—the new king, Charles X. At the performance of Molière's play on the 15th of January 1825, between ten and twelve people in the audience booed and hissed when the actor began his praise of the king, "We serve a Prince to whom all fraud is hateful." In a long letter to the minister of the interior the prefect used the history of politics and theater in Rouen to argue that plays which offered opportunities for critics to boo and hiss at the king explicitly should *not* be banned.

According to his summary, the height of unrest in the theater of Rouen was in 1820 and 1821, when "the bad spirit manifested by one part of the audience" was the subject of a number of reports which he had, at that time, submitted to the minister. Switching immediately to the reassuring tone so common in such police reports, the prefect jumped forward five years to the present and congratulated himself and his police force whose strict measures had "finally triumphed against the troublemakers."[14] He boasted that it had been two years since "the tranquillity had been troubled." The incident of two years ago to which the prefect subtly alluded was again a performance of *Tartuffe*. In 1823 the speech about the king was an occasion for some hissing, but in that incident it seems that "the spirit of the troublemakers was promptly squelched by the manifestation of good sentiments of the great majority of the spectators."[15] Still, the minister of the interior had reprimanded the prefect for failing to arrest the guilty parties back in 1823.[16] So it is not surprising that the prefect did not refer specifically to the incident of 1823 but instead used the current incident to demonstrate how much progress his police force had made in getting the theater under control.

Two years had passed, "and for more than two years, not only had the public tranquillity not been troubled, but the good citizens could express their sentiments when some allusions offered them the occasion, without any opposition whatsoever." This was a very important point for the prefect, and he stressed it by explaining to the minister that, for example, "at the time of the accession of the King, the allusions which could be seen as favorable to him were the object of marked applause." But since that time (in the past two months), the prefect suspected a change in opinion about the new king, and he explained the hissing and booing of January 1825 accordingly. He blamed the changing view of the king on the writers of *Le Constitutionnel* and other "newspapers of the same color" whose critical articles about the king explained why "the *parterre* permitted itself to show signs of disapproval."[17]

The rest of the letter explained why the prefect was not concerned about the most recent incident. He had already arrested one merchant thanks to a gendarme in disguise whom he had cleverly planted beside the culprit in the *parterre*. Although the other ten to twelve "guilty" parties could not be prosecuted, they were taken down to the police station and reprimanded. Such firm measures, he was confident, would prevent such an incident from repeating itself in the future. Besides, during the performance itself, "at the end of the passage cited earlier, applause erupted from all over the theater, and there were no further disruptions." It is at this point that he explained his view regarding censorship and the theater.

> These circumstances confirm my opinion that to squelch the opposition party, which is supported by only a few hotheads, it will suffice to demonstrate that we have no fear, and barring circumstances which I cannot predict in advance, I thought it preferable to authorize the performance in Rouen of all plays which are performed in Paris, but at the same time to take security measures to prevent any disturbance.[18]

Between January and April of 1825 many important events had taken place both in Rouen and Paris which affected his opinion. His own justification for the banning of *Tartuffe* refers to the pastoral letter of the local archbishop and a desire to avoid "the rude and disgusting allusions to which the performance would have given rise" as well as the scandalous impression that the local civil authorities approved of the popular religious anticlericalism. But his own concern for the timing of the incident—the fact that it coincided with the discussion in Paris of the Sacrilege Law and that it was just before the coronation of a king whom he suspected was becoming unpopular—suggests that it might have been the political allusions in the play which concerned him. Whatever his motivations actually were, his effort to protect the churchmen and the regime from verbal assaults during one performance of *Tartuffe* backfired. By trying *not* to ally himself with the people of Rouen against the clergymen, he made it look as if he were secretly allied with the churchmen against the people of Rouen. His censorship of Molière's play was seen as a clear sign that a local clerical plot was afoot.

For if the prefect was *apparently* responsible for the censorship, the people were sure that behind the scenes the archbishop or his vicar-general had forced his hand. One flyer distributed in the theater and apprehended by the police on the 20th of April made this assumption clear. It read:

> The Commissaire to those who demand a performance of *Tartuffe*.
> Messieurs, it is not by us
> that this play is prohibited
> and if you want to see Tartuffe or the hypocrite
> address yourselves to the grand vicar.[19]

Echoing the situation in Orgon's household, there were two serious issues which provoked organized resistance in Rouen. First, the churchmen (like Tartuffe) seemed to wield influence over the civil authorities (as over Orgon); it seemed that their power was being extended, and in a deceptive manner, into realms where it did not belong. Second, the values these churchmen were trying to impose, even as they gained influence in the secular realm, were anathema to the local population. Taken together, these issues set the population at large (as it did the weaker characters in the play) against the local clerical and civil authorities.

Various tactics were employed as critics of the local churchmen and civic officials organized their campaign to have *Tartuffe* performed in spite of the official ban. Songs were the most popular form of seditious material collected by the police. Songs mocking the *mandement* spread the word of that document's contents. Songs treating various aspects of the theater incident provided the population with a way of seeing the events around them as "Tartufferie." They also incited the population to action. To the tune of the "Marseillaise" the people of Rouen were encouraged not to take up arms but to whistle.

> Braves enfans de Normandie
> le Jour de siffler est venu
> Un prefet plein de tyrannie
> et de vils mouchards soutenu (bis)
> pourra-t-il bravent le parterre?
> pour un prêtre plein de fureur
> nous priver de voir l'imposteur
> ce chef-d'oeuvre de Molière?
> Aux sifflets, mes amis
> soyons donc bien réunis
> Crions Tartuffe et tous en choeur
> Oui nous serons vainqueurs.

> Brave children of Normandy
> the day to whistle has arrived
> A prefect, full of tyranny
> and his vile spies
> could he take on the parterre?
> for a priest full of fury
> deprives us of the imposter
> the masterpiece of Molière?
> In your whistling, my friends
> Be then, united
> Let's cry Tartuffe, and all in chorus,
> Yes, we will be the conquerors.[20]

Songs that had been rewritten to reflect revolutionary ideas in the 1790s such as "Mon père était pot,"[21] "Il pleut, Il pleut bergère,"[22] and "Femmes, voulez-vous éprouvez?"[23] were written anew with lyrics relating to the local drama. Bills were distributed in the theater or thrown on the stage expressing the demands of the people. Placards were posted all over town—outside the archbishop's residence, in the town square, in the halls of the theater, by the army barracks. On the 19th of April, after the second attempted performance of a play which was not *Tartuffe*, the director of the theater, M. Morel, was given a letter which summarized the campaign of the people of Rouen. The letter explained, "that in spite of the esteem in which the regular theatergoers hold [the director] . . .

they would not suffer any performance, even for the opening of the season, other than *Tartuffe* of Molière." This resolution, "adopted unanimously by citizens who have always and will always know how to resist the dishonorable bondage that one would like to impose on them,"[24] was acted out as the people of Rouen flocked to the theater every night for a week, preventing any play but *Tartuffe* from being performed, and when they were forced out of the theater they spent hours in the streets harassing the local officials, singing, and organizing further.[25]

Who was behind this organization? The authorities were quick to blame local liberals, working in cahoots with a national party. But the police based their assertion on very scanty evidence. The only testimony they had was that of one questionable spy who informed them that a group of liberal bourgeois was paying workers to come in from neighboring factory towns to swell the numbers at the theater.[26] In other reports on seditious material, the authorities admitted that they were clearly "popular" in nature. Words were badly misspelled, the handwriting was clearly unpracticed, icons often stood in for words. According to the police, "The style of these writings proves that they could only be the work of men of the lowest classes of the people."[27] In this entire affair only a small number of individuals was arrested, and therefore explicitly identified by the police. The authors of songs, placards, and *billets* were never apprehended; nor were the hundreds of people who went to the theater and demanded *Tartuffe* over the course of a month. We only know, from the reports of the prefect, that the participation was broad, including members from all parts of the political and social spectrum. In the theater the police were surprised to find that those seated in the expensive *secondes* and *troisièmes* whistled and stomped their feet along with those occupying cheaper seats.[28] The prefect explained that he was horrified to learn "that Royalists of all classes" were opposed to his efforts to prevent *Tartuffe*'s performance, as were "all the magistrates and even all of the functionaries in my jurisdiction."[29]

What made *Tartuffe* resonate in the town of Rouen in 1825? Why was it such a perfect weapon in the people of Rouen's struggle against what appeared to be a clerical plot? How did the events in Rouen look when refracted through this particular play? The most obvious lesson to draw from the play was that a Tartuffe was living in their midst—actually several Tartuffes—the archbishop, the vicar-general, and the many curés working with them. Almost all the seditious material collected by the police used "Tartuffe" interchangeably with the names of these men of the collar. Occasionally the resemblance between the priests and the main character was invoked as the reason for the play's banning. One placard, found on the main street in town on the night of 25 April 1825, read:

> People of Rouen, do you know why from seeing Tartuffe
> you are prevented?
> It's because Le Surre finds in the play his own portrait presented! [30]

Other placards made the connection between Tartuffe and the local prelates more comically, as in the following placard, which suggested that the archbishop fill in for the sick actor:

> Notice to the people of Rouen
> The [Director of the Theater], wanting to obviate any
> inconveniences which could result from the
> adjournment of the play, Tartuffe, informs the
> public that it will be performed at the opening of the theater season.
> PS. Mr. Le Sur, . . . given the indisposition of Mr. Saint Elmé,
> [the supposedly sick actor], will fill the role of Tartuffe. [31]

The recent *mandement* was easily compared to the rigid moral order which Tartuffe tried to impose on Orgon's household. As in the play, where numerous speeches are devoted to mocking Tartuffe's ridiculous objections to the family's life-style, the most onerous aspects of the archbishop's new religious regime were mocked again and again in various songs which circulated throughout the spring of 1825. The most popular song, "Le Mandement," described an invasive new system in which local curés acted as spies, carefully watching to see who gambled, worked, drank, or danced on Sunday, keeping track of who did and did not take communion. [32]

As in the play, the criticism quickly shifted from the new regulations themselves to the questionable motives and morals of their author. That ambition was behind the *mandement* was made clear in one song which accused Le Sur of seeking nothing short of canonization. [33] But greed motivated the prelates as well. In addition to its requiring strict adherence to Catholic practice, the *mandement* was criticized for calling for "expensive linens," "dishes of gold," and "other riches to do honor to our priests." [34] The greed and hypocrisy of the clerics were stressed in the numerous songs and placards which accused them of accepting bribes from those who wanted to avoid the rigors of the *mandement*. One placard, found at the fountain in front of the Church of Notre Dame, explained how to avoid the problem of not being allowed to be a godparent:

> The public is informed that it will find chez le Sr.
> Vinegar, also known as le Sur, Passage des canons, a

> complete assortment of godfathers and godmothers
> in a state of grace.
> At the lowest price![35]

In Molière's play, Tartuffe's hypocrisy was demonstrated by the contrast between his own behavior and the harsh moral standards he set up for everybody in Orgon's household. In Rouen, the attacks on the moral character of the local priests suggested the same type of hypocrisy. While one song accused Le Sur of "having affairs with more than one tender maiden,"[36] another attacked the prelate for a wider range of sins: "Raping virgins, incest / false testimony, . . . / Bestiality and the rest / are the privileged cases / reserved for the Monseigneur."[37]

Just as the chaos in Orgon's household was caused by the inappropriate influence wielded by the self-serving Tartuffe, so were the problems in Rouen caused by the unacceptable power of the church officials in civic affairs. One song complained, "Even in the theater / they wish to dictate the law";[38] but it was the collusion with the civil authorities which was worrisome, as another song explained:

> Or les gendarmes de France
> maris Chrétiens qu'ont du coeur
> avec nos dignes pasteurs
> ont fait sainte alliance.
> Les prêtres nous beniront
> les gendarmes empoigneront.

> The gendarmes of France
> Christians who have a heart
> have with our worthy pastors
> made a saintly alliance.
> The priests will bless us
> The gendarmes will seize us.[39]

Already controlling the civic authorities, and extending their control into arenas like the theater, what was to prevent the clerics from ruling completely in Rouen? As the same song noted,

> Conduisez vous prudement
> M. le Curé controle
> Vos principes religieux
> et politiques bien mieux.

> Conduct yourselves prudently
> Mr. le Curé controls
> Your religious principles
> and political principles, better still.[40]

Just as it was the responsibility of the weaker members of Orgon's family to make him see his error in allowing Tartuffe to reign over his household, so it was up to the people of Rouen to make the civic officials see the dangers of allowing the religious authorities too much power. That they were capable of such a task was stressed in a letter sent to the theater director which depicted the population as comprised of "citizens who, in all times and all places, have known and will always know how to resist the dishonorable bondage that one would like to impose upon them."[41] A similar point was made in a placard written to encourage the soldiers in Rouen to support the people who were "too enlightened" to be taken in by "these *calotins*, who, calling themselves ministers of God, are nothing but false men, only seeking to make a revolution, . . ."[42]

As the reference to "revolution" in the previous quotation suggests, the language and images of *Tartuffe* were used to describe what seemed like a serious change in the church and the relationship between church and state which stretched far beyond the problems experienced in Rouen. The letter to the director cited earlier contains a litany of expressions which described the situation in Rouen, but which could be used to assail a wide range of clerical abuses. The letter spoke of "deceptive appearances," "shameful means," and "the inquisitorial formulae" used by the "introducers of Jesuitism" who threatened "to impose bondage" on the good people of Rouen.[43]

In the end, the people of Rouen prevailed. On the 6th of May *Tartuffe* was finally performed. Why did the authorities change their minds? Why was the ban on the play finally lifted? In a *deus ex machina* scenario worthy of Molière, it was King Charles X himself who issued the order that the play be performed. The director of the theater of Rouen, M. Morel, took advantage of the break in the theater season at the end of April to go to Paris, where he pleaded his case before the minister of the interior for the right to perform *Tartuffe* in Rouen. He cited the appearance of Molière's play in Paris and Elbeuf and argued that it was unjust to ban the play in his town. The minister of the interior referred the case to the king, who finally authorized the production of *Tartuffe* in Rouen.[44]

For the long-awaited performance the theater was packed, and 300 people had to be turned away at the door. One official claimed that the most perfect order reigned, and he noted "that during the course of the play, all of the allusions were seized and applauded by the *parterre*, but in the fifth act, in the scene where one speaks of the justice of the King, unanimous applause erupted in every corner of the theater." [45] Why shouldn't they applaud? After a full month of agitation in Rouen, the people seemed content that they had exposed the local fraudulent priests. The very performance of *Tartuffe* was evidence that the prelates no longer reigned "at the same time in the church and in the theater," [46] and, especially, over the civil authorities. They could enjoy the play, knowing in advance the denouement. When the bailiff told Orgon, "Sir, all is well; rest easy, and be grateful. / We serve a Prince to whom all fraud is hateful," he might have been speaking directly to the people of Rouen. For had not their own king, in authorizing *Tartuffe,* proven himself to be deserving of Molière's words (disproving rumors circulating that he was a Jesuit-king)? "A Prince who sees into our inmost hearts, / And can't be fooled by any trickster's arts . . . / Nor does his love of piety numb his wits / And make him tolerant of hypocrites." [47]

The performance of *Tartuffe* was not the only victory enjoyed by the people of Rouen. On the 19th of May, Archbishop Le Croy issued a second pastoral letter which responded to the criticism of the people of the Seine-Inférieure. In it he explained that "our intention was not to establish a sort of inquisition," and that this second letter was intended to calm his parishioners. *Le Constitutionnel* immediately reprinted the new letter and added that "[this is] very reassuring . . . we are happy to reprint such examples of moderation and wisdom; they have much more influence on us than the worst threats . . . ." [48] The religious content of the letter frankly did not change very much, but the spirit was different; the assumption that the church could impose itself on the lives of the Rouennais was now absent. So the inhabitants of Rouen had reason to rejoice indeed.

However, in their effort to render clear the line dividing civil from religious authority in Rouen, and to reject efforts to enforce an unpopular new Catholicism in the spring of 1825, the people of Rouen developed a popular anticlerical discourse which could be called into action at the slightest provocation. A year after the events just described, such a provocation appeared in the form of a visiting mission. Stink bombs in churches and disruptions of religious processions were added to the repertoire of seditious tactics, materials, and language to create one of the largest expressions of anticlericalism in France during the Restoration.[49] But in 1826, when the people of Rouen demanded a performance of *Tartuffe,* the authorities showed that they had clearly learned a lesson from the previous year's incident. In a police report from May of 1826 the prefect explained, "The authorities, in order to avoid throwing themselves into another compromising situation, have announced that there will be no opposition to a performance of *Tartuffe*." [50] When the play was performed, the people of Rouen demonstrated that they still appreciated how germane Molière's play was for them. The police noted, "In the theater, where one performed *Tartuffe,* all of the allusions that one believed applicable to current circumstances were covered from the beginning of the play to the end with riotous applause and foot-stomping." [51]

From this report, which is the only one that exists about this performance, it is hard to tell whether the audience reacted positively or negatively at the end when the king's reputation was at issue. One can easily imagine that they took every opportunity to laugh at jokes at Tartuffe's expense, thinking of the missionaries visiting their town. But whether by the spring of 1826 their views of the king had changed is hard to say. In the fall of the same year, the king's day (Saint Charles's Day) offered some critics an opportunity to express their disapproval of the sovereign, but at least, according to the police, this view was not yet widespread. Again the theater was the site of an incident, and although *Tartuffe* was not the play performed, "couplets in honor of the king" again became an occasion for the people of Rouen to express their opinion of their ruler. The report noted: "The King's Day was celebrated in Rouen by public festivities, unmarred by any disorder; but at night in the theater, at the moment when the actor sang couplets in honor of the king, some signs of disapproval erupted from the *parterre,* and were mixed with applause from the rest of the audience." [52]

In 1827, with no apparent local instigation evident from the archives, *Tartuffe* was performed and was once again the occasion for a theater incident. By then the sentiment toward the king seemed to be changing. There was no longer the "unanimous applause" which the king enjoyed in the spring of 1825. In his report on this latest incident, the prefect described, once again, the response of the audience to the last scene. "As is the custom, all of the passages against false priests excited loud and affected applause. Then, when the actor began his elegy to the king some boos and a whistle were heard in the *parterre.*" [53] By 1827 the practice of using *Tartuffe* as a critical weapon against missionaries, local and national civil and ecclesiastical officials, and as a useful prism for making sense of their world had spread far beyond the limits of Rouen.

Tartuffe Incidents Throughout France, 1825–1829

Provoking "Tartufferie"

Rouen was hardly the only city where people were demanding *Tartuffe* and using its performances as an opportunity to express their disapproval of local priests, missionaries, and even the king. The incident in Rouen became a point of reference both for those in other towns who would emulate the Rouen theatergoers and for the local authorities trying to keep these incidents under control. The number of incidents resembling the one in Rouen, the frequency with which the incidents refer to one another, and the tendency of the participants in different towns to copy one another suggest a more concerted, and if not organized, at least loosely coordinated effort to confront the clericalism of the Restoration than has been previously appreciated.[54] Authorities everywhere were pricking up their ears at the end of Molière's play, pulling down placards using themes from *Tartuffe*, and reporting to Paris about the varied uses of this seventeenth-century play to criticize clericalism between 1825 and 1829. Between these years, at least forty-one incidents involving *Tartuffe* erupted, in twenty-three different departments. (See table.) These ranged in time from the length of one performance to up to a month of continuous agitation. Participation ranged from what the authorities called "a few troublemakers" (for which one should understand "liberals" or "revolutionaries") to a majority of the local population, including individuals of all political persuasions and social classes. A variety of specific, local circumstances prompted demands for, bannings of, the wide circulation of, or the ultimate performance of *Tartuffe* in different cities. For people in the urban centers of departments near Rouen, and even in cities as far away as Nantes and Toulon, it was the events in the Seine-Inférieure which seemed to spark minor incidents. In the same year a number of cities reacted against the Sacrilege Law—especially in towns with large Protestant communities such as Nîmes.[55] The local celebration of the elaborate coronation of Charles X or of the Papal Jubilee of 1826 often became the occasion of a Tartuffe incident.[56] An overzealous, greedy, corrupt, or simply unpopular church official could spark an incident.[57] The most common cause for the deployment of *Tartuffe* was the arrival in town of a mission.[58]

The incident in Rouen was itself a cause for theater disorders in neighboring departments. While the prefect of the adjacent department of the Eure expressed concern that the calumnies repeated against M. L'Abbé

1819	October–November	Brest, Finistère
1823	January	Rouen, Seine-Inférieure
1825	January	Rouen, Seine-Inférieure
	April–May	Rouen, Seine-Inférieure
	May	Fécamp, Seine-Inférieure
		Beauvais, Oise
		Nantes, Loire-Atlantique
		Bordeaux, Gironde
		Lyons, Rhône
	June	Toulon, Var
		Colmar, Haut-Rhin
		Lyons, Rhône
	August	Lyons, Rhône
		La Rochelle, Charente-Maritime
	December	Nancy, Meurthe-et-Moselle
		Nîmes, Gard
1826	January	Clermont-Ferrand, Puy-de-Dôme
	May	Angoulême, Charente
	June	Bordeaux, Gironde
		Rouen, Seine-Inférieure
	July	Tours, Indre-et-Loire
	August	Rouen, Seine-Inférieure
	October	Tours, Indre-et-Loire
		Strasbourg, Bas-Rhin
	October–November	Brest, Finistère
		Lyons, Rhône
		Paris, Seine
		Perpignan, Pyrénées-Orientales
	November	Clermont-Ferrand, Puy-de-Dôme
		Marseilles, Bouches-du-Rhône
		Rouen, Seine-Inférieure
	December	Toulouse, Haute-Garonne
1827	January	Perpignan, Pyrénées-Orientales
	January–March	Brest, Finistère
	February	Nantes, Loire-Atlantique
	March	Bordeaux, Gironde
		Besançon, Doubs
	May	Epinal, Vosges
	June	Rouen, Seine-Inférieure
	November	Nîmes, Gard
1829	August	Marseilles, Bouches-du-Rhône
	September	Angers, Maine-et-Loire
	November	Carpentras, Var

Le Sur were spreading and gaining popularity in Evreux in late April 1825,[59] the prefect of the Oise had a potential repetition of the events of Rouen on his hands. During a theater performance in Beauvais on the 1st of May in 1825, pamphlets were distributed among the audience and thrown on the stage between the two plays scheduled demanding a performance of *Tartuffe* and, as in Rouen, threatening that the *parterre* would not stand for the performance of any other play. The prefect defended the people of his department, calling them "eminently tranquil, and enemies of all disorder," and blamed outsiders, who "seek, now more than ever, to agitate the population, making them distrust the 'power of the Jesuits' and seizing upon the *mandement,* at the least inconvenient," to create disorder. Proclaiming the innocence of the native population, and underestimating the different ways one could become acquainted with *Tartuffe,* the prefect pointed out the complete ignorance of the inhabitants of Beauvais of Molière's masterpiece. "The best proof of the influence that one has exerted on the population, is that as far as I know this comedy has never been performed here, and that the majority of those who demand it, don't even know it at all."[60] He underlined this point by noting that the *billets* in the theater requesting *Tartuffe* misspelled the name of the play.

In two cases, in Nantes and Toulon, the events in Rouen seemed to render *Tartuffe* more popular, and certainly made the authorities careful about how they handled its performance. In Nantes, an opening performance of *Tartuffe* "helped the local population rediscover the road to the theater," which, according to the prefect, "they had long since forgotten." Reporting on the performance of the opening night, the prefect noted that "the number of spectators was considerable." The prefect was pleased to assure the minister of the interior that while the play was frequently applauded, it was always "without affectation" and "without tumultuous cries" and that the final, important speech "received its share of well-merited applause." Everything went so well in fact that the prefect never would have bothered reporting the "nonincident" associated with *Tartuffe* in Nantes had it not been for the fact that "in another city, no less important [Rouen], it had been the cause or the pretext of scandalous troubles."[61] In Toulon the events in Rouen inspired the director of the local theater to stage a production of *Tartuffe.* Given what had happened in Rouen, the prefect of the Var explained that he did not think it would be either necessary or prudent to oppose the performance, although he took all the preventive police measures which seemed appropriate given the circumstances. The prefect reported with "satis-faction" that "the performance of this play which took place last night [on the 20th of June 1825] was perfectly calm; nothing out of order, nothing reprehensible was reported to me, and offered, on the contrary, new evidence of the good spirit which guides the inhabitants of this city."[62]

Missionaries were a common target in *Tartuffe* incidents, especially after the example set by the people of Rouen in their reaction to the mis-sionaries in 1826. (However, as we saw in the case of Brest in 1819, this application of *Tartuffe* was hardly new.) In Angoulême the people used a performance of *Tartuffe* to dissuade the local authorities from allow-ing a mission to come to town. In June of 1826, the *parterre* demanded a performance of *Tartuffe*. While the actual performance "took place without disorders," many members of the audience warned the local of-ficials "that if they wanted to give a mission, . . . that they would behave like they did in Rouen."[63] In Angers, the arrival of missionaries in the fall of 1829 provoked someone to try to stir up a theater incident by posting the following placard in the corridor of the local theater: "Mes-sieurs, wanting to see a performance of Tartuffe, we invite you to add your voices to ours and demand it at the beginning of the second play."[64] In fact, no incident followed, but the local authorities arranged for full surveillance of the theater during the rest of its season just in case. In Nîmes, the arrival of the missionaries coincided with the arrival of a flood of cheap copies of *Tartuffe*, sold for only eight centimes per copy. Within eight days of the missionaries' arrival two performances of Mo-lière's play were staged. The local ecclesiastical authorities were so con-cerned about the potential disturbances in a town "in which one third of the population was comprised of Protestants" that the local archbishop banned all outdoor ceremonies during the course of the mission.[65]

Most reports on *Tartuffe* incidents in 1825 reveal that audiences re-sponded primarily to the barbs in the play which were directed against religious figures. The report in *L'Indicateur* on a minor incident in Bor-deaux was typical. It explained that "All the allusions which one could apply to false priests, who use religion for their own material gain, were seized and rigorously applauded."[66] But events such as the Sacrilege Law, the coronation, and the Jubilee of 1826 turned the audience's at-tention increasingly to the lines which focused on the person of the king. A report from the prefect of the Gironde concerning an incident in Bor-deaux which took place in the same city two years later, in 1827, was typical of this later period: "the speeches which offered allusions which satisfied the opposition were ardently seized, and that of the last act which begins with 'We live under a Prince, &c,' was interrupted by conversations, sneezing, and an affectation of noise which bespoke guilty intentions."[67] Aside from producing this general shift, these events themselves provoked incidents.

The passage of the Sacrilege Law of April 1825 provoked a number of incidents in Protestant regions, where it was seen as a sign of a return to persecution. In Colmar and Lyons, agitators were accused of spreading fear of persecution among Protestants that was linked to the growing intolerance of the Catholic clergy in conjunction with the recent Sacrilege Law. In an article of 5 June 1825, *Le Constitutionnel* made the connection for its liberal readers between the persecution of the Protestants and the usefulness of *Tartuffe* as a weapon against it: "Perhaps Tartuffe was performed intentionally in Colmar, the very night when not far from this city three Protestant travelers were forced to descend from their carriages and kneel before a procession. They undoubtedly feared the worst punishment threatened by the Sacrilege Law."[68] In Lyons, the authorities claimed that "one tries to stir up concern among Protestants, by spreading the rumor that some rural priests were preaching against them; one plots to get youths to go to the theater and tumultuously demand a performance of Tartuffe, which one performs anyway on the banks of the river."[69]

In the region of Nîmes the Sacrilege Law created quite a stir among Protestants. This is hardly surprising given the long history of struggle between Protestants and Catholics in the department of the Gard. In its most recent flare-up, in the White Terror of 1815, the Catholics of Nîmes used the return of the Bourbons to oust Protestants from office and kill them in the streets in a wave of violence not seen since the Revolution. The Protestants, no doubt, took very seriously the threat of persecution implicit in the Sacrilege Law.[70] In May of 1825 the police reported that one speech in the Chamber of Deputies against this law was distributed everywhere within the Cévennes and the Avonage. "Those who take it upon themselves to read and to comment upon this law, announce that one wishes to annihilate the Protestant religion."[71] According to the police, local Protestant ministers, acting on orders from their superiors, were contributing to the growing fear of persecution by Catholics.[72] There was no immediate *Tartuffe* incident in Nîmes associated with these events. However, as we saw earlier, by the fall of the same year when missionaries arrived in town, Nîmes was flooded with cheap copies of Molière's play, and two performances of the play were staged within eight days of the missionaries' arrival.[73]

The coronation of Charles X became the occasion for several performances of *Tartuffe* in the city of Lyons. In Rouen, as we saw, the authorities had demonstrated concern that the timing of the theater incidents coincided with preparations for the massive celebration at Reims. In Lyons the authorities similarly accused local troublemakers of capitalizing on the festivities surrounding the seemingly unpopular coronation to stir up religious controversies. The apathy of the local population in regard to the coronation was underlined in one report in which the local police complained that "the festivities given on the occasion of the coronation . . . have not produced the enthusiasm that one would expect in such a touching circumstance."[74] Another report acknowledged that "the working class even showed a singular indifference" to the celebration.[75] But the police further accused "troublemakers" of using this unpopular celebration to stir up "religious controversies" in all social classes. Blaming local liberals, the authorities claimed that "they try to organize opposition against the priests even within the ranks of loyal monarchists."[76] In conjunction with these efforts, three performances of *Tartuffe* were staged. "Enormous crowds attended the opening two performances," where the bust of Molière was crowned. By the third performance "the fervor had died down, in spite of the efforts to spread the news that the clergy protested against these performances."[77]

If the coronation upset some people in Lyons, Charles X's participation in the Jubilee of 1826 troubled French people in a number of cities all over France. In Lyons the Jubilee was opened on the 29th of October with a procession attended by the local authorities along with more than 40,000 spectators. The authorities reported that "this imposing solemnity, which lasted for more than six hours, took place without the slightest disorder." However, if the streets of Lyons were not filled with protesters during the procession, on the eve of the celebration the Théâtre des Celestins was. A dozen spectators demanded *Tartuffe*, but no major incident followed. The next day, however (the day of the procession), "at the end of the performance new cries, much more numerous than on the previous night, were heard and two to three hundred people insisted upon occupying the theater where they caused considerable damage. . . ." The crowd was ultimately dispersed by the authorities, and three men were arrested—a previous editor of the liberal newspaper *L'Eclaireur du Rhône,* a silk worker, and a traveling salesman from Geneva. But the theater disorders did not end there. The following night "the disorders were renewed with even more violence." The authorities were attacked with rocks and they in turn fired on the crowd, injuring some of the spectators.[78] A similar scene took place in Strasbourg. As in Lyons, the festivities surrounding the Jubilee prompted the demand for performances of *Tartuffe*. In Strasbourg, however, the performance was scheduled and the theater filled to capacity when the civil authorities tried to block the production. A regiment was sent in to prevent the performance by force, and fighting broke out between the spectators and the authorities. When some missionaries who were in town for the Jubilee left on the 24th of October 1826, they had to be protected by a military escort."[79]

In Marseilles the authorities were prepared for a similar theater disorder. One police report explained: "For some time now the municipal authorities noted that the coming Jubilee was fomenting opposition, and that troublemakers would take advantage of this fact and imitate the scenes of Rouen, Brest, and Lyons by demanding *Tartuffe*."[80] In fact the prefect of the Bouches-du-Rhône and the mayor of Marseilles decided in advance to refuse any request to have *Tartuffe* performed, and in cases where this refusal became an occasion for troubles, the authorities intended to arrest the perpetrators and subject them to the full vengeance of the laws.[81] A later report, submitted after the celebration of the Jubilee in Marseilles, demonstrated that the authorities had worried for nothing. Unlike the city of Brest, where disruptions inside and outside the churches and regular disorders in the theaters confronted the authorities with a town in revolt against the missionaries, there was no incident to speak of in Marseilles, either at the procession or at the theater the same night.[82] In Aix some troublemakers threw stones in two different churches during Vespers,[83] but otherwise the Jubilee festivities proceeded without a hitch.

In Besançon an incident was reported in conjunction with the Jubilee. A placard was erected on the doors of the college of the town on the day the Jubilee procession featuring its pupils was supposed to pass by it. The authorities suspected that the authors of this poster were the pupils who were unhappy about being forced to attend these processions. The placard, which took the form of a theater *affiche*, contained an announcement of the intention to perform *Tartuffe*, but also playfully used the themes and images of that comedy to mock the local situation in Besançon.

> By permission of the Mayor
> The privileged actors of the King, also belonging to
> the Great Jesuit Troupe of France

Will give today, Monday, 5 March 1827
For the benefit of the hypocrites of this city and the
Chapel of the Royal Collège
A second performance of the Grand universal Jubilee.
During the intermissions MM de Ch_ and du B_ The leading
hypocrites of this city will dance a *pas de deux*
with the nuns of Sacré Coeur de Jésus.
The spectacle will begin with Le Tartuffe
Comedy of Molière, important play for which
there is no need to offer praise
and will conclude with
The missionaries
Harlequinade of M. Forbin-Janson.[84]

Practicing "Tartufferie"

In all of the incidents which rocked the theaters of France between 1825
and 1829, many of the same tactics were employed: requests for the performance of *Tartuffe* were made to theater directors, *billets* were thrown
on the stage during other performances, placards were hung on the
walls, and the *parterre* simply began screaming for *Tartuffe* or distributing and reading pamphlet versions of the play in their seats. Plays
other than *Tartuffe* were prevented from being performed. Once performed, the same lines became an occasion for disruptions of the play.
As in Rouen, the contents of Molière's play offered a way of making
sense of local events, and fed a growing popular anticlericalism. But how
did the idea of using *Tartuffe* as a weapon in these local anticlerical incidents spread?

The authorities blamed local liberals for spreading this idea and in-
stigating incidents. Indeed, there seemed to be some justification for this
position. In Toulouse and Epinal, local liberals demanded *Tartuffe* of
the local theater director and so did instigate incidents.[85] In Toulouse, in
late December 1826, a journalist for *Le Constitutionnel* and medical
and law students made up the group of liberals behind the request. In
Clermont-Ferrand, in January of 1826, liberal lawyers were central to a
Tartuffe incident which took place in the theater, and stood together
helping to defend those parties arrested by the police.[86] So popular was
Tartuffe in these years that the local liberals of Nancy came up with the
idea of using a performance of the play as a fund-raiser for a subscription for the children of General Foy. The authorities blocked the effort.[87]
In many cases the local police just blamed liberals without any real
justification. Reports about an incident in La Rochelle in August of

1825 blamed the "revolutionary party," exactly the term used by the authorities in Carpentras to explain the motivating force behind an incident in their town four years later.[88] No substantiation for the accusation was offered in either case.

If individual liberals and liberal groups were themselves often involved in spreading the use of *Tartuffe* as a political weapon in these years, the liberal newspapers played an even more central role. As early as 1819 *Le Constitutionnel* informed its readers that Molière's masterpiece was relevant to their century: "People believe that Molière was excessive in his portrayal of Tartuffe; our century proves that he is far from having exaggerated his traits."[89] The liberal publications *Le Constitutionnel* and *L'Ami de la Charte* reported generously and supportively on incidents taking place all over the country. Reporting on the *Tartuffe* incident in Rouen in April of 1825, *Le Constitutionnel* encouraged its readers to draw a broad conclusion from the banning of *Tartuffe* in the Seine-Inférieure:

> A fact like this offers a beautiful portrait of an epoch. Isn't it a strange thing that a comedy which appeared under the auspices of Louis XIV, which has never been banned, even under the empire of P. Lachaise, should be prohibited under the ministries of Villèle, Francet, Corbière, and Frayssinous?[90]

These papers also played an important role in spreading the idea of demanding a performance of *Tartuffe*, of applying the themes and images of the play to local events, and informing the audience of which lines to respond to once the play was performed. An article of 5 June 1825 in *Le Constitutionnel* reported on eight different *Tartuffe* incidents and encouraged its readers "to go to the theater which offers so many contradictions, on the stage, go from the scenes of the missionaries to those of *Tartuffe*, join the crowd at performances of the great comedy of the day, seize with enthusiasm each allusion. . . ."[91]

According to the authorities, the liberal papers went beyond generally encouraging *Tartuffe* incidents. In Clermont-Ferrand *L'Ami de la Charte* was blamed by the police for "predicting" and thereby provoking an incident in the theater. In an article of 28 January 1826 the newspaper ran an article which applauded the decision of the theater director to stage *Tartuffe* the next day, and noted, "One can predict, with assurance, that there will be a huge crowd, and the administration should prepare itself to satisfy the demands of Molière's admirers to see the bust of their immortal author."[92] In the cover letter which accompanied a copy of this article, the prefect of the Puy-de-Dôme described the scene

at the theater on the 29th of January and directly blamed the article in
the liberal paper for provoking the demand to pay homage to Molière's
bust.[93] He also enclosed an article from the *Journal du Puy-du-Dôme*
which drew the same conclusion.

> Molière's *Tartuffe,* which was performed yesterday at our theater, was for
> some turbulent spectators an occasion to renew the cries and vociferations
> which, in a similar circumstance, shook the town of Rouen last year. . . . It
> seems to us that the frenetic admiration of the *parterre* should have been
> satisfied with all of the calculated applause given during each scene; *but it
> was necessary that they also fulfill the prediction of L'Ami de La Charte,*
> [and so the bust of Molière was requested].[94]

Hundreds of thousands of cheap, tiny copies of *Tartuffe* were made
available by liberal publishers. Like the newspapers, the prefaces to these
editions informed the readers about the relevance of *Tartuffe* to contemporary French society. They encouraged the people of France "to oppose
the Tartufe [*sic*] on the stage with the Tartufes of the world, . . . Don't be
content to applaud this play in the theater, read it, study it, carry it with
you as a new kind of protection against the sellers of amulets, like an
antidote against charlatans."[95] They even told their readers to identify
with the best characters in the play: "women should become like Elmire,
young men, like Damis, wise and religious men, like Cléante;" the consequence of their collective efforts would be "that soon, the Orgons and
the Pernelles would open their eyes."[96] According to one preface, the political circumstances of the day assured the popularity of this seventeenth-
century play. "It's Charles X who makes this play eminently germane today, and keeps it alive in the theater."[97] That the play would serve an
important political purpose was also stressed. "Today, when one finds fanaticism and superstition suddenly resurrected, and spread anew [by the
missionaries], they are confronted by Molière, always alive and in all of
his éclat, Molière with Tartufe [*sic*], and they no longer know how to play
their role."[98] The same preface also underlined the importance of publishing Molière's comedy in large numbers and for readers to repeat and
respond enthusiastically to certain verses. "Hypocrisy attacks us with
condemnations, with denunciations, with bailiffs and police officers; we
respond with 100,000 copies of Tartufe [*sic*]; and at the end, the French
will repeat as a family: 'We live under a Prince, to whom all fraud is hateful.'"[99] Another preface explicitly underscored the importance of making cheap copies available so as to educate the population at large about
the utility of Molière's comedy: "these were the intentions of the pub-

lishers of the small format of *Tartuffe;* they wanted virtuous men of all classes, . . . to have access to this excellent work." [100] The liberal newspapers helped to publicize these cheap editions by informing readers of their local availability.[101]

The men and women of France could learn about Molière's comedy not only by reading newspapers or special prefaces affixed to cheap pamphlet versions of the play; broadsheets featuring stock scenes from *Tartuffe* also publicized its contents. The broadsheet reproduced here was quite typical: the top part represents the moment from act 3, scene 3, when Tartuffe is seducing Elmire (and looking down her dress) and pronouncing "My God, but from this point of view, the work is marvelous!" But at the bottom is a four-stanza song, to the popular tune "la Colonne," which offers a brief history of the play, and invites those who would see and sing the song to go to the theater, applaud Molière's verses, crown his bust, and thereby continue the struggle against fanaticism, ignorance, and hypocrisy.[102] (See figure 7.) While this is the only such image I have found with a song as well, there were many examples of broadsheets representing the most popular scenes from the play. The scenes most commonly depicted seemed to have been those involving Elmire's seduction by Tartuffe, in act 3, scenes 2 and 3, and act 4, scene 5, as well as the scene in which Orgon discovers the truth about Tartuffe because from his hiding place under a table he overhears the hypocrite's final efforts at seduction.

Throughout the Restoration, although especially in the latter 1820s, French men and women were also treated to vaudeville adaptations which involved Molière or this particular comedy. The key scenes from *Tartuffe* were rendered accessible and memorable by playwrights who put key soliloquys to popular tunes. One play written by Henri Simon, entitled *Ninon, Molière, et Tartuffe,* was a one-act vaudeville performed in Paris in 1815, featuring a scene between Tartuffe and a servant, Annette, which was a direct imitation of the scene in which Tartuffe first seduces Elmire. Including a song called "Il est avec le ciel / des accomodemens," put to the popular tune "Mon père était pot," this play rehearsed all the stock insults and key phrases which were reproduced in one theater incident after another during the Restoration.[103] Another short play, *Un Trait de Molière: Prologue du Tartuffe,* written by Eugène de Pradel, again features Tartuffe as a character in conversation with Molière, and ends with Molière himself addressing the audience and pronouncing "that today, surely, Tartuffe will be of use to you." [104] Likewise,

Acte III Scene 3

1
You, whose sublime genius
Attacks the idiotic and the perverse,
Forcing hypocrisy to submit
Under the weight of your supple verses;
Molière receives the crown
Emblem of immortality,
Which in the name of beauty,
France unites to give to you.

2
Fanaticism and ignorance
Conspire in vain against you;
Through your verses reason asserts itself
And the evil-doer pales in fear.
We applaud you without fear
Because the real wisdom we all respect,
The torch of truth
Will burn all who would extinguish it.

3
Against the clamors of envy
A great prince protected you;
And from the calamitous attacks
His support at least avenged you.
He knew how to draw luster to himself
By making your beautiful verses triumph;
He knew how to enlighten the universe,
Having the sun as his emblem.

4
If you, sublime author,
Could leave the darkness of your tomb,
One would see ruse and crime
Die anew at your hands.
But alas! Vice prospers,
In this world where your verses shine forth
We still have evil-doers
But we have no more Molière.

Figure 7. "Oh, from here the work is marvelous!" (1827). Act 3, scene 3, *Tartuffe*. Bibliothèque Nationale, Paris. Photograph, Bibliothèque Nationale. Image and text in original; translation by Sheryl Kroen.

a three-act play featuring Molière, written in 1828 by M. F. Garnier, offers the following quotation on the title page, "It is to love one's country, to serve humanity / To expose for all to see, so much perversity." [105]

In Bordeaux in 1828 a censor rejected a play which had nothing to do with Molière or his comedies, but in which the author had tried to slip in the lines "We live under a King / To whom all Fraud is hateful" when describing the justness of the main character of the play, Charles V. The censors blocked the effort "to cite with regard to Charles V a verse written in the century of Louise XIV." [106] The play was written for a special performance to be given on the occasion of the duchesse de Berry's visit in Bordeaux. Presumably the censors were trying to avoid the problems which might ensue if the famous lines were repeated in her presence, particularly since just one year earlier audiences in that town had responded "guiltily" to the final act of *Tartuffe*.[107]

Although *Tartuffe* incidents were often provoked by liberals and encouraged by liberal newspapers and publications, these incidents were not strictly liberal affairs. In Protestant regions, ministers were often responsible for spreading the word, encouraging their congregations to protest the move in the direction of religious persecution represented by the Sacrilege Law.[108] Travelers or *colporteurs* who had passed through Rouen or another city where an incident had taken place often carried word of these events.[109] Fairs and especially large regional markets were feared by many authorities to be the places where information and seditious material were shared.[110] *Tartuffe* incidents were primarily portrayed as a middle-class affair, although whenever other social groups were involved the authorities quickly became alarmed. Lawyers and journalists were often involved,[111] as were students and officers.[112] Artisans participated in large numbers in the incident in Angoulême.[113] But the participants who most concerned the authorities were workers. In Rouen, as we saw, the authorities blamed middle-class liberals for the participation of workers. In Nîmes there was a particularly turbulent performance of *Tartuffe* because it was held on a Sunday, intentionally enabling workers to come.[114] In almost all cases, whoever was responsible for planting the idea of bringing *Tartuffe* to bear on a local situation, the event usually sparked an incident and inspired broad participation, beyond the local liberal and middle-class circles whom the authorities were always happy to blame.

In Angoulême, for example, the authorities blamed prominent liberals for provoking a *Tartuffe* incident in 1826, at least in their early reports. However, by the time the affair was complete, after the incident in the theater was followed by trials for those apprehended, the authorities were forced to amend their portrait of the events in their final reports. One report claimed that upwards of 2,000 people were involved in the incident. On the night of the theater incident itself all efforts to apprehend the supposed liberal troublemakers were blocked by the assembled crowd. Once the parties were apprehended and the trial carried out, everyone refused to cooperate, even the civil authorities. According to the prefect's rendition of the "scandalous" trial, there was not a single person willing to testify against the four people actually taken into custody by the gendarmes.

> I cannot hide from Your Excellency that the defense was truly scandalous by the tone which the witnesses adopted as almost all of them proclaimed that they had yelled and demanded Tartuffe like the others, by the plea of the defense attorney whom the President had to reprimand, and by the weakness of the gendarmes who spent two hours in the middle of disorder, but who declared in court that they recognized no one, even though there was one who had lived in Angoulême for fifteen years, and others who had been there for many years, and therefore must have been eminently capable of identifying the troublemakers.[115]

Interpreting "Tartufferie"

What did all these incidents involving *Tartuffe* accomplish? For one thing, audiences were treated to plenty of performances of *Tartuffe* in the last years of the Restoration, even, as was the case in Rouen, thanks to the direct intervention of the king. In some cases, specific churchmen were driven out of town. In Nîmes, as we saw, the anticlerical sentiment expressed in and around the theater led the ecclesiastical authorities to prohibit any external ceremonies, usually the high point of the mission.[116]

These *Tartuffe* incidents seemed to have had a long-term impact in certain regions. A look at the geographical distribution of these incidents reveals a striking similarity with the distribution of "mission cross incidents," studied by Michael Phayer, which took place after the 1830 Revolution.[117] It is not a coincidence that attacks on mission crosses which immediately followed the Revolution of 1830 took place in the same areas where *Tartuffe* incidents had taken place earlier. Of the forty-one *Tartuffe* incidents included in this study, twenty-two took place in cities which also experienced mission cross incidents a few years later. To some degree, the geographic distribution of *Tartuffe* incidents can be explained by patterns of religious practice. The incident in Rouen was provoked by a pastoral letter in a region where religious practice had be-

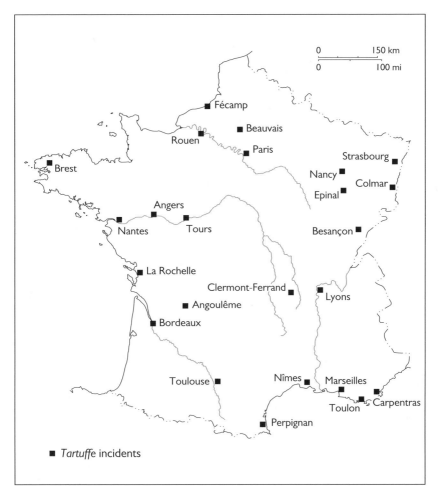

Geographical distribution of *Tartuffe* incidents.

come quite lax. Incidents in Nîmes can be explained by the large number of Protestants residing in that city. If one looks at the geographical origins of church personnel in this period, one finds that *Tartuffe* incidents and attacks on mission crosses corresponded geographically with the regions which provided the smallest number of recruits for the church on the eve of the July Revolution.[118] Whatever the reason for the initial participation in *Tartuffe* incidents, they seemed to leave an important anticlerical legacy. The geographical distribution of these incidents also corresponds to those areas of France which in 1905 did *not* object to the Law of the Separation of Church and State (see map).[119]

In the 1820s what was significant was the fact that people all over France were acting in concert, using the same means to criticize local manifestations of the regime's increasingly unpopular clericalism. Images of priests as Tartuffe-type hypocrites and of the king as a dupe to such impostors became widespread. Even the police began to adopt the language and logic of Molière's comedy to talk about apparently unrelated things. One extraordinary example of this comes from a censor's report on a play proposed for the celebration of Saint Charles's Day in Arras in 1827. Criticizing the manner in which the play mocked minor civil officials, the censor commented, "These accusers of the police daily applaud the bailiff who carts Tartuffe off to prison in place of the good man whom he had defrauded. To whom then do we owe this act of justice on behalf of a king 'to whom all fraud is hateful' if it's not the police who know how to expose the maneuvers of the impostor?"[120]

Equally important, the responses of the civil authorities to the troubles in the theater allow us to see the degree to which the population's "Tartufferie" came to shape the way the government too came to see the missions (as well as the problem of politics and opposition more generally). In some instances this was quite clear, when authorities themselves began to adopt the derisive language of theatricality when referring to the missionaries. This was also obvious in the tactics the police adopted when contending with the troublemakers in the theater, which were exactly analogous to their (often futile) efforts to discipline or provide security for the missionaries. As they had tried to avoid evening ceremonies and to postpone missions until after the popular carnival season, so did they try to control the "timing" of performances of *Tartuffe,* either by postponing them until after the missionaries left town, until after the epoch of the coronation, the Sacrilege Law, or the Jubilee, or simply by allowing the performance on evenings known to be unpopular for theater attendance.[121] They tried to control the theater itself in much the same way as they tried to control the interiors of the churches during the missions: just as they tried to hold the missionaries to a previously accepted script for their sermons, so did they try to prevent actors from departing from the text of their plays either by responding to *billets* thrown on the stage or to requests for repetitions of popular lines or by seizing an opportunity to crown a bust of Molière. Just as they put secret agents in churches, so did they place police officials in the *parterre,* both to listen carefully to what the actors (and the missionaries) said and to gauge the responses of their audiences (and followers). Outside the theaters, as outside the church, they stationed troops to ensure the dispersal of troublemakers and to prevent performances of *Tartuffe* (like ceremonies of the missionaries) from becoming opportunities for large crowds to express overt opposition to the ecclesiastical as well as the civil authorities. As was the case with the disorder occasioned or portended by the arrival of the missions, the threatened or real evidence of theater incidents led civil officials all over France to coordinate their efforts in the name of public tranquillity; they demonstrated that they appreciated the degree to which both the revival and the disorders they precipitated in the theater riots were national problems, to be dealt with as often as possible in a coherent, organized way. Finally, just as the ineffective efforts to control the missionaries left them to preach as they saw fit in the name of freedom of religion and thereby cast themselves as the "arbiters of France's future," so did the administrators' ineffective efforts to prosecute offenders in the theater riots open up a clear space within which men and women could openly defy their government and insist upon their own rights to organize and to express their own vision of the political order.

As people responded to the Sacrilege Law, the Jubilee celebration, and visiting missions—with their placards, their songs, and their demands for *Tartuffe*—a truly popular anticlericalism spread all over the country. With this popular anticlericalism went a spirit of resistance. Seditious acts of all kinds multiplied—even those directed specifically against the king. When the civil authorities tried to put down anticlerical incidents, they were often met by a population willing to respond with force. People from different cities began to mimic one another, and this contributed to a growing sense of unity among the people against the government. Despite the gravity of their seditious acts, the people involved were rarely fined or imprisoned. Acquittals were much more common, often owing to the explicit collaboration of the civil authorities. Newspapers and reprinted trial proceedings gave the people of France a sense that "Tartufferie" was national, and that their political futures were tied to the outcome of these events. In Clermont-Ferrand the lawyers defended the right of the people to demand a play, and argued that it was the police's responsibility to defend, not to stifle, the rights and pleasures of the people. Summarizing the argument made first in the theater, and later in the courtroom, the *Ami de la Charte* asked its readers:

> Why can't we do in Clermont what is being done every day in all the cities of France. The rights of the people of Strasbourg, are they different from the rights of the people of Clermont? and that which is permitted there, can it be

prohibited elsewhere? The rules of the theater, aren't they always the same? The police in Lyons, do they have other instructions than those given to the police in Clermont? No, without a doubt, everywhere the police, . . . show themselves willing to restrain our rights and our pleasures when they should be defending them.[122]

When cases came to trial they became forums for the expression of more revolutionary arguments, such as in Angoulême, where the defense attorney and his client "established the principle that one could resist authority when it gave arbitrary and unjust orders, and that, in this case, one could oppose force with force." [123] It was in the context of the highly publicized trial of the troublemakers apprehended for their part in the theater disturbance in Brest in 1826 that the defense attorneys most clearly articulated the deeper political stakes involved in the theater incidents which shook the entire nation between 1825 and 1829.

Brest, September, 1826–March, 1827

In 1819, as we saw in chapter 3, the people of Brest, deploying charivaris, an expanded meeting of the municipal council, and a deputation to the bishop of Quimper, successfully chased the missionaries from town. While they also arranged for a command performance of *Tartuffe* in 1819, this played a relatively minor role in their efforts to enforce their "general will." By 1826, *Tartuffe* had assumed a new importance; it had become the most commonly used tool in an increasingly national anticlericalism. Thus, when the missionaries returned to Brest in 1826 on the occasion of the Papal Jubilee, it is no surprise that their critics turned to the theater and demanded this play in order to express their opposition.

In many respects, the anticlerical outburst which greeted the missionaries in Brest on the occasion of the Jubilee, between September and late October of 1826, was an outgrowth of the kinds of struggles that erupted all over France whenever missionaries came to town. As in the many cases evoked in chapter 3, the anticipation of disorder prompted the civil authorities of the Finistère to commence negotiations with the bishop of Quimper and the missionaries about their planned revival in Brest. The prefect (with the support and advice of the minister of the interior) tried to prevent evening services, to limit the length of the mission, and even to give the municipal council the role of determining the placement of the mission cross.[124] All of their disciplinary efforts failed, and the prefect explained that he decided "not to insist in the fear of establishing an open struggle between the administration and the clergy, a circumstance which the troublemakers would seize to justify their efforts to undermine the success of the mission." [125] Instead, the prefect called for the full deployment of the forces at his disposal in order to ensure the tranquillity of the revival which would, ultimately, be orchestrated as the missionaries saw fit. In a letter to the minister of the interior, the subprefect of Brest explained the full range of security measures to be taken by the local authorities under his and the mayor's direction: first, the director of the theater was clearly instructed that he was not to accede to demands for *Tartuffe,* but rather was to explain that the play was not in the repertoire, and that the actors did not know it; second, the officers of the armed forces and employees of different administrations were directed to appear, in uniform, at all of the Jubilee ceremonies; third, a continuous surveillance would be practiced against those traveling salesmen and independent men who only three months before had tried to stir up trouble on the occasion of the trial concerning the anticlerical pamphlet of M. Montlosier.[126] These measures were expanded to include special surveillance of an actor who arrived during the course of the mission, who was familiar with Molière's comedy and who had made this fact known to the audience.[127]

If the civil authorities appeared determined to deploy military force and the law to protect the missionaries, the fact that the people of Brest had a right to negotiate over the mission was publicized by those opposing the mission, the liberal press reporting generously on these acts, and tacitly acknowledged by the authorities, who in fact were remarkably lenient when it came to pursuing the troublemakers. From the day that the missionaries arrived in Brest (at the end of August), a mannequin was hung in town, representing their leader, the Père Guyon, holding in his hand a small pamphlet containing the history of the laws against the Jesuits. Songs and placards began to circulate deriding the priests and expressing the opposition's determination to disrupt the revival; troublemakers stationed themselves within the church, where they set off stink bombs and congregated outside the church and yelled "Down with the missionaries!" and squirted those exiting from the church with black ink and wax.

At the same time, people took to the theater and began to demand *Tartuffe.* In fact, a ritualized protest emerged in the city of Brest. Every day, for about two weeks, those protesting against the missions went back and forth between the church, where they sang and interrupted religious services with firecrackers and stink bombs, and the theater, where many of the same men repeatedly demanded *Tartuffe*. While the authorities carefully kept tabs on all the activities of the troublemakers, and repeatedly took down their names and occupations, they arrested no one until the night of October 12th, when the theater erupted into full-scale violence. In the theater itself the authorities engaged in a continuous public negotiation with the spectators demanding *Tartuffe*. The mayor represented the local civil administration; on the 2nd of October, in response to the first *billet* thrown on the stage formally requesting *Tartuffe*, the mayor explained (as he had planned in advance) that he had to refuse to allow the performance in the current month because it did not figure in the repertoire, but that he hoped it could be performed the following month (when, although he did not explicitly say so to the audience, he expected the missionaries to have left town). Before he could promise this, however, he said he needed to consult with his superiors. On the 8th of October the request for *Tartuffe* was repeated, again by a *billet* thrown on stage; this time the mayor responded that the prefect had decided not to permit *Tartuffe*, even after a month. That this was because the missionaries had decided to extend their stay in Brest, and thus would still be in town, was evident and clearly articulated by the audience. As a result, screaming, foot-stomping, the banging of umbrellas and canes, and general disorder broke out in the theater, and the refusal of the audience to calm down, despite repeated, rather patient efforts on the part of the mayor and the police commissioner to convince them to do so, forced the authorities to evacuate the theater. The same scene was repeated two days later, on October 10th. Now, for the first time, the authorities tried to make arrests; however, all the men they apprehended were freed by the assembled crowd. Apparently the effort to arrest the men calmed the crowd sufficiently to permit the performance to go ahead; however, at this point pamphlet versions of *Tartuffe* were distributed within the *parterre*, and while the actors performed another play on stage, those in the *parterre* read Molière's play aloud.[128] Finally, on the 12th of October the same scene was repeated, but this time the mayor and the police commissioner, again after extensive efforts to convince the people to allow the performance to go forward, or leave peaceably, authorized the introduction of troops into the theater. General violence broke out—the people screamed "Down with the Mayor of Brest, Assassin of the people of Brest!" as they threw anything they could get their hands on, including benches, at the soldiers threatening them with force. On this night the officials successfully arrested fourteen men, who would be held in custody until they stood trial in January of 1827.

The civil administration's whole approach to handling the disorders in the church and the theater derived from its interpretation of the anti-clerical opposition as the machinations of outsiders, "traveling sales-men," "strangers to the town," taking advantage of such missions to spread rumors and provoke disorder all over the nation.[129] This inter-pretation of the situation was made evident by the placard posted by the prefect after the night of October 12, an official pronouncement which appealed to the *pères de familles* and respectable citizens (precisely those people who had comprised the opposition to the missionaries in 1819) to aid him in his efforts to restore tranquillity in 1826.

> Inhabitants of Brest, look around you and consider your situation: calm reigned within our walls, strangers have come determined to excite a small number of you to acts of disobedience against our laws; they will not be long in escaping this town once they have succeeded in creating divisions and causing trouble; they have left you to bear the burden of their guilty actions; and already the justice system has been turned against you.
>
> We are convinced that the order in our town will be troubled no longer: we hope that all the good citizens, the heads of families and businesses will stop, by their own good example, these imprudent people who may be tempted to initiate new disorders. If their good advice will not be heeded we warn the troublemakers that our laws are severe, and we have the firm in-tention of executing them.
>
> *Brest 17 October 1826, Prefect.*[130]

Subsequent events led the prefect to change his view of the opposi-tion. Between October, when the "troublemakers" were apprehended, and January 1827, when they were tried in Brest, and March 1827, when they were tried on appeal in Quimper, pamphlets in favor of those arrested began to articulate the rights of the theatergoers, and the unjust and abusive use of force by the local authorities, all in the name of the respectable men and inhabitants of Brest who were unjustly accused and held in custody. *Le Constitutionnel* reported generously and critically on the affair, clearly placing all the blame for the disorders in Brest not on the "outsider troublemakers" associated with their paper but on the missionaries. Indeed, in its way of articulating the responsibility of the missionaries, this paper even implied that the civil authorities had not wanted the mission, and in so doing encouraged its readers to place the events in Brest within the broader context of struggles with missionaries in which the civil authorities had been participating for years. *Le Constitutionnel* reported on the events of 12 October 1826 in Brest and drew the following conclusion.

> The members of the Congregation and the Jesuits will not fail to take part in this affair on behalf of the missionaries and against the citizens. But they need to respond to one simple observation: no one in Brest felt the need for a mission, the authorities themselves would have preferred to avoid welcoming them, and if they had not installed themselves in this town, would there have been such disorder and misfortune? Why is it that almost everywhere the missionaries present themselves people demand again and again a performance of *Tartuffe*? [131]

The lawyers defending those arrested would make a similar argument, shifting blame for the whole affair back onto the missionaries who evaded and flouted every rightful effort of the civil authorities to control them. [132] A letter from an unnamed member of the civil administration to the minister of the interior, dated 24 October 1826, criticized *Le Constitutionnel*'s portrait of the situation in Brest. It says: "[*Le Constitutionnel*] wants to know why one demands *Tartuffe* wherever the missionaries preach. The answer is quite simple: it's because whenever a mission begins one is sure to find readers of *Le Constitutionnel*, imbued with its principles." He goes on to refute the paper's depiction of the "imposition" of a mission against the wishes of the local authorities, and directly responds to the argument later made by the defense attorney, Isambert: "The mission did not 'install itself' in Brest; it was installed by a bishop of the diocese and the misfortunes produced by the mission are reduced to the arrest of a small number of young men who need to learn respect and obedience that one owes to those authorities responsible for maintaining order and public tranquillity." [133]

In fact, the events which transpired between October, when the fourteen men were arrested, and March, when most of them were acquitted on appeal, demonstrated that the misfortunes were not restricted to a few troublemakers, that the administration was not unwilling to negotiate with the opposition of Brest about the issues raised over the previous two months, and that these issues cut right to the heart of the major political struggles of the Restoration. Immediately after their arrest in October, the lawyers for the defense began to circulate in Brest several key documents, the most important of which were, first, the legal request that those arrested be freed on bail until their trial, and second, an official complaint and suit brought by the defendants against the mayor and commissioner of police for their unjust and abusive behavior on the night of October 12. The combined effect of these two documents was to publicize throughout the town a wide range of legal arguments and ways of understanding the rights of citizens in regard to their civil and ecclesiastical officials. In January the defendants were tried and condemned, but temporarily freed while awaiting their appeal; at that time another performance of *Tartuffe* was organized which gave the citizens of Brest an opportunity to show their support for the "troublemakers" and their continued opposition to the civil authorities. When the mayor and the police commissioner arrived at the theater that night they were greeted with boos and hisses. After the play, which was attended by the fourteen condemned men, the audience threw a *billet* on the stage requesting that the orchestra play "Ou peut-on être curieux." Permission was accorded and, in the words of the prefect, "the authorities present thus implicated themselves in the expressions of esteem and interest which this seditious public wished to offer to those individuals which our justice system had just flattered with arrests." By a second *billet* the public demanded permission to crown a portrait of Molière; again the authorities gave their permission and "therefore made possible a most ridiculous ceremony; crowns fell in great number, and it was easy to see that one wanted to give homage to more than one man, more than one head."[134] Another official was more explicit in his account of this second request: "It was clear to all present that those crowns were addressed to the condemned men sitting in the audience."[135] In a later letter the prefect described the increasing popularity of those crowned during the performance of the 26th of January: "the condemned men are represented as the victims of a partial justice system, sold to the Jesuits; they were greeted in the theater with a sort of ovation. Every day fêtes and balls are given in their honor; they are to come to Quimper [for their appeal] accompanied by supporters from all of the communes which they will traverse; here in Quimper people are quarreling over who will have the honor of lodging them during their trial."[136] If by their continued willingness to concede to the audience's requests to pay homage to the condemned men in the theater, the mayor and the commissioner of police acknowledged the kinds of "rights" of theatergoers which the trial had publicized, the ultimate acquittal of ten of the men in March, and the lenient sentencing of the remaining four, sent a clear message that the superior court chose to see the events in Brest according to the narrative offered by the defense team and *Le Constitutionnel*.[137]

Seeing Through the Prism of Tartuffe

Many officials reported on the events in Brest in the fall of 1826 and the winter of 1827, but none so thoroughly or so interestingly as Commissaire de Police Parison. Other officials (the mayor of Brest, the prefect of Finistère, the subprefect of Brest) gave regular reports on events; but Parison's sixty-seven-page "Analytical Report on the Events in Brest during the Mission" offers an elaborately detailed account, unquestionably motivated by his desire to exonerate himself of charges that he had unjustly used force against the people of Brest; he wrote his report as the suit brought against him by the defendants was being considered by superior officials in Brest. This report is most interesting, however, because of the way in which it is framed; more than any other document I have identified, it testifies to the degree to which *Tartuffe* and the "Tartufferie" it inspired in the late 1820s affected the way people, even unsympathetic public officials, viewed the world around them. For *Com. Parison* to make sense of the events in his town he seemed to feel the need to step back and offer his superiors a broad frame of reference defined by the principle of theatricality. He cast everything that happened in his city of Brest in terms of a duel between two theaters: the church, where the missionaries were preaching, and the theater, where their opponents regularly demanded performances of *Tartuffe*.[138]

The text is organized around the opposition between these two venues: long paragraphs given the subtitle "MISSION" are immediately followed by others subtitled "SPECTACLE" (theater). What took place in the context of the "MISSION" was not relegated to the interiors of churches; these paragraphs also address grand processions in the streets of Brest as well as other venues relevant to the mission, such as the square in front of the main church and the presbytery where the visiting missionaries were lodged during their stay. Likewise, the "SPECTACLE" sections of the report contained information on events in the interior of the theater, but also followed the agitators outside the theater when protest spilled into the streets, or an actor when he went to see the mayor at city hall, or leading liberals in the café where they had organized a banquet. There is also a lot of slippage between the two venues: sections on the "SPECTACLE" often make mention of the troublemakers inside the church, while sections on the "MISSION" refer back to events in the theater. So "MISSION" and "SPECTACLE" represented more than opposing sites, although quite often the report simply evoked what did correspond to a face-off between the church and the theater.

Clearly it made sense for Commissioner Parison to think about the mission in terms of the theater, because events in the latter venue were a direct response to the churchmen's activities in the former. He himself said of the protesters against the mission that "the theater was the battleground in which they directed their efforts."[139] From the day the mission was announced and the missionaries first arrived in town (26 August 1826), the authorities anticipated a response in the theater.[140] It was not long in coming. On September 3, the official opening of the Jubilee, marked by a procession in which "all the civil authorities, the judicial authorities, the army and the navy, and a considerable number of followers of all ranks and ages" took part, was met with the first demand for *Tartuffe* at the "SPECTACLE." The very same day, "given what had just transpired in relation to the religious ceremonies, the opposition party made itself obvious for the first time, with a *billet* thrown on the stage containing a request for *Tartuffe*."[141] This was but the first of ten disruptions at the theater occasioned by demands for Molière's comedy. As Parison's account opened with the start of the mission and the expected demands for *Tartuffe,* so did his narrative conclude with the final demand for the play on October 25th, when the request was actually granted. Here, underlining the opposition's use of the theater and Molière's play to respond to the missionaries, the commissaire reported that many "voices from the *parterre* and the *premières* responded many times, and quite loudly, 'We don't need it any more, the Tartufes [*sic*] have left; no more Tartufe.'"[142]

One benefit of Parison's report is that it allows us to see the degree to which the struggles in Brest (and elsewhere where the same practice was followed) did involve a direct negotiation between people in two theaters (the mission and the theater). The missionaries were not only aware of what was going on in the theater in Brest; they directly addressed what the troublemakers were doing. Initially, the missionaries launched tirades against the troublemakers explicitly interrupting the church services by stink bombs.[143] As Parison's report shows, the very same men who were throwing stink bombs and greeting the followers outside the church with showers of ink and wax were assembling in the theater at night and asking for *Tartuffe*. But in the context of the sermons given on October 3rd, Abbé Guyon issued a threat which directly concerned the people in the theater. Parison explains: "On this occasion the orator spoke vehemently against the troublemakers, exposing the indecency and inconvenience of their conduct, and observing that if their intention was to stop the mission, he would, on the contrary, prolong it."[144] Given the fact that the negotiations going on within the theater between the mayor and the audience demanding *Tartuffe* rested on the delicate question of when the missionaries would be gone, and therefore when it would be safe in the mayor's opinion to allow the play to be performed, such a threat had direct import for the people in the theater. In the changing content of their *billets* the theatergoers made it clear that they understood the Abbé Guyon's threat and the fact that he was using his power to lead events beyond the "MISSION" and into the realm of the "SPECTACLE." On October 5, *Tartuffe* was demanded for the fifth time, with a *billet* which ironically suggested the possibility that the civil administration might be working on behalf of the missionaries. It read, "We would like to believe, Mr. Mayor, that the authorization to allow *Tartuffe* which you have requested has been granted; we cannot imagine any reasons why you would refuse our wishes, nor that you would be guided by the fear of an insolent hypocrite, who extends his effrontery to attacking all authorities who do not follow his mission from his pulpit." [145] Previous *billets* implied the role which the missionaries in general played in preventing performances of *Tartuffe*, and employed the rhetoric of the clerical plot so common in these years. [146] But this *billet* directly referred to the missionaries' preaching and directly invoked the Abbé Guyon (in the guise of an insolent hypocrite) as the cause of the refusal to allow *Tartuffe*'s performance. They were more explicit on the 8th of October when, to the ultimate refusal to allow *Tartuffe*, the theatergoers responded, "It is the Abbé Guyon who governs us." [147] They were not completely wrong. The abbé made good on his threat; the mission was extended, and as a result the performance of *Tartuffe* was prohibited by order of the prefect, which led to the more and more serious outbreaks in the theater until October 12th, when violence led to the arrest of the fourteen men and the closing of the theater until the end of the mission.

Parison's account enables us to see quite vividly how the theater was constituted as a venue where those opposing the mission could directly challenge the power of the missionaries and, in particular, their ability to exert pressure on the civil authorities and, thereby, to "dictate the law" in their town. In a context where the civil authorities had decided to cast their lot with the missionaries, the anticlerical opponents used the theater to continue to press their cause, to encourage the authorities to try to end the mission as quickly as possible, or at least to give them the right to publicly express their own opposition. While in Brest they failed to convince the authorities to insist upon ending the mission earlier than the missionaries would have liked, they did, for a time, accomplish the latter goal, for the authorities, as we have seen, allowed the protests in the SPECTACLE to go on unhindered, at least until mid-October. To some degree this was because the authorities viewed the theater as a kind of pressure valve, offering the possibility for the opposition to express itself without directly threatening the religious exercises. This way of viewing the theater was articulated in the early discussion in September as to whether to prohibit *Tartuffe;* at that time it was agreed that closing the theater entirely would backfire and that it would be better merely to avoid performances of problematic plays.[148] In late October the prefect expressed himself quite clearly on the relationship between the MISSION and the SPECTACLE: "in closing the theater one runs the risk of extending the focus of the troubles to points much more dangerous for the religious exercises."[149] In the end they did close down the theater; during the disorders of the 12th of October the mayor pronounced quite clearly his intention to apply force and thereby demonstrate "that the authorities cannot and should not allow the people in the theater to dictate the law."[150] The mayor did not, however, announce the closure of the theater before the assembled public but, rather, the next day (October 13th) in a placard posted all over town. The one in front of the church was quickly defaced so that next to the mayor's signature were the words, "Assassin of the people of Brest."[151] In fact, the authorities were incorrect in assuming that the closing of the theaters would lead the troublemakers to turn to other venues to express their opposition to the missionaries. In the remaining ten days of the mission there were threats to stage charivaris outside the presbytery and to accompany the missionaries as they left town, but neither was carried out. The same kind of disruptions which had taken place in the church since the beginning of the mission continued, but Parison's final report underscores the "complete order" which reigned during the final ceremony marking the culmination of the mission; and that more than 10,000 people witnessed the erection of a cross with "a spirit of profound respect."[152] On the 25th of October the theater was reopened, and the offer to permit *Tartuffe* was made by the authorities, and quickly rejected by the theatergoers who saw no need for the performance now that "the Tartuffes have left." So Parison's narrative ends.

Aside from enabling us to see how opponents of the missionaries used the theater to exert pressure on the authorities and assert their "rights" vis-à-vis the ecclesiastical and civil authorities, Parison's report allows us to see how successful anticlerical protesters were in transforming the theater into a "carnivalesque reiteration" of the mission.[153] It is not so much the format of Parison's report which allows us to appreciate this as it is the approach he adopts to analyzing what went on inside the dueling theaters. What is most important, he addresses the MISSION just as he does the SPECTACLE; he analyzes the performance on the stage (the precise sermon given, the talent with which the orator delivered it) just as he was attentive to its reception. In one particularly moving passage describing the ceremony on the 10th of October, Parison evokes the atmosphere created by the missionaries and the emotion inspired among (what he calls) the spectators as they took in the effects of the 4,000 candles carefully placed on the altar and all over the church.[154] Parison was not overtly, self-consciously analyzing the theatrical tactics of the missionaries or their effects on the audience in the derisive way so many anticlerical pamphlets and placards suggested. Rather, by organizing his narrative in the way he did, and treating the MISSION itself as a theater to be analyzed in the same way he analyzed the SPECTACLE on the other side of town, this official demonstrated how widespread had become the tendency to see the world through the prism suggested by *Tartuffe*.

At the beginning and the end of his "Analytical Report" Parison prefaced and concluded his narrative with this interpretation of the political significance of the "Tartufferie" which he both describes and seems to have learned from. He opened his account by placing the events in Brest in 1826 in a longer historical perspective: "France, which for 30 years now has triumphed against the attempts which the Revolution has made upon her peace, her power, and her glory, could not expect to find itself under attack during the reign of its legitimate monarch, within the walls of Brest; . . . this is, however, exactly what has happened on the occasion of the mission associated with the Jubilee."[155] If he was writing a lengthy account of what happened in Brest, it was "to alert not only the inhabitants of Brest, but of France as a whole," in order to avoid the most dangerous and pernicious consequences which could result should the authorities not immediately and forcefully "remedy" the situation.[156] After his day-by-day account of the mission, he returned to this general discussion and characterized the disorders in Brest as the work of "enemies of the august Bourbon family" who want nothing less than "to excite hatred against the state religion and the government which protects it."[157] Having evoked the "revolutionary" aims of the men whom he had successfully arrested and placed in custody, Parison depicts the new battleground onto which they have transposed their struggle. He directly cites the documents being circulated by the defense attorneys of the accused and publicized by newspapers trying to "deceive France as a whole, and to excite other cities to reproduce the disorders recently experienced in Brest." [158] Here he referred to the two documents mentioned earlier: first, to the petition signed by many of Brest's notables (who, according to Parison, "show no respect for the color of our *Lys*") requesting the provisional liberty of those arrested until their trial; and second, to the denunciation deposed against the mayor of Brest and himself for their allegedly abusive conduct toward the citizens of Brest, in particular their illegal deployment of force against them in the theater on the 12th of October. In fact, Commissaire de Police Parison concludes his official report there, having evoked the stakes in this confrontation between the "enemies of the government," on the one hand, and the civil authorities determined to defend the "peaceful order which has reigned for 30 years" in France, on the other. He appended to his report, however, the full texts of these two documents, and in the margins offered a line-by-line response to the arguments of the defense attorneys. While his own direct negotiation with the theatergoers was over as of the 12th of October, he continued to respond meticulously to the arguments made on their behalf, not publicly in the *parterre*, but in the margins of the documents sent on to his superiors. As we now turn to the arguments made publicly in the courtrooms of Brest and, later, Quimper, and to the ultimate decisions of the judicial authorities, we will see how successful the "revolutionary" Tartufferie proved to be.

Tartufferie on Trial

When the accused were initially tried and condemned in January of 1827, it was not only for the crimes committed within the theater on the 12th of October, 1826, but for the whole range of disorders which took place from the beginning of the mission in early September to the outbreak of violence in the theater in October. Taken together, this wide range of anticlerical practices was interpreted as an overt and organized act of opposition to the government; the men charged were accused of having offended and having sought to undermine the state religion and the mission which the government had authorized; they were also charged with outrages against the local civil authorities, including both their verbal abuse and their threats and real use of physical force. Initially, the fourteen men were convicted of these extremely serious crimes. But over the course of the following two months arguments were

made in their defense which resulted in an appeal, and finally an acquittal for ten of the fourteen accused, and very lenient sentences for the
reduced crimes of the four men found guilty. Looking closely at the original court proceedings, and the initial framing of "Tartufferie" by the
prosecution, and following the different arguments proffered by the defense between January and March, we will see how in the particular context of Brest in 1827 a truly national "Tartufferie" was analyzed by its
supporters and used to insist upon certain key political principles and
rights and, in the process, to articulate some of the broader consequences of the struggles analyzed in previous chapters.

In the initial trial in Brest on the 12th of January 1827, the prosecutor adopted the approach suggested by Parison's narrative. The events in
Brest between the opening of the mission and October 12th were seen
as evidence of a "plot, formed in hatred for the religion of the state and
its ministers, and a seditious obstinacy in demanding the performance of
Tartuffe in spite of the well-known prohibition proclaimed by compe-
tent local authorities." [159] When laying out the specific charges against
the accused, the prosecution defined the terms of the struggle which
would take place in legal briefs and courtrooms for the following two
months. Several key principles were established. First, the prosecution
cited the Corcordat in order to justify the missionaries' presence in Brest
in 1826 and to establish the legal and official character of this religious
revival. [160] Second, they established a more general principle regarding
the proper and legal means of expressing opposition to such "official"
proceedings in order to define the "Tartufferie" in Brest as clearly outside the law.

> On the occasion of the authorized mission there erupted one of these tumul-
> tuous oppositions which, far from being constitutional, are evidently con-
> trary to all constitutions, since it is the nature of constitutional governments
> that if there is an opposition, this opposition can only manifest itself in the
> Chambers, which an individual can address, by means of petitions, either to
> rectify a wrong which resulted from a violation of the law, or in the name of
> the general interest; but that any open and tumultuous manifestation of op-
> position on the part of one or several individuals is essentially illegal, and
> tends to do nothing short of establishing a right which is monstrous and sub-
> versive of the social pact. [161]

Third, the court established that all of the seditious acts committed since
September (including firecrackers and stink bombs set off inside the
church, gatherings outside the church which mocked followers of the
mission, and the repeated demands for *Tartuffe* at the theater) demon-

strated the determination of the accused to "make guilty allusions to the missionaries in order to trouble public peace and excite hatred against a class of persons."[162] To justify this charge the prosecution cited the specific texts of the *billets* thrown on the stage at the theater which explicitly attacked the Jesuits and suggested their control over local civil officials. Fourth, the court argued that the authorities made themselves clear about the impossibility of permitting a performance in Brest, and that the insistence of the public on seeing this play on the 12th of October, and the fact that the disorder spilled over and extended to the church itself, was evidence of "a plot formed in hatred against the religion of the state and its ministers."[163] Fifth, it was asserted that violence was committed against the armed forces brought in to arrest the seditious parties and evacuate the theater; if the officers themselves committed any violence it was in order to defend themselves. Finally, the accused were charged with "publicly proffering insults against the Mayor of Brest and the Commissaire de Police, Parison, in the exercise and on the occasion of the exercise of their functions." In particular, the mayor was called a "*scélérat*" (scoundrel) and "an assassin of the people of Brest," and the commissaire de police, an assassin.[164]

For the original trial I do not have the full arguments made by the defense. A printed version of the "Judgment given during the course of the debates," however, offers some information about the tenor of this initial trial and the approach the defense adopted on behalf of its clients. Most important, the lawyers seem to have continued the "Tartufferie" of the accused in order to undermine the accusations of the prosecution. They consistently questioned the legitimacy of the missionaries in Brest and, in particular, the spectacular processions which (in their words) were nothing but an "insult to religion." They also sought to undermine the testimonies of the civil officials, making them out to be deceptive and intending to turn criticism onto the accused (who were part of a crowd of generous and good-natured men), when in fact it was their inappropriate and unjust use of force which was actually responsible for the violence on October 12th. The court regularly reprimanded the lawyers for their tone and their own injurious discourse against the state religion and the officers of the civil administration.[165] This is all we know about the opening salvos of the defense, aside from the fact that they were clearly a failure. After this first trial the court handed down stiff sentences to all of the fourteen men accused.

In the brief which they prepared in order to get an appeal, the lawyers for the defense developed their arguments with more precision. First, they began to undermine the court's presentation of the events in Brest as "an organized plot, a planned meeting of more than twenty armed men intending to threaten public tranquillity," by emphasizing the improvised and defensive posture of the accused. Second, they challenged the notion that the accused sought to incite hatred and organize opposition to a "class of persons." Here they adopted different tactics. First, they isolated the specific *billets* and cries in order to demonstrate that in calling the Abbé Guyon a Jesuit, and criticizing the Jesuits, the accused were merely stating facts that were constantly being presented in newspapers and pamphlets circulating in France. Second, they cited the various laws of the realm which hindered the actions of the Jesuits (a decree from 1804, the law of 1827, and the discussion of May 1825 which prohibited men's religious orders) and offered their own interpretation of the Concordat, which stressed the rights and the authority of regular priests to preach, but not those of outsiders, and especially Jesuits. They went on to make the kind of argument which civil officials all over France used as they tried to police the missionaries throughout the Restoration. In particular, they offered the following portrait of a group of unauthorized outsiders, illegally stepping outside their churches, troubling public tranquillity, and trying to extend their influence into a realm where it did not belong. "The ceremonies of the Jubilee could be performed only by the resident priests of Brest; one has the right to refuse to recognize the missionaries or the Jesuits who did not fulfill the formalities required by law." [166] What were these?

> The missionaries left the church; they orchestrated numerous outdoor processions in a city which has many Protestants; they preached in the streets and public square and caused trouble in families; they had a cross produced, without proper legal deliberations; they had it placed on a public thoroughfare, on communal land. . . . L'Abbé Guyon pressured the mayor to prohibit *Oedipus,* and convinced him to break his promise to the people regarding the performance of *Tartuffe.* [167]

Not only were the people in the theater *not* insulting and arousing hatred against a "class" in their demands for *Tartuffe,* they were criticizing only the unauthorized and illegal ceremonies of the missionaries on behalf of their legitimate priests. In short, "if there was provocation on the part of the [missionaries for exciting the hatred or distrust of them], all of the accused are innocent." Finally, they disputed the fact that a mere request for *Tartuffe* could be interpreted as incitement to hatred, arguing that "all comedies attack the vices of one class or another, and it would be impossible to perform any of them" if one accepted that the local authorities had the right to censor plays on this basis.[168]

Finally, the defense lawyers turned to the charge that the accused committed violent acts against the armed forces and verbally insulted the local authorities. Here, as with the arguments developed earlier, the defense would lay out its case more clearly at the trial in March; in this request for an appeal they established the basic principle that the accused were merely defending themselves against an unjust and brutal use of force. They cited the law and ordinance of 19 October 1820 forbidding the use of force when no "offensive resistance" has been made; and underscored the fact that in this instance military forces entered the theater and, without proper orders, began to "attack unarmed citizens who opposed them with only purely passive resistance."[169] Correspondingly, they argued that the defendants did not break any law when they challenged the authority of the mayor and the police commissioner. "The Magistrate," they explained, "has the right to respect and obedience whenever he speaks in the name of the law, and so long as he acts in accordance with the law, because in respecting him it is the law itself which one obeys." But, the lawyers continued, "If the magistrate forgets his duties, if he transgresses the law, if he compromises the safety of his citizens by orders given against the law, or not conforming to the formalities it presents, then the injury and the outrage lose their criminal character; they dwindle into simple reproaches; sometimes this reproach can be a civic act authorized by the law . . . ."[170] Here the defense lawyers laid out the arguments which formed the basis for their separate suit against the mayor and police commissioner. In particular, they cited the Martial Law of 1789, and the subsequent law and ordinance of 29 October 1820 for the gendarmerie, which requires that before deploying force, the mayor must three times formally invite the population to disband and stop resisting the authority. They offered to provide witnesses to prove that the mayor did not adhere to this formality required by law. The court had also contended, in its judgment, that the mayor never gave the order to attack the citizens of Brest and yet was injuriously called an "Assassin of the people of Brest." To this, the defense simply stated that if he never gave the order, it was still his responsibility to protect his citizens from such abuses. The mayor, "present at the moment of the tumult . . . should have, on the one hand, invited the peaceable citizens to clear the theater, and on the other hand, forbidden the soldiers from maltreating them."

The mayor, in not executing the law properly, is responsible for the events [of October 12]; the citizens, hit by butts of rifles and with their lives in real danger, had the right to address themselves to the one who had turned the armed forces against them, and to offer the most serious reproaches; it was at least excusable to do so, for they were in a posture of natural defense.[171]

The appeal was granted, the condemned men were temporarily freed while they awaited their new trial in Quimper, and during the two-month interlude the population of Brest treated them to a performance of *Tartuffe*, banquets and balls, while word of the case spread all over France thanks to the reprinting and distribution of the brief which won the appeal by the leading defense attorney, M. Duval. When the lawyers returned to the courtroom in Quimper in March of 1827, they were doing more than defending fourteen men; they were self-consciously defending the national outbreak of "Tartufferie" of which Brest was but a very good example. They made this eminently clear in their extensive pleas, which referred as often as possible to similar incidents elsewhere, and to the general principles being established in these and other kinds of struggles taking place all over France.

The lawyer Duval opened the proceedings with a long and heated defense of the rights of the people of Brest; in his detailed narrative of the negotiations between the theatergoers and the mayor of Brest, the defense attorney completely turned the prosecution's primary principle on its head. Far from "subverting the social pact," the opposition which developed in the theater between September and mid-October was the direct result of the mayor's breach of promise and illegal refusal to permit *Tartuffe,* and represented an effort on the part of the people to ensure the political order which the civil authorities were supposed to defend. The lawyer's narrative was prefaced by the statement that "Tranquillity reigned in Brest before the 3rd of September 1826, before the arrival of the Jesuit missionaries," and that it was restored immediately after their departure.[172] Having established that the missionaries were the real cause of the disorder, the lawyer laid out the principal facts in the case. He began with the statement that "during the course of September a right was exercised at the theater of Brest by the public which frequents it; *Tartuffe,* a play which is in the general repertoire, was demanded at different times." "This," he continued, "is the legal act which the judgment would turn into a crime, by imputing motives to its authors, and by linking this to acts committed outside of the theater."[173] Having successfully separated the demands for *Tartuffe* from the broader "Tartufferie" of which his clients were accused, Duval developed the main thrust of his argument. In particular, he established the fact that the first formal demand for *Tartuffe* was met with the following promise by the mayor of Brest: "This play is not in the repertoire for the week, but I will have it added." "Voilà the promise, and voilà its terms, voilà what six hundred people heard." Everything that happened between September and October 12 followed directly from the pact established between the audience and the mayor: "If the public insisted [in its demand for *Tartuffe*] it was because the mayor had promised it." The lawyer then went on to "prove" that if there was any trouble in the theater it was because the people came to understand that the mayor had forgotten or was reneging on his promise. The first evidence of this was given when the mayor explained that he had referred the decision to his superiors. "This was the first mistake, the first departure from a solemn promise." On the 8th of October the public demanded *Tartuffe* anew, and the police commissioner told the crowd, "the mayor will bring the response, and this response will satisfy you." A few moments later the mayor arrived and announced, "the authority refuses; the response is absolutely negative." [174] The effect was expected, not surprising, "the public was unhappy and expressed that." On the 9th, one saw the "same effort to obtain the promised play." On the 10th, "tired of refusals of the promised play," young men arrived, "each one with a little *Tartuffe* in his hand, and marched around in the middle of the *parterre* and produced uproarious laughter." [175] Duval underscored the fact that before the 12th of October, "there was neither posted, nor published, nor adopted any munipal *arrête* contrary to the promise given," and thus when the public arrived at the theater they expected to see the mayor's promise fulfilled. Duval's portrait of the night of October 12 is that of a public engaging in a peaceful negotiation with its administrators, trying to get them to acknowledge and satisfy the promise of the mayor. "That was the subject of great public speeches." These speeches were quickly ended by the introduction of force, foreign soldiers [a regiment of Hohenlohe] who spoke only German, who began to attack "without provocation." [176] Duval ended his account with the final breach of promise, when the mayor not only failed to allow *Tartuffe* but actually announced the closing of the theater on the 13th of October; the attorney entered the placard announcing this fact as vital evidence for the defense.

The next day (March 7th), Duval pursued a different line of argument, taken up by his colleagues in their subsequent pleas. This was to place the opposition to the Jesuits in a long historical context in which the people of Brest, in particular, had consistently shown themselves

willing to defend the city against the dangerous machinations of this illegal order. Interestingly, he did not refer back to the events in 1819,
when the people of Brest exerted their "general will" and chased the missionaries from town, but rather went back to a decree from 1703, when
the Parliament of Brittany responded favorably to a petition against Jesuits "troubling consciences by their speeches and sermons." [177]

On the same day, the second lawyer took the stand; M. Bernard
opened his plea with long and gracious praise for this tribunal which
had already accorded the accused provisional liberty and had shown itself to be "impartial" and determined to defend the law alone rather
than fall victim to "passions" and the all "too ardent zeal" which could
so easily have motivated the judge's decisions. At the end of his plea he
was even more direct in identifying the dangerous party who threatened
the law and the very foundation of the realm, and invited the judge to
consider his decision regarding the accused in light of his responsibility
to protect the people of France against this threat. In his words:

> At this moment, when all of our most precious rights are thrown into ques-
> tion, when one menaces the very pact on which our destinies depend, you
> have the power to calm the agitation which is felt all over France. You will
> join with the rest of our Magistrates, the hope of our nation, and with the
> high Chamber, to whom we already owe such gratitude. You will prove, at
> last, that if there is a dangerous faction, which is continually at war with our
> laws, there are at least judges who know how to deal with them.[178]

He ended his plea by offering a portrait of the effect produced by the
court's initial decision to hear an appeal, and provisionally free the fourteen accused men during the trial: "Did you hear the sounds of public
gratitude! They celebrate the justice of our sovereign so justly served!
The day of general reconciliation has arrived, and it will be because of
your work!" Thus, for the first time one of the defense team enlarged the
field of struggle to include the whole of France, and to directly acknowledge the war waged by the missionaries against the laws of the land, and,
borrowing their language of "reconciliation," asked the judge to ensure
this by deciding against the missionaries and for the defendants and
thereby protect the "very pact on which our destinies depend." [179]

The body of Bernard's defense was more narrowly conceived. He restricted himself to disproving, first, that by their repeated demands for
Tartuffe the accused tried to excite hatred against a class of persons; and
second, that they physically assaulted the soldiers of the Hohenlohe regime and verbally insulted the mayor in the exercise of his functions.
The latter charge he dismissed by quickly repeating the argument of

M. Duval as to the people having acted in legitimate self-defense. The lion's share of his plea was devoted to demonstrating that not only were his clients innocent of a vast plot against the state religion and the government, but they were, in fact, working on behalf of their government, and their religion, to put down the real plot which was afoot in France —that of the Jesuits. His presentation of this argument was masterful. He opened by inviting his audience to acknowledge that the issues presented in the case seem "so easy to resolve, at first view," and are attached to or mixed up with the great issues which agitate all spirits today, namely the questions of religious freedom and civil liberty." [180] While it would appear he was still talking about the crimes of which his clients were accused, the ambiguity quickly fell away. Recapitulating the initial judgment of the court of Brest in January, and evoking the interpretation which, as we saw, Commissioner Parison certainly applied to the opposition in Brest, the lawyer summarized the "plot" of which his clients were accused, and which he turned against the missionaries: "Hatred for the state religion, outrages against its ministers, the overthrow of religion, the triumph of the Revolution, these are the spirit, the means, and the aims of the authors of this plot." [181] He quickly warned the tribunal, "Believe me . . . you must be careful not to let yourself be carried away by words. The Revolution, always the Revolution. I see only two things: on the one side the unanimous spirit of the nation, reasserting its rights which have so long been disregarded, and on the other, the excesses of factions who step by step have been taking over power." Finally he exposed his real argument:

> If when one speaks with horror of this Revolution, one thinks only of the blood which flowed, we also turn our faces away from this horrible memory. But if we confound with these excesses that we all suffered, the sacred rights to which it gave rise, and then attacking it without end, we attack those very rights. So it is not merely the evils that it caused that we must discuss, but the good things of which it was the source which we still want. Let us try to forget the tears and blood which it produced and know how to protect its positive legacies. [182]

He continued to argue that the arrested men never sought to attack Catholicism but, rather, in their minor acts of opposition to the Jesuits in Brest, showed themselves to be part of a widespread movement to put down a plot to undermine precisely those positive legacies of the Revolution which the laws of the land are supposed to defend. In his words:

> In the ranks of the clergy, so worthy of our respect, slither members of a famous society, which has been working for more than a century, first in the

shadows, and now in broad daylight, to seize power, to resurrect its destroyed temples, to repossess among us the dangerous privileges which royal authority has taken away. Its goal is well-known. There is no mystery there. It proclaims that the Christian polity of France can be saved only with and by it. But at the same time it doesn't hide the fact that certain obstacles stand in its way, the most important of which is an immense public opinion which protests with terror against the rehabilitation of this society.[183]

It is to overcome this "resistance," he argued, that the Jesuits staged the missions of the type seen so recently in Brest. The lawyer did not explicitly allude to the specific legacies of the Revolution which the missionaries assailed, nor to the specific political order which their revival quite explicitly sought to resurrect. Instead, he restricted his arguments to the hated Jesuits, so easily cast as outside the law, being the real authors of "Revolution" which the tribunal in Quimper was to put down.

It is in this general context that he discussed his clients' demand to see *Tartuffe* in the theater during the course of the Jesuits' mission in Brest. Because this play could only be offensive to those priests who saw themselves represented by a character who is "a scoundrel, exploiting the mask of religion in order to deceive a benefactor," the accused were clearly not seeking to excite hatred against the entire clergy, or the Catholic Church, but only the Jesuits, and even then, only if those attending the performance "chose to seize the applicable lines, the allusions, each in his own manner." [184] At this point he repeated the argument of Duval: "what would become of our theater if we prohibited all plays which might excite hatred against a class? What profession, what class of society, from the lawyer of Bruey and the doctors of Molière, to the Marquis of Regnard, and the financiers of Lesage, have not been slain at the altar of the *parterre?*" [185]

Bernard concluded this lengthy plea by evoking the stakes involved in maintaining the judgment against the accused, in particular for the innocent and completely legal expression of their mere desire to see Molière's masterpiece in the theater. He took up the terms used by the prosecution, that the "opposition" manifested in the theater was illegal and subversive of the social pact, and (like Duval) turned it on its head: "One observation will suffice to make apparent how strange this doctrine is; that is that it forbids us to speak, and that it effaces from the Charter the right of all French citizens to publish their opinion." [186] He continued his argument by citing a recent publication by M. Cottu, Conseiller de la première Cour royale du royaume, "honored with the confidence of the government," which directly attacked the national missionary movement, and which he portrayed as threatening the very foundations on which the monarchy rests. "Did any one think to see [in this publication] the crime of exciting hatred against the clergy? And we, for having demanded *Tartuffe,* for this inoffensive act of opposition, for this fact so simple in itself, but transformed into a sort of sacrilege, we are pursued, accused of grave crimes, given rigorous sentences, and presented to our fellow citizens as criminals and authors of a plot tending to subvert the government. You will do justice to this cruel exaggeration." [187]

Continually narrowing the "crime" of which his clients were convicted from full-fledged, overt opposition to the priests and the state religion to the simple act of having asked for a masterpiece of Molière, the lawyer was able at the same time to evoke the enormous political struggles in which the nation as a whole was engaged. While he limited his main narrative to specific attacks against the dangerous and illegal Jesuits, by invoking the positive heritage of the Revolution, by citing M. Cottin's pamphlet which defended this heritage against the missionaries in general, and by appealing to the judges to act in defense of "our most precious rights," "the very pact on which our destinies depend," M. Bernard placed the seemingly minor offenses committed in Brest in the context of the vital political controversies of the Restoration. His colleague, M. Grivart, was even more overt, more self-conscious in his determination to elaborate the stakes involved in the judgment of the court he was addressing.

The final plea by M. Grivart, which began on the 10th of March, was conceived as a summation, and was proffered as a final response to the prosecution's case. In his opening salvo, this lawyer, like all his colleagues, employed the language and tactics of "Tartufferie" to undermine the court's position.

> After seeing the lively and profound impression which has been produced on the numerous and imposing audience by the eloquent pleas on behalf of the defense I though there would be little left for me to do; I thought my task would be neither long nor difficult; I thought that since I was so moved, so convinced, that the same conviction would have reached everyone, that it would have reached even so far as the prosecutor's bench: I was wrong; the prosecution has not backed off. What does it matter, Sirs, I'm not at all afraid to say, and out loud. Whatever their attitude, they are defeated. The attorneys for the condemned men have spoken, . . . they have said to you, "Look, look at what they pronounce against us!" They ripped up all the evidence, they threw it on the ground. The prosecutor then returned, and with a talent which we must permit ourselves to acknowledge, he picked up all the debris which he saw strewn all over the floor of the courtroom, he reunited it, re-

assembled it, and with great *art,* no doubt, he has even given it the form and the general air of a judgment; but this is but *a vain appearance.* There is really nothing there; the judgment is broken.[188]

The plea which followed this eloquent and artful preface was long, passionate, and apparently convincing, given the outcome of the trial. The argument, however, can be reduced to one simple point, elaborately and forcefully articulated: "The plot of which my clients are accused"—which is not limited to the theater, or even to Brest, but "which manifested itself at the same time in many points in the realm"—of what did it consist? How did it manifest itself? "Someone demanded Tartufe [*sic*] in Lille, in Lyons, in Brest. Is that all? Yes. . . . And that, that's a plot! . . . ."[189] For a response to this ironic and clearly rhetorical question, M. Grivart turned his audience's attention to the real plot threatening France, that of the Jesuits, "for whom religion is not an end, but a means"; for it is they who "threaten our security," who threaten the very legal foundation of the nation.[190] Not once after this initial evocation of the supposed plot of which his clients stood accused did the lawyer return to the events in Brest. Rather, the rest of his plea turned the judgment of the court into a decision in favor of or against the Jesuits and, more important, the Charter, which, he argued, was the sole protection which the French people (from Lille, to Lyons, to Brest) had against the Tartuffes. He concluded:

> The Charter, that is all we want, but we tremble that there are those who would ravish it. We have living among us men who work today in the shadows, but in a few days, perhaps in broad daylight, trying to chop down the very trunk of this sacred tree under whose shade France demands the right to rest. It was planted by one of our kings. His successor, in the name of God, placed it under his protection. Men of power, chase those who have sworn to ruin it; do not mistrust salutary warnings. France is agitated; irritated, yes, without a doubt; but if you wish to dissipate her alarm, calm her irritation, accomplish her wish, which is that of all peoples: constitutions, everywhere, Jesuits, nowhere."[191]

Theater as Politics

The fourteen men were either acquitted or given lenient sentences. Pamphlets publicizing the pleas of the defense attorneys were distributed and sold all over the country. What was their impact? What significance did this extraordinary defense and victory of "Tartufferie" have? I have not ended this chapter, or this part of the book, with the trial in Brest because I believe in itself it had any great impact; even if it did, it would be very hard, if not impossible, to measure or prove. Rather, I have concluded with this trial because it allows us to see how the national preoccupation with the clerical plot, exposed most cogently through the prism of *Tartuffe,* allowed a wide range of people "of both sexes and all ranks" (as the authorities so often remind us) to engage in a public, continuous negotiation with the government, outside the formal channels of government, about the capital political issues of the day. The very political struggles which were enacted in the correspondence between the church and state over the missions were replayed continuously in theaters, explained and justified in courtrooms, and at least tacitly condoned by the verdicts handed down by the judiciary system. The legal foundations for subjugating the church, honed by civil authorities as they tried to police the missions, were clearly articulated and enacted in public confrontations all over France. The legacy of the Revolution—and in particular, the secular, liberal principles on which the nation came to be constituted—was defended and increasingly embraced, not only by literate liberals directly engaged in official politics, but by the diverse practices by which people exposed and denounced the plot to subvert them.

But what can we say about the deeper crisis of legitimacy which I have been arguing "Tartufferie" exposed? By turning the theater not only into a carnivalesque reiteration of the missions, but of the political order itself, by exposing to criticism the "Jesuit-king" whose right to rule rested only upon the ability of appearances to deceive, did the theatergoers resolve the crisis of representation which I have argued was the most important legacy of the Revolution? Not entirely, and not yet. But I would argue that the politics of the theater laid the groundwork for such a resolution to emerge in France. The heightened sensitivity to theatricality, the obsession with the clerical plot, the extraordinary popularity of *Tartuffe* all bespeak a growing awareness of and anxiety about the fact that legitimate authority was no longer a given, but something that had to be constituted, fabricated. But to this political problem, the "opposition" developed an extraordinarily rich response, which would bear fruit in the long term. First, by their continuous evocation of the twenty-five-year interregnum which their regime would have had them forget, French men and women insisted upon the relevance and necessity of constituting the political order on the basis of ideals and laws and around emblems and practices which derived from the revolutionary period. Second, by protesting against the missionaries and, in particular, their effort to resurrect Christian monarchy, the people forced the state to develop tactics which would ultimately secure the secular and liberal basis of the political order. Third, by finding innumerable ways to practice politics in spite of the strictures of the official political system, the population insisted on its basic right to participate in the negotiation over the nature of this political order. Indeed, in very surprising contexts (struggles over mission crosses, or defenses of the right to demand *Tartuffe*), a resounding argument was made about the social pact itself being absolutely dependent upon just such a public and continuous negotiation. All this, I would argue, is the stuff out of which a resolution to the problematic "theatricality of politics" would emerge. If the obsession with the Jesuits and the clerical plot bespoke a desire for a kind of magical, *deus ex machina* type of resolution, which would simply purify the nation of the rot within, the practices invented in the context of the struggles of the Restoration allowed for a more complex legacy. They allowed the French to move beyond a simple denunciation of politics because it was "theatrical," because it did not allow "transparency" to reign; they offered many new ways for the population both to express itself and to get beyond its anxiety about this new reality of modern political life.

Conclusion

My restaging of the Restoration sheds new light on the Revolution of 1830 and the July Monarchy which it brought to power. Like the Restoration, although for different reasons, the Revolution of 1830 has been understudied by comparison with the Revolution of 1848. For a long time, the Three Glorious Days, which successfully and rapidly exchanged the Bourbon King Charles X for the Orleanist King Louis-Philippe, have been treated primarily as a Parisian phenomenon, which could be explained by the political events immediately preceding July 1830, and which had minimal long-term political consequences. Charles X's July Ordinances, which signaled a rejection of the basic rules of constitutional monarchy and the freedoms associated with the Charter, have been seen as sufficient to explain the rejection of the Bourbons, although some inquiries into the propaganda wars since 1825 and the social and economic crises of these years have helped historians to explain the temporary coalition between political elites and the masses which made the Revolution possible.[1] Pamela Pilbeam summarizes the literature on 1830 and explains that very basic assumptions precluded a more extensive analysis of either the origins or the consequences of this event. Historians on the right have tended to depict the July days as a dangerous, but ultimately contained, resurgence of the revolutionary spirit of 1789, or as an unfortunate accident linked to Charles X and his ministers' miscalculations in 1829 and 1830; meanwhile, historians on the left, as seen most clearly in Marx's own writings on the nine-

teenth century, have characterized the Revolution of 1830 as a failed
bourgeois revolution which offered little real hope for political or social
changes for the masses of the nation. Whatever the reason for their interpretation of this event's insignificance, the result has been a historiography that largely ignores the long-term conflicts which were played
out between 1830 and 1848, which have their origins in the Restoration, many of which took place outside of Paris.[2]

Pilbeam's own analysis of 1830 represents a welcome rethinking of
the Revolution: her book takes seriously the political unrest which shook
the whole nation during and after 1830, and tries to find antecedents and
explanations for the events of these years in the history of the Restoration. While her study includes an extensive analysis of the social and economic causes and consequences of the Revolution of 1830 as well, it is
her attention to the anticlerical dimension of popular protest after 1830
that moves in the direction which my own interpretation of the Restoration suggests. In particular, Pilbeam tries to make sense of the repeated
violent attacks on mission crosses between 1831 and 1834, which she in-
terprets as part and parcel of this Revolution. Her efforts to understand
these expressions of popular anticlericalism sent her back to the Restoration. Rather than merely considering the Ordinances of 1830 which
precipitated the Three Glorious Days in Paris, she argues that to understand the broader political opposition which emerged during the Restoration one must go all the way back to 1815. In a chapter entitled "The
Political Crises of the Bourbon Restoration," she offers an interpretation
which is complementary to my own restaging of the Restoration.

The crises she highlights are those key political events which transformed the practices of official politics, and which primarily affected the
small fraction of the population actively engaged in the administration
of the nation or electoral politics. The White Terror of 1815 is the first
crisis she considers, a crisis which she argues left "a legacy of imprisonment, summary justice, including murder and the subsequent exclu-
sion from public office of Bonapartist partisans of the Hundred Days,
robbing the new king of a vast array of experienced officials." Echoing
the argument made forcefully by Robert Alexander in his study of the
Fédérés during the Restoration, she reminds us, "It is no accident that
victims of the White Terror were often the leaders of both the liberal opposition in the 1820s and the Revolution of 1830."[3] The second crisis
she discusses arose from the murder of the duc de Berry in 1820, which
precipitated an emotional backlash which, "although less violent than
the White Terror, allowed the Ultra minority to trim the constitution

more to their taste."[4] Here Pilbeam focuses on the changes in electoral laws which gave the wealthiest quarter of the population a second vote. The years between 1820 and the next political crisis of 1827 are depicted by Pilbeam as a period when Bonapartism and republican ideals became blurred, and were articulated in a series of failed conspiracies hatched within the Carbonari, studied previously by Alan Spitzer.[5] Anticlericalism was a dimension of this growing opposition to the Bourbon monarchy, and it is in this context that she briefly evokes the Missions to the Interior, as well as the clerical policies of the regime pursued after 1825 (the law indemnifying émigrés and especially the Sacrilege Law). The final crisis of the regime which Pilbeam underscores was precipitated by another modification in electoral procedure. Between 1827 and 1829 electoral practices shifted once again, when prefects and especially the episcopacy became involved in campaigning and actively controlling elections in favor of the king's men, the ultraroyalists. The clerical dimension of this shift is stressed by Pilbeam, who here emphasizes the pronounced social elitism which dictated clerical appointments during the Restoration. The clergy, which was enjoined to work for the election of ultraroyalist candidates in the last years of the Restoration, were led by an episcopacy which was uniformly noble (the older and more senior the better), devoted to the principles and social order of the Old Regime, and explicitly opposed to the Revolution of 1789 and its legacy. The political machinations of Charles X in 1829 and 1830—the dissolution of the Parliament and the ordinances of 1830—are thus presented as the last in a series of acts which proved that the regime was defined by an unquestionable alliance between the king, the Ultras, and this counterrevolutionary episcopacy, which was utterly opposed to the principles of constitutional monarchy. For Pilbeam these "crises" explain the gradual emergence of a growing elite opposition to the monarchy which led it to support a revolution, even though its goals and basic predilections were hardly "revolutionary"; it also explains the anticlerical dimension of protest after 1830.

Her rendering of the anticlerical protests between 1831 and 1834 focuses primarily on the wave of violent attacks on mission crosses which immediately followed the Revolution of 1830 and on the struggles which were precipitated by the government's efforts to force the clergy to incorporate prayers for the new king into their regular liturgy. She highlights the role of a memorial ceremony for the duc de Berry, organized by legitimists against the wishes of the new government, in precipitating widespread anticlerical violence; thus she connects the wave of violence from 1831 to 1834 to the second political crisis of 1820. But most important, she underscores the degree to which church-state struggles constituted a fundamental aspect of the Revolution of 1830, and looks at shifting government policies regarding the mission crosses, the prayers for the king, and the changing nature of the episcopacy after this revolution to demonstrate this.

My rendering of the Restoration and the Revolution of 1830 dovetails beautifully with Pilbeam's, although it differs in certain critical respects. The struggles between church and state, which she sees being played out in the post-1830 period, were equally significant in the context of the Restoration. She does not deny tensions between altar and throne during the Restoration, but my emphasis on the differences between the missionaries and the regime, and the ensuing struggles throughout fifteen years over the missions, offers a long-term perspective for appreciating the struggles she highlights in the post-1830 period. After the Three Glorious Days, when the regime commenced negotiations with the clergy over the fate of mission crosses and the proper representation of the regime within their temples, it was not a departure from, but a continuation of, previous practices. After the Revolution of 1830, mission crosses, sprinkled throughout the kingdom, became the emblems of counterrevolution par excellence and served as rallying points for both extremes of the political spectrum. In response to the potential and real disorder they inspired, the government once again turned to its prefects and their staffs, as well as to the archbishops and their subordinates, to work out an approach to these religious and eminently political emblems.

In the years immediately following the Revolution of 1830, mission crosses became the focus of violent attacks and fierce struggles between competing political factions.[6] Supporters of the new regime destroyed existing crosses and replaced them with liberty trees and monuments to the Three Glorious Days.[7] Others simply defaced the crosses, leaving no clear evidence of their political agendas. Some civil officials transferred the crosses to the interiors of local churches as a deterrent or, in the case of an actual attack, announced their intention to do so. Meanwhile, defenders of the crosses staged demonstrations to denounce civil officials responsible for the removal of crosses or to enlist the support of local governments in the prosecution of "troublemakers" responsible for their destruction. As was true for the missions themselves during the Restoration, a national policy regarding what to do with these symbols of legitimate monarchy emerged piecemeal in response to complaints about specific incidents all over the country. Once again, civil and ecclesiastical officials negotiated the fundamental question of the state's jurisdiction in religious matters. And once again, in the interest of maintaining "order," the government ultimately gave the upper hand to civil officials. The policy of the regime was to avoid a general ban on crosses; rather, it was left to local civil authorities—in consultation with ecclesiastical authorities—to determine whether or not removing them was politically necessary.

In response to individual efforts to remove crosses, the ecclesiastical officials of the July Monarchy invoked the persecution of 1793, threatening that such actions would send priests in the Vendée back to the *bocage* (woods) and would spread fears among the population that the government was once again supporting an attack on religion.[8] The bishop of Belley, for example, expressed his concern to the minister of ecclesiastical affairs that the people in his region would immediately expect the government to come in and destroy the church bell towers, as they had in 1793, if they learned of the regime's intention to remove the local mission crosses.[9] Such allusions to the worst persecution of the Revolution were more frequent after 1830, when the regime was clearly less sympathetic to the church than it had been during the Restoration, but as we have seen in the correspondence from prelates in chapters 2 and 3, they were not new.

They became more vociferous, however, as the July Monarchy tried to enforce its policy of requiring priests to say prayers for Louis-Philippe in the context of their regular devotions.[10] Likening this demand to the oath required of priests during the Revolution, clergymen all over France tried to avoid adding the name Ludovicum Philippum to the *Domine Salvum* usually included in masses. Some priests defied the new regime, continuing prayers for Charles X as if the Revolution of 1830 had never happened. Others simply mumbled the part of the prayer that included the king's name, making it impossible for the congregation to know where they stood. Popular protests greeted priests whether they defied or abided by the new law. As the regime used its prefects, subprefects, and mayors to enforce the saying of this prayer, it honed the tactics once deployed to control the missionaries during the Restoration. Everywhere civil officials checked up on the clergymen in their jurisdiction, employing police spies when the latter objected to the obvious presence of police officials in their churches.[11] Correspondence about local priests went via Paris and represented efforts on the part of ecclesiastical and civil officials to negotiate their rights in religious affairs.

The approaches the July Monarchy adopted to mission crosses and to prayers for the king show it to have been a regime that continued to revolutionize church-state relations in the manner of its more reactionary predecessor. In 1830, crosses did not have to be razed as an ideological gesture against a powerful political opponent (as they had been in 1793). Rather, the selective and respectful transferral of mission crosses to the interiors of churches were the actions of a pragmatic regime interested in maintaining social peace. In this respect the regime pursued the same moderate goals that had set the state against the church during the Restoration. But in its determination to force priests to say a prayer for the king as a part of their regular services, the regime went further than its predecessors. Not content to intervene in the exceptional ceremonies of traveling missionaries, the regime now insisted on its right to alter the regular liturgy of the Catholic church. Here the July Monarchy mimicked Napoleon, who had required such prayers; it then used the former emperor's administrative structures, well oiled throughout the Restoration, to enforce them.

Pilbeam's analysis of the clerical policies of the July Monarchy further substantiates and strengthens my interpretation of the anticlerical character of this regime. In her discussion of the episcopacy of the postrevolutionary period, she argued, "The age of the noble-cleric was over; the bourgeois-bureaucrat bishop had arrived. Louis-Philippe, predictably, chose far less socially-elevated bishops and concentrated on individuals with a proven record as efficient administrators. Increasingly the episcopacy took on the character of the religious arm of the bureaucracy." [12] But again, this shift makes more sense when considered in light of the extensive negotiations with, and efforts to discipline, the missionaries during the Restoration; the regime's frustrating efforts to discipline the missionaries quite naturally led to the effort to replace an intransigent church hierarchy with a group of men willing to act as the "religious arm of the bureaucracy."

The other, more fundamental difference between my understanding of the Restoration and Pilbeam's, which also has important ramifications for making sense of anticlerical protest after 1830, regards the way in which we conceive of the clerical problem in relation to politics, and especially popular political expression. Rather than seeing the clerical problem in terms of high politics, I have focused on the Missions to the Interior and the degree to which they engaged the broader population in a protracted struggle over the nature of the sacred. This led me to consider a broader repertoire of political practices which involved more of the population, and which help to explain the fears of a clerical plot, the characterization of Charles X as a Jesuit-king, and the growing unpopularity of the regime. This allows me to explain the popular support for the Revolution of 1830 in a way that does not need to rely on propaganda campaigns from the center or from above. This also offers a long *durée* in which to understand the anticlerical violence against mission crosses between 1831 and 1834, and the determination to resurrect liberty trees in their proper place, which sent Pilbeam back to the Restoration in the first place. These expressions of popular anticlericalism beg for an analysis of the sort I have attempted for the Restoration, one that would discuss them in terms of the general political problem still critical in the context of the July Monarchy, namely resolving the crisis of legitimacy from which this postrevolutionary monarchical regime continued to suffer.

Another recent book on the Revolution of 1830 points in this direction. In his *Forest Rites: The War of the Demoiselles in Nineteenth-Century France,* Peter Sahlins shows us how the rites of charivari and carnival were deployed by the *demoiselles* of the Ariège to defend ancient rights and practices associated with the forest; in his reflection on the Revolution of 1830, however, he argues that this "language" of popular festive protest was transposed to the national bourgeois scene after 1830. As evidence for this shift, he cites the carnivalesque tactics and "language" which infused the illustrated bourgeois periodicals *Le Charivari* and, later, *La Caricature,* as well as the tendency of youthful middle-class opponents of the *juste-milieu* to adopt the specific practices of festive protest as they orchestrated charivaris and mock serenades in provincial cities after 1832.[13] For Sahlins (unlike most historians of nineteenth-century France), the July days represented a key political turning point precisely because the peasants of the Ariège adopted the national language of revolutionary liberty in their ancient struggles over the forests, while the middle class turned to the codes of popular culture to oppose the July Monarchy. "The parallel use by peasants and middle-class republicans of the respective languages of protest," he writes, was made possible by "the dissolution and reconstitution of the political order during and after the July Revolution. . . . The July Revolution opened up a space and a time in which the language and practices of the political underwent an important and enduring transformation."[14]

My analysis of the Restoration supports Sahlins's emphasis on the importance of the popular language of the carnivalesque and the degree to which this came to be integrated into a national, bourgeois political discourse. He does a masterful job of portraying 1830 as a critical turning point because, as his evidence of the increasingly "political" significance of charivari and of the new illustrated *Charivari* and *La Caricature* make clear, this transposition had reached new levels by 1832. However, I would argue that to explain this shift one must turn back to the Restoration, and consider the many practices both of popular anticlerical protesters using the traditional tactics of charivari and carnival and of the adaptation of this "language" in national political protests, particularly, although not exclusively, in the context of the theater. In his final chapter, Sahlins cites reports from the later 1820s in which prefects commented on the increasingly widespread tendency to rely upon carnivalesque tactics in disputes with missionaries and local officials. In this sense, he clearly points in the direction of the argument presented in this book. But the applicability and relevance of the "carnivalesque" after 1830 can be even more fully understood by thinking about the religious revival against which it was most consistently deployed and the crisis of legitimacy besetting any monarch who tried to assert his right to rule in the wake of the French Revolution. The missionaries of the Restoration played a critical role in "politicizing" the festive language of protest and turning it into the perfect vehicle for defending the "liberal and secular values" that Sahlins shows the peasants of the Ariège deployed by 1830. In other words, the missionaries become the critical missing piece which helps us understand the long-term process by which Ozouf's "transferral of sacrality" from the revolutionary decade was finally accomplished, first during the Restoration and then, as Sahlins has shown, with greater vigor during the July Monarchy. But the carnivalesque mode of criticizing the regime clearly also bears a resemblance to that of the Restoration period, which I would argue is related to the fact that both the Restoration and the July Monarchy were faced with the impossible problem of representing the king as natural, as legitimate, in the wake of the Revolution. The "Jesuit-king," Charles X, is clearly an early incarnation of the "bourgeois-king," Louis-Philippe, impossible and illegitimate precisely because he was fabricated, because his identity, his authority, and the basis for his rule were open to question. Indeed, another direction in which my work points, and which the more recent work of Jo Burr Margadant already pursues, is the problem of representing monarchy in this period within this assumed crisis of representation. In her effort to chart the "Family Romance" of the Orleanist Louis-Philippe, Margadant has demonstrated how much we have to learn about this period by applying the insights and approaches of Old Regime cultural historians to the images, scandals, and ceremonial innovations of the nineteenth-century monarchs.[15]

The Revolution of 1830, like the July Monarchy as a whole, should be studied together with, rather than in opposition to, the Bourbon Restoration. Both regimes were defined by the crisis of legitimacy which was the primary legacy of the French Revolution. There is extraordinary continuity both in the practices adopted by the successive regimes to deal with this problem and in the repertoire of practices by which the population as a whole participated in bringing about its resolution. My way of conceptualizing the "unofficial politics" of the Restoration could be usefully extended to the July Monarchy as a whole, when the majority of the population was still formally excluded from politics but nonetheless increasingly participated in ways which had serious political and ideological consequences. Both periods must be inserted into an analysis which tries to understand the emergence of democracy in France, not only because they represented "institutional apprenticeships" in parliamentary democracy, but because the practices of the ruling authorities (the church and the state) and the population at large allow us to appreciate the struggles through which the transition from monarchy was finally achieved. Such an analysis also allows us to appreciate the particularities of French history which emerged from these struggles: the importance of popular anticlericalism, and the peculiar blend of republicanism and Bonapartism which defined democratic ideology, and which enabled the Republic of 1848 to become the Second Empire of 1851.[16] Most important, I believe that such an approach allows us to understand how France came to be constituted on an entirely new political foundation or, in other words, how ideologies were invented and secured through the practices of everyday life. While such an approach clearly demands that we integrate "reactionary" periods like the Restoration into any analysis of the emergence of democracy in France, it also suggests that we move away from big political events (such as the Revolutions of 1830 and 1848) and major institutional changes (like the creation of universal suffrage) and instead attend to the manifold and surprising practices and venues through which the key ideological issues of the day were exposed and worked out.

Implicit in my rendering of the Restoration is a way of approaching the study of politics which contributes to current debates among historians about the benefits of cultural history in a discursive mode. My mainly political analysis of the Restoration rests entirely upon an inter-

pretation of a wide range of cultural practices: the ceremonial and commemorative practices of a regime trying to assert its claim to rule in spite
of the previous twenty-five years; the ritual and symbolic practices of
Catholic missionaries staging a spectacular national revival throughout
the fifteen years of the Restoration; and the wide range of practices by
which the men and women of France confronted the representatives of
the state and the clerics, and in the process participated in the complex
negotiation over legitimate authority which I argue constituted the political culture of the years between 1815 and 1830. My theoretical claim
is that an analysis of material, historically contingent cultural practices
holds the key to reconciling many of the contradictions and tensions
which seem to trouble cultural history. In particular, I would argue that
a focus on cultural practices allows us to identify coherent systems of
meaning, while at the same time insisting upon conflict and struggle.[17]
While such an approach privileges understanding the logic which governs a wide range of practices, it need not abandon the quest to understand causality, nor suffer from the erasure of the human subject and human agency.

In my analysis of the competing commemorations favored by the
state and the missionaries, I have emphasized the coherent visions which
defined them and placed these two pillars of the Restoration in opposition. However, because I derive my broad frameworks of *oubli,* as opposed to expiation, from the actual practices of local officials and missionaries, I have also been able to demonstrate the degree to which
improvisation was continually involved in the orchestration of monarchy. In other words, it should be clear that perfect *oubli* and perfect expiation were never actually enacted or accomplished, but that they represented poles in a struggle which did shape the terrain in which the
population was, in way, incited to negotiate with its civil and ecclesiastical officials over the future of France's political order. Likewise, while
I have emphasized the fact that one can see a certain coherence in
the anticlerical protests against the missionaries, that they represent a
struggle over the sacred which goes back to the struggles of the revolutionary decade, I am certainly not arguing that everyone who protested
against the missionaries was actually defending a secularized conception
of monarchy, or that they were all necessarily attacking a sacred conception of the monarch tied to the Eucharist. But I am arguing that perhaps their intentions did not matter, that whatever their reasons were
for crushing Hosts in churches, disrupting the missions, attacking mission crosses, or expressing concern about the identity and authority of

their king, it can be shown that there was a pattern to this web of oppositional practices, and that identifying that pattern helps us to understand critical ideological dilemmas of the postrevolutionary period.[18] It also helps us to understand very concrete institutional changes in the relationship between the church and the state which took place during the Restoration and which hitherto have been ignored.

Likewise, to argue that one can see coherence in the "Tartufferie" of the post-1825 period is not to claim that everyone who participated in a theater riot, or defaced a coin of the realm, or wore a tricolor watchband was consciously expressing anxiety about the crisis of representation suffered by the regime, and turning to the theaters to resolve the problems of modern democracy. But thinking about diverse practices deployed for all kinds of reasons in terms of a coherent discourse does allow us to understand certain problems faced by this regime and the July Monarchy, and it also permits us to appreciate how a very broad cross section of the population participated in transforming and consolidating key legacies of the French Revolution. In other words, it allows us to consider the problems associated with political theory, not as they developed in the writings of elite political actors directly engaged in the process of writing constitutions, or reflecting on contemporary politics, but as they were confronted and defined through the practices of everyday life.[19]

My discursive analysis of the cultural practices of the Restoration does not abandon the quest to understand causality, nor need it deny the human subject or human agency. To be sure, by focusing on cultural practices I am putting an analytical emphasis less on the agents of history than on their actions and particularly the material traces of them to which we have access in the archives. Yet my focus on such material practices helps me to include in my narrative a broad range of actors hitherto ignored in political histories of the Restoration, in spite of my admission that their identity (their specific social class or sex) and their intentions are less important to me than their practices. Here, I believe, I am following a long tradition, especially of early modern cultural Marxist historians who, borrowing the tools of structural and symbolic anthropology, have focused on rituals and practices of popular culture as a way of integrating various dispossessed groups—peasants, workers, women—back into a history in which they participated and helped to negotiate.[20] If a cultural history focused on practices expands the historical stage to include actors previously excluded from our narratives, it also forces us to widen our understanding and analysis of the political, and to imagine various arenas where ideological struggles and

innovations took place. Here my debt is more clearly to poststructural-
ists, who have helped us to think about the past in terms of broader webs
of signification in a way which eschews a hierarchy of economic, political, and cultural levels. But this need not lead us to abandon all hope of
making arguments about causality.

I may have no unified framework for explaining causality—Marxist,
liberal, or otherwise—but because of my focus on material, historically
contingent practices, I can certainly make arguments about change over
time, about causes and consequences. The practices of the sort I am analyzing have a history which can be traced and within which they must
be situated. The church and state had been struggling over the constitution of legitimate public authority for many centuries. The Revolution
of 1789 fundamentally transformed that struggle in ways which can
be clearly demonstrated. The radical counterrevolutionary agenda and
practices of the missionaries, the more moderate practices of their supposed allies in the state, and the many practices by which men and
women protested against both are all tangible pieces of evidence which
allow me to make new arguments about the political legacy of the
French Revolution during the Restoration. Because of my "openness"
regarding sources of conflict, the basis for historical change, I found
"causality" in surprising places—in the religious revival of the missionaries, for example.[21]

In the end, I suppose I am announcing the "comic" ending which
Lynn Hunt predicted in 1986 in her discussion of the future of cultural
history; at that time she foresaw the "reconciliation of all contradictions
and tensions in the pluralist manner most congenial to American historians."[22] That wouldn't be surprising coming from an author who sees
Tartuffe as a reasonable way to make sense of history. But I hope I have
made it clear that such a "comic" ending is no simple matter, but requires a certain kind of cultural history, one that remains attentive to
material, historically contingent cultural practices. But it may also be
that this approach to doing history is particularly fruitful for periods
which, like the Restoration, are defined by a crisis of legitimacy. I can
insist upon conflict and struggle over coherence, and political agency
and innovation precisely because the Restoration was a period when
so many of the cultural and political "givens" were open to question.
Whether I borrow the language and insights of Pierre Bourdieu and talk
about ideology or habitus, or turn to Gramsci's notion of hegemony, I
am talking about a moment in history when, far from being "natural-
ized" by the practices of everyday life, such practices served both to

challenge an older, apparently arbitrary, even fraudulent, order and to constitute a new, more desirable one.[23]

One example from Bourdieu will suffice to demonstrate the peculiar condition of "crisis" which characterized the Restoration. In his *Outline for a Theory of Practice,* Bourdieu used the example of the school-teacher to explain how it is that the dominant social order is reproduced. He argues that this occurs "not so much by the teacher speaking 'ideologically' to the students, but by the teacher being perceived as in possession of an amount of 'cultural capital' which the student needs to acquire. The educational system thus contributes to reproducing the dominant social order not so much by the viewpoints it fosters [by its teachers] but by this regulated distribution of cultural capital."[24] In the Restoration, whether we consider the missionaries, local government officials, or the king himself, it is clear that merely reproducing the dominant order was impossible precisely because these authority figures were no longer assumed to be the arbiters of that order or, in Bourdieu's language, they were no longer vested with "cultural capital." Indeed, precisely because of their questionable authority, the viewpoints and practices they encouraged became the focus of struggle, which had tangible consequences. Precisely because the "givenness" of monarchy and the power and authority of the church were no longer accepted, but suspected of being arbitrary and fraudulent, cultural practices which might have served to legitimize or consolidate power became the means of negotiating and constituting a new order.

Similarly, rather than following Gramsci and thinking primarily about the ways in which a governing power wins "consent" for its rule from those it subjugates, and thereby consolidates its power, I have accented the whole arena of culture, defined in the broadest everyday sense, in which changes in that order were negotiated throughout the Restoration.[25] If I have taken pains to elaborate the realm of "unofficial politics," it was to insist upon the innovative capacity of cultural practices to transform and ultimately constitute a new public sphere which grew out of the struggles of the revolutionary era.[26] My account of the struggles of the Restoration goes beyond imagining cultural practices as merely reactive; the wide range of practices of the state and the missionaries, and the men and women who protested against them, paved the way for the new political order which would be consolidated over the course of the nineteenth century.[27]

If my way of approaching the Restoration illustrates some of the benefits which a cultural history of "practices" has to offer to historians in general, my approach to the problem of commemoration, in particular, may be useful to the growing number of scholars interested in this historical problem. My insistence on looking for and taking seriously competing commemorations, in this case of the church and state, represents a direction in which historians of commemoration already appear to be moving. Particularly historians of the twentieth century, who are confronted with commercial commemorations which clearly undermine the official narrative offered by the state, have been forced to conceptualize the politics of commemoration in these terms.[28] However, my emphasis on the "improvisational" nature of commemorations, even when orchestrated by modern states, would undermine some of the apparently "totalitarian," or at least hegemonic, consequences which historians assume derive from national commemorations in the age of mass politics.[29] My efforts to understand the reception of the commemorative efforts of the church and state, and the degree to which the audience's oppositional practices were determined by these national spectacles, and how these in turn affected the performances of the missionaries and their state officials should be useful in this regard.

For those interested in commemoration in general, this study of the Restoration identifies certain narrative strategies which have reappeared repeatedly in history when regimes (and established churches) have been confronted with the problem of dealing with revolutionary events. In the Restoration I have identified two primary narratives—the politics of *oubli* of the regime, which depends upon forgetting past historical events in order to ensure a certain future, and the politics of expiation, which insists upon remembering, confessing, and expiating for past historical sins in order to make possible another kind of historical future. These modes are by no means peculiar to the Restoration within French history, nor to France more generally. In France itself, "forgetting" was quite clearly adopted immediately after the fall of Vichy; and "expiation" could be adopted by secular republicans, as was clear after the Commune, when the expiatory Sacré Coeur was erected, and especially later in the Fourth and Fifth Republics when expiation regarding the Vichy past came to be seen as the only way to ensure France's republican future.[30] Outside of France similar modes have been adopted for dealing with painful historical events. Unlike the way in which the Restoration regime handled the regicides of 1793, the regicide in England was represented by the restored Stuart monarchy according to an expiatory narrative. Charles I was represented as the martyr king in exactly the way the missionaries represented the Bourbons.[31] The contemporary era offers endless fascinating examples of "forgetting" and "expiating" the painful past. In 1989 the regimes of Eastern Europe attacked the problem of their respective revolutions by different versions of forgetting and expiating, and, more recently still, the government of South Africa created its truth commissions, and offered a particularly amazing example of expiation being practiced in an organized, bureaucratic mode.[32]

It was the men and women of France who took to the theaters in the 1820s who turned my study of the Restoration into an analysis which could be of interest to other historians working in any number of times and places where, as with the Restoration, the emergence of democracy became tangled up in and expressed most clearly in the politics and rhetoric of the theater. Returning now to the place where I began—taking my cue from *Tartuffe*, and especially from the two cartons of police reports evoking the ways in which the theater became the primary forum for negotiating politics in the 1820s—I will conclude with a reflection on the usefulness of theatricality for understanding the emergence of democracy, and not just in France.

When Marx wrote his account of the Revolution of 1848 in France, the theatrical metaphor was absolutely critical to his understanding of this historical event. Opening with Hegel's remark "That all facts and personages of great importance in world history occur, as it were twice," Marx noted, "He forgot to add: the first time as tragedy, the second as farce." [33] Going on to make his famous statement, "Men make their own history, but they do not make it just as they please," he immediately reverted to the language of theater to explain the constraints which limit men's actions: ". . . precisely in such periods of revolutionary crisis [men] anxiously conjure up the spirits of the past to their service and borrow from them names, battle cries, and costumes in order to present the new scene of world history in this time-honoured disguise and this borrowed language." [34] Jean-Christophe Agnew's study of market and theater in Anglo-American thought offers one important perspective from which to understand Marx's preoccupation with theatricality in the mid-nineteenth century. For Agnew, Marx was but the most famous of a long line of writers who had expressed their anxiety about the new social relations associated with capitalism by drawing attention to the falseness and hypocrisy of the world around them.

Agnew traces the history of the relationship between the market and the theater, demonstrating how in actual theaters, in the drama of the seventeenth through the nineteenth centuries, but also in the writings of political economists of the same period, the discourse around theater

flourished. In the seventeenth century, when the innovations of capitalism were most troubling, "theatricality" was applied to the social world
in negative terms: "theatricality itself had begun to acquire renewed
connotations of invisibility, concealment, and *mis*representation, connotations that were at once intriguing and recriminating." [35] Looking at
the literature of social instruction in the sixteenth and seventeenth centuries, Agnew found that authors heightened their readers' suspicions of
fraud and facetiousness in the world around them, even as they offered
the means of protecting themselves against it. "The popular handbooks
acknowledged the onset of a national, if not global, crisis of representation, one wherein traditional social signs and symbols had metamor-
phosed into detached and manipulable commodities. Copyholds could
be tested in the courts, but where was the tribunal that could try the
'copies' men and women made of their countenances?" Agnew continued: "The playwrights' answer was, of course, the stage, and in a sense
their contemporaries agreed, for not only did the former seize upon the
problem of social representation and misrepresentation as the theme
and touchstone of their drama, but their audiences, equally perplexed by
the fluidity of social relations, used the idiom of the theater to frame the
problem for themselves. 'Man in business is but a Theatricall person,
and in a manner but personates himselfe,' the poet John Hall wrote,
adding that 'in his retired and hid actions, he pulls off his disguise, and
acts openly.'" [36]

If the sixteenth- and seventeenth-century handbooks and drama expressed anxiety about theatricality, Agnew, like Richard Sennett before
him, finds the eighteenth century to be a period when the theatrical perspective "recovered its appeal for the literate classes not because it re-
called the ritual entreaty to a divine order, but because it implied the
conventional fabrication of a secular order." [37] No longer bent on "pulling off the disguise," the theatrical metaphor now "reappeared in literary circles of this epoch," "to serve poets and philosophers, bent on domesticating the somber legacy of its meaning. In their hands, a metaphor
long used to question the very foundation of perception came to be incorporated within a general philosophical outlook that, by the latter
half of the eighteenth century, could proudly call itself Common Sense.
Like so many other aspects of culture in that time, the deconstructive
practices of the theatrical perspective were restrained and recast in a
more manageable form; it too, was 'settled,' albeit imperfectly and im-
permanently." In short, Agnew argues that this preoccupation with theatricality allowed for "a socio-cultural accommodation with an expan-

sive system of capital formation in commodity exchange. In these years the theater became a laboratory of and for the new social relations of agricultural and commercial capitalism"[38]

If Agnew's analysis of the relationship between emergent capitalism and the preoccupation with theatricality offers one critical perspective on the explanatory and narrative power of theatricality for Marx's analysis of the Revolution of 1848, the political transformations highlighted in this book offer another. Just as the natural, divine order of things appeared to be corrupted or unmoored by the transformative power of capitalism, so in the same period was the political order undermined. As the "givens" of the absolutist political order came under attack—the sacrality of the king, the absolute union of altar and throne in the constitution of a Most Christian King and kingship—the metaphor of theatricality emerged initially to express anxiety about this new situation; but, as with the discourse of market and theater, that of politics and theater also eventually made accommodation to the new realities of political life possible.

In the late seventeenth century, when Molière wrote his *Tartuffe* for the court of Louis XIV, it was to flatter a monarch whom most people accepted as legitimate; yet the play offered a critical language of theatricality which could and would be turned against the monarch over the course of the eighteenth and nineteenth centuries, as social and political changes served to weaken the foundations upon which monarchy was built. As with the transformations wrought by the rise of capitalism, the struggles between the church and the state, the rise of a critical enlightened discourse imagining a contractual rather than a divine basis for the political order, and changes in popular practices associated with both the church and the state served to make the negative discourse of theatricality relevant as a way of expressing anxiety about the dilemma of legitimate political authority. In the eighteenth century, Saint-Simon, Montesquieu, and, later, Rousseau all extended the theatrical metaphor to analyze and criticize the world around them.[39] By the end of the century this critical perspective on monarchy helped to fuel a revolution, but one that was itself destined to see the political dilemma facing France in terms of the critical discourse on theatricality. As Lynn Hunt has shown, the rhetoric of conspiracy permeated revolutionary political culture; imbued with the same obsession with the gap that could separate private intentions from public appearances, this led revolutionaries to reject conventional politics in the name of the higher ideal of transparency. It was precisely because of their "ambivalence toward organized politics, especially in the form of parties and factions, [that] new symbols and ceremonies became the most acceptable medium for working out political attitudes . . . the revolutionaries' passion for the allegorical, the theatrical, and the stylized was not simply a bizarre aberration, but rather an essential element in their effort to mold free men."[40] In the particular context of the French Revolution, where tradition had "lost it givenness" and where the revolutionaries "found themselves acting on Rousseau's conviction that the relationship between the social and the political (the social contract) could be rearranged," theatricality served both to express anxiety about this unprecedented political reality and to shape the specific practices which defined the Revolution and its legacy.[41]

When the Bourbons were returned to the throne in the nineteenth century it is hardly surprising that the idiom of theatricality would be turned against them or their supporters in the Catholic church. The Revolution had proven that no natural or divine order existed, but that the political order could be constructed according to various ideologies. Yet the state and the church sought to unmake this critical legacy either by returning the king's subjects to a world where ideology did not exist through the politics of forgetting, or by encouraging French men and women to repent, confess, and thereby resurrect Christian monarchy. Both efforts served only to underscore the crisis of legitimacy faced by the monarchy in these years, and provoked protest not only in a theatrical idiom but in real theaters, around Molière's eminently germane *Tartuffe*.

The practices by which men and women protested against the church and state during the Restoration continued to express anxiety about the theatricality of politics, but they also served to accommodate French citizens to this reality of modern political life. The direct attacks on missionaries for their theatricality, and the obsession with the clerical plot clearly illustrate that theatricality was still being deployed in a negative, critical way. The king was potentially illegitimate precisely because he seemed to rule by deception; while he appeared to be a Bourbon king, it seemed he was really just a front for "Tartuffes" who in fact were ruling in France. In Rouen, *Tartuffe* was demanded and became the focus of a month-long protest because it enabled the people of this town to expose the local clerical plot and restore the proper order of things (in which priests did not "rule in the theater as well as the church," in which a prefect did not ban performances because he was under the thumb of the archbishop, in which the king himself would step in and allow Molière's play against the wishes of the local "Tartuffes"). When defending the fourteen men accused in the theater incident in Brest, the defense attorney likewise invoked the language of plots and conspiracies, although it was to identify the real threat to France's future—the Jesuits. But by the 1820s the people of France had made strides toward accommodating themselves to the theatricality of politics; rather than rejecting political authority as illegitimate simply because it was theatrical, the men and women of France developed a set of practices which enabled them to come to terms with this new fact of modern politics.

In an age in which official political participation was limited to the one in 360 men who could vote, anyone—man or woman—could go to the theater and clamor for a performance of *Tartuffe* or disfigure the coinage of the realm, and thereby encourage their fellow citizens to be vigilant in their identification of legitimate authority. But they could also traffic in symbolic seditious objects, and thereby use these material reminders to keep alive the very real ideological alternatives to monarchy which they would soon insist become the basis of their political order. In the context of *Tartuffe* incidents, critics of the missionaries adamantly asserted the audience's right to shape the action on the stage—both in the "mission" and in the "spectacle." In short, the men and women of France used the theater and the wide range of tactics I have called "Tartufferie" to expose (and thereby condemn) the theatricality of politics, as well as to articulate the ways in which they could control the theater which politics had become. Whether by determining which play was performed in any one theater at any one time or place, or by using this theater to force the other spectacle—that of the missionaries—out of town, or by insisting on the role they were to have in identifying and defining legitimate authority right up to their king, the people of France made tentative steps toward resolving the regime's crisis of legitimacy.

That the "Tartufferie" of the 1820s was a key turning point on the road to modern democratic politics is testified to by the theatrical perspective not only of Marx in 1852, but also of other political figures from this period, who saw not only the theater, but particularly Molière, as critical for understanding the events transpiring around them. In 1847, Baron Isidor Taylor, a key political figure from the 1820s through the 1870s and an active organizer of artists, put together an extraordinary collection of documents which he published at his own expense under the title *Scenes Imitated from the Works of Molière*.[42] This collection contains clippings from major national newspapers from the years between 1832 and 1835, each of which offers a rewrite of one or another scene from Molière's plays, recast with historical figures and allusions from the Revolution of 1830 and its aftermath. The majority of these imitations are adaptations of the most popular scenes from *Tartuffe*. In 1850, J. Cénac-Moncaut published *Before and During,* a work that features two imitations of Molière—this time *The Doctor in Spite of Himself* and *The School for Husbands/Wives*—to make sense of the events "before" the Revolution of 1848, or 1847, and "during" the Revolution itself. These rewrites of Molière, entitled *The Police Commissioner in Spite of Himself* and *The School of Deputies,* offer a full-scale recasting of the events of the Revolution of 1848 through the prism of Molière's comedies. Cénac-Moncaut argues in his preface that "if Molière were alive today . . . he would have applied his satire regarding doctors to the ambitious political man . . . . and he would have improvised his portrait of the jealous tutor to represent parliamentarians." He continues, "We have therefore applied to two contemporary subjects the thoughts, the forms, and even the expressions of Molière."[43] A year later, George Sand penned a play improvising on the life of Molière and arranged for it to be performed in one of the theaters of the boulevard, precisely so that it could have a positive political influence on the popular classes.[44]

Marx was but one of many authors who after 1848 saw the theater as critical for making sense of the social and political changes wrought by recent events. But like Baron Taylor, who was inspired by imitations of *Tartuffe* flourishing in the press in the 1830s, and George Sand, who made reference to the critical role Molière's comedies and the politics of the theater played in shaping France's destiny, Marx may very well have relied on the theatrical metaphor because so many French men and women had actively turned the theater into "a laboratory of and for the new cultural and political relations of modern democratic politics."[45]

France in the 1820s was hardly the only context in which the theater and the theatrical metaphor played a key role in negotiating the shift to a democratic political culture. Historians of the American Revolution have long highlighted the heightened sensitivity, even "paranoia," regarding the theatricality of politics in the early republic; more recently, they have begun to underscore the more positive role which theaters, festivals, the symbolic, and the allegorical actually played in resolving political dilemmas in these years.[46] In so many contexts the theater has been critical to expressing anxiety about the breakdown of a traditional political order, but also in the accommodation and constitution of a new, more democratic one. A recent article on Vaclav Havel and the revolution in Czechoslovakia suggests just one famous example of this: "It was intensely symbolic that the Civic Forum, the movement that led the Velvet Revolution, was born, and Czech democracy reinvented in a theater."[47] Symbolic? Certainly. Surprising? Not really. The two cartons of police documents which inspired this book help us to see why it was perfectly fitting that Molière's *Tartuffe,* used to flatter and promote absolute monarchy in the seventeenth century, would be the perfect vehicle for bringing about its ultimate demise in the 1820s. But the men and women who took to the theater in those years, and inspired the police to collect this precious evidence, allow us to understand why the theater would become the perfect venue for negotiating the complex transition to democracy in France and elsewhere.

Notes

Introduction

1. Karl Marx is only the most famous writer to have cast French history in particular in these terms, when he took Hegel's notion that all facts and personages of great importance in world history occur, as it were, twice, and added, "the first time as tragedy, the second time as farce," and then used this theatrical metaphor to analyze Louis Napoleon's "farcical" reenactment of his uncle, Napoleon. *The 18th Brumaire of Louis Bonaparte* (New York: International Publishers, 1963), p. 1. Based on an 1869 translation from the 1852 original.

2. Jean Baptiste Poquelin de Molière, *Tartuffe*, trans. Richard Wilbur (New York: Harcourt, Brace & World, 1961), p. 11.

3. Ibid., pp. 161–62. Following Colin Jones's suggestion, I have changed Wilbur's translation slightly: he translated "fraude" as sham, and I have retained the more direct "fraud" because of its importance to my argument.

4. Geoffrey Cubitt, *The Jesuit Myth: Conspiracy Theory and Politics in Nineteenth-Century France* (Oxford: Clarendon Press, 1993); Réné Rémond, *L'Anticlericalisme en France de 1815 à nos jours* (Paris: Fayard, 1976).

5. Archives Nationales (hereafter AN), F7 6693, dossier Rouen, song and placard included with letter from the Prefect of the Seine-Inférieure to the Minister of the Interior, 7 May 1825.

6. Molière, *Tartuffe*, p. 162.

7. Ibid., p. 161.

8. Preface to Molière, *Tartuffe* (Paris: Baudouin Frères, 1825), pp. 4–5, signed "C. L."; attributed to Claude Langlois in other versions.

9. Peter Burke, *The Fabrication of Louis XIV* (New Haven: Yale University Press, 1992).

10. Molière, *Tartuffe*, p. 121.

11. The history of Molière's play is treated in Henri D'Alméras, *Le Tartuffe de Molière* (Paris: SFELT, 1946). Two previous versions which did not contain the fifth act were banned. The play lived a sort of shadow existence, being performed and read in the homes of nobles. But it was not until Molière added the fifth act that the play was approved for performance at court.

12. Roger Chartier summarizes these arguments in chap. 6 of his *The Cultural Origins of the French Revolution,* trans. Lydia G. Cochrane (Durham, N.C.: Duke University Press, 1991).

13. Lynn Hunt, *Politics, Culture, and Class in the French Revolution* (Berkeley: University of California Press, 1984).

14. Louis Marin, *Portrait of the King* (Minneapolis; University of Minnesota Press, 1988); Marin's general argument about the functioning of a eucharistic model of kingship under the reign of Louis XIV is summarized in Chartier, *Cultural Origins,* pp. 128–30.

15. Mona Ozouf, *Festivals of the French Revolution,* trans. Alan Sheridan (Cambridge, Mass.: Harvard University Press, 1988), esp. the conclusion.

16. Guillaume de Bertier de Sauvigny's general study, *La Restauration* (Paris: Flammarion, 1955) is the most widely used analysis of this period. It is absolutely typical in the degree to which high politics, changing ministries, and shifts in the balance of power between ultraroyalists and liberals dictate the entire narrative of the period. Other "political" histories which conceptualize the period in similar ways and restrict their analysis to institutions and key national figures include Pierre de la Corce, *La Restauration: Louis XVIII* (Paris: Plon, 1926); Vincent Beach, *Charles X of France* (Boulder, Colo.: Pruett, 1971); Jean Fourcassié, *Villèle* (Paris: Fayard, 1954); works on parliamentary democracy/constitutional monarchy which include the Restoration: Felix Ponteil, *Les Institutions de la France de 1814 à 1870* (Paris: Presses Universitaires de France, 1966) and *La Monarchie parlementaire, 1815–1848* (Paris: Colin, 1949), and Paul Bastid, *Institutions politiques de la monarchie parlementaire française, 1814–1881* (Paris: Sirey, 1954); works which focus on the history of the press as fundamental to politics: Irene Collins, *The Government and the Newspaper Press in France, 1814–1881* (London: Oxford University Press, 1959) and Charles Ledré, *La Presse à l'assault de la monarchie, 1815–1848* (Paris: A. Colin, 1960).

17. Alan Spitzer, *The French Generation of 1820* (Princeton, N.J.: Princeton University Press, 1987); Jonathan Beecher's biography/social/intellectual history, *Charles Fourier: The Visionary and His World* (Berkeley: University of California Press, 1986), along with Spitzer's work, does a beautiful job of evoking this period among this group of men participating in a certain intellectual/political milieu. Stanley Mellon, *The Political Uses of History: A Study of Historians in the French Restoration* (Stanford, Calif.: Stanford University Press, 1958); Françoise Parent-Lardeur, *Les Cabinets de lecture: La lecture publique à Paris sous la Restauration* (Paris: Payot, 1982); Edgar Newman, "The Blouse and the Frock Coat: The Alliance of the Common People of Paris with the Liberal Leadership and the Middle Class During the Last Years of the Bourbon Restoration," *Journal of Modern History* 47 (March 1974): 26–59.

18. Robert Alexander, *Bonapartism and Revolutionary Tradition in France: The Fédérés of 1815* (Cambridge: Cambridge University Press, 1991). This excellent book innovates in its attention to the transformation of left-wing ideologies (in particular the merging of Bonapartism and republicanism) as a result of the confrontations of this period.

19. Alan Spitzer's *Old Hatreds and Young Hopes: The French Carbonari Against the French Restoration* (Cambridge, Mass.: Harvard University Press, 1971) focuses on the subversive French Carbonari; Daniel P. Resnick's *The White Terror and the Political Reaction after Waterloo* (Cambridge, Mass.: Harvard University Press, 1966) looks at popular acts of retribution as well as the legal repression which followed the Hundred Days; similarly interesting, but limited in scope, is Gwyn Lewis's "The White Terror of 1815 in the Department of the Gard," *Past and Present* 58 (1973): 108–35, which considers the same period in the context of the age-old religious conflicts between Protestants and Catholics in the Gard.

20. Réné Rémond, *L'Anticlericalisme en France de 1815 à nos jours* (Paris: Fayard, 1976); Newman, "The Blouse and the Frock Coat"; Mary S. Hartman, "The Sacrilege Law of 1825 in France: A Study in Anticlericalism and Mythmaking," *Journal of Modern History* 44, 1 (1972): 21–37; J. Michael Phayer, "Politics and Popular Religion: The Cult of the Cross, 1815–1840," *Journal of Social History* 11, 3 (Spring 1978): 346–65. The last article does look at popular acts of violence against the mission crosses, but in and around the Revolution of 1830.

21. Patricia Pilbeam, *The Revolution of 1830 in France* (New York: St. Martin's Press, 1991) and Peter Sahlins, *Forest Rites: The War of the Demoiselles in Nineteenth-Century France* (Cambridge, Mass.: Harvard University Press, 1994) will be discussed at length in the Conclusion, where the Revolution of 1830 is treated.

22. Bertier de Sauvigny's *La Restauration* includes separate chapters on "religion," and in these he treats the Missions to the Interior; but they are never integrated in a serious way with a discussion of "politics" because, as the chapter entitled "La Vie Politique" makes clear, politics is defined in very narrow terms as the institutions of government (see esp. pp. 268–99); almost all histories of the Restoration, particularly those which take anticlericalism seriously, allude to the missions; however, until now no one has done a thorough *political* analysis of this national revival. Geoffrey Cubitt's *The Jesuit Myth: Conspiracy Theory and Politics in Nineteenth-Century France* (Oxford: Clarendon Press, 1993) argues that the missions were central for understanding the rise of anti-Jesuitism, which had profound political consequences (including the fall of the regime in 1830); but even in this rendering, which clearly dovetails with my interpretation, the missions occupy not the foreground but the background, with the most important discussions focused on the debates in the legislature, the press wars, and debates over popular pamphlets such as the work of Montlosier. Currently completing a dissertation at Princeton University, Maria Riasanovsky will shed new light on this understudied revival. For the prehistory of this worldview, already circulating among the antiphilosophes of the eighteenth century,

see the dissertation and work of Darrin M. McMahon, *Enemies of the Enlightenment: The French Counter-Enlightenment and the Birth of the European Right, 1778-1830* (forthcoming, Oxford University Press). The theater incidents are the focus of a couple of short articles: Alain Corbin, "L'Agitation dans les théâtres de province sous la Restauration," in *Popular Traditions and Learned Culture in France from the Sixteenth to the Twentieth Century,* ed. Marc Bertrand (Stanford, Calif.: Stanford University Press, 1985) and Paule Salvan, "Le Tartuffe de Molière et l'agitation anticléricale en 1825," *Revue de la Société d'Histoire du Théâtre* (1960): 7-19; otherwise they are invoked, like the Missions to the Interior, to give a general sense of anticlericalism, as in Remond, *L'Anticlericalisme,* or of anti-Jesuitism, as in Cubitt, *The Jesuit Myth,* pp. 286-90.

23. Ernest Sevrin, *Les Missions religieuses en France sous la Restauration, 1815-1830,* vol. 1: *Le Missionnaire et la mission* (St. Maudé: Procure des Prêtres de la Miséricorde, 1948) and vol. 2: *Les Missions, 1815-1820* (Paris: Librairie Philosophique J. Vrin, 1959). This author was very sensitive to the political aspects of the missions, but he also took great pains to distinguish the spiritual agenda of the missionaries from the rather secondary, and what he saw as their unfortunate, political content and consequences. Thomas Kselman, *Miracles and Prophecies in Nineteenth-Century France* (New Brunswick, N.J.: Rutgers University Press, 1983); Michael J. Phayer, "Politics and Popular Religion: The Cult of the Cross in France, 1815-1840," *Journal of Social History* 11, 3 (Spring, 1978): 346-65. Phayer's work clearly addresses the political aspects of the missions, but focuses mainly on the fact that the crosses came to be signs of legitimacy and the return to the Old Regime; moving in the direction of my interpretation, he emphasizes the lack of national coherence in the individual acts of violence against crosses before 1830, and does not put these incidents in the context of other anticlerical practices which I consider. Martyn Lyons, "Fires of Expiation: Book-Burnings and Catholic Missions in Restoration France," *French History* 10, 1: 1-27, looks primarily at book burning in the context of the missions, using some of the archival materials which are featured in my analysis of the missions.

24. Again I am referring to Pilbeam, *Revolution of 1830* (interested in anticlericalism) and Sahlins, *Forest Rites* (interested in carnivalesque practices), both of which are addressed in the Conclusion.

25. Emmanuel de Waresquiel and Benoît Yvert, *Histoire de la Restauration, 1814-1830: Naissance de la France moderne* (Paris: Perrin, 1996); Pierre Rosanvallon, *La Monarchie Impossible: Les Chartes de 1814 et de 1830* (Paris: Fayard, 1994). The title of the first part of the latter book illustrates my point perfectly: "The Charter of 1814 and the Apprenticeship in Parliamentary Government" (my translation).

26. One important exception to this would be the dissertation of E. L. Newman, "Republicanism During the Bourbon Restoration in France, 1814-1830" (Ph.D. dissertation, University of Chicago, 1969), as well as his two articles which do seek to find aspects of the republican legacy in the context of the Restoration: "Republicanism," in *Historical Dictionary of France from the 1815 Restoration to the Second Empire* (New York and Westport, Conn.: Greenwood

Press, 1987), and "Lost Illusions: The Regicides in France During the Bourbon Restoration, 1815–1830," *Nineteenth-Century French Studies* 10 (1981–1982): 45–74. Likewise, the recent work of Robert Alexander, *Bonapartism and Revolutionary Tradition in France: The Fédérés of 1815* (Cambridge: Cambridge University Press, 1991), looks at the political opposition during the Restoration in order to understand the blurring of Bonapartism and republicanism as liberalism during this period.

27. André-Jean Tudesq, *Les Grands Notables en France (1840–1849): étude historique d'une psychologie sociale.* (Paris: Presses Universitaires de France, 1964).

28. Isser Wolloch, *The New Regime: Transformation of the French Civic Order, 1789–1820s* (New York: Norton, 1994).

29. For a discussion of the general shift in the direction of "political culture" in studies of both the Old Regime and the French Revolution, see the introductions to the first two volumes of *The French Revolution and the Creation of Modern Political Culture:* Keith Michael Baker, introduction to vol. 1: *The Political Culture of the Old Regime* (Oxford: Pergamon Press, 1987), pp. xi–xxiv; and Colin Lucas, introduction to vol. 2: *The Political Culture of the French Revolution* (Oxford; Pergamon Press, 1988), pp. xi–xvii.

30. *The French Revolution and the Creation of Modern Political Culture,* François Furet and Mona Ozouf, eds., vol. 3: *The Transformation of Political Culture, 1789–1848* (Oxford: Pergamon Press, 1989), p. xvii. This surge of interest in political theory as a historical problem in France has produced scholarly publications on the subject as well as new editions of the original writings of early-nineteenth-century political thinkers. Pierre Rosanvallon's *Le Moment Guizot* (Paris: Gallimard, 1985) is one of the most impressive contributions from this group of historians/political theorists who were grouped primarily at the Centre Raymond Aron in Paris, where Furet and Ozouf regularly conducted seminars on related topics.

31. Edward Berenson, author of *Populist Religion and Left-Wing Politics in France, 1830–1852* (Princeton, N.J.: Princeton University Press, 1984), contributed "A New Religion of the Left: Christianity and Social Radicalism in France, 1815–1848," and William Sewell, Jr., author of *Work and Revolution in France: The Language of Labor from the Old Regime to 1848* (Cambridge: Cambridge University Press, 1980), contributed "Beyond 1793: Babeuf, Louis Blanc and the Genealogy of 'Social Revolution'," both of which are in Furet and Ozouf, eds., *The Transformation,* pp. 543–60 and pp. 509–26.

32. Réné Rémond's *The Right Wing in France from 1815 to De Gaulle* (Philadelphia: University of Pennsylvania Press, 1966) is an older example of the right wing being studied as a whole, which has been brought up to date by the recent multivolume series, *Les Droits françaises De la Revolution à nos jours,* sous la direction de Jean-François Sirinelli (Paris: Gallimard, 1992). As we shall see below, it is primarily the republican tradition which has been studied in this way, with periods when the right returned to power being ignored. One excellent book which demonstrates the critical role of the Restoration period in cementing the popular counterrevolutionary tradition of remembering the Revolution in the West is Jean-Clément Martin, *La Vendée de la mémoire (1800–*

1980) (Paris: Editions du Seuil, 1989). See especially chap. 3, "La société du souvenir, 1815–1830."

33. This is an allusion to the most recent volume of Maurice Agulhon's study of the symbol of the republic, Marianne, which begins in the Third Republic and is entitled *Marianne au Pouvoir: L'imagerie et la symbolique républicaine, 1880–1914* (Paris: Flammarion, 1989); the first volume, which treated this key symbol from the Revolution to the Third Republic, appeared in 1979, and in an English translation by Janet Lloyd as *Marianne into Battle: Republican Imagery and Symbolism in France, 1780–1880* (Cambridge: Cambridge University Press, 1981).

34. Rosamonde Sanson, *Les 14 Juillets, fêtes et conscience nationales, 1789–1975* (Paris: Flammarion, 1976); Rita Hermon, "Fêtes révolutionnaires, fêtes républicaines une tradition retrouvée," *Nouvelle Revue Socialiste* 53 (1981): 42–56.

35. Pierre Nora, ed., *Les Lieux de Mémoire,* vol. 1: *La République* (Paris: Gallimard, 1984), which includes Raoul Girardet, "Les trois Couleurs"; Bronislaw Baczko, "le Calendrier républicain"; Michel Vovelle, "La Marseillaise"; and Maurice Agulhon, "Le 14 juillet." The article by Girardet on the tricolor does mention (p. 19) that this symbol was popularized by the Restoration's adoption of the white flag, but the analysis still focuses largely on periods when the tricolor was in power.

36. Agulhon, *Marianne into Battle,* p. 37.

37. Françoise Wacquet, *La Fête royale sous la Restauration, ou l'Ancien Regime retrouvé* (Geneva: Groz, 1981), my translation.

38. Anne M. Wagner, "Outrages: Sculpture and Kingship in France after 1789," in Ann Bermingham and John Brewer, eds., *The Consumption of Culture, 1600–1800: Image, Object, Text* (London and New York: Routledge, 1995), pp. 294–318; Elisabeth Fraser, "InCivility: Eugène Delacroix and the Private History of Romanticism," unpublished manuscript.

39. For a beautiful discussion of this wave of writing in France, which involves the works of Maurice Agulhon, André Armengaud, Alain Corbin, and Philippe Vigier, among others, see the introduction to Berenson, *Populist Religion,* pp. xiv–xvii.

40. As Berenson noted, both Agulhon and Vigier were also interested in political issues, but were not interested in the interplay of national political organization and ideology, on the one hand, and local politics, on the other—a subject which has been more central for American historians of France.

41. Charles Tilly, "How Protest Modernized in France, 1845–1855," in W. Aydelotte, ed., *The Dimensions of Quantitative Research in History* (Princeton, N.J.: Princeton University Press, 1972), pp. 192–255.

42. Ted W. Margadant, *French Peasants in Revolt: The Insurrection of 1851* (Princeton, N.J.: Princeton University Press, 1979).

43. Berenson, *Populist Religion.* Not all historians agree that this integration had made significant strides this early. Eugen Weber's *Peasants into Frenchmen: The Modernization of Rural France, 1870–1914* (Stanford, Calif.: Stanford University Press, 1976) argues that the modernization and "civilizing" of France's isolated rural society did not take place until between 1870 and 1914;

Michael Burns, in *Rural Society and French Politics: Boulangism and the Drey-fus Affair, 1886–1900* (Princeton, N.J.: Princeton University Press, 1984), looks at the Boulanger Affair and the Dreyfus Affair to show that national events were received unevenly at the local level in the late nineteenth century.

44. I would add here the interesting works of Peter McPhee, "The Seed-time of the Republic: Society and Politics in the Pyrénées-Orientales, 1846–1851," *Australian Journal of Politics and History* 22 (1976): 196–213, "Popular Culture, Symbolism, and Rural Radicalism in Nineteenth-Century France," *Journal of Peasant Studies* 5 (1978): 238–53, and the extensive discussion and bibliography on the Second Republic he offers in his *Social History of France, 1780–1880* (London: Routledge, 1992), as well as the articles in Roger Price, ed., *Revolution and Reaction: 1848 and the Second French Republic* (London: Croom Helm; New York: Barnes and Noble Books, 1975). Also Ronald Gosselin, *Les Almanachs Républicains: Traditions révolutionnaires et culture politique des masses populaires de Paris (1840–1851)* (Paris: Editions L'Harmattan, 1992).

45. Susanna Barrows, "Laughter, Language, and Derision: Seditious Speech and Popular Political Culture in Mid-Nineteenth-Century France," unpublished manuscript, p. 4; her forthcoming work on this period will help to fill in this eerie silence.

46. Margadant, *French Peasants in Revolt,* p. 335.

47. John Merriman, *The Agony of the Republic: The Repression of the Left in Revolutionary France, 1848–1851* (New Haven and London: Yale University Press, 1978).

48. Maurice Agulhon, Gabriel Désert, and Robert Specklin, *Histoire de la France Rurale,* vol. 3: *Apogée et crise de la civilisation paysanne, 1789–1914* (Paris: Editions du Seuil, 1976); this quotation comes from a section written by Agulhon, pp. 143–45 (my translation).

49. Alain Corbin, "L'Agitation dans les théâtres de province sous La Restauration," in Marc Bertrand, ed., *Popular Traditions and Learned Culture in France from the Sixteenth to the Twentieth Century* (Stanford, Calif.: Anma Libri, 1985), p. 112, n. 86.

Introduction to Part I

1. Ernst H. Kantorowicz, *The King's Two Bodies: A Study in Medieval Political Theology* (Princeton, N.J.: Princeton University Press, 1957).

2. Ibid., p. 196.

3. Ibid., pp. 196–97.

4. Ibid., p. 196.

5. Ernst Kantorowicz, "Mysteries of State: An Absolutist Concept and Its Late Mediaeval Origins," *Harvard Theological Review* 48 (January 1955): 90, citing Simon of Tournai.

6. Kantorowicz, *The King's Two Bodies,* p. 197.

7. Kantorowicz, "Mysteries of State," p. 91.

8. Rogier Chartier discusses Bloch's work in *The Cultural Origins of the French Revolution,* trans. Lydia G. Cochrane (Durham, N.C.: Duke University Press, 1991), p. 121. Also explained in Jeffrey W. Merrick, *The Desacralization*

of the French Monarchy in the Eighteenth Century (Baton Rouge: Louisiana State University Press, 1990), p. 17, who includes the formula intoned on such occasions, which made manifest the relationship between God and his earthly Prince: "The King touches you; God heals you."

9. Kantorowicz, "Mysteries of State," quoting Lucas de Penna, p. 81.

10. Ralph E. Giesey, *The Royal Funeral Ceremony in Renaissance France* (Geneva: Librairie E. Droz, 1960), p. 189.

11. Ibid., p. 190.

12. Ibid., p. 191.

13. Ibid., p. 192.

14. Summarized in Chartier, *Cultural Origins,* pp. 124–27. See also Sarah Hanley, *The lit de justice of the kings of France: Constitutional ideology in legend, ritual, and discourse* (Princeton, N.J.: Princeton University Press, 1983).

15. Michel Fogel, *Les Cérémonies de l'information dans la France du XVIe au milieu du XVIIIe siècle* (Paris: Fayard, 1989), p. 243; cited in Chartier, *Cultural Origins,* pp. 127–28.

16. From Chartier, *Cultural Origins,* citing Michèle Fogel, "Propagande, communication, publication: points de vue et demande d'enquête pour la France des XVIe–XVIIe siècle," in *La Culture et l'idéologie dans la genèse de l'Etat moderne. Actes de la table ronde organisée par le Centre de la recherche scientifique et l'Ecole française de Rome, Rome, 15–17 October 1984* (Rome: Ecole française de Rome, 1985), pp. 325–36, statistics on pp. 328–29. Chartier lists the number of *Te Deums* celebrated over time, p. 128: "Although it was used in Paris to celebrate victories only rarely before 1620, there were eighteen such occasions between 1621 and 1642, twenty-two during the minority of Louis XIV, eighty-nine between 1661 and 1715, and another thirty-nine between 1715 and 1748."

17. Chartier, *Cultural Origins,* p. 131.

18. Chartier, *Cultural Origins;* both information about Versailles and its decoration and quotation from Edouard Pommier, "Versailles, l'image du souverain," in Nora, *Les Lieux de mémoire,* vol. 2, p. 213. Also see Peter Burke, *The Fabrication of Louis XIV* (New Haven, Conn.: Yale University Press, 1992), for a discussion of this transformation, which also emphasizes the criticism to which it exposed the monarchy once events failed to conspire to glorify the person of the king.

19. Chartier, *Cultural Origins,* p. 133, where he summarizes his own "From Ritual to the Hearth: Marriage Charters in Seventeenth-Century Lyons," in *The Culture of Print: Power and the Uses of Print in Early Modern Europe,* ed. Roger Chartier, trans. Lydia G. Cochrane (Princeton, N.J.: Princeton University Press, 1989), pp. 174–90.

20. Louis Marin, *Portrait of the King* (Minneapolis: University of Minnesota Press, 1988), p. 13. Marin's analysis is summarized in Chartier's discussion in *Cultural Origins,* pp. 128–30.

21. Marin, *Portrait of the King,* p. 285. Marin relates his own elaboration of the eucharistic model of kingship from Kantorowicz's "Two Bodies of the King" in the following way, p. 15: "To prolong in all modesty the work accomplished by Kantorowicz for the Middle Ages, my study would propose the following

hypothesis for 'classical' absolutism: the king has only one body left, but this sole body, in truth, unifies three, a physical historical body, a juridico-politico body, and a semiotic sacramental body, the sacramental body, the 'portrait,' operating the exchange *without remainder* (or attempting to eliminate all remainder) between the historical and political bodies."

22. Chartier, *Cultural Origins*, on pp. 131–32, has a very useful discussion of the effectiveness of monarchical authority at its height, drawing upon the work of Pierre Bourdieu as well as Louis Marin. The quotations here are taken from p. 132.

23. Merrick, *Desacralization of the French Monarchy*, p. 1. The following discussion is based on the first two chapters of Merrick's book.

24. Cited in Merrick, *Desacralization*, p. 7.

25. Ibid., p. 8.

26. Ibid., p. 28.

27. Ibid., pp. 32–33.

28. Ibid., p. 43.

29. Chartier, *Cultural Origins*, p. 103.

30. Merrick, *Desacralization*, p. 44; also see Chartier, *Cultural Origins*, pp. 103–5.

31. Merrick, *Desacralization*; and Dale Van Kley, *The Damiens Affair and the Unraveling of the Ancien Regime, 1750–1770* (Princeton, N.J.: Princeton University Press, 1984) and *The Jansenists and the Expulsion of the Jesuits from France, 1757–1765* (New Haven: Yale University Press, 1975).

32. Merrick, *Desacralization*, p. 167.

33. Ibid., p. 25.

34. Ibid., p. 26.

35. Ibid., p. 30.

36. Ibid., p. 34.

37. Ibid., pp. 38–39. Merrick here offers a spectacular example of a case in 1766, when, by the implementation of a law of 1666 which made various acts of sacrilege punishable by increasingly severe forms of corporal punishment, a man was executed for blasphemy precisely to make the point that "the most noteworthy fact about the death sentence . . . was its exceptional character."

38. Ibid., p. 40.

39. Ibid., p. 42.

40. The following paragraphs from *Desacralization* paraphrase Merrick's conclusions, p. 167.

41. There is a rich literature evoking and analyzing the *mauvais discours* against the monarchy in the eighteenth century, and this process of desacralization: for a general discussion, see Chartier, *Cultural Origins*, pp. 113–24; and Merrick, *Desacralization*, pp. 20–22; see also Sarah Maza, *Private Lives and Public Affairs: The Causes Célèbres of Prerevolutionary France* (Berkeley: University of California Press, 1993); and Lynn Hunt, *The Family Romance of the French Revolution* (Berkeley: University of California Press, 1992).

42. Merrick, *Desacralization*, p. 26.

43. Kantorowicz, "Mysteries of State," p. 91.

44. See Hunt, *Family Romance*, pp. 44, 49, and esp. 51.

45. On the problem of "embodying" the nation after 1791, see Lynn Hunt, *Politics, Culture, and Class in the French Revolution* (Berkeley: University of California Press, 1984), esp. chap. 3, "The Imagery of Radicalism"; and Dorinda Outram, *The Body and the French Revolution: Sex, Class and Political Culture* (New Haven: Yale University Press, 1988). On the transfer of sacrality, see Mona Ozouf, *Festivals and the French Revolution,* trans. Alan Sheridan (Cambridge, Mass.: Harvard University Press, 1988), or the original *La Fête, révolutionnaire, 1789–1799* (Paris: Gallimard, 1976).

46. Ozouf, *Festivals and the French Revolution,* esp. the conclusions, p. 282; in his *Cultural Origins,* Chartier convincingly presents the argument, pp. 92 and 109, that this transferral of sacrality was already begun before the events of 1789.

47. Hunt, *Politics, Culture, and Class,* p. 12: "Rather than expressing an ideology . . . revolutionary politics brought ideology into being."

48. Molière, *Tartuffe,* p. 98.

Chapter One

1. Archives Départementales de la Seine-Inférieure (hereafter ADSI), 1 M 173, speech included in a letter sent by the subprefect of Yvetot to the prefect of the Seine-Inférieure on 18 June 1816, the day after the festivities.

2. ADSI, 1 M 173, speech, with letter, 18 June 1816.

3. ADSI, 1 M 173, letter, 18 June 1816.

4. ADSI, 1 M 173, from the speech.

5. ADSI, 1 M 173, from the letter.

6. Article 11 of the Charter of 1814, cited in Guillaume de Bertier de Sauvigny, *La Restauration* (Paris: Flammarion, 1955), p. 71.

7. *Journal de l'Empire,* 6 July 1815.

8. The effort to purge the bureaucracy and elective bodies of those men associated with the Revolution will not be covered here, as they are amply discussed in D. P. Resnick, *The White Terror and the Political Reaction after Waterloo* (Cambridge, Mass.: Harvard University Press, 1966); and Alan B. Spitzer, "The Ambiguous Heritage of the French Restoration: The Distant Consequences of the Revolution and the Daily Realities of the Empire," in J. Pelenski, ed., *The American and European Revolutions, 1776–1848: Sociopolitical and Ideological Aspects* (Iowa City: University of Iowa Press, 1980): 208–26.

9. For the specific policies adopted against the Fédérés, and the subsequent impact of the White Terror, see Robert Alexander, *Bonapartism and Revolutionary Tradition in France: The Fédérés of 1815* (Cambridge: Cambridge University Press, 1991), and Pamela Pilbeam, *The 1830 Revolution in France* (New York: St. Martin's Press, 1991).

10. Report from the prefect of the Dordogne, 22 September 1815, instructing local commanders of the gendarmerie to arrest anyone expressing support for Napoleon in these ways, in response to reports that military personnel in the area had recently committed such acts. A cover letter informed the minister of police that publicity was given to this order to ensure that anyone, military or otherwise, who "allowed themselves to wear distinctive emblems of the previous

government, or proffer seditious cries," would be pursued by the authorities. Archives Departementales de la Dordogne (hereafter ADD) 1 M 64.

11. *Arrêté* of the mayor of Bordeaux dated 30 October 1815, AN, F/2 (I) 135.

12. "Loi relative à la répression des cris séditieux et des provocations à la révolte," *Collection complète des lois, décrets, ordonnances, réglements, avis du conseil d'état,* vol. 20, 2d ed. (Paris: A. Guyot et Scribe, 1837), pp. 107–8.

13. Resnick, *The White Terror,* esp. chaps. 4, "Repressive Legislation," and 6, "Political Arrests and Convictions."

14. ADSI, 1 M 173, circular from the Ministère Secrétaire d'Etat au Departement de la Police Générale du Royaume, 24 November 1815.

15. ADSI, 1 M 173, circular, 24 November 1815.

16. Every departmental archive has a folder within its police dossiers on the Restoration entitled *"Mise-en-Place,"* containing correspondence between the national authorities and various local representatives, and between the prefect and his subordinates in his department. Detailed reports of local ceremonies can also be found in these folders, usually sent from mayors to their subprefects, and from the subprefects on to the prefects. On the national level, one can find evidence of the *mise-en-place* in the minister of the interior's files. One folder in particular, F/2/I 135, contains all the correspondence between national and local authorities on this campaign, including detailed descriptions of individual ceremonies conducted all over France. The following section is based primarily on this folder bringing together evidence of the *mise-en-place* all over the country, but also on documents from the ADSI and ADD. While these documents never explain why the government pursued its *mise-en-place* in the way it did, Achille de Vaulabelle's *Histoire des Deux Restaurations,* 3d ed. (Paris: Perrotin, Editeur de Béranger, 1855), suggests that it might have been a reaction against the occupying armies who, during the summer of 1815, "rounded up tricolor flags and everything else they could find . . . and kept them as trophies." Vol. 4, pp. 383–84.

17. ADSI, 1 M 173, letter from the subprefect of the Arrondissement of Rouen to the mayors of the same arrondissement, 18 December 1815.

18. A response to this circular from one mayor demonstrates that this new order was put into effect in his commune: "I will first employ persuasion, and if this should fail, I will identify the recalcitrant parties to you." ADSI, 1 M 173, letter from the mayor of Betteville, arrondissement of Rouen, to the subprefect of Rouen, December 1815 (no day given in original).

19. ADD, 2 Z 22, letter to the subprefect of Montron from the prefect of the Dordogne, 20 December 1815.

20. ADSI, 1 M 173, letter from the minister of police to the prefect of the Seine-Inférieure, 12 April 1816.

21. ADSI, 1 M 173, letter from the minister of the interior to the prefect of the Seine-Inférieure, 12 February 1816.

22. ADD, 2 Z 22, letter from the mayor of the Commune of Champagnac to the subprefect of Montron, 19 April 1816.

23. In addition to the shorter references in the procès-verbaux to objects collected and destroyed all over France, I have located five extensive inventories of

such objects: 1) ADSI, 1 M 173: compiled in Rouen by a special committee which met for the purpose of gathering and cataloguing seditious articles; the committee consisted of the keeper of the Museum of Rouen, an architect, and the police commissioner; their list was dated 17 January 1816; 2) AN, F/2 (I) 135: included in the procès-verbal from the prefect of the Loiret, dated 22 February 1816; 3) AN, F/2 (I) 135: in a report from local officials to the prefect of the Dordogne, dated 31 March 1816; 4) AN, F/2 (I) 135: letter from the prefect of the Saône-et-Loire to the minister of the interior, 26 April 1816; 5) AN, F/2 (I) 135: report by the mayor of St-Jean Pied-de-Port to the prefect of the Basses-Pyrénées, 19 May 1816. See below for a more detailed discussion of these inventories.

24. ADSI, 1 M 173, letter from the captain commanding the Royal Guard to the prefect of the Seine-Inférieure, 15 April 1816; AN, F/2 (I) 135, letter from the prefect of the Nièvre, 7 March 1816, to the minister of police, reporting that gendarmes had been sent to communes to see that flags and busts had been removed from all public edifices.

25. ADSI, 1 M 173, letter from the mayor of Buchy to the prefect of the Seine-Inférieure, 6 April 1816.

26. AN F/2 (I) 135, letter from the prefect of the Oise to the minister of police, 1 March 1816.

27. ADSI, 1 M 173, letter from the curator of the Musée de Rouen to the prefect of the Seine-Inférieure, 17 January 1816.

28. AN, F/2 (I) 135: Haute-Marne, letter from the prefect to the minister of police, 19 February 1816; Nord, letter from the prefect to the minister of police, 17 February 1816.

29. ADSI, 1 M 173, correspondence between a gendarme in Duclair and the prefect of the Seine-Inférieure, May to July 1820.

30. ADSI, 1 M 173, letter from the minister of the interior to the prefect of the Seine-Inférieure, 29 November 1815. A brief article on the traffic in seditious prints during the Restoration beautifully evokes the drama of visits by the police to booksellers and the range of practices which were used to "amend" problematic images and texts. See Paul Cordonnier-Detrif, "Imagerie et Colportage," *La Revue Historique et Archéologique du Marne* 33 (1953): 3–51.

31. ADSI, 1 M 173, letter from the subprefect of Rouen to the mayors of the same city, 26 December 1815.

32. ADSI, 1 M 173. One report from the police commissioner of the 6th arrondissement of Rouen, 22 December 1815, indicates both types of actions. His list includes the following information: "names of merchants," "*qualité*" (i.e., printer or bookseller), "address," "number of copies found," and "*observations*" (what was done with the books). Out of a total of 759 copies, 359 were "put under government seal," 25 were confiscated outright, and 375 remained on the shelves with the problematic chapter removed.

33. ADSI, 1 M 173, letter from the mayor of Le Havre to the subprefect of Yvetot, 19 February 1816. The mayor reported that sixty-nine books with such songs were located, and in all of them "we have carefully removed all allusions to the family of Bonaparte."

34. ADD, 2 Z 22, letter from the mayor of the Commune of Lusson to the subprefect of Montron, 15 April 1816. An argument of the same genre was proffered in a letter from the mayor of a neighboring town trying to excuse his seeming support for Napoleon during the Hundred Days. He explained that although he did hang a tricolor flag outside his city hall, "I had an old flag put up which had served the National Guard, which was almost entirely white . . . " ADD, 2 Z 22, letter from the mayor of the Commune of Champagnac to the subprefect of Montron, n.d.

35. ADSI, 1 M 173, letter from the mayor of Boisguillaume, Canton of Darnétal, to the prefect of the Seine-Inférieure, 6 July 1816.

36. ADSI, 1 M 173, letter from the mayor of Rouen to the prefect of the Seine-Inférieure, 31 May 1816.

37. ADSI, 1 M 173, letter from the subprefect of Dieppe to the prefect of the Seine-Inférieure, 26 February 1816. The folder F/2 (I) 135 contains formulaic accounts regarding these ceremonies from all over France. Where particular details stood out, or where speeches were included, I have analyzed them separately.

38. AN, F/2 (I) 135, letter from the prefect of the Marne to the minister of the interior, 17 February 1816.

39. For example, in one case in the Côte d'Or, the mayor of the small town of Montmoyen stood up in the church at the end of a mass and "read acts concerning general security and the repression of seditious cries, and then gave orders for tricoloured flags and sashes to be burnt in the public square." The mayor then ended his speech with "Citizens, the colours of usurpation are banned forever! Let us fling these signs of rebellion into the flames, and woe betide those who try to wear them or have them revived!" Cited from *Journal de la Côte d'Or,* 6 December 1815, in Irene Collins, ed., *Government and Society in France, 1814–1848* (London: Edward Arnold, 1970), p. 18.

40. AN F/2 (I) 135, letter from the prefect of the Charente-Inférieure to the minister of the interior, 8 April 1816.

41. ADD, 2 Z 22, letter from the mayor of the Commune of Champagnac to the subprefect of the arrondissement of Montron, 26 February 1816, describing the incident which took place the previous July.

42. AN, F/2 (I) 135, letter from the prefect of the Loire to the minister of the interior, 5 March 1816, written in advance to the minister to ask for approval of this plan; letter of 23 March 1816 from the prefect of the Somme to the minister of the interior, written after the fact, offers a positive account, stressing that this gave the inhabitants of his department an opportunity to show their love of their monarch.

43. AN, F/2 (I) 135, the prefect of Gers to the minister of the interior, 5 April 1816.

44. Ibid.

45. AN, F/2 (I) 135, letter from the mayor of St-Jean Pied-de-Port, 19 May 1816, forwarded by the prefect of the Basses-Pyrénées to the minister of the interior.

46. AN, F/2 (I) 135, letter from the prefect of Basses-Pyrénées to the minister of the interior, 31 March 1816.

47. AN, F/2 (I) 135, report to the prefect of the Basses-Pyrénées from the subprefect of the city of Orthez, 19 May 1816. Sent on to the minister of the interior by the prefect.

48. AN, F/2 (I) 135, the prefect of the Saône-et-Loire to the minister of the interior, 26 April 1816.

49. AN, F/2 (I) 135, the prefect of the Haut-Rhin to the minister of police, 2 February 1816, describing the *mise-en-place* in Colmar.

50. ADSI, 1 M 173, list compiled by the curator of the Museum of Rouen, an architect, and the commissaire de police of Rouen, 17 January 1816.

51. ADSI, 1 M 173, procès-verbal from the gendarmerie royale, describing a visit to the commune of Bonville in the arrondissement of Rouen, 20 July 1816. The flag is described in great detail, and although they say that it was taken from a private home, they do not say whose.

52. ADSI, 1 M 173, list compiled by the curator of the Museum of Rouen, an architect, and the commissaire de police of Rouen, 17 January 1816.

53. ADSI, 1 M 173, letter from the mayor of Boisguillaume to the prefect of the Seine-Inférieure, 6 July 1816; another example took place in Neufchâtel on 15 December 1815, ibid., letter from the subprefect of Neufchâtel to the prefect of the Seine-Inférieure, 18 April 1816.

54. AN, F/2 (I) 135, the prefect of the Loiret to the minister of police, 22 February 1816.

55. ADSI, 1 M 173, speech included in the letter from the subprefect of Yvetot to the prefect of the Seine-Inférieure; the ceremony was on 17 and 18 June 1816.

56. ADSI, 1 M 173, circular sent from the subprefect of Yvetot to the mayors of his arrondissement, 7 May 1816.

57. AN, F/2 (I) 135, the prefect of Basses-Pyrénées to the minister of the interior, copy of report from the mayor of Orthez, 19 May 1816.

58. ADSI, 1 M 173. The mayor of la Houssaye wrote two letters to the prefect of the Seine-Inférieure asking for information about changes in costume to accompany the change in regime, 19 August 1816 and 20 March 1817. The first one received no response; the second one received notification that a law from October 1814 states that mayors should wear white belts; response from prefect, 24 May 1817.

59. ADSI, 1 M 173, letter from the subprefect of Neufchâtel to the prefect of the Seine-Inférieure, 18 April 1816, describing this ceremony which took place on 15 December.

60. ADSI, 1 M 173, letter from the subprefect of Neufchâtel to the prefect of the Seine-Inférieure, 25 December 1815.

61. ADD, 2 Z 22, letter from the mayor of the Commune of Champagnac to the subprefect of Montron, 19 April 1816. The curé, according to the letter, was present when the tree was chopped down, and asked at that point if he could have permission to erect a large, stone cross in its place at his own cost. The mayor agreed.

62. ADSI, 1 M 173, letter from the mayor of St-Saud to the subprefect of Montron, 6 February 1816. While I have never found evidence of this in my own research, Vaulabelle depicts a *mise-en-place* ceremony which took place during Carnival, and during which the local officials explicitly orchestrated the cere-

mony as a carnivalesque presentation of the new "court" or administration. Vaulabelle never actually refers to the *mise-en-place,* but the example he offered fits within this spectrum of ceremonies. When discussing this particular ceremony he explicitly makes the contrast between the destruction of revolutionary and imperial objects he is describing and festivals of the French Revolution which they mimicked. Vaulabelle, *Histoire des deux Restaurations,* vol. 4, pp. 230–34.

63. ADSI, 1 M 173, procès-verbal and letter from the mayor of St-Gilles de Crelot, arrondissement of Yvetot, sent to the prefect of the Seine-Inférieure, 2 February 1816.

64. David Higgs, "Discursive Shouts: Marginals and Bonapartists in Restoration Toulouse," presented at the Annual Meeting of French Historical Studies, Vancouver, March 1990 (mimeographed), pp. 6–7.

65. *Journal de L'Empire,* 6 July 1815.

66. ADSI, 1 M 173, speech included in a letter sent by the subprefect of Yvetot to the prefect of the Seine-Inférieure on 18 June 1816, the day after the festivities.

67. Ibid.

68. My argument is based on the premise asserted by Lynn Hunt that ideology was born in the French Revolution precisely because monarchy, tradition, indeed everything lost its "given-ness." It is my view that by trying to return to the moment prior to that of radical regeneration and "construction," the representatives of the Restoration regime sought (hopelessly) to evade the problem of "constructing" monarchy. *Politics, Culture, and Class in the French Revolution* (Berkeley and Los Angeles: University of California Press, 1984), pp. 12–13.

69. ADSI, 1 M 173, circular from the minister of police addressed to all prefects, entitled "Destruction des signes proscrits," 12 February 1816 (emphasis my own).

70. ADSI, 1 M 173, letter from the mayor of Gouy to the prefect of the Seine-Inférieure, 17 July 1816 (emphasis my own).

71. ADD, 2 Z 22, letter from the mayor of Champagnac to the subprefect of the arrondissement of Montron, 26 February 1816 (emphasis my own).

72. Nowhere in the orders of the minister of police was destruction by fire even suggested, yet this was almost universally adopted by local officials.

73. AN, F 2 (I) 135, letter from the prefect of the Basses-Pyrénées to the minister of the interior, 31 March 1816 (emphasis my own).

74. Higgs, "Discursive Shouts," p. 6.

75. The following discussion focuses on the possible resistance to this effort without considering the support which certainly existed, especially in some regions, because that has already been studied by historians under the rubric of the White Terror. See, for example, Daniel Resnick, *The White Terror,* and David Higgs, *Ultra-Royalism in Toulouse: From Its Origins to the Revolution of 1830* (Baltimore and London: Johns Hopkins University Press, 1973); and, more recently, Alexander, *Bonapartism and Revolutionary Tradition.*

76. The difference between these formulaic, basically unpopular ceremonies and the spontaneous attacks on Catholic and Protestant symbols that were common during the Wars of Religion is quite striking. See Natalie Zemon Davis,

"The Rites of Violence," *Society and Culture in Early Modern France* (Stanford, Calif.: Stanford University Press, 1975), pp. 152–87.

77. ADSI, 1 M 176, correspondence between a gendarme in Duclair, the Chef d'Escadron Commandant de la Garde Royale, and the prefect of the Seine-Inférieure, May through June 1820.

78. AN, F/2 (I) 135, report from the subprefect of Orthez to the prefect of the Basses-Pyrénées, 19 May 1816.

79. ADD, 2 Z 22, letter from the mayor of St-Saud to the subprefect of Montron, 6 February 1816.

80. ADSI, 1 M 173, list compiled by a committee consisting of the curator of the Musée de Rouen, an architect, and a commissaire de police, 17 January 1816.

81. AN, F/2 (I) 135, letter of 4 April 1816, from the prefect of Meurthe-et-Moselle responding to the circular of 12 February 1816 from the minister of police, reminding him of the need to enforce the *mise-en-place*. But usually such reports also make allusions to the severe repercussions which have been threatened for those who tried to elude the state's effort, implying at least that there was some evidence of this kind of evasion.

82. ADSI, 1 M 173, letter from the mayor of Gouy to the prefect of the Seine-Inférieure, 17 July 1816.

83. ADSI, 1 M 173, letter from the mayor of Bosquerard to the subprefect of Rouen, 31 December 1815.

84. "The Old Flag," by Béranger, cited in translation in Irene Collins, *Government and Society in France, 1814–1848* (London: Edward Arnold, 1970), pp. 28–29. According to Collins, Béranger was imprisoned for three months and fined 400 francs for publishing this song. There was actually a case in La Rochelle of an old soldier doing precisely what this song said. A young man kept three *drapeaux tricolores* "decorated with emblems of the Republic and the Empire" in his possession, "and has shown them to officers [of the National Guard]." The man was not charged with any offense. The police report concluded that there was nothing "alarming" about this incident; since the veteran demonstrated "an unseriousness which borders on folly," his actions were merely excused as "a new act of dementia." AN, F7 3796, Bulletin de Police, No. 29, 15 May 1824, La Rochelle, 8 May 1824.

85. Cited in Jean-Marie Darnis, *Les Monuments expiatoires du supplice de Louis XVI et Marie-Antoinette sous l'Empire et la Restauration* (Paris: J. M. Darnis, 1981), p. 25, from *Le Moniteur Universel,* 9 December 1815, p. 1365.

86. Darnis, *Les Monuments expiatoires,* p. 26, cited from the *Moniteur Universel,* 28 December 1815, p. 1436. This amendment was proposed by Hyde de Neuville.

87. *Bulletin des Lois,* 7e série, t. 11, 1816, p. 77. According to this law, monuments were also to be erected in memory of Louis XVII, Marie Antoinette, and Madame Elisabeth.

88. ADSI, 1 M 366, included in circular sent to the archbishops of France, 20 December 1815.

89. Last Will and Testament, ADSI, 1 M 366, included in circular sent to archbishops of France, 20 December 1815.

90. Sarah Maza, "The Diamond Necklace Affair Revisited (1785–1786): The Case of the Missing Queen," pp. 63–89, and Lynn Hunt, "The Many Bodies of Marie Antoinette: Political Pornography and the Problem of the Feminine in the French Revolution," pp. 108–30, in Lynn Hunt, ed., *Eroticism and the Body Politic* (Baltimore and London: Johns Hopkins University Press, 1991).

91. AN, F7 9890, letter adjoined to circulars sent out to prefects by the minister of police, 10 October 1817.

92. AN, F7 9890, report from the Prefect of the Bouches-du-Rhône to the minister of police, 31 January 1818.

93. AN, F7 9890, circular sent to all subprefects and mayors of the Manche, 14 January 1817.

94. AN, F7 9890, placard posted in the town of Troyes containing the regulations for the celebration of the 21st of January 1821, 17 January 1821.

95. AN, F7 9890, circular sent to subprefects and mayors of the Manche regarding the celebration of 21 January 1817; circular sent to subprefects and mayors in the department of the Drôme regarding the celebration of 21 January 1816.

96. On the importance of the oath in festivals during the Revolution, see Ozouf, *Fête révolutionnaire,* and Hunt, *Politics, Culture, and Class,* p. 21, referring to Jean Starobinsky, *1789: Les Emblêmes de la Raison* (Paris: Flammarion, 1979), pp. 66–67.

97. ADSI, 1 M 173, minutes from the meeting of the Municipal Council of Dieppe, 7 May 1816; in the Seine-Inférieure the prefect received reports from the mayors of Darnetal, Rouen, Caudebec, and Yvetot in 1816 regarding the circulation of similar registers: ADSI, 1 M 173, Darnetal, 15 March 1816; Rouen, 8 March 1816; Caudebac, 1 March 1816; and Yvetot, 18 June 1816.

98. AN, F7 9890, circular from the prefect of the Drôme to the subprefects and mayors of his department, regarding the celebration of 21 January 1816.

99. AN, F7 9890, letter from the prefect of the Manche to the minister of the interior, 28 January 1817.

100. AN, F7 9890, letter from the prefect of the Hautes-Alpes to the minister of police, 29 January 1823.

101. AN, F7 9890, letter from the prefect of the Aisne to the minister of police, 24 January 1816.

102. AN, F7 9890, letter from the prefect of the Côte d'Or to the minister of police, 28 January 1817.

103. AN, F7 9890, letter from the mayor of the Commune of Petersback in the Bas-Rhin to the minister of police, 10 December 1818.

104. AN, F7 9890, letter from the prefect of the Lot-et-Garonne to the minister of police, 23 February 1816.

105. AN, F7 9890, letter from the commissariat special de police en Corse to the minister of police, 11 November 1816.

106. ADSI, 1 M 366, letter from the subprefect of Le Havre to the prefect of the Seine-Inférieure, 16 October 1823.

107. AN, F7 9890, letter from the prefect of the Haut-Rhin to the minister of police, 19 October 1822; ibid., letter from the prefect of Tarn et Garonne to the minister of police, 18 October 1822.

108. AN, F7 9890, letter from the prefect of the Haut-Rhin to the minister of police, 19 October 1822.

109. AN, F7 9890, letter from the prefect of Indre to the minister of the interior, 17 October 1823.

110. ADSI, 1 M 366, letter from the prefect of the Seine-Inférieure to the subprefect of Rouen, 16 October 1822.

111. The discussion of the failure to accomplish this monument is in Darnis, *Les Monuments expiatoires,* chap. 8, "Le Monument Expiatoire, Place Louis XV," pp. 77–95. Darnis sees the failure to erect this monument strictly as a result of bureaucratic problems. The failure to erect a monument to the king can also be understood in the context of the regime's general difficulties in representing monarchs in sculpture. See Anne M. Wagner, "Outrages: Sculpture and Kingship in France after 1789," in Ann Bermingham and John Brewer, eds., *The Consumption of Culture, 1600–1800: Image, Object, Text* (London and New York: Routledge, 1995), pp. 294–318.

112. Roger-Armand Weigert, *La Madeleine* (Paris: Les Editions du Cerf, Nefs et Clochers, 1962), p. 10.

113. Ibid., p. 12.

114. Pierre Nora, ed., *Les Lieux de mémoire,* vol. 1: *La République* (Paris: Gallimard, 1984).

115. François Macé de Lépinay et Jacques Charles, *Marie-Antoinette du Temple à la Conciergerie* (Paris: Editions Tallandier, Caisse Nationale des Monuments Historiques et des Sites, 1989), p. 75.

116. Ibid. All changes described on pp. 79–81.

117. Ibid., p. 80. Also discussed in Darnis, *Les Monuments expiatoires,* p. 59.

118. de Lépinay et Charles, *Marie-Antoinette du Temple,* p. 80.

119. Ibid., p. 81.

120. Marie-Claude Chaudonnent in *Aux armes, aux arts* (1988), cited in *Marie-Antoinette du Temple,* p. 81.

121. Darnis, *Les Monuments expiatoires,* p. 60. In this book there is an illustration of an extraordinary sculpture of the queen, "Marie-Antoinette Soutenue par la Religion," which demonstrates the effort to make her seem almost saintly. This sculpture, not commissioned until the 1860s, and placed in the Chapel of Louis XVI in 1868, demonstrates the lasting power of this effort. See p. 142.

122. The establishment of the Charter, the departure and return of Louis XVIII before and after the Hundred Days, the marriage and death of the duc de Berry, the birth of the duc de Bordeaux, and the coronation of Charles X were events that were commemorated graphically on medals engraved by Bertrand Andrieu and Jacques Eduoard Gatteaux. See Jean Babelon, *La Médaille en France* (Paris: Librairie Larousse, 1948), pp. 95–96.

123. Jean-Marie Darnis, "Les sept médailles commemoratives officielles à la mémoire de Louis XVI et de Marie-Antoinette sous la Restauration," in Catalogue d'Exposition, *La Monnaie: Miroir des Rois,* Musée Monétaire, Hôtel des monnaies et médailles, Paris, 1 fevrier–30 avril, 1978, pp. 389–416.

124. Babelon, *La Médaille en France,* contains a general discussion of the most famous of these medals, pp. 79–80; the article by Jean Marie Cannoo, "Les Emissions des émigrés après la mort de Louis XVI," *Helvetische Meunzen Zeitung* 9, 3 (1974): 106–12, contains a more complete list of the different medals issued by émigrés as well as illustrations of many of them.

125. Inscription quoted from a medal by Daniel Friedrich Loos, a German; discussed in Cannoo, "Les Emissions des émigrés," p. 108.

126. Medal by the Austrian, Lauer; this medal contained a bust of Louis XVI on the other side with the inscription, "Lud. XVI Rex Galliae Natus 23 August 1754"; Cannoo, "Les Emissions des émigrés," p. 107.

127. Medal by Abraham Abramson from Berlin, in Cannoo, "Les Emissions des émigrés," p. 109.

128. Series of medals by Daniel Friedrich Loos, cited in Cannoo, "Les Emissions des émigrés," pp. 108–9.

Chapter Two

1. The following account of the mission at Marseilles is derived from Ernest Sevrin's account in *Les Missions religieuses en France sous la Restauration,* vol. 2: *Les Missions (1815–1820)* (Paris: Librairie Philosophique J. Vrin, 1959), pp. 477–500; and from the correspondence between local civil and ecclesiastical authorities and the minister of the interior, AN, F7 9792, Dossier Bouches-du-Rhône.

2. These are the terms used by supporters of the missionaries to explain why a mission was so badly needed in Marseilles in 1820. See Sevrin, *Missions,* vol. 2, pp. 477–78.

3. Cited in Sevrin, *Les Missions,* vol. 2, p. 487.

4. Sevrin, *Missions,* vol. 2, p. 492.

5. AN, F7 9792, letter from the prefect of Bouches-du-Rhône to the minister of the interior, 3 May 1820, referring to an earlier letter of 3 February 1820 on the same issue.

6. AN, F7 9792, letter from the prefect of Bouches-du-Rhône to the minister of the interior, 10 January 1820.

7. AN, F7 9792, *Le Phocéen,* 16 February 1820, included in dossier Bouches-du-Rhône.

8. *Le Phocéen,* 16 February 1820.

9. AN, F7 9792, letter from the prefect of Bouches-du-Rhône to the minister of the interior, 22 January 1820.

10. AN, F7 9792, letter from the archbishop of Aix to the prefect of Bouches-du-Rhône; copy sent to the minister of the interior, 11 December 1819.

11. As described in AN, F7 9792, letter from the prefect of Bouches-du-Rhône to the minister of the interior, 15 February 1820.

12. AN, F7 9792, letter from the prefect of Bouches-du-Rhône to the minister of the interior, 17 February 1820. The civil officials' authority is not explicitly alluded to in this quotation, but the reason that the prefect included this report in his letter to the minister of the interior was precisely to underscore the

impression that the missionaries had no obligations to the civil authorities and that they could act with impunity, explicitly ignoring all efforts on the part of the prefect to intervene in their activities.

13. Ernest Sevrin, *Les Missions religieuses en France sous la Restauration, 1815–1830,* vol. 1: *Le Missionnaire et la mission* (St. Maudé: Procure des Prêtres de la Miséricorde, 1948); vol. 2: *Les Missions, 1815–1820* (Paris: Librairie Philosophique J. Vrin, 1959).

14. Currently completing a dissertation on the missions at Princeton, Maria Riasanovsky will soon allow us to have the full portrait of the missions which Sevrin began.

15. For figures, see Henri Guillemin, *Histoire des Catholiques français au XIXème siècle, 1815–1905* (Geneva, Paris, Montreal: Editions du Milieu du Monde, 1947), p. 16n.

16. Sevrin, *Missions,* vol. 1, p. 22.

17. Sevrin, *Missions,* vol. 1, summarizes this portrait offered in *L'Ami de la Religion et du Roi,* in his section "Etat Religieux de la France après l'Empire," pp. 22–24. Although this description was given in order to convince readers of the need for a mission, as we saw in the Introduction to Part I, this portrait corresponds to the findings of historians regarding the relative decline in the practices of Christianity in the eighteenth century.

18. Cited in Sevrin, *Missions,* vol. 1, p. 25.

19. Ibid.

20. Ibid., p. 26.

21. Ibid., p. 29.

22. Ordinance cited in Sevrin, *Missions,* vol. 1, p. 33. The only financial support the missionaries received from the government came through the funds set up for the "prêtres de secours"; thus, on a material level, this was the only justification offered by the government for its official participation in the missions.

23. Given the king's role in nominating prelates, this ordinance doubly ensured his control over the missions—indirectly through his nomination of the prelates who had to request the missions, and directly because his express authorization was also required.

24. Sevrin, *Missions,* vol. 1, p. 35.

25. See Geoffrey Cubitt, *The Jesuit Myth: Conspiracy Theory and Politics in Nineteenth-Century France* (Oxford: Clarendon Press, 1993), pp. 60–61, for a discussion of the connection between the Jesuits and the missionaries during the Restoration.

26. Sevrin discusses each of these organizations in detail, and in particular recounts the specific struggles of individual leaders to try to found such seminaries. Most important among such leaders were the Abbé de la Mennais, working out of Rennes; the Cardinal de Clermont-Tonnerre, in Toulouse; and the Cardinal Fesch, whose seminary at Chartreux was at the center of a national missionary movement during the Empire but, after it was closed in 1808, it never succeeded in recovering this status during the Restoration. See *Missions,* vol. 1, pp. 36–48.

27. Sevrin, *Les Missions,* vol. 1, p. 48.

28. Ibid., pp. 45–46.

29. See ibid., pp. 84–85, for a general portrait of the missionaries.

30. Pamela Pilbeam, *The Revolution of 1830 in France* (London: St. Martin's Press, 1991), p. 102.

31. According to Sevrin, this number is probably modest. Estimates of the numbers of missions from this period vary. Grivel, a Jesuit and a participant in the missions of the Restoration who wrote his account in the 1830s, offered the number 1,500. Omodéo, a critic of the missionaries who wrote a separate history, placed his estimate at 1,200. Sevrin identified 300 missions in the pages of *L'Ami de la Religion et du Roi,* and almost 600 in his research in the National Archives. Sevrin accepts the number 1,500 as the most likely estimate of the missions in this period. *Missions,* vol. 1, p. 50.

32. Sevrin, *Missions,* vol. 1, p. 50, makes this argument using only the numbers he has gathered himself. Of the 560 missions he has identified, 64 took place in departmental capitals, another 111 in capitals of arrondissements or bishoprics, whereas the remaining 385 took place outside these larger towns. Since the more rural missions were less likely to be reported either in the press or by police officials, the percentage of missions in the countryside as opposed to the city is probably even higher than Sevrin's own statistics indicate.

33. Sevrin, *Missions,* vol. 1, p. 68.

34. Ibid., p. 114.

35. Sevrin, *Missions,* vol. 1, pp. 118–23, gives several examples of discord between missionaries and local clergymen at the lower levels, and explains this either by invoking the jealousy of the local curé, frustrated by the power and popularity of outside preachers, or occasionally by citing the support of the lower clergy for the local population's religious practices under attack from the rigorist missionaries.

36. Sevrin, *Missions,* vol. 1, p. xxix.

37. Ibid., p. 91.

38. Ibid., p. 177.

39. Ibid., p. 167.

40. Ibid., p. 92.

41. Sevrin, *Missions,* vol. 1, p. 105, cites the missionaries' own writings when he describes their tactics in these terms.

42. Sevrin, *Missions,* vol. 1, p. 175.

43. Cited at length in Sevrin, *Missions,* vol. 2, p. 274. The term *terrible predicateur* is his.

44. For a general discussion of the efforts to limit access to the sacraments over this period and the protest this engendered, see Réné Rémond, *L'Anticlericalisme en France de 1815 à nos jours* (Paris: Fayard, 1976), p. 76; Thomas Kselman's "Popular Religiosity," in Edgar L. Newman, ed., *Historical Dictionary of France from the 1815 Restoration to the Second Empire* (New York and Westport, Conn.: Greenwood Press, 1987), vol. 2, pp. 812–17; Adrien Dansette, *Religious History of Modern France,* vol. 1: *From the Revolution to the Third Republic* (New York: Herder and Herder, 1961), p. 193.

45. The church establishment encouraged parishioners to take advantage of

this exceptional opportunity to ensure their salvation. In his official placard announcing the coming of the mission in Besançon, the archbishop listed all the churches where services and confessions would be held from 5 A.M. to 5:30 P.M. and enjoined the inhabitants of his town to participate in the mission by resorting to the fire and brimstone language so typical of the missionaries: "Inhabitants of the city of Besançon! a mission is a memorable moment in the life of a Christian; . . . [it offers the choice between] happiness or eternal damnation." AN, F7 9792, Dossier Doubs, placard dated 8 January 1825.

46. Cited in Sevrin, *Missions,* vol. 1, pp. 286–87.

47. Cited in ibid., p. 183.

48. Sevrin, *Missions,* vol. 1, p. 184.

49. AN, F7 9792, letter from the prefect of Allier to the minister of police générale, 17 April 1817.

50. Sevrin, *Missions,* vol. 1, pp. 289–96, tries to estimate the "success" of the missions in terms of conversions. Particularly in vol. 2, where he cites statistics for every mission regarding participation in the sacraments, it becomes obvious that the missionaries achieved some spectacular successes, and consistently high participation.

51. For an analogous discussion of the effects of the Counter-Reformation, see Merrick, *Desacralization of the Monarchy,* p. 44; and Chartier, *Cultural Origins,* pp. 95, 105.

52. According to one prefect, one of the missionaries directly assaulted the Concordat, when he clearly differentiated his own from the pope's more conciliatory stance vis-à-vis the Revolution and its legacy. In the prefect's words, "one of them evoked the specter of the persecutors whom the Pope himself had approved, and called the one who led this persecution a new Nero." AN, F7 9792, the prefect of the Bouches-du-Rhône to the minister of the interior, 10 January 1820.

53. AN, F7 9792, letter from the prefect of Hautes-Alpes to the minister of the interior, 1818.

54. AN, F7 9792, letter from the commissaire de police of Arles to the minister of police, 3 December 1819. The man in question was suspected by the missionaries of "secretly fanning the flames of Jacobinism." Because he was a wealthy man who had donated much money in his town for charity, he was well liked, and the excommunication of this benevolent man who had asked to have the last rites displeased the civil authorities as well as many of the beneficiaries of his good works.

55. Sevrin, *Missions,* vol. 1, p. 254. In vol. 2 of his study, Sevrin cites exactly how many people renewed their marriage vows during the course of the different missions.

56. In Rémond, *L'Anticlericalisme,* p. 13, the author underscores this "religious" interpretation of explicitly political acts as critical to the growing threat of clericalism in France, since it provided evidence of the blurring of temporal and spiritual matters and the role of the clerics in each.

57. Thomas Albert Kselman, *Miracles and Prophecies in Nineteenth-Century France* (New Brunswick, N.J.: Rutgers University Press, 1983), pp. 68, 75, 76–77. This book, which analyzes the prophetic literature and demonstrates

how widespread it was in this period, complements the following discussion of the missions, since it points to other ways in which the central message of the missions was propagated during the Restoration. Darrin M. McMahon's forthcoming book on the "antiphilosophes" likewise offers insight into the literature circulating in the Restoration which echoed the missionaries' message; indeed, in this case, the missionaries can be seen as popularizers of a view which the "anti-philosophes" had been propagating since the late eighteenth century. Darrin M. McMahon, *Enemies of the Enlightenment: The French Counter-Enlightenment and the Birth of the European Right, 1778–1830* (forthcoming, Oxford University Press).

58. AN, F7 9792, letter from the archbishop of Aix to the prefect of Bouches-du-Rhône; copy sent to the minister of the interior, 11 December 1819.

59. Sevrin, *Missions,* vol. 1, p. 101; and Henri Guillemin, *Histoire des Catholiques,* p. 23, wrote, "The missionaries thought it good to give to their efforts the allure of an official political propaganda; they were careful to multiply proofs of their cooperation with civil powers; they demanded of prefects and of the military authorities their assistance and their participation in the pompous and theatrical ceremonies which they organized."

60. AN, F7 9794, *mandement* of the bishop of Strasbourg, 10 October 1825.

61. Mona Ozouf, *The Revolutionary Festival, 1789–1799* (Cambridge, Mass.: Harvard University Press, 1988).

62. AN, F7 9794, *mandement* of the bishop of Strasbourg, 10 October 1825.

63. F7 9792, letter from the prefect of the Allier to the bishop of Clermont, 9 December 1819.

64. Martyn Lyons, "Fires of Expiation: Book-Burnings and Catholic Missions in Restoration France," *French History* 10, 1: 1–27.

65. It is in these *autos-da-fé* that the missionaries most clearly expressed the views of the antiphilosophes studied by McMahon in *Enemies of the Enlightenment.*

66. Sevrin, *Missions,* vol. 2, p. 169.

67. Sermon given in Grenoble in 1818, cited by Sevrin, *Missions,* vol. 2, p. 93.

68. Sevrin, *Missions,* vol. 2, p. 234.

69. Ibid., p. 366.

70. Ibid., p. 67.

71. Ibid., p. 119. There are many such cases, and the police reports in particular always stress the divisions which such attacks necessarily created, even within the church establishment. October 16 often served as a useful occasion for raising this delicate problem, since many priests took it upon themselves to note that Marie Antoinette had refused the ministering of a constitutional priest during her final days; the authorities were quick to reprimand such priests, and in this context generally discussed the inconveniences of raising this particularly painful legacy of the Revolution.

72. AN, F7 9792, letter from the prefect of the Hautes-Alpes to the minister of the interior, 18 October 1818.

73. AN, F7 9792, the prefect of Bouches-du-Rhône to the minister of the interior, 1 February 1819.

74. Sevrin, *Missions,* vol. 2, pp. 126–27.

75. AN, F7 9792, letter from the prefect of Bouches-du-Rhône to the minister of the interior, 26 January 1820, regarding the sermon given on the 21st of January by the mission in Marseilles.

76. AN, F7 9792, letter from the prefect of Charente-Inférieure to the minister of the interior, 22 January 1818.

77. Sevrin, *Missions,* vol. 2, pp. 206, 209, 226; carriers of the cross also went barefooted.

78. Sevrin, *Missions,* vol. 2, p. 269.

79. Cited in Sevrin, *Missions,* vol. 1, p. 194.

80. Ralph Giesey, *The Royal Funeral Ceremony in Renaissance France* (Geneva: Librairie E. Droz, 1960), esp. p. 190.

81. Art historians Elisabeth Fraser and Anne M. Wagner both underscore the difficulty which the regime had in representing the actual bodies of the king in painting and statuary respectively. See Elisabeth Fraser, "InCivility: Eugène Delacroix and the Private History of Romanticism," unpublished manuscript, and Anne M. Wagner, "Outrages: Sculpture and Kingship in France after 1789," in Ann Bermingham and John Brewer, eds., *The Consumption of Culture, 1600–1800: Image, Object, Text* (London and New York: Routledge, 1995), pp. 294–318.

Chapter Three

1. Cited in Ernest Sevrin, *Les Missions religieuses en France sous la Restauration, 1815–1830,* vol. 2: *Les Missions, 1815–1820* (Paris: Librairie Philosophique J. Vrin, 1959), p. 295.

2. Guillaume de Bertier de Sauvigny, *La Restauration* (Paris: Flammarion, 1955), pp. 315–16; Adrien Dansette, *Religious History of Modern France,* vol. 1: *From the Revolution to the Third Republic* (New York: Herder and Herder, 1961), pp. 182–84.

3. Jeffrey W. Merrick, *The Desacralization of the French Monarchy in the Eighteenth Century* (Baton Rouge and London: Louisiana State University Press, 1990), p. 36.

4. Dansette, *Religious History,* p. 183.

5. Ibid., pp. 183–84. According to Odile Krakowitch, censorship of plays that attacked religion was more consistently applied. *Le Théâtre soumis à la censure, 1815–1830* (Paris: National Archives, 1984).

6. Merrick, *Desacralization of the French Monarchy,* pp. 38–39.

7. Dansette, *Religious History,* p. 184; Bertier de Sauvigny, *La Restauration,* pp. 378–79. For debates on this law in the chambers, see James Kieswetter's "Law of Sacrilege," in Edgar L. Newman, ed., *Historical Dictionary of France from the 1815 Restoration to the Second Empire,* 2 vols. (New York and Westport, Conn.: Greenwood, 1987), vol. 2, p. 606.

8. Cited in Bertier de Sauvigny, *La Restauration,* p. 379.

9. Geoffrey Cubitt, *The Jesuit Myth: Conspiracy Theory and Politics in Nineteenth-Century France* (Oxford: Clarendon Press, 1993), p. 67, and his discussion of Bertier de Sauvigny, *Le Conte Ferdinande de Bertier, 1782–1869, et l'énigme de la Congrégation* (Paris: Presses Continentales, 1948); Mary S. Hart-

man, "The Sacrilege Law of 1825 in France: A Study in Anticlericalism and Mythmaking," *Journal of Modern History* 44, 1 (1972): 21–37.

10. Dansette, *Religious History,* p. 184.

11. Merrick, *Desacralization of the French Monarchy,* p. 169.

12. For a discussion of the degree to which this effort of Fraysinnous backfired, see Cubitt, *The Jesuit Myth,* p. 85.

13. Bertier de Sauvigny, *La Restauration,* p. 417.

14. Françoise Waquet, *La Fête Royale sous la Restauration, ou l'Ancien Régime retrouvé* (Geneva: Droz, 1981).

15. Clearly the public ceremonies considered in chapter 1, and the contrast already evoked between the regime's commemoration of the Revolution and the missionaries' expiatory spectacles, complicate Waquet's analysis somewhat. Taking seriously the *mise-en-place* ceremonies and the regime's reluctance to commemorate regicide, as well as the critical importance of the missions themselves as public spectacles of this period, forces us to differentiate the monarchs of the Restoration from their predecessors of the Old Regime, and demonstrates how impossible it was to effect a mere "return" to the Old Regime. Waquet's analysis, however, focuses only on national festivals in Paris, and mostly on the way in which the decorative arts were used to legitimize the monarchy through the practices and images of its ancestors. Within this narrow conception of the problem, the author's argument holds.

16. Waquet, *La Fête Royale,* p. 52.

17. In her article "Outrages: Sculpture and Kingship in France after 1789," in Ann Bermingham and John Brewer, eds., *The Consumption of Culture, 1600–1800: Image, Object, and Text* (London and New York: Routledge, 1995), Anne M. Wagner underscores the difficulty the Restoration regime faced in representing either the sacred body of past kings or the actual body of the obese King Louis XVIII by looking at its decision to resurrect the statue of Henri IV on the Pont Neuf. Using the example of royal statuary, this article complements the arguments I make here regarding the ceremonial choices of the regime. See especially pp. 295–98 and 309.

18. For a full discussion of how Charles X celebrated his coronation in comparison with earlier monarchs, see Richard A. Jackson, *Vive le Roi!: A History of the French Coronation from Charles V to Charles X* (Chapel Hill: University of North Carolina Press, 1984).

19. Whereas the percentage of festivals which were religious was generally 29.8% for the whole Restoration, and peaked in 1821 with the mourning around the duc de Berry's death to 58.3% and reached 38.2% in 1826 because of the Jubilee, the proportion of religious festivals declined to 19.5% between 1826 and 1829. Statistics from Waquet, *La Fête Royale,* p. 52.

20. Merrick, *Desacralization of the French Monarchy,* p. 28.

21. AN, F7 9792, the prefect of Hautes-Alpes to the minister of the interior, 18 October 1818.

22. Cited in Sevrin, *Les Missions,* vol. 2, p. 166.

23. AN, F7 9792, letter from the police commissioner to the minister of the interior, 16 May 1818. He continued to argue in terms which are interesting and critically important for us to remember: "That this fact is true or not, it is

generally accepted to be so. This is one of the reasons why they are so desired in Dijon by the Ultras, and why they are descried by the independents and acquirers of *biens d'émigrés,* which form the mass of this department." Whether true or not, the rumors that the missionaries spoke out vehemently against the laws of the land created a political divide among the population, leading the Ultras to side with them and the "independents" or those who benefited from the revolutionary settlement to see them as threatening the very legal foundations of their nation.

24. AN, F7 9792, letter from the prefect of the Côte-d'Or, 29 May 1819, to the minister of the interior.

25. AN, F7 9792, letter from the prefect of the Allier to the minister of police, 17 April 1818.

26. AN, F7 9792, letter from the prefect of Allier to the bishop of Clermont, 9 December 1819.

27. AN, F7 9792, the prefect of Bouches-du-Rhône to the minister of the interior, 20 December 1817.

28. AN, F7 9792, letter from the archbishop of Aix to the prefect of Bouches-du-Rhône, enclosed in letter from the prefect to the minister of the interior, dated 11 December 1819.

29. The archbishop of Aix to the prefect of Bouches-du-Rhône, AN, F7 9792, 11 December 1819.

30. Sevrin, *Missions,* vol. 2, p. 18. In this quotation Sevrin promises to cover this point at greater length in later volumes, which he unfortunately never completed. But all the evidence I have found substantiates this view.

31. AN, F7 9792, letter from the prefect of Allier to the minister of the interior, 20 December 1819.

32. AN, F7 9792, "Note," 5 March 1829, no author indicated.

33. Cited in AN, F7 9792, letter from the prefect of Allier to the minister of the interior, 20 December 1819. Although I haven't found a full letter from the minister of the interior regarding this request, in the margins of the prefect's original letter the words *très certainement* are marked next to the prefect's question, "today, when one makes religion an affair and an arm of a party, does this convention still have force?"

34. Cited in "Note" on policies regarding the missions applied by the minister of the interior, in AN, F7 9792, dated 5 March 1829 (no author identified).

35. All cited in "Note," AN, F7 9792, 5 March 1829 (no author indicated).

36. Cited, for example, in letter from the minister of the interior to the prefect of Ain, 4 April 1820, AN, F7 9792.

37. Cited in AN, F7 9792, letter from the prefect of Hautes-Alpes to the minister of police, 18 October 1818, regarding which laws could be used against ministers speaking out against civil marriage.

38. Law of 11 November 1815, *Collection complète des Lois, décrets, ordonnances, Réglemens, avis du Conseil-d'état,* vol. 20, 2d ed. (Paris: A. Guyot et Scribe, 1837), pp. 107–8; emphasis mine.

39. AN, F7 9792, letter from the conseiller de préfet délégué to the minister of police, April 18, 1817; AN, F7 9792, letter from the prefect of Drôme to the minister of police, 12 January 1820.

40. AN, F7 9793, letter from the prefect of Loire-Inférieure to the minister of the interior, 7 May 1827. What is fascinating about this set of suggestions is the degree to which they mimic the general procedures which would also be suggested in the policing of the theater, as we shall see in chapters 4 and 6 below.

41. AN, F7 9793, reply from the minister of the interior to the prefect of Loire-Inférieure, 11 May 1827.

42. AN, F7 9793, letter from the minister of ecclesiastical affairs to the minister of the interior, 5 July 1827.

43. AN, F7 9792, letter from the prefect of the Allier to the minister of the interior, 15 May 1821; here we see an example of a local official using the argument that the local bishop had not properly approved the mission. In this case, the accusation was spurious, but it still inspired vigorous efforts by the prefect to prevent the mission on these grounds.

44. AN, F7 9793. The letter of 7 May 1829 from the prefect of the Loire-Inférieure (the author of the suggested national policy) complains bitterly of the refusal of missionaries to cooperate with the authorities even by just informing them of their plans. In his words: "It was agreed at the beginning of this mission that the municipal authorities would be told about all plans for sites and timing of religious exercises, in order to allow us to provide the surveillance and intervention necessary to preserve order. More than once the authority was only informed after the fact, and then by public rumors." This kind of evasion was a constant complaint of civil authorities trying to ensure order in the missions. In the following two notes from the prefect of the Bouches-du-Rhône in 1820, we see different ways in which the local authorities could interpret such evasion. In one note the prefect complained that "the missionaries do not have a proper idea of the obligations they have to the authorities, and they are ignorant of the laws which in fact define such obligations." But the following day, describing one missionary's ceremony in the cemetery, an outdoor spectacle which the administration tried unsuccessfully to block, the prefect ascribes a more deliberate motive to the priest's evasion: F7 9792, the prefect of Bouches-du-Rhône to the minister of the interior, letters of 14 February 1820 and 15 February 1820.

45. The following letter from the prefect of Allier to the minister of the interior is typical in the way it conjures examples from surrounding areas as it presents the problems expected to erupt in the town of Moulins: "The reports that Your Excellency will have received from Nevers, Bourges, Clermont and Grenoble will have without a doubt made you aware of the effect that the missions produce wherever they go. . . ." In this case, "such reports" led the prefect to open negotiations with the minister of the interior about the kinds of laws he could invoke to block a mission in Moulins, and, when that failed, to control the mission and its message. AN, F7 9792, letter of 17 April 1818.

46. Sevrin, *Missions*, vol. 2, p. 256.

47. AN, F7 9793. The quotations from protesters in the charivari are from the prefect of Finistère's letter to the minister of the interior, 26 October 1819.

48. AN, F7 9793. The discussion of the special charivari for the mayor and his participation in the delegation to the bishop of Quimper is in a letter from the prefect of Finistère to the minister of the interior, 6 November 1819. The crowd assembled outside the mayor's residence and screamed, "Send away the

missionaries! or leave your job; you are too weak; get out of here with your Jesuits!" As we shall see, different reports offer contradictory estimates of the number of men signing the declaration, reaching over a thousand according to the liberal pamphlet to be discussed below. I have counted 186 signatures on the actual document from the archives.

49. AN, F7 9793, letter from the prefect of Finistère to the minister of the interior, 16 September 1819.

50. AN, F7 9793. These two songs are contained in the letter from the prefect of Finistère to the minister of the interior, 8 October 1819. The general themes of hypocrisy and theatricality dominate the first song, "La Mission," a so-called "Christian song," which portrays the missionaries as "the sons of Midas," who lead a battalion of priests in a revival announced by "a trumpet, leading the processions, belting out a favorite tune from the opera." The second song, also entitled "The Mission," is more derisive still, mocking the hypocritical priests for their efforts to get back the *biens nationaux* and for burning Voltaire and Rousseau, and directly accusing the missionaries of dividing families.

51. AN, F7 9793, letter from the prefect of Finistère to the minister of the interior, 8 October 1819.

52. AN, F7 9793, letter from the minister of the interior to the prefect of Finistère, 1 November 1819.

53. AN, F7 9793, letter from the prefect of Finistère to the minister of the interior, 29 October 1819.

54. On the decrease in powers actually lodged in the municipal council during the Restoration, which help to explain why its use in this context was considered problematic, see Isser Wolloch, *The New Regime: Transformations of the French Civic Order, 1789–1820s* (New York: W. W. Norton, 1994), pp. 142–43.

55. AN, F7 9793, letter from the prefect of Finistère to the minister of the interior, 10 November 1819.

56. AN, F7 9793, letter from the prefect of Finistère to the minister of the interior, 29 October 1819.

57. "Trois Jours d'une Mission à Brest," p. 10, by Edouard Corbière, enclosed in letter from the subprefect of Brest to the minister of the interior, 5 November 1819, AN F7 9793.

58. "Trois Jours d'une Mission à Brest," pp. 11–12.

59. Ibid., p. 12.

60. AN, F7 9793, letter from the prefect of Finistère to the minister of the interior, 6 November 1819. After 1825, civil officials always reported quite extensively on performances of *Tartuffe*, even when they were not popular or seized by the population as a vehicle for expressing their opinion regarding visiting missions, or the local civil or ecclesiastical establishment. This counterexample of the prefect of Finistère is interesting because it shows that the play had not yet acquired the status which would define it after 1825.

61. "Trois Jours d'une Mission à Brest," pp. 14–15.

62. Ibid., p. 14. The following document republished in the pamphlet gave weight to this argument since it included both the deliberations of the municipal

council and the signatures of the members and the *pères de familles*. The author, as we have mentioned, seems to have exaggerated the number of signatures.

63. "Trois Jours d'une Mission à Brest," p. 15.

64. Ibid.

65. Ibid., p. 18.

66. Ibid., p. 20.

67. Ibid., p. 21.

68. AN, F7 9793, cover letter from the prefect of Finistère to the minister of the interior sent along with the pamphlet "Trois Jours d'une Mission à Brest," 5 November 1819.

69. AN, F7 9793, letters from the prefect of Finistère to the minister of the interior, 2 December 1819 (regarding his intention to prosecute and carefully select the jury) and 22 January 1820 (in which the failure of this attempt is reported).

70. AN, F7 9794, letter from the prefect of Haute-Vienne to the minister of the interior, 31 January 1828.

71. AN, F7 9794, letter from the prefect of Haute-Vienne to the minister of the interior, 4 February 1828.

72. AN, F7 9794, enclosed in letter from the prefect of Haute-Vienne to the minister of the interior, 22 March 1828.

73. AN, F7 9794, letter from the prefect of Haute-Vienne to the minister of the interior, 29 April 1828.

74. Ibid.

75. Sevrin, *Les Missions,* vol. 1, discussion in "Inconveniences of evening exercises," pp. 162–64, quotation from p. 163.

76. AN, F7 9792, *Le Phocéen,* 16 May 1820; the article also applauds the efforts to block the service in the cemetery.

77. AN, F7 9792, dossier Drôme: a case from Tain in 1819.

78. AN, F7 9792, letter from the prefect of Bouches-du-Rhône to the minister of the interior, 22 January 1820.

79. AN, F7 9792, letter from the prefect of Charente-Inférieure to the minister of the interior, 22 January 1818.

80. AN, F7 9792, letter from the prefect of Bouches-du-Rhône to the minister of the interior, 6 December 1819 regarding the gathering of information about sermons from local inhabitants.

81. The decision not to prosecute was based on a variety of factors: according to AN, F7 9792, letter from the prefect of Drôme to the minister of the interior, May 1818, the decision to drop charges against a missionary was based on the fact that it was impossible to prove that he made his "seditious" comments in public; in the Bouches-du-Rhône the prefect complained that he could find no one willing to testify against the missionaries, AN F7 9792, letter from the prefect of Bouches-du-Rhône to the minister of the interior, 26 January 1820.

82. AN, F7 9792, extract from a report on the situation in l'Izère, 19 January 1821, recounts a meeting between the prefect of the Drôme and the missionaries before they began preaching in Grenoble, at which the prefect exacted a promise from them not to treat political subjects, a promise which was apparently adhered to; AN, F7 9792, letter from the prefect of Aveyron to the minister of the interior, 2 May 1824, recounts another case in which advance nego-

tiation and surveillance appeared to be successful, since the prefect reported, "Sermons didn't touch upon politics except to encourage love for the king, and respect for all of the laws which he has given us." AN, F7 9792, letter from the prefect of Bouches-du-Rhône to the minister of the interior, 6 December 1819, explained that recent sermons by the preacher Desmazure were more *sage* than earlier sermons, and he accounts for this change by the police spies which he has made visible in the churches where Desmazure was preaching.

83. As reported in *Le Phocéen,* 16 May 1820, AN, F7 9792.

84. Ferté-sous-Jouarre, Sevrin, *Missions,* vol. 1, p. 316; Tarascon, AN, F7 9792, letter from the prefect of Bouches-du-Rhône to the minister of the interior, 16 May 1819.

85. AN, F7 9792, letter from the prefect of the Drôme to the minister of the interior, 12 January 1820, reports, "There have been some debates on the subject of the placement of the cross, but this did not lead to significant problems, although the local authority regrets the opposition which had been expressed to the missionaries' plans." Likewise in AN, F7 9792, the prefect of Bouches-du-Rhône to the minister of the interior, 3 February 1820, the prefect discusses the kind of security issues which often led local officials to disagree with the missionaries' sites for their crosses.

86. AN, F7 9792, letter from the prefect of Côte d'Or to the minister of the interior, 8 September 1819. The prefect explained that the only measure to take in these circumstances "is to prohibit all outdoor public ceremonies."

87. AN, F7 9792, letter from the prefect of the Bouches-du-Rhône to the minister of the interior, 19 November 1817.

88. AN, F7 6769, letter from the prefect of the Gard to the minister of the interior, Nîmes, 12 December 1825. It was the fact that over a third of the population was Protestant, and was disturbed by the recent law, that led the ecclesiastical authorities to adopt this measure.

89. AN, F7 9793, letter from the prefect of the Loire-Inférieure to the minister of the interior, 20 March 1829.

90. Cited in Sevrin, *Missions,* vol. 2, pp. 343–47. Also see AN, F7 9792, letter from the prefect of Bouches-du-Rhône to the minister of the interior, 4 February 1819.

91. AN, F7 9792, letter from the conseiller de préfet délégué, acting in the absence of the prefect of the Drôme, 18 April 1817.

92. AN, F7 9792, letter from the conseiller de préfecture délégué (in the absence of the prefect of the Drôme) to minister of police, 15 April 1817.

93. AN, F7 9792, letter from the captain of the Gendarmerie Royale de la Drôme to the minister of the interior, 23 December 1818.

94. Guillemin's *Histoire des catholiques,* p. 23, cites two examples: the mission in 1817 at Reims, where a colossal cross was carried by hundreds of men, promenaded across the city behind the music of military bands; and Cherbourg, where in the same year the missionaries presided over the launching of a new vessel for the navy.

95. Sevrin, *Missions,* vol. 2, p. 197.

96. Ibid., p. 198.

97. AN, F19 5557, the bishop of Dignes to the minister of the interior, 29 April 1819, cited in Sevrin, *Missions*, vol. 2, p. 205.

98. Sevrin, *Missions*, vol. 2, p. 256.

Introduction to Part II

1. Lynn Hunt, *Politics, Culture, and Class in the French Revolution* (Berkeley: University of California Press, 1984), p. 53.

2. Mona Ozouf, *Festivals of the French Revolution*, trans. Alan Sheridan (Cambridge, Mass.: Harvard University Press, 1988).

3. Suzanne Desan, *Reclaiming the Sacred: Lay Religion and Popular Politics in Revolutionary France* (Ithaca, N.Y.: Cornell University Press, 1990).

4. Maurice Agulhon, *Marianne into Battle: Republican Imagery and Symbolism in France, 1789–1880*, trans. Janet Lloyd (Cambridge: Cambridge University Press, 1981; originally 1979), pp. 36–37.

Chapter Four

1. Isser Woloch, *The New Regime: Transformations of the French Civic Order, 1789–1820s* (New York: W. W. Norton, 1994), pp. 142–43.

2. AN, F7 3796, Bulletin de Police, No. 101, 21 December 1825, Grenoble, 15 December 1825.

3. Departmental police records (series M) and the series on Theater (T) were consulted in the Seine-Maritime, the Dordogne, the Haute-Garonne, and the Haut-Rhin. Otherwise, all references come from police records (F7) in Paris at the Archives Nationales, most of which represent local reports that have been sent on to the Ministries of the Interior and the Police.

4. Maurice Crubellier, *Histoire culturelle de la France, XIXe et XXe siècles* (Paris: Armand Colin, 1974), chap. 3, "Système de la culture populaire," section 2, "Les Travaux et les fêtes—le cycle annuel," pp. 59–65; Georges Duby, gen. ed., *Histoire de la France rurale*, vol. 3: *Apogée et crise de la civilisation paysanne, 1789–1914* by Maurice Agulhon, Gabriel Désert, and Robert Specklin (Paris: Editions du Seuil, 1976), pp. 145–47. Both books rely upon the crucial work of Arnold Van Gannep, *Manuel de folklore français contemporain*, 9 vols. (Paris: Picard, 1943–1958). For an excellent summary of the folkloric calendar and, in particular, its importance in shaping festive forms of protest and contestation, see "The Drama of Peasant Time," in chap. 2, "Festive Revolt," in Peter Sahlins, *Forest Rites: The War of the Demoiselles in Nineteenth-Century France* (Cambridge, Mass.: Harvard University Press, 1994), pp. 70–74.

5. For a discussion of the comparable national festive calendar in the provincial context during the Old Regime, see Robert A. Schneider, *The Ceremonial City: Toulouse Observed, 1738–1780* (Princeton, N.J.: Princeton University Press, 1995).

6. See chap. 18, "Un Roi à Verrières," Stendhal, *Le Rouge et le Noir* (Paris: Gallimard, 1972; originally published 1830), pp. 108–20.

7. AN, F7 6767, dossier 8, letter from the prefect of the Ardèche to the minister of the interior, 14 July 1827.

8. AN, F7 3798, Bulletin de Police, No. 65, Cahors, 5 August 1829.

9. Described in Higgs, "Discursive Shouts: Marginals and Bonapartism in Restoration Toulouse." Paper presented at Annual Meeting of French Historical Studies, Vancouver, March 1990, p. 7.

10. ADSI, 1 M 176, letter from the mayor of Rouen to the prefect of the Seine-Inférieure, 15 September 1825, regarding events in Manneville. This statue had been given to the church by a woman whom Napoleon had saved during the Terror; while it had been destroyed at some point (the date is not given) rumors were spreading that three figures had appeared in its place and that a huge crowd was assembling to see this apparition.

11. ASDI, 1 M 176, 1MP3358.

12. Susanna Barrows, "Language, Laughter, and Derision: Seditious Speech and Popular Political Culture in Mid-Nineteenth-Century France," unpublished manuscript, p. 7, uses this idea of a popular *anti-fête* to discuss the timing of seditious cries during the Second Empire, which tended to be provoked by national celebrations.

13. Both the "scandalous but not dangerous" merrymaking and this example in F7 9890, letter from the prefect of the Lot-et-Garonne to the minister of police, 23 February 1816.

14. ADSI, 1 M 173, n. d., from the Commune of Bois Guilbart in the Canton of Bouchy. The letter with it refers to this having been repeated.

15. AN, F7 6704, Dordogne, no correspondence, simply the placard with the inscription "found January 1822 in Périgueux."

16. Higgs, "Discursive Shouts," p. 19.

17. AN, F7 9897, letter from the prefect of the Puy-de-Dôme to the minister of the interior, 28 August 1819.

18. AN, F7 9898, letter from the prefect of the Haut-Rhin to the minister of the interior, 6 November 1829.

19. AN, F7 9898, extract from a report from the prefect of the Ardèche, 12 November 1825, describing the festivities in Privat.

20. AN, F7 9898, letter from the prefect of the Isère to the minister of police, 26 August 1821.

21. AN, F7 9898, letter from the prefect of the Haute-Garonne to the minister of the interior, 18 September 1822.

22. AN, F7 9898, letter from the prefect of the Seine-Inférieure to the minister of police, 27 August 1820.

23. AN, F7 9898, Colonel de la 18e Légion to the minister of police, 28 August 1821.

24. AN, F7 9898, letter from the prefect of the Loire-Inférieure to the minister of the interior, 26 August 1823.

25. AN, F7 9898, letter from the prefect of the Basses-Pyrénées to the minister of police, 30 August 1823.

26. AN, F7 3796, Bulletin de Police, No. 92, 29 November 1825, Privas, 12 November 1825.

27. AN, F7 9898, report from the prefect of Bouches-du-Rhône to the minister of the interior, 5 November 1829.

28. ADSI, 1 M 17, letter from the subprefect of Dieppe to the prefect of the Seine-Inférieure, 28 August 1816; AN, F7 6706, letter from the prefect of the Seine-et-Oise to the minister of the interior, 14 November 1825.

29. AN, F7 3796, Bulletin de Police, No. 90, 12 November 1825, Angers, 7 November 1825.

30. ADSI, 1 M 175, report from the mayor of Rouen to the prefect of the Seine-Inférieure, 28 September 1820. The original French, which ends, that's to *voler à la gloire,* can also be translated according to the expression *travailler à la gloire,* which means "work for nothing." Thus perhaps it was the double meaning that made people boo and applaud.

31. AN, F7 9898, letter from the prefect of the Seine-Inférieure to the minister of the interior, 6 November 1824.

32. AN, F7 3796, Bulletin de Police, No. 90, 12 November 1825, Saint-Quentin, 11 November 1825.

33. AN, F7 9898, letter from the prefect of Finistère to the minister of the interior, 5 November 1827.

34. AN, F7 9898, letter from the prefect of Landes to the minister of the interior, 31 August 1824.

35. AN, BB 22, 15–23, dossier S4 2824.

36. ADSI, 1 M 176, letter from the subprefect of Dieppe to the prefect of the Seine-Inférieure, 4 September 1816.

37. AN, BB22, 15–23, dossier S6362, request for pardon by a worker condemned to two years of prison for seditious cries against the duchesse d'Angoulême on the occasion of her visit in the Herault in 1823.

38. The coronation and its reception in the press and other printed sources has been well studied. See J. P. Garnier, *Le Sacre de Charles X et l'opinion publique en 1825* (Paris: Jouve, 1927); the article in *Le Constitutionnel,* 3 June 1825, offers a typical critical account, as does Béranger's famous popular song, "The Crowning of Charles the Simple."

39. Regarding seditious speech on this occasion: AN, F7 3796, Bulletin de Police, No. 49, 19 May 1825, Colmar, 25 May 1825; regarding "plot" of liberals: several letters from the prefect of the Seine to the minister of the interior in April and May of 1825, AN, F7 6772, dossier 1, Seine.

40. AN, F7 6738, from the prefect of the Gers to the minister of the interior, describing events in the town of Mirande, 2 June 1825.

41. AN, F7 6738, found on 29 May and 5 June 1825 on City Hall in St-Cere in Lot.

42. AN, F7 6738, report from 14 June 1825.

43. See, for example, Higgs, who in "Discursive Shouts," pp. 9–10, describes the political geography of Toulouse, citing a royalist café and a pharmacy which were known meeting places for royalists; the police reports from all over France indicate an overall awareness of the political complexion of different public establishments and neighborhoods.

44. AN, F7 3797, Bulletin de Police, No. 80, 2 September 1826, Digne,

26 August 1826; Bulletin de Police, No. 85, 15 September 1826, Digne, 7 September 1826; Bulletin de Police, No. 96, 28 October 1826, Digne, 19 October 1826.

45. Peter Stallybrass and Allon White analyze these two functions of the fair in *The Politics and Poetics of Transgression* (Ithaca, N.Y.: Cornell University Press, 1986), p. 37. The rest of this paragraph is informed by their very interesting discussion.

46. AN, F7 6729, initial circular sent out by the minister of the interior, director of the police to prefects, 15 December 1815.

47. AN, F7 6727, circular dated 2 March 1823.

48. Many of the incidents of seditious cries and songs discussed below took place in cafés; for the importance of cafés and cabarets during the repressive Second Empire, see Barrows, "Laughter, Language, and Derision," pp. 3–5.

49. Newspapers were far too expensive for most people to subscribe to themselves (three months, the minimum subscription time, cost the equivalent of a factory worker's monthly wage). Thus the cafés and the "cabinets de lecture" of the bigger cities "assure . . . the public diffusion of the press." Parent-Lardeur, *Les Cabinets de Lecture: La lecture publique à Paris sous la Restauration* (Paris: Payot, 1982), pp. 109–10.

50. AN, F7 6729, letter from the prefect of Mayenne to the minister of the interior, 17 March 1823.

51. All examples which follow are from ADSI. One café owner in Rouen, a retired military man, provided a gathering place for military men and workers and was suspected of spreading Bonapartist ideas: ADSI, 1 M 175, confidential report from the mayor of Rouen to the prefect of the Seine-Inférieure, 5 June 1822; one cabaret owner denounced two men for having "uttered seditious speech and sung couplets in honor of Napoleon," report from the mayor of Rouen to the prefect of the Seine-Inférieure, 16 March 1820; example of another denunciation which was ignored because of the bad blood that existed between the denouncer and the alleged perpetrator of seditious crimes, letter from the prefect of the Seine-Inférieure to the mayor of Rouen requesting information, 14 January 1822; response from mayor explaining the situation, 22 January 1822. ADSI, 1 M 173: case of a café owner keeping an imperial eagle hanging in his bar; correspondence between a gendarme in Duclair, the Chef d'Escadron Commandant de la Garde Royale, and the prefect of the Seine-Inférieure, May to July 1820.

52. ADSI, 1 M 175, letter from the mayor of Rouen to the prefect of the Seine-Inférieure, no day or month, 1821, discussed the difficulty of getting people in a café to testify; ADSI, 1 M 175, report from the mayor of Rouen, 23 January 1822; extract sent to prefect dated 29 January 1822, which gives details of conversations held in a café, was typical of the reports provided by informers. AN BB 22/19, dossier S4 553, request for pardon in Morbihan, 30 March 1818; ibid., 22/15–23, dossier S4 270, request for pardon in Ardèche, 4 February 1818; ibid., dossier S4 2824, request for pardon in Doubs, 29 April 1819; in all three cases pardons were granted on the basis of inebriation.

53. See, for example, Jeffrey S. Ravel, *The Contested Parterre: Public The-*

ater and French Political Culture, 1680–1789 (Ithaca, N.Y.: Cornell University Press, 1999).

54. ADSI, 4 T 81, ordinance dated 5 May 1821, issued in response to requests from the minister of police and then the prefect of the Seine-Inférieure that the mayor get the theater of Rouen under control. These requests contain evidence that most of the provisions of the ordinance were violated in Rouen alone in the two years preceding its enactment. See ADSI, 4 T 81, letter from the prefect of the Seine-Inférieure to the mayor of Rouen, 1 December 1820; letter from the minister of police to the prefect of the Seine-Inférieure, May 1820 (no exact date in original).

55. ADSI, 1 M 175, letter from the prefect of the Seine-Inférieure to the minister of the interior, 21 September 1820; AN, F7 9898, prefect of the Seine-Inférieure to the minister of the interior, 6 November 1824.

56. ADSI, 1 M 175, procès-verbal from the commissaire de police in Elbeuf, 2 November 1823.

57. According to Alain Corbin, "L'Agitation dans les théâtres de province sous La Restauration," in Marc Bertrand, ed., *Popular Traditions and Learned Culture in France from the Sixteenth to the Twentieth Century* (Stanford, Calif.: Anma Libri, 1985), p. 111; agitators in the theater threw tomatoes, apples, chestnuts, olives, oranges, potatoes, mud, hay, and wood, but never metal or stones.

58. Corbin, "L'Agitation dans les théâtres," pp. 93–114. See especially "La Lutte pour le contrôle de la salle," pp. 102–6.

59. Corbin, "L'Agitation dans les théâtres," p. 107.

60. Cited in ibid., p. 110.

61. Corbin, "L'Agitation dans les théâtres," p. 110; my translation.

62. Ibid., p. 112, n. 86.

63. ADSI, 1 M 175, letter from the prefect of the Seine-Inférieure to the mayor of Rouen, 22 May 1821, describes an incident in which people who had been disruptive in a café left and sang the "Marseillaise" in the streets; AN, F7 6768, dossier 9, Côte d'Or, letter from the prefect of the Côte d'Or to the minister of the interior, 22 December 1828, describes an incident in which people left a café and walked by a public gallery of statues of Napoleon and his family and began screaming, "Vive Napoléon!"

64. Corbin, "L'Agitation dans les théâtres," pp. 111–13, gives examples of theater incidents spilling over into the streets.

65. Roger Chartier, *The Cultural Uses of Print in Early Modern France*, trans. Lydia G. Cochrane (Princeton, N.J.: Princeton University Press, 1987), pp. 230–31.

66. One placard, which read "LONG LIVE THE EMPEROR, SHIT FOR LOUIS XVIII, THE STUPIDEST OF KINGS, LONG LIVE DANGOULÈME, LONG LIVE THE COUNT DARTOIS, LONG LIVE NAPOLEON II, LONG LIVE MARIE LOUISE, shit for all the Royalists" was even smaller than a 3 × 5 index card. ADSI, 1 M 176, found in Elbeuf, included in prefect's file from 1817, otherwise undated. All errors and capitalization as in original.

67. In ADSI, 1 M 176, a full subdossier is devoted to "*inscriptions sédi-*

tieuses," precisely describing the transformation of public edifices into placards by the writing on them of simple slogans, most commonly "Vive Napoleon," "Vive le Roi de Rome," and "au mort Louis XVIII." Sites of slogans included the ramparts of the town, the door of the city hall, one in a theater loge; in Haute Vienne, antimissionary slogans were inscribed on the doors of various officials, and on the walls and doors of all the houses situated on the main marketplace of Limoges, F7 9794, letter from the prefect of Haute-Vienne to the minister of the interior, 4 February 1828.

68. In a report on a placard found in Paris, on 20 May 1827, the prefect of the Seine describes the combination of a large, easily readable message with little details visible only upon closer scrutiny: "At 11 P.M. a placard was found on the Wall of the House of the Baker of the King, Rue Notre Dame des Victoires. 16 inches in width, a foot in height, written in pencil, very large, very readable, the words 'Francais, la Patrie, Crie Vengeance, Vive Napoleon II, Aux Armes'; in the four corners one reads 'Courage, Gloire, Patrie, Honneur.'" AN, F7 6706, dossier 3, Seine.

69. In the context of the Rouen incident in 1825, the prefect noted that placards found on the door of the archbishop's palace were also arriving by post at the homes of various local officials. AN, F7 9793, letter from the prefect of the Seine-Inférieure to the minister of the interior, 22 April 1825.

70. In Digne, for example, a police report describes thirteen placards with the same contents, written by the same hand, posted at different points in town: AN, F7 3797, Bulletin de Police, No. 55, 16 June 1826, Digne, 8 April 1826 (the precise contents of the placard are not described, only that they "insult authority"). In Rouen, three copies were posted of a placard which read "To the Devil, the King, Death to the priests, the deputies and the Nobility. Long live Napoleon II": ADSI, 1 M 176, found in Rouen on 13 March 1816. In the Haute Vienne, in response to word that missionaries were coming to Limoges, many public edifices were turned into placards, for example, the door of the residence of Mr. le premier President and the door of the Hôtel de Poste (one of the sites most frequented by the public). The report explains: "These writings have been reproduced, and have multiplied; a great number of houses on the marketplace have written on their doors and their walls: 'Down with the missionaries, down with the Jesuits.' It appears that the perturbers profit from the obscurity of the night when they write their slogans which are all of the same handwriting and are conceived in the same terms." AN, F7 9794, letter from the prefect of the Haute Vienne to the minister of the interior, 4 February 1828.

71. It is obvious, from looking at the majority of placards, that they were written in block letters, meant to have the effect which one would produce today by cutting and pasting letters from a magazine. Demonstrating the efforts to track down culprits by checking on the handwriting used was the subprefect of Yvetot, who got the director of the Post Office to allow the police commissioner to come and inspect all letters and packages in an attempt to find handwriting which matched the seditious placards he had seen in his town: ADSI, 1 M 176, letter from the subprefect of Yvetot to the prefect of the Seine-Inférieure, 16 December 1816; in another case the subprefect of Dieppe accused the author of a

placard of faking bad handwriting to throw the police off track, ADSI, 1 M 176, letter to the prefect of the Seine-Inférieure, 24 August 1816.

72. AN, F7 6706, dossier Seine, report from lt. general commandant la 1ère division militaire de la Seine, 19 September 1825, to the minister of the interior. The message was written using coal.

73. AN, F7 6693, letter from the prefect of the Seine-Inférieure to the minister of the interior, 25 April 1825, which also contained the text and picture described.

74. ADSI, 1 M 176, found on the door of the Eglise St-Vivien, the night of 14–15 August 1818.

75. AN, F7 6704, dossier Dordogne, no correspondence, simply the placard, with the remark "found, January 1822 in Périgueux."

76. ADSI, 1 M 176, placard included in a letter from the subprefect of Dieppe to the prefect, found during the night of 18–19 May 1816.

77. A placard announcing the celebration of Saint Charles's Day which was simply destroyed is described in AN, F7 3796, Bulletin de Police, No. 90, 12 November 1825, Angers, 7 November 1825.

78. AN, F7 9898, placard included in letter from the prefect of the Côtes-du-Nord to the minister of the interior, 8 November 1825.

79. AN, F7 6704, in a letter from the prefect of the Doubs to the minister of the interior, 7 March 1827, the text reads: "Dans les entr'actes MM. de Ch_ et du B_ Doyens des hypocrites de cette ville danseront un pas de deux avec les religieuses du Sacre Coeur de Jesus."

80. The full text read "Archbishopric of Rouen, for rent or for sale," sent among seditious writings circulating in this turbulent month, many of which fleshed out the themes of this economical placard, in the prefect of the Seine-Inférieure to the minister of the interior, 22 April 1825, AN, F7 6693.

81. AN, F7 3797, Bulletin de Police, No. 43, 30 May 1826, Rouen, 29 May 1826.

82. AN, F7 6705, placard included in letter from the prefect of the Moselle to the minister of the interior, 19 September 1826, which had been posted on the door of the Eglise de Longwy.

83. ADSI, 1 M 176, letter from the subprefect of Dieppe to the prefect of the Seine-Inférieure, 15 December 1816.

84. AN, F7 6705, dossier 18, Rhin-Bas, in letter from the prefect of Bas-Rhin to the minister of the interior, 8 April 1826.

85. David Higgs, "Discursive Shouts," p. 11.

86. Ibid., p. 16.

87. Susanna Barrows, "Laughter, Language, and Derision: Seditious Speech and Popular Political Culture in Mid-Nineteenth-Century France," unpublished manuscript, pp. 4, 6.

88. In the following chapter we will look more closely at the specific seditious cries inspired by the missions.

89. ADSI, 1 M 175, letter from the subprefect of Le Havre to the prefect of the Seine-Inférieure, 5 April 1820; this incident took place in a café.

90. AN, BB 22/15–23, dossier S6 362, request for pardon in a case in which

a man was imprisoned for two years for insulting the duchesse d'Angoulême during a procession in her honor, 7 May 1823; Higgs, "Discursive Shouts," p. 17, refers to a similar incident, when someone shouted, "the Duchesse of Angouleme is nothing but a whore."

91. The police did, occasionally, apprehend people for seditious cries on the basis of a denunciation. In one case, in the Dordogne, a man and his son were denounced by two people who heard them say at the market, "that we will have to pay the dîme, and other feudal taxes, that the émigrés would have their *biens* restored, and that the king wants to put all the French into slavery." Letter to the prefect of the Dordogne, from Périgueux, 11 January 1817, ADD, 1 M 64. Much more commonly, the police would try to get the people in the crowd to denounce those perpetrating such crimes, but to no effect.

92. We already saw, in the section on the *mise-en-place* ceremonies, how often the songs "most loved by the French" were incorporated into those celebrations; reports on local festivities almost always include references to songs and, occasionally, to special verses when they were composed for the occasion. Two years in a row, for example, one subprefect from Verdun wrote special verses for the celebration of Saint Louis, which he included in his reports, AN, F7 9897, letters from August 1817 and 1818, including verses to two songs, the 1817 song to the tune of "Le Vin, les Femmes, et la Gloire."

93. The police were particularly attentive to songs circulating in this period precisely because they could reach the entire population. In the circular by which the minister of police informed his prefects about the measures to take to control peddling of all manner of seditious materials, one sees special attention devoted to the extensive influence of small compositions (which included almanacs as well as songs), but songs are singled out in the following way: "The influence of these little works has always been extremely profound on the people, and a collection of all the popular songs would offer a rather accurate portrait of the diverse variations in the *esprit public.*" AN, F7 6729, circular from the minister of police to all prefects, 15 December 1815.

94. On the peculiar importance of songs and singing, see Laura Mason, *Singing the Revolution* (Ithaca, N.Y.: Cornell University Press, 1997); Regina Sweeney, "Harmony and Disharmony: French Musical Politics during the Great War," forthcoming manuscript; Walter J. Ong, *Orality and Literacy: The Technologizing of the Word* (London and New York: Routledge, 1982), p. 34.

95. AN, F7 6693. The longer song was included in a letter from the prefect of the Seine-Inférieure to the minister of the interior, 30 April 1825; the shorter song was sent in a later letter, 7 May 1825.

96. AN, F7 6693, letter from the prefect of the Eure to the minister of the interior, 27 April 1825.

97. AN, F7 3796, Bulletin de Police, No. 7, 31 January 1824, Lyons, 27 January 1824.

98. "Marseillaise" rewrite, F7 6693, contained in a letter from the prefect of the Seine-Inférieure to the minister of the interior, 7 May 1825. In Rouen in 1825, the authorities reported seditious rewrites of three popular drinking songs, "Mon père était pot," "Il pleut, il pleut bergère," and "Femmes, voulez-vous éprouvez?" which also had many incarnations during the Revolution ac-

cording to Constant Pierre, *Les Hymnes et Chansons de la Revolution: Aperçu général et catalogue avec notices historiques, analytiques et bibliographiques* (Paris: Imprimerie National, 1904), pp. 1007, 1004, and 1003. I thank Laura Mason for having made me aware of this catalogue, and helping me to identify the historical background of many of the songs collected by the police in this period.

99. F7 6770, letter from the prefect of the Haute-Loire to the minister of the interior, 9 March 1822.

100. AN, F7 6706, dossier Seine, unsigned letter, included in a report from the commissaire of police to the prefect of the Seine, dated 4 July 1826, about an incident which took place on 29 June 1826.

101. ADD, 1 M 64, letter from capitaine commandant la Gendarmerie Royale de la Dordogne, not addressed, although probably sent to the prefect of the Dordogne, dated 30 June 1818, describing events of the previous night. Emphasis in original.

102. The following letter from the prefect of the Seine-Inférieure regarding a song he was forwarding to the minister of the interior was quite typical in this regard: "[This new song] . . . has circulated in public these last few days. It is the only one that I could procure since the 30th, even though I had been told that many others had also appeared at that time." AN, F7 6693, 3 May 1825.

103. AN, F7 3798, Bulletin de Police, No. 60, 25 July 1829, Nord 12 July 1829. In this case one man was imprisoned for a month and fined 50 francs for singing a seditious song in public.

104. ADSI, 1 M 174, Rouen, 18 March 1822, letter from the prefect of the Seine-Inférieure to the mayor of Rouen asking him to keep trying to identify authors of songs circulating in town.

105. Most accounts in the police archives of seditious singing follow the general lines of this report from Rouen, when an incident is simply mentioned in passing, with no evidence of prosecution: ADSI, 1 M 175. Here the mayor of Rouen, describing a café scene where seditious things were said against the king, concluded his report with the mention that, at the end of the evening, the individuals in question "left the café . . . and went up the street singing the marseillaise [*sic*]." Or in a case from Chateauroux, in 1822, the prefect of the Indre sent in a copy of a seditious song, recently sung in a café, to show "that he neglected nothing in his efforts to discover the maneuvers of troublemakers," but in fact he had no traces of the authors of the song or of the singing in question: AN, F7 6727, letter to the minister of the interior, 9 February 1822.

106. AN, F7 6772, dossier 3, Seine, report dated 12 September 1829. The end of the report identifies two musicians and a singer who traveled together in an effort to get other police officials' help in tracking down these instigators.

107. AN, F7 7604, dossier Jura, letter from the prefect of the Jura to the minister of the interior, 13 October 1819.

108. Several letters between officials in the Eure-et-Loir and Paris refer to a prosecutor who refused to prosecute traveling singers who sold brochures containing texts of their songs; the prefect complains that this set up a system which put the police administration in continual contradiction with the judicial ad-

ministration, which makes the government look ridiculous, at the same time as it clearly condones the traffic in seditious songs. AN, F18, 551; letters: 12 January 1826, from the prefect of the Eure-et-Loir to the minister of the interior; 19 February 1827, from the minister of the interior to the garde de Sceaux; 28 February 1827, from the minister of justice to the minister of the interior.

109. Irene Collins, *The Government and the Newspaper Press in France, 1814–1881* (London: Oxford University Press, 1959); Charles Ledré, *La Presse à l'Assault de la Monarchie, 1815–1848* (Paris: A. Colin, 1960).

110. Announcement of the complete works of Voltaire (described as the "patriarch of philosophy") in 8, in 12 volumes, in *Le Journal du Commerce, de Politique, et de Littérature,* no. 477, 12 November 1818.

111. This calculation of the *Mémorial Catholique* is cited in Henri Guillemin, *Histoire des Catholiques français au XIXe siècle (1815–1905)* (Geneva, Paris, Montreal: Editions du Milieu du Monde, 1947), p. 21.

112. This language of "fortifying the good spirit of the century" is taken from the announcement cited above concerning the works of Voltaire, in *Journal du Commerce,* 12 November 1818.

113. Other historians have written about this extraordinary traffic in pamphlets. Among them, Edgar Leon Newman uses this explosion of pamphlet literature after 1825 to support his argument for a growing alliance between the working class and the middle class in the years leading up to 1830 in his "The Blouse and the Frock Coat: The Alliance of the Common People of Paris with the Liberal Leadership and the Middle Class During the Last Years of the Bourbon Restoration," *Journal of Modern History* 46 (March 1974): 43; see also Réné Rémond, *L'Anticlericalisme en France de 1815 à nos jours* (Paris: Fayard, 1976), p. 51; and, on the "Battle of the Books," from the missionaries' perspective, see Martyn Lyons, "Fires of Expiation: Book-Burning and Catholic Missions in Restoration France," *French History* 10, 1 (1996): 1–27.

114. Most reports quote the price of 10 sous. This was the price quoted in the report from Paris regarding 5,000 copies of Voltaire's *Candide* and 3,000 copies of a small history of the Inquisition, Bulletin de Police, No. 62, 1 July 1826. A report from Tours cites two small books, *Melahie* of La Harpe and Mirabeau's "Discourse sur le droit d'Ainesse," at 6 sous, Bulletin de Police, No. 21, 22 March 1826, Tours, 17 March 1826. A report from Paris on two volumes of Voltaire, *The Philosophical Dictionary* and *La Pucelle,* mentions that "one even sees some books of this type circulating for 5–10 sous," Bulletin de Police, No. 53, 12 June 1826, Paris, 11 June 1826. Another report quoting the price of 5 sous, Bulletin de Police, No. 59, 26 June 1826, mentions that "to regularize and perpetuate the publication in 32 at 5 sous, the Librairie Touquet announced another series of little books of this genre."

115. This calculation is cited from Newman, "The Blouse and the Frock Coat," p. 43.

116. AN, F7 3797, Bulletin de Police, No. 31, 26 April 1826, Paris, same date.

117. AN, F7 3797, Bulletin de Police, No. 32, 29 April 1826, Paris, same date.

118. Voltaire's works are cited continually in the police reports of this period. A few examples: AN, F7 3797, Bulletin de Police, No. 53, 12 June 1826, Paris, 11 June 1826; No. 78, Paris, 30 August 1826 (also Rousseau).

119. *Les Jesuits:* AN, F7 3797, Bulletin No. 30, Paris, 22 April 1826; *Civil Constitution of the Clergy:* AN, F7 3797, Bulletin de Police, No. 59, Paris, 26 June 1826; *Liberties of the Gallican Church:* AN, F7 3797, Bulletin de Police, No. 59, Paris, 26 June 1826; No. 62, Paris, 1 July 1826; No. 69, Paris, 24 July 1826 (a version containing the Civil Constitution of the Clergy).

120. *Feudal Dictionary:* AN, F7 3797, Bulletin de Police, No. 61, Paris, 29 June 1826; Mirabeau's essay: AN, F7 3797, Bulletin de Police, No. 30, Paris, 22 April 1826; *Biography of the Women of the Court:* AN, F7 3797, Bulletin de Police, No. 62, Paris, 8 July 1826; No. 71, Paris, 29 July 1826 also mentions *The Adventures of the Duke of Roquelaure.*

121. General histories: AN, F7 3797, Bulletin de Police, No. 59, Paris, 26 June 1826; *History of the Revolution:* AN, F7 3797, Bulletin de Police, No. 80, Paris, 2 September 1826.

122. AN, F7 3797, Bulletin de Police, No. 62, Paris, 8 July 1826 mentions a volume of Béranger songs which had been seized and sent to the minister of justice; AN, F7 3797, Bulletin de Police, No. 109, Paris, 13 December 1826, notes: "The most impious and revolutionary songs of Béranger are being sold clandestinely, not only printed, but also illustrated in a volume now appearing in Paris which reassembles all of the verses which had been carefully removed for the approved publication."

123. Pamphlets regarding debates in chambers: Montlosier's famous essay regarding the Sacrilege Law is only the most well-known pamphlet of this genre. Reported in AN, F7 3797, Bulletin de Police, No. 30, Paris, 22 April 1822; again in Bulletin de Police, No. 68, Paris, 22 July 1826; and yet again in Bulletin de Police, No. 104, Paris, 25 November 1826, along with new printings of Voltaire and Rousseau. In another report a month later, other pamphlets "in the same spirit as Montlosier's" are described, AN, F7 3797, Bulletin de Police, No. 109, Paris, 13 December 1826. Pamphlets regarding trials: AN, F7 3796, Bulletin de Police, No. 69, Paris, 18 August 1825 notes 1,200 copies of a defense lawyer's plea in a recent case against a curé; in the Brest incident, which we will consider at length in chap. 6, the court proceedings and the pleas of the defense lawyers were likewise published, although I do not know how many copies were produced. AN, F7 9793, dossier Brest 1826–27.

124. For the most recent summary of the literature on the "good books" side of this battle, see Darrin M. McMahon's *Enemies of the Enlightenment: The French Counter-Enlightenment and the Birth of the European Right, 1788–1830* (forthcoming, Oxford University Press); on the prophetic literature widely circulating in this period, see Thomas Kselman, *Miracles and Prophecies in Nineteenth-Century France* (New Brunswick, N.J.: Rutgers University Press, 1983) and, for a shorter treatment of the same issue, Kselman's "Popular Religiosity," in Edgar L. Newman, ed., *Historical Dictionary of France from the 1815 Restoration to the Second Empire* (New York and Westport, Conn.: Greenwood Press, 1987), p. 813.

125. On the 'oeuvre' of Good Books in Bordeaux, see McMahon, *Enemies of the Enlightenment;* on the Catholic Good Book Society, see Adrien Dansette, *Religious History of Modern France,* vol. I: *From the Revolution to the Third Republic* (New York: Herder and Herder, 1961), p. 190.

126. David Longfellow, "Society for Good Studies, 1828–1833," in Edgar L. Newman, *Historical Dictionary of France from the 1815 Restoration to the Second Empire* (New York and Westport, Conn.: Greenwood Press, 1987), p. 995; Françoise Parent-Lardeur, *Les Cabinets de lecture: La lecture publique à Paris sous la Restauration* (Paris: Payot, 1982).

127. From *Ami de la Religion*, 1 February 1819, cited in Martyn Lyons, "Fires of Expiation: Book-Burning and Catholic Missions in the French Restoration," *French History* 10, 1: 12.

128. *Le Constitutionnel*, No. 108, 18 April 1825, p. 3.

129. *Le Constitutionnel*, No. 145, 25 May 1825, p. 2.

130. Cited in Henri Guillemin, *Histoire des Catholiques français*, p. 21.

131. As we shall see in the trial of the instigators of the *Tartuffe* incident in Brest in 1826, the lawyers would make precisely this kind of argument. The proceedings from this trial were themselves published in cheap pamphlet form and circulated. A wonderful pamphlet in the police files on the missions, entitled "Letter to the Missionaries," beautifully illustrates the use of the reasoning of the philosophes against the missionaries. Here the author accuses the missionaries of all the crimes for which they held the philosophes responsible. AN, F7 9792, loose piece between dossiers Ardennes and Eure-et-Loir, dated 7 February 1818.

132. AN, F7 9792, letter from the commissaire de police from La Rochelle to the minister of the interior, 14 January 1818.

133. *Le Constitutionnel*, 19 October, 1826, p. 3.

134. AN, F7 3797, Bulletin de Police, No. 46, 5 June 1826, Paris, 3 June 1826, citing an article from the *Mercure* from that date. Both Newman, "Blouse and the Frock Coat," and Paul Salvan's "Le Tartuffe de Molière et l'agitation anticléricale en 1825," *Revue de la Société d'Histoire du Théâtre*, vol. 12 (Paris: 1960) emphasize the importance of these pamphlets in Tartuffe incidents all over France.

135. AN, F7 3797, Bulletin de Police, No. 35, 18 May 1826.

136. Robert Justin Goldstein, *Censorship of Political Caricature in Nineteenth-Century France* (Kent, Ohio: Kent State University Press, 1989), offers a wonderful complement to this discussion.

137. Paul Cordonnier-Detrif, "Imagerie et Colportage," extract from *La Revue Historique et Archéologique du Marne* 3 (1953): 3–51.

138. AN, F7 6705, letter from the prefect of Mayenne to the minister of the interior, 29 August 1819.

139. AN, F7 6704, from the prefect of Ille-et-Vilaine to the minister of the interior, 25 January 1820, circulating in Rennes; AN, F7 6704, from the prefect of Haute Garonne to the minister of interior, 5 October 1819; 8 October 1819; 21 October 1819; and 27 November 1819, circulating in Toulouse; AN, F7 6705, letter from the commissaire de police to the prefect of Sarthe, 3 September 1819, regarding seditious print purchased in Le Mans on 20 August 1819; AN, F7 6706, letter from the prefect of Seine to the minister of the interior, 28 January 1819; 6 February 1819, reporting successful condemnation of the distributor of these prints in Paris to three months in prison and a fine of 50 francs. This letter mentions that the price of the print was 4 F.

140. AN, F7 6705, from the prefect of Morbihan to the minister of the inte-

rior, 7 May 1824, describing razors which were being sold in the city of Vannes bearing the names and portraits of Voltaire and Montesquieu.

141. Scarves: AN, F7 6706, letter from the prefect of the Seine to the minister of finance, 21 June 1827; ties: Musée des Archives Nationales, Hôtel Soubise, AEV, No. 312, also cited in dossier 5506 in AN, F7 6704, Nantes, March 1828; umbrellas: AN, F7 6705, from the prefect of the Rhône to the minister of the interior, 19 June 1827.

142. AN, F7 6704, dossier 2, Aisne, letter from the prefect of the Aisne to the minister of the interior, 5 October 1820.

143. Busts: ADSI, 1 M 173, letter from the prefect of the Seine-Inférieure to the minister of the interior, 27 December 1822; AN, F7 3796, Bulletin de Police, No. 87, 26 October 1825, Lyons, 20 October 1825; No. 2, 12 January 1824, Lille, 8 January 1824; plateware: ADSI, 1 M 173, letter from the prefect of the Seine-Inférieure to the minister of the interior, 27 December 1822.

144. ADSI, 1 M 173, correspondence between the director of police and the mayor of Rouen, 24 November 1821 and 12 December 1821; letter from the prefect of the Seine-Inférieure to the minister of the interior, 20 November 1822. Such articles of clothing were also spotted in Perpignan and in Roanne in the Loire, AN, F7 3706, Bulletin de Police, No. 104, 30 December 1825. Another report of a similar incident came from the Lot-et-Garonne, AN, F7 6705, letter to the prefect of the Lot-et-Garonne from the minister of the interior, 30 April 1822.

145. AN, F7 6704, letter from the prefect of Doubs to the minister of the interior, 27 May 1826. The prefect thought they were produced in Alsace.

146. AN, F7 6705, Marne, 18 December 1822.

147. AN, F7 6704, dossier 3, Allier, letter from the prefect of Allier to the minister of the interior, 2 January 1820.

148. AN, F7 6706, letter from the prefect of Var to the minister of the interior, 7 January 1828; the prefect sees the selling of these particular boxes of candy as part of a broader effort, taking different forms, "to corrupt the spirit of the garrison and the inhabitants of Toulon."

149. Watchbands: ADSI, 1 M 176, letter from the mayor of Rouen to the prefect of the Seine-Inférieure, 20 July 1819; swimsuits: ADSI, 1 M 176, letter from the prefect of the Seine-Inférieure to the director of police, 29 August 1821; neckties; ADSI, 1 M 176, report of the central office of the mayor of Rouen, 15–16 August 1823.

150. ADSI, 1 M 176: The confiscation of the chairs was initially announced in a police report from Rouen sent to the director of police, 4 May 1820; in a letter from the director of police to the prefect of the Seine-Inférieure, 17 May 1820, the local authorities were ordered to return the chairs to their owner. In the Musée de l'Hôtel de Ville (Museum of the National Archives) AEV 331, thirty-seven different Bonapartist and liberal wine labels can be found, many featuring the tricolor; also cited in AN, F7 6956, dossier 11801.

151. AN, F7 6704, Aisne, St-Quentin, 25 April 1829.

152. Ribbons: ADSI, 1 M 176, report from commissaire de police of Rouen to the prefect of the Seine-Inférieur, 20 July 1819; ADSI, 1 M 176, 1 M 174, letter from the mayor of Rouen to the prefect of the Seine-Inférieure, 8 July 1822.

153. AN, F7 6704, letter from the prefect of Ille-et-Vilaine to the minister of the interior, 18 December 1825.

154. AN, F7 3797, Bulletin de Police, No. 80, 2 September 1828, Digne, 26 August 1826; Bulletin de Police, No. 85, 15 September 1826, Digne, 7 September 1826; Bulletin de Police, No. 96, 28 October 1826, Digne, 19 October 1826.

155. ADSI, 1 M 176, letter from the mayor of Montvillier to the prefect of the Seine-Inférieure, 11 October 1819; ADSI, 1 M 176, letter from the prefect of the Seine-Inférieure to the minister of the interior, 27 January 1821.

156. ADSI, 1 M 173, letter from the mayor of Authieux about Port St-Oeun, July 1816 (no exact date in original).

157. ADSI, 1 M 177 contains a dossier of over twenty pieces describing attacks on busts in front of the city hall in Rouen in 1819–20. Anne M. Wagner gives other examples of attacks on busts of both Louis XVIII and Charles X in her "Outrages: Sculpture and Kingship in France after 1789," in Ann Bermingham and John Brewer, eds., *The Consumption of Culture, 1600–1800: Image, Object, Text* (London and New York: Routledge, 1995), pp. 311–12.

158. AN BB22, 15–22, dossier 53 4208, request for a pardon, 23 October 1817, for a crime committed on the night of 9–10 May 1816 in the town of St-Jean Pied-de-Port in the Basses-Pyrénées.

159. ADSI, 1 M 176, letter from the subprefect of Dieppe to the prefect of the Seine-Inférieure, 4 September 1816, regarding the arrest of a man for crushing a white cockade under his shoe.

160. See Susanna Barrows, "Laughter, Language, and Derision," for a critical discussion of the role of humor and derision in nineteenth-century protests in general.

161. AN, F7 6693, song enclosed in letter from the prefect of the Seine-Inférieure to the minister of the interior, 7 May 1825.

162. AN, F7 6693, placard enclosed in letter from the prefect of the Seine-Inférieure to the minister of the interior, 25 April 1825.

163. For example, in Rouen, when the first letter of each line of one seditious text was read vertically, it spelled out "LESUR GRAND VICAR DE ROUEN"; when read normally, it contained twenty-two lines of insults aimed at that same official. AN, F7 6693, text enclosed in letter from the prefect of the Seine-Inférieure to the minister of the interior, 27 May 1825.

164. General references to the "rude" and "obscene" nature of placards: AN, F7 3796, Bulletin de Police, No. 101, 21 December 1825, Melun, 20 December 1825; reference to obscene songs, AN, F7 3796, Bulletin de Police, No. 41, 26 May 1826, Rouen, 23 May 1826; example cited above in which the official placard for the Saint Charles's Day celebration was defaced with the words, "The civil and military authorities will kiss the asses of the ecclesiastical authorities," AN, F7 9898, included in a letter from the prefect of the Côtes-du-Nord to the minister of the interior, 8 November 1825; "shit for Louis XVIII" placard cited above, ADSI, 1 M 176, 1817, otherwise undated; different songs in the *Tartuffe* incident in Rouen accuse churchmen of incest, bestiality, attacks on young virgins, AN, F7 6693.

165. AN, F7 6693, placard sent in a letter from the prefect of the Seine-Inférieure to the minister of the interior, 7 May 1825.

166. In three different letters in the correspondence of the prefect of the Seine-Inférieure, one finds the danger of the *colporteur* explained, ADSI, 1 M 175: 1) letter from the mayor of Rouen to the prefect, 17 April 1821, about a particular *colporteur* who exaggerated the news as he read it in public; the mayor noted his intention to prevent him from selling but admitted that "experience has shown me the impossibility of getting this individual to adhere to the conditions which we impose upon him." 2) letter from the prefect to the sub-prefect of Le Havre, 19 June 1823, about another *colporteur* specializing in news sheets who spoke out publicly against the war in Spain and the king and in favor of Napoleon. He repeated these words in front of 300 people as they came out of the church. 3) letter from the mayor of Elbeuf to the prefect, 6 May 1826, about a *colporteur* who was spreading news of workers' attacks on machines in England among textile workers in Normandy: "We know the danger of such publications among an uneducated working-class population, and what consequence they could have." One popular work of fiction represented the *colporteur* as a serpent and as a corrupter of youth. See *Le Colporteur au Village,* par l'Abbé . . . , 3d ed. (Tours: Ad. Mame. et Cie, 1849), pp. 51–56.

167. Other historians have rightly criticized the tendency of the police to portray politics in this way. See especially Peter Sahlins, *Forest Rites: The War of the Demoiselles in Nineteenth-Century France* (Cambridge, Mass.: Harvard University Press, 1994).

168. The police seemed especially concerned whenever workers were involved, and usually ended their reports with requests for special surveillance, which was not the case with other groups. See, for example, ADSI, 1 M 175, letter from the prefect of the Seine-Inférieure to the mayor of Darnetal, 6 March 1823, about a café near textile factories which was frequented by workers.

169. Corbin, "L'Agitation dans les théâtres," pp. 95–98; see chap. 5 below for a discussion of the social composition of those involved in *Tartuffe* incidents.

170. In a letter written to the director of the theater and posted in public in Rouen in the spring of 1825, the following postscript was featured: "Women are asked not to present themselves at the theater until further orders, if they wish to avoid the disagreeableness which they will inevitably confront." AN, F7 6693, letter from the prefect of the Seine-Inférieure to the minister of the interior, 23 April 1825.

171. ADSI, 1 M 176, 1817, otherwise undated.

172. ADSI, 1 M 174, letter from the prefect of the Seine-Inférieure to the mayor of Rouen, 18 March 1822.

173. Roger Chartier evokes the degree to which written forms played a role in the lives of illiterate people in *The Cultural Uses of Print,* p. 343.

174. AN, F7 6693, placard sent in a letter from the prefect of the Seine-Inférieure to the minister of the interior, 7 May 1825.

175. AN, F7 3797, Bulletin de Police, No. 98, 4 November 1826, Lyons, 2 November 1826.

176. ADSI, 4 T 81, report from the Bureau Central de Police, Mairie de Rouen, 12 February 1821. Not only were 2,000 people in the theater but between 200 and 300 were turned away at the door.

177. AN, F7 6692, letter from the prefect of the Charente to the minister of the interior, 22 July 1826.

178. Robert Alexander, *Bonapartism and Revolutionary Tradition in France: The Fédérés of 1815* (Cambridge: Cambridge University Press, 1991).

179. AN, F2 (I) 135, letter from the prefect of the Basses-Pyrénées to the minister of the interior, 31 March 1816 (emphasis my own). In her "Outrages: Sculpture and Kingship," Anne Wagner gives a fabulous example which is perfectly analogous to the fleur-de-lis fold-up, or the everyday objects bearing concealed Bonapartist images, in the statue of Henri IV erected on the Pont Neuf. While to all appearances this statue represented the resurrection of monarchy, it turns out that one of the team of founders who cast the statue "literally filled it with Napoleonica—all potentially contraband and seditious. He deposited a statuette of Napoleon in the ruler's right arm . . . and in the horse's belly what he calls 'several boxes filled with various papers, like songs, inscriptions, diatribes—monuments to the flavor of the times which I wanted to conserve for history.'" Concluding about the significance of these mementos, hidden in the entrails of the giant bronze, Wagner argues, "Unreadable, unseeable, nonetheless they need simply be lodged in the king's vitals to work their special predictive magic. There they embody the revolutionary Other, giving it form in the figure of Napoleon, and voice as seditious speech." Citing the founder, pp. 312, 313.

Chapter Five

1. Mona Ozouf, *Festivals of the French Revolution,* trans. Alan Sheridan (Cambridge, Mass.: Harvard University Press, 1988), p. 282.

2. AN, F7 6742, articles cited from 25 May 1825, enclosed in letter from subprefect of Issoire, 28 October 1825.

3. AN, F7 9792, dossier Bouches-du-Rhône, letter from commissaire de police to the minister of the interior, 3 December 1819.

4. AN, F7 3797, Bulletin de Police, No. 4, 14 January 1826, Niort, 9 January 1826.

5. "Le Mandement," in AN, F7 6693, dossier Rouen, in a letter from the prefect of the Seine-Inférieure to the minister of the interior, dated 25 April 1825. The letter explicitly describes this song as widely circulating and popular. The English translation does not do justice to the rhyme scheme or the humor of the French version, which goes:

1

Pour être bon catholique,
Ecoutez le mandement
de l'archévêque de Rouen,
vous verrez comme il s'explique
en homme de qualité
qui a de l'humanité

2

à Dieu né dans une crèche
il rend grace, y a de quoi,
d'être pair, prince de Croy,

Chimonier, même archévêque,
Commandeur du St. Esprit
Primicier [*sic*] de St. Denis.

3

Pour les habits, redingottes
couleur claire, il fait du bruit.
que les prêtres soient bien mis,
dit-il, qu'ils aient des culottes
les pantalons de nanssin [*sic*]
lui font beaucoup de chagrin.

4

les curés qui auront des nièces
faudra les mettre en garni;
les jeunes bonnes aussi
qui auront eu des faiblesses
les filles de quarante ans
servent sans inconvénient.

6. "Le Mandement," stanzas 5–7.

7. In "Le Mandement," stanzas 9–12 explain the kinds of riches this new brand of priest requires; for example, 9: "The tabernacle must be decorated / with riches . . . wallpaper is cheap, one must use satin." Stanza 10 applies the same logic to the linens necessary for the altar, and stanza 11 to the dishes from which the monseigneur should be served: "no more dishes of copper . . . only gold will do . . . " Stanza 13 explicitly alludes to the Jesuits.

8. "Le Mandement," stanzas 14–18: the public chastisement for such offenses would take the form of having one's name listed on the church wall.

9. "Le Mandement," stanza 19.

10. "Le Mandement," verses 23–30.

11. "Le Mandement," verses 31–33; quotation from 33.

12. AN, F7 6693, included in letter from the prefect of the Seine-Inférieure to the minister of the interior, 23 April 1824; AN, F7 6693, song included in letter from the prefect of the Seine-Inférieure to the minister of the interior, 7 May 1825. Song described as having "circulated these last days in the city." Stanza 11: "Those who during the Revolution / forged a profane union / will be remarried. . . ." Stanza 13: "To Confession everyone will go / and at Easter will take communion, or they will be excommunicated." Stanza 16: "To satisfy my desire / I want to trouble your pleasures. . . ." 17: "even today I see they're representing me on stage / I see *Tartuffe* in the *affiche* here / what an abomination . . . ;" 18: "I do not want them to perform this / the police will obey me / for I will threaten them with eternal damnation . . . ;" 19: "Bravo, the city is rife with rumors / and me I'm the author! / soon the pope will hear about it."

13. AN, F7 3796, Bulletin de Police, No. 98, 12 December 1825, Blois, 25 November 1825.

14. AN, F7 3797, Bulletin de Police, No. 16, 4 March 1826.

15. AN, F7 3796, Bulletin de Police, No. 89, 5 November 1825, Bar-le-Duc, same date. In a later bulletin, No. 91, 17 November 1825, it was reported that the three offenders were sentenced to three months of prison and a fine of 300 francs

for "having performed a sacrilegious parody of the sacrament of extreme unction in a cabaret."

16. AN, F7 3797, Bulletin de Police, No. 3, 12 January 1826, Le Puy, 6 January 1826. Several days later, some visiting missionaries preached against these sacrilegious acts, and the people involved in the incident denied the missionaries' accusations and "seized this pretext to complain about the missionaries."

17. AN, F7 3796, Bulletin de Police, No. 99, 14 December 1825, Epinal, 9 December 1825.

18. AN, F7 3797, Bulletin de Police, No. 28, 15 April 1826, Bar-le-Duc, 7 April 1826.

19. AN, F7 3797, Bulletin de Police, No. 100, 11 November 1826, Nancy, 3 November 1826.

20. E. P. Thompson, "Le Charivari anglais," AESC 27 (1972): 285–312; and Natalie Zemon Davis, Society and Culture in Early Modern France (Stanford, Calif.: Stanford University Press, 1975). For a clear, concise summary of the vast literature on this subject, see Peter Sahlins, Forest Rites: The War of the Demoiselles in Nineteenth-Century France (Cambridge, Mass.: Harvard University Press, 1994).

21. Ozouf, Festivals of the French Revolution, esp. "A Shameful Ethnology," pp. 218–22.

22. The failure of this project during the Revolution is discussed by Ozouf, Festivals, in "History of a Failure," pp. 223–31; on the Napoleonic approach, see Maurice Agulhon, La Vie Sociale en Provence Intérieure au lendemain de la Revolution (Paris: Société des Etudes Robespierristes, 1970), pp. 413–14.

23. Law published in Le Moniteur Universel, No. 318, 18 thermidor, an X (6 August 1802).

24. It seems that state officials were also still trying to get certain folkloric practices under control, such as the charivari, which was deemed illegal by a special arrêté of the prefect of the Côte d'Or in 1818, announced in Le Journal du Commerce, de politique, et de littérature, No. 195, 3 February 1818, p. 3.

25. AN, F7 9792, letter explaining this from the prefect of Bouches-du-Rhône to the minister of the interior, 6 December 1819.

26. All quotations from Le Phocéen, 16 February 1820, included in AN, F7 9792, dossier Bouches-du-Rhône.

27. AN, F7 9792, letter from commissaire de police, La Rochelle, to the minister of the interior, 14 January 1818.

28. AN, F7 9897, from the prefect of the Creuse to the minister of police, 29 August 1818.

29. AN, F7 3798, Bulletin de Police, No. 57, 18 July 1829, Côtes du Nord, 28 May 1829.

30. AN, F7 3798, Bulletin de Police, No. 63, 4 August 1829, Côtes du Nord, same date.

31. AN, F7 9792, letter from the conseiller de préfecture délégué to the minister of police, 15 April 1817.

32. All quotations from AN, F7 9792, letter from the conseiller de préfecture délégué to the minister of police, 15 April 1817.

33. In Pierrevillères in the Moselle, Vespers was disrupted by scandalous singing which forced the clergymen to withdraw from the church, AN, F7 3797, Bulletin de Police, No. 25, 4 April 1826, Metz, 30 March 1826; in Draguignon, in February of 1826, services were disrupted when some young men coming from a masquerade party entered the church in Cuers, dressed as women, AN, F7 3797, Bulletin de Police, No. 11, 14 February 1826, Draguignon, 7 February 1826.

34. AN, F7 3797, Bulletin de Police, No. 12, 18 February 1826, Draguignon, 6 February 1826; see Réné Rémond, *L'Anticlericalisme en France de 1815 à nos jours* (Paris: Fayard, 1976), p. 36, for a discussion of the common use of the symbol of the *éteignoir*.

35. All of the major anticlerical disturbances evoked in the police records cite this common practice of throwing petards into the church. See, for example, reports on the Marseilles mission of 1820; Rouen, 1826. In Strasbourg, firecrackers were thrown at the procession organized by missionaries in celebration of the Jubilee: AN, F7 3797, Bulletin de Police, No. 86, 23 September 1826, Strasbourg, 18 September 1826. Creuse in 1828: F7 9792, letter from the prefect of the Creuse to the minister of the interior, 29 November 1829; Eure, 1828; Limoges in 1828.

36. Sevrin, *Missions,* vol. 2, p. 236.

37. AN, F7 3797, Bulletin de Police, No. 11, 14 February 1826, Draguignon, 7 February 1826. On the widespread and multivalent practice of sexual inversion, see Davis, "Women on Top," in *Society and Culture,* p. 129.

38. AN, F7 9792, letter from the prefect of Côte d'Or to the minister of the interior regarding the incident in Beaune, where men disguised in this way both destroyed the base of the mission cross and posted anticlerical placards in town, 20 December 1820.

39. AN, F7 9793, from the prefect of Finistère to the minister of the interior, 26 October 1819.

40. AN, F7 3797, Bulletin de Police, No. 86, 30 September 1826, Brest, 25 September 1826.

41. AN, F7 3797, Bulletin de Police, No. 88, 4 October 1826, Quimper, 30 September 1826.

42. Besançon: AN, F7 3796, Bulletin de Police, No. 21, 12 March 1825, Besançon, 8 March 1825; Rouen: AN, F7 3797, Bulletin de Police, No. 37, 22 May 1826, Rouen, 21 May 1826.

43. AN, F7 9792, letter from the prefect of Doubs to the minister of the interior, 8 March 1825, describing a procession in Besançon.

44. AN, F7 9792, *Le Phocéen,* 18 February 1820, included in correspondence between the prefect of Bouches-du-Rhône and the minister of the interior.

45. *Le Constitutionnel,* 9 May 1825, cited and translated in Irene Collins, *Society and Government in France, 1814–1848* (London: Edward Arnold, 1970), p. 49.

46. Le Baron D'Henin de Cuvillers, *Des Comédiens et du clergé, suivi de refléxions sur le mandement de Mgr. L'Archêveque de Rouen* (Paris: P. Dupont Delannay, et les marchands de nouveautés, 1825), p. 376. This pamphlet calls vo-

ciferously for a subjugation of the churchmen orchestrating such theater and publishing such unreasonable *mandements* as that of the archbishop reprinted here.

47. AN, F7 9792, Correspondence from Lt. de Police sur la Mission of 1820, n.d.

48. AN, F7 9793, "Analytical Report on the events in Brest during the Mission, 1826–1827," by Commissaire de Police Parison. See chap. 6 for a full discussion of this extraordinary document.

49. AN, F7 9792, letter from the prefect of Charente-Inférieure to the minister of the interior, 22 January 1818.

50. See especially Mary Hartman, "The Sacrilege Law of 1825 in France: A Study in Anticlericalism and Mythmaking," *Journal of Modern History* 44, 1 (1972): 21–37; Edgar L. Newman, "The Blouse and the Frock Coat: The Alliance of the Common People of Paris with the Liberal Leadership and the Middle Class During the Last Years of the Bourbon Restoration," *Journal of Modern History* 47 (March 1974): 26–59. For a particularly interesting interpretation of the clerical plot and its significance, see Geoffrey Cubitt, *The Jesuit Myth: Conspiracy Theory and Politics in Nineteenth-Century France* (Oxford: Clarendon Press, 1993).

51. AN, F7 6772, dossier 16, letter from the prefect of the Vosges.

52. AN, F7 6767, dossier 5, Allier, letter from the prefect of Allier to the minister of the interior, 20 July 1827.

53. AN, F7 6705, Bas-Rhin, accompanying a letter from the prefect to the minister of the interior, 8 April 1826 from Strasbourg. The placard read "*A Bas Charles X / A bas le Clergé Catholique / Vive la Liberté / Français ne dormez pas.*"

54. AN, F7 6704, dossier 25, Haute-Garonne, copies of placards found on 1 January 1827, sent in letter from the prefect to the minister of the interior, 2 January 1827.

55. AN, F7 3797, Bulletin de Police (no number), 21 April 1825.

56. Cubitt, *The Jesuit Myth*, p. 3.

57. Davis, *Society and Culture*, p. 153. Caroline Ford, in her response to the forum on "Religion and Violence in the Nineteenth Century," in which my own work on the missionaries appeared, supported my way of understanding the missionaries and the anticlericalism of the Restoration when she argued that historians need to make the connection between the religious wars of the sixteenth century and the struggles ensuing from the sacralization of the nation and its politics in the nineteenth century. "Violence and the Sacred in Nineteenth-Century France," *French Historical Studies* 21, 1 (Winter 1998): 101–12, esp. 110–12.

58. This number includes all the incidents reported in Bulletins de Police contained in cartons F7 3796, F7 3797, and F7 3798 at the AN. This does not include attempted or suspected robberies, only "successful" efforts.

59. The reports of these incidents are all similar to the following report on the incident in Cambray, AN F7 3796, Bulletin de Police, No. 55, 18 June 1825: "Robbers entered the Church of Anneux (Arrondissement of Cambray) during the night of 9 June, and took a sacred vase and a chalice after having thrown down the sacred hosts contained within." Other similar incidents: F7 3796, Bul-

letin de Police, No. 100, 17 December 1825, in Versailles; F7 3796, Bulletin de Police, No. 93, 22 November 1825, in Dieppe; F7 3797, Bulletin de Police, No. 56, 19 June 1826, in Nantes; F7 3797, Bulletin de Police, No. 85, 19 September 1826, in Morlaux.

60. AN, F7 3797, Bulletin de Police, No. 23, 28 March 1826.

61. AN, F7 3797, Bulletin de Police, No. 38, 15 April 1826.

62. Cited in Sevrin, *Missions,* vol. 1, p. 316.

63. AN, F7 9792, letter from the prefect of Drôme to the minister of the interior, 25 April 1821.

64. AN, F7 3798, Bulletin de Police, No. 22, 17 March 1826, Bouches-du-Rhône, 9–10 March 1826.

65. AN, F7 3797, Bulletin de Police, No. 41, 26 May 1826, Montargis, 22 May 1826.

66. Michael J. Phayer, "Politics and Popular Religion: The Cult of the Cross in France, 1815–1840," *Journal of Social History* 11, 3 (Spring 1978): 346–65.

67. Louis Marin, *The Portrait of the King* (Minneapolis: University of Minnesota Press, 1988), p. 285.

68. One cartoon, published in "La Silhouette," and drawn by Philipon, featured Charles X wearing ecclesiastical bands and a skullcap, with the inscription "Un jésuit." Cited in Cubitt, *The Jesuit Myth,* p. 100, and James Cuno, "The Business and Politics of Caricature: Charles Philipon and La Maison Aubert," *Gazette des beaux arts* 106 (1985): 97–98. Also discussed in Robert Justin Goldstein, *Censorship of Political Caricature in Nineteenth Century France* (Kent, Ohio: Kent State University Press, 1989), pp. 113–16.

69. Report of 2 April 1827, referred to in letter from the prefect of the Moselle to the minister of the interior, 17 May 1827.

70. AN, F7 6705, letters from the prefect of the Moselle to the minister of the interior, dated Metz, 23 June 1827. This dossier contains only a stain from the original cookie, but the cookie itself can still be found in AEV 314, Musée des Archives Nationales, Hôtel Soubise.

71. AN, F7 6704, copy of a letter, dated 21 July 1826, from the capitaine de la Gendarmerie de l'Aube to the prefect of that department sent in a letter to the minister of the interior on 31 July 1826.

72. AN, F7 6706, letter from the prefect of the Meurthe in Nancy to the minister of the interior, 29 November 1826.

73. AN, F7 6706, letters describing the circulation of such coins in one dossier: St-Lô, 19 October 1827; Poitiers, 29 January 1827 and 23 April 1827; Digne, 16 May 1827; Quimper, 12 May 1827; Vannes, 19 and 28 April 1827; Arras, 5 April 1827; Orléans, 17 March 1827; Toulouse, 9 February 1827; Lille, 9 February 1827; Bordeaux, 9 January 1827; Carcassonne, 16 December 1826; Marseilles, 16 January 1826, 28 June 1826, and 25 September 1826; Besançon, 15 September 1826; Bourg, 4 September 1826; Avignon, 28 April 1826; Limoges, 12 January 1827.

74. AN, F7 6706, Rouen, 13 March 1827.

75. AN, F7 6706, Rouen, 5 March 1827.

76. AN, F7 6706, Bordeaux, 9 January 1827; Bourg, Ain, F7 3797, Bulletin

de Police, No. 83, 9 September 1826, Bourg, 4 September 1826. In the Hôtel Soubise, the Museum of the National Archives, one can still find coins of the variety defaced by wax in AEV 337.

77. Marin, *Portrait of the King,* p. 128.

78. Ibid., p. 127.

79. Ibid., p. 126.

Chapter Six

1. Most of the information on this incident has been compiled from various reports from local authorities in Rouen, sent to the minister of the interior in Paris, in AN, F7 6693, dossier Rouen. The seditious materials confiscated by the police were sent to Paris from April through June of 1825.

2. AN, F7 6693, letter from the Baron de Baussay, prefect of the Seine-Inférieure, to the minister of the interior, 7 May 1825. Today the Seine-Inférieure is the Seine-Maritime.

3. AN, F7 6693, letter from the prefect to the minister of the interior, 7 May 1825.

4. AN, F7 6693, letter from the prefect to the minister of the interior, 4 May 1825.

5. AN, F7 6693, letter from the prefect to the minister of the interior, 20 April 1825.

6. Croy (Gustave, Maximilien, Juste, Prince de), *Instruction Pastorale et ordonnance de S. A. Mgr. l'archevêque de Rouen, primat de Normandie* (Rouen: Méjard Imp., in-4, 19 Mars 1825).

7. Chaline, "Une Image du Diocèse de Rouen sous l'Episcopat de Monseigneur Le Croy (1823–1844)," *Revue historique de l'Eglise de France* 58 (1972): 53–71. Earlier in 1825, Monseigneur Le Surre wrote "Observations sur l'état moral du seminaire de Rouen," criticizing the failure among seminarians to observe basic rules. This report led to the expulsion of several seminarians and to a change in the leadership at the seminary.

8. Chaline, "Une Image du Diocèse de Rouen," p. 71. This article offers statistics demonstrating the low level of participation in the sacraments of the parishioners of Rouen and the surrounding areas. In the textile manufacturing district nearest to Rouen, Darnétal, the number of people taking the sacraments was as low as 4%.

9. Pierre Pierrard, *La Vie quotidienne du prêtre français au XIXème siècle, 1801–1905* (Paris: Hachette, 1986), p. 171.

10. Paule Salvan, "Le Tartuffe de Molière et l'agitation anticléricale en 1825," *Revue de la Société d'Histoire du Théâtre,* vol. 12 (Paris: 1960), p. 8.

11. AN, F7 6693, dossier Rouen, letter from the prefect of Eure to the minister of the interior, 27 April 1825. According to Chaline, "Une Image du Diocèse de Rouen," note, p. 68, the diocese of Evreux shared Rouen's low level of participation in the sacraments and tendency to anticlericalism. It is therefore not surprising that it too would bristle under the new religious regime of Archbishop Le Croy.

12. AN, F7 6693, song included in letter from the prefect to the minister of the interior, 30 April 1825.

13. AN, F7 6693, letter from the prefect to the minister of the interior, 20 April 1825.

14. AN, F7 6693, letter from the prefect to the minister of the interior, 18 January 1825.

15. ADSI, 4 T 81, letter from the minister of the interior to the prefect of the Seine-Inférieure, 8 February 1823.

16. ADSI, 4 T 81, response from the minister of the interior to the prefect, 8 February 1823; the minister wrote that "it is regrettable that one couldn't discover the authors of this guilty maneuver." He went on to recommend that the prefect arrange for the *parterre* to be seated as a way of getting it under control.

17. AN, F7 6693, letter from the prefect to the minister of the interior, 18 January 1825.

18. Ibid.

19. AN, F7 6693, contained in letter from the prefect to the minister of the interior, 21 April 1825.

20. AN, F7 6693, song sent in letter from the prefect to the minister of the interior, 7 May 1825.

21. According to Constant Pierre, *Les Hymnes et Chansons de la Revolution: Aperçu général et catalogue avec notices historiques, analytiques et bibliographiques* (Paris: Imprimerie Nationale, 1904), p. 1007, this song existed in twelve different versions between 1789 and 1801, eleven versions being from the revolutionary period.

22. According to Pierre, *Les Hymnes et Chansons,* p. 1004, this song existed in six versions between 1792 and 1795.

23. According to Pierre, *Les Hymnes et Chansons,* p. 1003, this song existed in ten versions between 1793 and 1799.

24. AN, F7 6693, placard, addressed to M. Morel, the director the theater in Rouen, sent in a letter from the Prefect to the Minister of the Interior, 23 April 1825.

25. The seditious writings, placards, and songs collected by the police break down as follows: 1 billet thrown on stage in theater; 14 placards erected in public, of which 4 contained both an icon and text; 3 letters sent to different authorities; 10 songs (although the authorities admit that this is but a fraction of what was circulated and sung at the time); 12 seditious writings, for a total of 40 pieces seized by the police and forwarded to the minister of the interior in Paris.

26. AN, F7 6693, report from the colonel commandant de la 3e légion de gendarmerie royale to the prefect, 5 May 1825. The report explained, "[the young rich men] have joined together to support lots of workers from the factories of Darneal, Louvier, Elbeuf, and the valley of Maronne. . . . These revelations come to me via a young man who is an unreliable intriguer; . . . ." This was the only evidence the police had that the middle class was organizing the workers' participation in the events of the spring of 1825; yet it completely dominated their interpretation of these events. A year later, when antimission incidents

rocked the city of Rouen, the same interpretation was used to explain events, in exactly the same terms, without any supporting evidence. See AN, F7 3797, Bulletins de Police from May 1826. This corresponds to what I described as the "liberal plot theory" in chap. 4, which many officials used to explain popular forms of protest.

27. AN, F7 3796, Bulletin de Police, No. 34, 27 April 1825.

28. AN, F7 6693, dossier Rouen, commissaire de police, report of 21 April 1825, submitted in a letter of the prefect to the minister of the interior, 21 April 1825.

29. AN, F7 6693, letter from the prefect to the minister of the interior, 7 May 1825.

30. AN, F7 6693, included in the letter from the prefect to the minister of the interior, 25 April 1825, found at 4 A.M., rue Nationale, on house #22.

31. AN, F7 6693, included in a letter from the prefect to the minister of the interior, 27 April 1825, found on the 26th of April at 4:15 A.M. at the corner of the Grande rue and rue d'Houret.

32. AN, F7 6693, sent in a letter from the prefect to the minister of the interior, 30 April 1825. Another song which mocked the *mandement* contained twenty-two verses, and was sent in a later letter, 7 May 1825. The contents of this song were discussed at length in chap. 5.

33. AN, F7 6693, contained in a letter from the prefect to the minister of the interior, 7 May 1825; this song was sent with two others.

34. AN, F7 6693, from "The Mandement," in letter dated 30 April 1825.

35. AN, F7 6693, sent in a letter from the prefect to the minister of the interior, 23 April 1825. The placard was found on 22 April 1825.

36. AN, F7 6693, sent in a letter, 7 May 1825, from the prefect to the minister of the interior.

37. Ibid.

38. AN, F7 6693, in a letter from the prefect to the minister of the interior, 25 April 1825.

39. Ibid.

40. Ibid.

41. AN, F7 6693, text of letter sent to the director of the Theater of the Arts, M. Morel, enclosed in letter of 23 April 1825 from the prefect to the minister of the interior.

42. AN, F7 6693, placard included in letter from the prefect to the minister of the interior, 23 April 1825. The placard, entitled "The People of Rouen to the brave soldiers of the 6th regiment of the Royal Guard," was found on a column in the port, at the end of the bridge. It was removed at 7 A.M., 22 April 1825.

43. AN, F7 6693, placard in letter from the prefect to the minister of the interior, 23 April 1825.

44. Salvan, "Le Tartuffe de Molière," p. 12, citing Bouteiller, *Histoire des théâtres de Rouen,* p. 231.

45. AN, F7 6693, dossier Rouen, letter from the colonel commandant de la 3e légion de la gendarmerie royale to the minister of the interior, 8 May 1825.

46. AN, F7 6693, song included in letter from the prefect to the minister of the interior, 3 May 1825.

47. Molière, *Tartuffe,* trans. Richard Wilbur, pp. 161–62.

48. *Le Constitutionnel,* No. 139, 19 May 1825.

49. Information about the popular response to the mission of Rouen in the spring of 1826 can be found in AN, F7 3797, in the Bulletins de Police.

50. AN, F7 3797, Bulletin de Police, No. 41, 26 May 1826, Rouen, 25 May 1826.

51. AN, F7 3797, Bulletin de Police, No. 42, 27 May 1826, Rouen, 26 May 1826.

52. AN, F7 3797, Bulletin de Police, No. 100, 11 November 1826, Rouen, 10 November 1826.

53. AN, F7 6693, letter from the prefect to the minister of the interior, 19 June 1827.

54. In particular, I am taking issue with Phayer's portrayal of the late 1820s as a period when anticlericalism was still disorganized and local in nature as compared with the two years following the Revolution of 1830 when the mission cross incidents that he studied took place. See J. Michael Phayer, "Politics and Popular Religion: The Cult of the Cross in France, 1815–1840," *Journal of Social History* 11, 3 (Spring 1978): 346–65.

55. Nîmes: AN, F7 3796, Bulletin de Police, No. 57, 25 June 1825.

56. Coronation: Lyons: AN, F7 6671, dossier 11; Rhône: item 112, Lyons, 22 June 1825; AN, F7 3796, Bulletin de Police, No. 54, 14 June 1825 and No. 57, 25 June 1825; Papal Jubilee: Lyons: AN, F7 3797, Bulletin de Police, No. 98, 2 November 1826 and 4 November 1826; Besançon: F7 6704, letter from the prefect of the Doubs to the minister of the interior, 7 March 1827; Strasbourg: incident cited in Henri Guillemin, *Histoire des Catholiques français au XIXe siècle (1815–1905)* (Geneva, Paris, Montreal: Editions du Milieu du Monde, 1947), p. 27.

57. Lyons: AN, F7 3796, Bulletin de Police, No. 61, 13 July 1825.

58. Nîmes: AN, F7 3796, Bulletin de Police, No. 101, 21 December 1825; Lyons: AN, F7 3797, Bulletin de Police, No. 98, 4 November 1826; Marseilles: AN, F7 3797, Bulletin de Police (no number), 13 November 1826; Besançon: AN, F7 6704, letter from the prefect of the Doubs to the minister of the interior, 7 March 1827; Angers: AN, F7 6692, letter from the prefect of the Maine et Loire to the minister of the interior, 17 September 1829; Strasbourg: incident cited in Guillemin, *Histoire des Catholiques,* p. 27; Rouen: AN, F7 3797, Bulletins de Police, No. 41, 26 May 1826, Rouen, 25 May 1826, and No. 42, 27 May 1826, Rouen, 26 May 1826.

59. Evreux: AN, F7 6693, dossier Rouen, letter from the prefect of the Eure to the minister of the interior, 27 April 1825, also explains that at the town square copies of the *mandement* in manuscript and several songs *contre les jésuites* were exchanged.

60. AN, F7 6693, letter from the prefect of the Oise to the minister of the interior, 2 May 1825.

61. AN, F7 6692, letter from the prefect of the Loire-Inférieure to the minister of the interior, 14 May 1825.

62. AN, F7 6693, letter from the prefect of the Var to the minister of the interior, 21 June 1825.

63. AN, F7 3797, Bulletin de Police, No. 45, 2 June 1826, Angoulême, 30 May 1826.

64. AN, F7 6692, dossier, Maine et Loire, placard posted 13 September 1829, sent in a letter from the prefect of the Maine et Loire to the minister of the interior, 17 September 1829.

65. AN, F7 6769, letter from the prefect of the Gard to the minister of the interior, 12 December 1825.

66. Cited in *Le Constitutionnel*, No. 150, 30 May 1825, p. 2.

67. Bordeaux: AN, F7 6692, report of the prefect of Gironde submitted to the minister of the interior, 8 March 1827.

68. AN, F7 6742, article from *Le Constitutionnel*, 5 June 1825, p. 2, included in police files.

69. AN, F7 6771, dossier 11, Rhône, item 113, letter from the prefect of the Rhône to the minister of the interior, 16 May 1825.

70. Gwyn Lewis, "The White Terror of 1815 in the Department of the Gard: Counter-Revolution, Continuity, and the Individual," *Past and Present* 58 (1973): 108–35.

71. AN, F7 3796, Bulletin de Police, No. 48, 28 May 1825.

72. AN, F7 3796, Bulletin de Police, No. 57, 25 June 1825, from Nîmes, 20 June 1825, which includes the text of the inflammatory sermon.

73. AN, F7 6769, letter from the prefect of the Gard to the minister of the interior, 12 December 1825; AN, F7 3796, Bulletin de Police, No. 101, 21 December 1825, 4 December 1825.

74. AN, F7 6771, dossier 11, Rhône, item 112, 22 June 1825.

75. AN, F7 3796, Bulletin de Police, No. 57, 25 June 1825.

76. AN, F7 6771, dossier 11, Rhône, item 112, 22 June 1825.

77. AN, F7 3796, Bulletin de Police, No. 57, 25 June 1825.

78. AN, F7 3797, Bulletin de Police, No. 98, 2 November 1826.

79. Incident described in Henri Guillemin, *Histoire des Catholiques*, p. 27.

80. AN, F7 3797, Bulletin de Police (no number), 13 November 1826.

81. AN, F7 9792, letter from the prefect of the Bouches-du-Rhône to the minister of the interior, 13 November 1826.

82. AN, F7 3797, Bulletin de Police, No. 109, 6 December 1826.

83. AN, F7 3797, Bulletin de Police, No. 111, 20 December 1826.

84. AN, F7 6704, letter from the prefect of the Doubs to the minister of the interior, 7 March 1827.

85. Toulouse: AN, F7 6692, report of the mayor of Toulouse to the director of police, 31 December 1826, and an extract from a report of the prefect of the Haute Garonne, 4 January 1827. Epinal: AN, F7 6693, letter from the prefect of the Vosges to the minister of the interior, 24 May 1827.

86. AN, F7 6693, dossier Puy-de-Dôme, letter from the capitaine commandant de la Gendarmerie Royale du Puy-de-Dôme to the minister of the interior, 30 January 1826; *Journal du Puy-de-Dôme*, 31 January 1826.

87. AN, F7 3796, Bulletin de Police, No. 99, 14 December 1825. In 1821, *Tartuffe* and a short skit entitled "Un Trait de Molière, Prologue du Tartuffe," by Eugène de Pradel, were similarly performed as a benefit to raise money for "la famille B***" at the Théâtre de la rue Chantereine in Paris. Explained in

frontispiece of Eugène de Pradel, "Un Trait de Molière, Prologue du Tartuffe, en vers" (Paris: chez Ladvocat, Librairie au Palais Royal, et chez Barba, 1821).

88. La Rochelle: AN, F7 6692, from the prefect of the Charente-Inférieure to the minister of the interior, 12 August 1825. Carpentras: AN, F7 6693, letter from the prefect of the Vaucluse to the minister of the interior, 15 December 1829; another unjustified accusation of liberals was made in Angoulême: AN, F7 6692, letter from the prefect of the Charente to the minister of the interior, 10 June 1826.

89. *Le Constitutionnel,* No. 193, 12 July 1819.

90. *Le Constitutionnel,* No. 110, 20 April 1825.

91. *Le Constitutionnel,* 5 June 1825, p. 2.

92. *L'Ami de la Charte,* 28 January 1826, included in a letter from the prefect of the Puy-de-Dôme to the minister of the interior, 30 January 1826, in AN, F7 6693.

93. AN, F7 6693. In a letter from the prefect of the Puy-de-Dôme to the minister of the interior, the prefect compared the uneventful performances of *Tartuffe* in the past with that of the previous night, and blamed the article in *L'Ami de la Charte* for the difference.

94. AN, F7 6693, article from *Journal du Puy-du-Dôme,* 30 January 1826, included in letter from the prefect of the Puy-du-Dôme to the minister of the interior, 30 January 1826 (my emphasis).

95. Preface to *Tartuffe* (Paris: Baudouin Frères, 1825), pp. 4–5, signed, C. L., attributed to Claude Langlois in other versions. In his important article "The Blouse and the Frock Coat: The Alliance of the Common People of Paris with the Liberal Leadership and the Middle Class During the Last Years of the Bourbon Restoration," Edgar Newman stresses the importance of the liberal press and publishing houses in spreading anticlericalism during the Restoration. *Journal of Modern History* 47 (March 1974): 26–59, esp. pp. 43–46. Savran's "Le Tartuffe de Molière" also looks at the distribution of *Tartuffe,* pp. 13–14.

96. Langlois, "Preface," *Tartuffe,* p. 5.

97. Ibid., p. 3.

98. Ibid., p. 4.

99. Ibid., p. 6.

100. *Tartuffe* (Paris: Imprimerie et Fonderie de J. Pinard, 1825) has a particularly interesting "Preliminary Discourse," although it is unsigned.

101. In *L'Ami de la Charte,* VII année, No. 9, 31 January 1826, an article describing the incident in Clermont-Ferrand ended with such an advertisement: "At the moment when the police prohibit us from crowning the bust of Molière, it is not without relevance to remember that one can find magnificent editions of Molière's complete works in six volumes, in-8, adorned with the author's portrait, and a number of illustrations, at the bookstore of Auguste Veysset, for 5F per volume, and smaller editions in six volumes in-16 at 1F per volume. A new shipment of Tartuffe, for 25 centimes is expected at the same bookstore."

102. "Mon Dieu que de ce point L'ouvrage est Merveilleux," lithograph by H. Brunet of Lyons, 1827. Bibliothèque Nationale (hereafter BN), Salle des Estampes, Tb mat 1a. This dossier contains an extraordinary range of such images, each presenting a summary of a particular scene. The original French text of the

song accompanying Brunet's lithograph in figure 7 is given below (and translated in the figure).

1

Toi, dont le sublime génie,
Frappant les sots et les pervers,
Fit succomber l'hypocrisie
Sous le poids de tes molles vers;
Molière recoit la couronne
Emblême d'immortalité,
Quand par les mains de la beauté
La France entière te la donne.

2

Le fanatisme et l'ignorance
Se liguent en vain contre toi;
De tes vers la raison se lance
Et le méchant palit d'effroi.
Nous t'applaudissons sans rien craindre,
Car du vrai sage respecté,
Le flambeau de la verité
Brule celui que veut l'éteindre.

3

Contre les clameurs de l'envie
Un grand prince te protegea;
Et des coups de la calomnie
Son suffrage au moins se vengea.
Il sut pour s'illustrer lui-même
Faire triompher tes beaux vers;
It dut éclairer l'univers.
Ayant le soleil pour emblême.

4

Si tu pouvais auteur sublime,
Sortir de la nuit des tombeaux,
On verrait la ruse et le crime
Mourir encor [sic] sous tes pinceaux.
Mais, hélas! Le vice prospère,
Dans ce monde où brillent tes chants
Nous avons encor [sic] des méchans
Mais nous n'avons plus de Molière.

103. Henri Simon, *Ninon, Molière, et Tartuffe* (Paris: Barba, 1815), 36 pages, a vaudeville in one act performed at the Théâtre de Vaudeville, 26 April 1815. These vaudeville performances, and the popularization of Molière which resulted from them, approximates the American experience of Shakespeare as described by Lawrence Levine for the same period, *High Brow/Low Brow: The Emergence of Cultural Hierarchy in America* (Cambridge, Mass.: Harvard University Press, 1988).

104. de Pradel, *Un Trait de Molière*. The anniversary of Molière's birthday provided the occasion for a similar one-act production at the Théâtre de l'Odéon in Paris in January 1815. Written by Mr. Samson, an actor of the royal

theater, and entitled *La Fête de Molière,* this play celebrates all of Molière's famous characters, of which one is, of course, Tartuffe.

105. François Garnier, *Le Mariage de Molière ou le Manteau du Tartuffe* (Paris: J-N Barba; Lyons: Cambit, fils, Oct. 1828).

106. F21 998, from the prefect of the Gironde to the minister of the interior regarding the play *The Voyage.* Censor report dated 10 July 1828.

107. AN, F7 6692, from the prefect of the Gironde to the minister of the interior, 8 March 1827.

108. Nîmes: AN, F7 3796, Bulletin de Police No. 57, 25 June 1825.

109. Tours: AN, F7 3797, Bulletin de Police No. 89, 7 October 1826.

110. Perpignan: AN, F7 6693, letter from the prefect of the Pyrénées-Orientales to the minister of the interior, 15 November 1826; Angoulême: AN, F7 6692, letter from the prefect of the Charente to the minister of the interior, 27 May 1826.

111. Lawyers were prominent in the Angoulême incident, AN, F7 6692, dossier Charente, letter from the prefect of the Charente to the minister of the interior, 22 July 1826. For the participation of journalists, see my earlier discussion of the impact of newspapers on Tartufferie.

112. Toulouse: AN, F7 6692, dossier Haute-Garonne, extract from a report from the prefect of the Haute-Garonne, 4 January 1827.

113. AN, F7 6692, letter from the prefect to the minister of the interior, 10 June 1826.

114. AN, F7 6692, letter from the prefect of the Gard to the minister of the interior, 13 November 1827. For a general discussion of the social composition of theater incidents of all kinds in the provinces, see Alain Corbin, "L'Agitation dans les théâtres de province sous la Restauration," in *Popular Traditions and Learned Culture in France From the Sixteenth to the Twentieth Century,* ed. Marc Bertrand (Stanford, Calif.: Anma Libri, 1985), pp. 93–114.

115. Angoulême: AN, F7 6692, letter from the prefect of the Charente to the minister of the interior, 22 July 1826.

116. AN, F7 6692, letter from the prefect of the Gard to the minister of the interior, 13 November 1927.

117. See Phayer, "Politics and Popular Religion," map, p. 356.

118. Phayer, "Politics and Popular Religion," based his analysis of priestly vocations on Emmanuel Le Roy Ladurie, *Le Territoire de l'historien* (Paris: Flammarion, 1973), pp. 45–46 and 65.

119. In "Politics and Popular Religion," Phayer based his discussion of the Law of the Separation of Church and State of 1905 on Gabriel Le Bras, "La Religion dans la société française," in *Aspects de la société française,* ed. André Siegfried (Paris: Librairie Générale de Droit et de Jurisprudence, 1954), pp. 221–40; and the maps in F. Boulard and J. Rémy, *Pratique Religieuse urbaine et régions culturelles* (Paris: Les Editions Ouvrières, 1968).

120. AN, F7 998, report on play proposed for Saint Charles's Day, Arras, 4 May 1827.

121. It was the prefect of the Gironde who decided to allow *Tartuffe* at long intervals, on unpopular evenings. AN, F7 6692, letter from the prefect of the Gironde to the minister of the interior, 8 March 1827. The minister of the interior

responded and applauded the prefect's wise approach of avoiding total prohibition (which had caused so many problems elsewhere) while at the same time avoiding scandal. In the case of Marseilles, already cited, the prefect banned *Tartuffe* for the duration of the Jubilee. The same would be true, as we shall see, in Brest in the same year.

122. AN, F7 6693, newspaper article included in letter from the prefect of Puy-du-Dôme to the minister of the interior, 2 February 1826; *L'Ami de la Charte,* VIIe année, No. 9, 4 January 1826.

123. AN, F7 6692, letter from the prefect of the Charente to the minister of the interior, 22 July 1826; in the same case, the authorities were unable to make arrests because of the refusal of civil officials to offer information about the alleged protesters despite the fact that they were present during the incident and saw everything.

124. AN, F7 9793, letter from the prefect of Finistère to the minister of the interior, 2 September 1826 (on evening services and length of mission); 1 October 1826 (on role of municipal council in determining placement of mission cross).

125. AN, F7 9793, letter from the prefect of Finistère to the minister of the interior, 24 October 1826.

126. AN, F7 9793, letter from Subprefect Gueracz to the minister of the interior, 1 September 1826.

127. AN, F7 9793, letter from the prefect of Finistère to the minister of the interior, 24 October 1826.

128. AN, F7 9793, "Analytical Report on the Events in Brest during the Mission, written by M. B. Parison, Police Commissioner of Brest, with one of his colleagues, Monsieur Lejeune, 1826 to 1827," included in dossier Brest, with cover letter submitted to the minister of the interior by the subprefect of Brest, 20 February 1827, p. 39.

129. AN, F7 9793, letter from the prefect of Finistère to the minister of the interior, 21 September 1826, stresses that "not a single inhabitant of the city" took part in the troubles either in the church or the theater.

130. AN, F7 9793, placard issued by the prefect of Finistère, 17 October 1826.

131. *Le Constitutionnel,* 18 October 1826, p. 3.

132. AN, F7 6693, printed "Consultation" of proceedings of 12 January 1827, p. 7, by Isambert, lawyer for the defense, distributed in Brest according to letter from the subprefect of Brest to the minister of the interior, 13 May 1827.

133. AN, F7 9793, no author, letter to the minister of the interior, 24 October 1826.

134. AN, F7 9793, from the prefect of Finistère to the minister of the interior, 30 January 1827 regarding performance of 26 January 1827.

135. AN, F7 9793, letter from the subprefect of Brest to the minister of the interior, 26 January 1827.

136. AN, F7 9793, letter from the prefect of Finistère to the minister of the interior, 1 February 1827.

137. AN, F7 9793, letter from the prefect of Finistère to the minister of the interior regarding the sentences handed down, 20 March 1827. Those who were

sentenced were given the minimum sentence allowable, two months in prison (which had already been served), and a fine of 100F.

138. AN, F7 9793, "Analytical Report." I have underscored the author's name "Com. Parison" because his name prefigures the approach he would adopt in his narrative of events in Brest. I thank John Western for pointing out this wonderful irony.

139. Parison, "Analytical Report," p. 4.

140. AN, F7 9793, letter from the subprefect of Brest to the minister of the interior, 1 September 1826 regarding anticipated demands for *Tartuffe*.

141. Parison, "Analytical Report," p. 6.

142. Ibid., p. 59.

143. Ibid., p. 26 (1 Oct.).

144. Ibid., p. 27 (3 Oct.).

145. Ibid., p. 28. *Billet* also cited during trial, and therefore republished in pamphlet form after January 1827.

146. Parison, "Analytical Report," alludes to the *billet* thrown on the 2nd of October, but is vague about its contents. It is described in the transcript of the trial, AN, F7 9973, "Tribunal Correctional de Brest," 12 January 1827, p. 5: "The public begs humbly for permission to allow the director to put on a performance of *Tartuffe*; we hope that France as a whole will not be able to say that our municipal authorities are in league with the Jesuits to deprive us not only of tranquillity in the interior of our homes, but also of the pleasures which we seek beyond the doors of our abodes."

147. Parison, "Analytical Report," p. 31 (Oct. 8).

148. It was in this spirit that the administration also decided to ban *Oedipus*, for which see AN, F7 9793, letter from the prefect of Finistère to the minister of the interior, 1 October 1826.

149. AN, F7 9793, letter from the prefect of Finistère to the minister of the interior, 24 October 1826.

150. Parison, "Analytical Report," p. 46 (Oct. 12).

151. Ibid., p. 54 (Oct. 13).

152. Ibid., p. 58 (Oct. 22).

153. Here I am borrowing Alain Corbin's term for the theater, which, as I explained in chaps. 4 and 5, is particularly useful when the theater incidents are considered in light of the missions to which they were most often a response. Corbin, "L'Agitation dans les théâtres," p. 110.

154. Parison, "Analytical Report," pp. 36–37 (Oct. 10).

155. Ibid., p. 1.

156. Ibid., pp. 4–5.

157. Ibid., pp. 61–62.

158. Ibid., p. 63.

159. AN, F7 9793, "Tribunal Correctionnel de Brest: Audience ordinaire publique de Tribunal Correctionnel séant à Brest," 12 January 1827, p. 6.

160. Ibid., p. 4.

161. Ibid., pp. 4–5.

162. Ibid., pp. 5–6.

163. Ibid., p. 6.

164. Ibid., p. 7.

165. AN, F7 9793, "Judgment given during the course of the debates," p. 20 (included at the end of "Tribunal Correctionnel de Brest," 12 January 1827).

166. AN, F7 9793, "Consultation pour Messieurs SPREAFICO, LAVALLEE, jeune, LAVALLEE, aîné, CONRIER, BARAZER, LE BRETON, SIMON (Marc), DESCHEZ, MAZURIE, DELOBEAU, LOYER, jeune, HUREL et MONGIN, all residents of Brest, condemned by the court of this city, the 12th of January 1827, deliberated in Paris, the 8th of February 1827, by l'Avocat au Conseil de Roi et à Cour de Cassation, ISAMBERT, printed in Brest, 24 février 1827," Y. Duval, Avocat, p. 7.

167. "Consultation," pp. 7–8.

168. Ibid., p. 9.

169. Ibid., p. 10.

170. Ibid., p. 11.

171. Ibid., p. 12.

172. AN, F7 9793, "Tribunal séant à Quimper, Chambre Correctionnelle jugeant par appel presidence de M. Germain, Affaire du Spectacle de Brest, Audience du 7 March 1827," Duval's plea, p. 2.

173. Ibid.

174. Ibid., p. 3.

175. Ibid., p. 4.

176. Ibid., p. 7.

177. Ibid., 8 March 1827, Duval's plea, p. 12.

178. Ibid., Bernard's plea, p. 22.

179. Ibid.

180. Ibid., p. 15.

181. Ibid.

182. Ibid.

183. Ibid., p. 16.

184. Ibid., pp. 19 and 20.

185. Ibid., p. 20.

186. Ibid.

187. Ibid., p. 21.

188. Ibid., 10 March 1827, Grivart's plea, p. 24 (emphasis mine).

189. Ibid., p. 25.

190. Ibid., p. 26.

191. Ibid., p. 31. The general effort to cast the modern magistracy in an inherited anti-Jesuit role was typical of many lawyers of this period, as Cubitt makes clear in *The Jesuit Conspiracy,* p. 71.

Conclusion

1. Edgar L. Newman, "The Blouse and the Frock Coat: The Alliance of the Common People of Paris with the Liberal Leadership and the Middle Class During the Last Years of the Bourbon Restoration," *Journal of Modern History* 47 (March 1974): 26–59; and John Merriman, ed., *1830 in France* (New York:

New Viewpoint, of Franklin Watts, 1975) treat the pamphlet wars of 1825 and the social and economic origins of the Revolution of 1830, respectively.

2. Pamela Pilbeam, *The 1830 Revolution in France* (New York: St. Martin's Press, 1991), chap. 1, "Historians and the Revolution," offers a more extended analysis of this diverse historiography.

3. Pilbeam, *The 1830 Revolution in France*, p. 14; Robert Alexander, *Bonapartism and the Revolutionary Tradition in France: The Fédérés of 1815* (Cambridge: Cambridge University Press, 1991).

4. Pilbeam, *The 1830 Revolution in France*, p. 16.

5. Alan Spitzer, *Old Hatreds and Young Hopes: The French Carbonari Against the French Restoration* (Cambridge, Mass.: Harvard University Press, 1971).

6. Michael J. Phayer, "Politics and Popular Religion: The Cult of the Cross in France, 1815–1840," *Journal of Social History* 11 (1978): 346–65, gives a summary of the types of violence committed in defense of and against these crosses; the author also discusses the regime's "flexible" policy that emerged for dealing with this.

7. All of the following examples come from AN, F19 5561, containing documents from the minister of religion concerning the mission crosses after 1830. The specific incidents alluded to here took place in Dijon in September of 1830 and Loches in the Aube in May of 1831.

8. AN, F19 5561, letter from the bishop of Lucon, 4 October 1830, makes the specific claim about priests returning to the *bocage* (woods).

9. AN, F19 5561, letter of the bishop of Belley to the minister of ecclesiastical affairs, 17 October 1830.

10. AN, F19 5566, circular no. 25, from the minister of public instruction and of religion to clergymen throughout France, 23 February 1831, entitled "Ajouter à la prière d'usage pour le Roi les noms *Ludovicum Philippum*." (Add to the prayer for the King the name Louis Philippe.)

11. When the bishop of Marseilles complained that police surveillance infringed religious autonomy, the prefect planted spies in the churches in his department. AN, F19 5566, letter from the prefect of the Bouches-du-Rhône to minister of public instruction and religion, 24 April 1831.

12. Pilbeam, *The 1830 Revolution in France*, p. 118.

13. Peter Sahlins, *Forest Rites: The War of the Demoiselles in Nineteenth-Century France* (Cambridge, Mass.: Harvard University Press, 1994), p. 115.

14. Sahlins, *Forest Rites*, p. 121.

15. Jo Burr Margadant, "The Duchesse de Berry and Royalist Political Culture in Postrevolutionary France," *History Workshop Journal* 43 (Spring 1997): 23–52. In her forthcoming study of Delacroix, Elizabeth A. Fraser treats precisely these issues of representing the monarchy in painting during the Restoration. See "InCivility: Eugène Delacroix and the Private History of Romanticism." Unpublished manuscript.

16. It is no great innovation to imagine studying the period 1815–1848 as a block, as all institutional political histories tend to group the two monarchies of the nineteenth century together; it is rather seeing them together in relation to

the legacy of the Revolution and as a critical prehistory to 1848 and the emergence of democracy in the nineteenth century that is different.

17. Here, like Suzanne Desan, I am arguing that cultural history in the ethnographic grain, inspired by Clifford Geertz and widely adopted by historians, need not imagine community or meaning as singular, but can actively seek out evidence of struggle and multiple meanings. Suzanne Desan, "Crowds, Community, and Ritual in the Work of E. P. Thompson and Natalie Davis," in Lynn Hunt, ed., *The New Cultural History* (Berkeley: University of California Press, 1989), pp. 47–71. If searching for meaning can tend to efface differences in the appropriations and uses of cultural forms, as Roger Chartier has argued, it need not be so if one is attentive to multiple interpretations. For a discussion of Chartier's critique, see Lynn Hunt's Introduction in *The New Cultural History*, pp. 12–13.

18. In a talk given at the American Historical Association meeting in Seattle in 1998, Marjorie Beale pointed to Judith Walkowitz's clear articulation of the ways in which historians can find causality and agency without focusing on intentionality. Marjorie Beale, "Poststructuralism and the New Cultural History: Problems and Promise," citing Judith Walkowitz, *City of Dreadful Delight: Narratives of Sexual Danger in Late-Victorian London* (Chicago: University of Chicago Press, 1992), esp. pp. 9–10.

19. In this sense my approach is a riposte to the third volume of *The French Revolution and the Creation of Modern Political Culture, The Transformation of Political Culture, 1789–1848,* ed. François Furet and Mona Ozouf (Oxford: Pergamon Press, 1989), p. xvii, which restricted itself to "study[ing] the ways in which the French Revolution has been portrayed in European thought and how its legacy influenced the development of political philosophy in the nineteenth century."

20. Natalie Zemon Davis and E. P. Thompson are only the most illustrious in a long line of historians who have followed their example and used the tools of cultural anthropology and a focus on rituals and popular practices to integrate such groups as active agents of history.

21. One of Michel Foucault's most important lessons to historians has been to encourage us to look in "the most unpromising places" to understand the workings of power. See Patricia O'Brien's "Michel Foucault's History of Culture," in Hunt, ed., *The New Cultural History*, pp. 25–46, as well as Hunt's own discussion in her Introduction, p. 37.

22. Lynn Hunt, ed. and author of the Introduction to *The New Cultural History* (Berkeley: University of California Press, 1989), p. 21.

23. Terry Eagleton discusses Pierre Bourdieu's notion of habitus as part and parcel of the naturalizing process; he cites different formulations Bourdieu proposed for defining legitimacy. Two definitions, legitimacy as "history turned into nature," and legitimacy as "the misrecognition of arbitrariness," define precisely the opposite of what was going on during the Restoration. Eagleton, *Ideology: An Introduction* (London: Verso, 1991), p. 157.

24. Eagleton, citing Bourdieu, *Ideology,* pp. 157–58.

25. Eagleton, in *Ideology,* p. 113, summarizes the benefits of Gramsci's notion of hegemony for understanding historical change as well as dominant or-

ders: "Implied in this vision is its corollary that revolution or change is dependent on contestation in the whole arena of culture, defined in the broadest everyday sense." Raymond Williams's interpretation of hegemony, as described in *Marxism and Literature* (Oxford: Oxford University Press, 1977), p. 112, emphasizes the dynamic nature which I find most useful for making sense of how political legitimacy is challenged and constituted: "Hegemony does not just passively exist as a form of dominance. It has continually to be renewed, recreated, defended, and modified. It is also continually resisted, limited, altered, challenged by pressures not at all its own."

26. I offer my portrait and definition of a "public sphere" as an alternative to Habermas's vision, which can imagine democratic consequences for the eighteenth century, when it is still comprised of an elite, challenging the singular power of the monarch, but offers a pessimistic forecast about the undemocratic nature of the public sphere in the age of mass culture. My "unofficial politics" explores a public sphere which is neither exclusively elite nor in the grip of mass culture. While my study ends in 1830, I think this way of conceiving of the public sphere would be more productive than Habermas's even later in the nineteenth century, when the advent of mass culture does change the conditions of political participation, but not necessarily in the undemocratic direction he predicted. Jurgen Habermas, *The Structural Transformation of the Public Sphere: An Inquiry into a Category of Bourgeois Society,* trans. Thomas Burger (Cambridge, Mass.: MIT Press, 1993; originally appeared in 1962).

27. Here I am trying to differentiate myself from Michel De Certeau, whose *Practices of Everyday Life* generally accords with my way of thinking about political history as best understood through cultural practices of everyday life. However, his work circumscribes the possibility for real innovation and change more than I would like; practices in his analysis can be used to "resist" or "poach" within the dominant order, but one is left with the sense that this does not seriously challenge the dominance of that order. Indeed, as with Gramsci, he believes that the ability of the dominant order to sustain that kind of resistance gives it greater strength. By contrast, I believe that such cultural practices as I present in this book did more than merely shore up the dominant order; they contributed to constituting a very different one. Michel De Certeau, *Practices of Everyday Life,* trans. Steven Randall (Berkeley: University of California Press, 1984).

28. Fitzhugh Brundage, currently working on a manuscript on memory in the U.S. South, explicitly adopts an approach which stresses competing commemorations; likewise, Alon Confino's recent work on commemoration since 1871 in Germany considers the wide range of organizations (local and national) as well as commercial interests that shaped the narrative of Germany history which appeared in textbooks and museums between 1871 and the end of World War I. Alon Confino, *The Nation as a Local Metaphor: Württemberg, Imperial Germany, and National Memory, 1871–1918* (Chapel Hill: University of North Carolina Press, 1997). Likewise, Frederick Corney's "Writing October: History, Memory, Identity, and the Construction of the Bolshevik Revolution, 1917–1927" (Ph.D. dissertation, Columbia University, 1997) looks exclusively at the repeated and competing commemorations of the October Revolution.

29. I am thinking most specifically of the assumption underlying George Mosse's *Nationalization of the Masses* (Ithaca, N.Y.: Cornell University Press, 1975), namely that the effort to embody the general will in the orchestration of mass festivals led in a direction that was necessarily totalitarian. Many historians have since tempered this view; however, there is still an overwhelming propensity to imagine that regimes accomplish what they set out to represent, or what they prescribe, rather than seeing their spectacles as helping to define the terrain in which a negotiation of that question would be carried out. See, for example, Eric Hobsbawm and Terence Ranger, eds., *The Invention of Tradition* (Cambridge: Cambridge University Press, 1983).

30. See the master's thesis of Allison K. Jones regarding the expiatory narrative and how it served to legitimize Pétain's rule, "Deliver us from evil: Maréchal Pétain and Extreme Right-wing Politics Cast in an Expiatory Mode during Vichy Regime France" (M.A. thesis, University of Florida, 1999); although the author doesn't present it in exactly this way, Henry Rousso's *The Vichy Syndrome: History and Memory in France since 1944,* trans. Arthur Goldhammer (Cambridge, Mass.: Harvard University Press, 1991) certainly contains material to support this way of showing how the Fourth and Fifth Republics have dealt with the problem of Vichy, and especially the treatment of the Jews. Francine Muel-Dreyfus, *Vichy, et l'Eternel féminin* (Paris: Seuil, 1996) specifically treats the Vichy period in terms of an expiatory narrative, here focused on the sins of the nation concerning women.

31. Paul Hammond, "The King's Two Bodies: Representations of Charles II," in *Culture, Politics, and Society in Britain, 1660–1800,* ed. Jeremy Black and Jeremy Gordon (Manchester: Manchester University Press, 1991), pp. 12–48; John Spurr, "Virtue, Religion, and Government: The Anglican Uses of Providence," in Tim Harris, Paul Seaward, and Mark Goldie, *The Politics of Religion in Restoration England* (London: Basil Blackwell, 1990), pp. 31–47.

32. In his comment, "De la violence religieuse," on the forum on Religion and Violence in *French Historical Studies* 21, 1 (Winter 1998), p. 119, in which he responded to my opposing narratives of forgetting and expiation, Claude Langlois aptly noted that the expiatory mode would be useful for thinking about the events in South Africa today.

33. Karl Marx, *The Eighteenth Brumaire of Louis Bonaparte* (New York: International Publishers, 1963), p. 15.

34. Ibid.

35. Jean-Christophe Agnew, *Worlds Apart: Market and Theater in Anglo-American Thought, 1550–1750* (Cambridge and New York: Cambridge University Press, 1986), p. 40.

36. Ibid., p. 97.

37. Ibid., p. 160; Richard Sennett, *The Fall of Public Man* (New York: W. W. Norton, 1977), pp. 39–41.

38. Agnew, *Worlds Apart,* p. 161.

39. In his memoirs, Saint-Simon stressed the extraordinary rituals around the king and the court, and thereby criticized the monarchy for its excessive theatricality; for example, see Louis, duc de Saint-Simon, *Versailles, the Court, and Louis XIV,* selected and translated by Lucy Norton (New York: Harper and

Row, 1988). Montesquieu's *Persian Letters,* trans. C. J. Betts (London: Penguin Books, 1973), also written in the 1720s, contained a similar view of monarchy and court culture which was likened in this epistolary novel to the despotic, irrational, and titillating world of the Oriental harem. Jean-Jacques Rousseau extended the theatrical critique beyond court life to Old Regime society and politics in general. His *Discourse on the Origin of Inequality,* written in 1755, beautifully mirrors Molière's comedy in its development of a model of a transparent order of things which is presented, first, in order to criticize its opposite, the reign of "haughty pomp and deceitful knavery" in the real world, and, second, in order to serve as an ideal toward which mankind should strive. This ideal is worked out more clearly in *The Social Contract,* written in 1762. For a fuller analysis of Rousseau's critical discourse on theatricality and its opposite, transparency, see Jean Starobinski, *Jean Jacques Rousseau: La Transparence et l'obstacle* (Paris: Gallimard, 1971, originally published 1959) and also his *1789: Les Emblêmes de la raison* (Paris: Flammarion, 1979).

40. Lynn Hunt, *Politics, Culture and Class in the French Revolution* (Berkeley: University of California Press, 1984), p. 55.

41. Hunt, *Politics and Culture,* pp. 12–13. In her recent work on the legal *causes célèbres* of the prerevolutionary period, Sarah Maza raises issues concerning the importance of the theater in the context of the political crisis of the 1770s which both help to explain the Manichaean rhetoric of the French Revolution and set the stage for the social and political struggles of the early nineteenth century. In particular, she analyzes the widespread use of the melodramatic mode prior to the Revolution, both in theaters and in widely circulating legal memoirs, which popularized what Peter Brooks has called the "mode of excess." Following Brooks, Maza argues that the waning of the authority of the church and state as arbiters of right and wrong led to aesthetic innovations in the genre of melodrama—innovations such as the adoption of hyperbolic expressions and gestures, complicated plotting, and emphatic moral didacticism; but she shows that these were adopted not only in plays but also in legal briefs in the prerevolutionary period. In her words, "the melodramatic mode thus represents the urge to resacralize a postsacral world, and to do so in terms that are both intensely personal and universally intelligible; in late eighteenth-century France the adoption of this new style by playwrights and lawyers testifies to the impulse to reach out to, and shape, an emergent 'public sphere.'" Maza's interesting efforts to analyze the important relationship between the theater and the courtroom, between dramatic productions and legal briefs, and the general discussion about both in the eighteenth century dovetails with my argument; however, where I highlight the uses of the theater and the critical discourse on theatricality to draw attention to and resolve the *political* crisis of legitimacy, her focus is on the ways in which the theater and particularly the melodramatic mode served to work through changing social relations and representations (or the "intensely personal") in the context of a political crisis. She rightly points out that these issues were still being negotiated in the early nineteenth century, when melodrama became most popular, and when the newly available *Gazette des Tribunaux* adopted and more broadly popularized this mode in the legal context. It would be very interesting to consider the significance of melodrama

in this sense and its role in "resacralizing a postsacral world" alongside the actual cultural practices (in and around theaters, but also around the religious revival) which have been the focus of this book. Peter Brooks, *The Melodramatic Imagination: Balzac, Henry James, Melodrama and the Mode of Excess* (New Haven: Yale University Press, 1976; reprint, New York: Columbia University Press, 1985), esp. chap. 1; Sara Maza, *Private Lives and Public Affairs: The Causes Célèbres of Prerevolutionary France* (Berkeley: University of California Press, 1993), pp. 66–67; for a relevant discussion of theater and the "Social Imagery of Political Crisis," see chap. 1.

42. *Scènes imitées de Molière, facéties politiques extraites du Figaro, du Revenant, du Corsaire, de la Caricature, du Charivari, et du Bridolson* (Paris: Bibliothèque de M. le Baron Taylor, 1847).

43. J. Cénac-Moncaut, *Avant et Pendant: Comédies Politiques en vers et imitées de Molière* (Paris: Comptoir des Imprimeurs Unis, 1850), pp. xix–xx. This is also a clever imitation of Scribe's *Avant, Pendant, et Apres* (Paris: Bezou et aimé andré Librairies, 1829), which represents "before, during, and after" the Revolution of 1789.

44. George Sand, *Molière: Drame en cinq actes* (Paris: E. Blanchard, 1851).

45. This is an adaptation of Agnew's formulation about theater being "a laboratory of and for the new social relations of agricultural and commercial capitalism," which I have cited above, Agnew, *Worlds Apart*, p. 161.

46. For a full discussion of this rich literature on the early American republic, see David Waldstreicher's *In the Midst of Perpetual Fetes: The Making of American Nationalism, 1776–1820* (Chapel Hill: University of North Carolina Press, 1997), which itself presents a very interesting view of the role of festive practices in constituting the American nation that is very complementary to my own portrait of politics in France. Those who most directly engage this debate about theatricality, transparency, and the transition to democracy are Jay Fliegelman, *Declaring Independence: Jefferson, National Language, and the Culture of Performance* (Stanford, Calif.: Stanford University Press, 1993); Simon Newman, *Parades and the Politics of the Street: Festive Culture in the Early American Republic* (Philadelphia: University of Pennsylvania Press, 1997); Jeffrey Richards, *Theater Enough: American Culture and the Metaphor of the World Stage, 1607–1789* (Durham, N.C.: Duke University Press, 1991); and Michael Warner, *The Letters of the Republic: Publication and the Public Sphere in Eighteenth-Century America* (Cambridge, Mass.: Harvard University Press, 1990). For a related discussion in the context of Restoration England, see Paula R. Backscheider, *Theatrical Power and Mass Culture in Early Modern England* (Baltimore: Johns Hopkins University Press, 1993).

47. Jacques Rupnik, "Vaclav Havel," in *Civilization*, April–May 1998, p. 46.

Selected Bibliography

Archival Sources

Archives Départementales de la Dordogne (ADD). Series M, Police. 1 M 64. Seditious objects.

———. 1 Z 22. *Mise-en-Place.*

Archives Départementales de la Seine-Inférieure (ADSI). Series M, Police. 1 M 173. 1 M 174. *Mise-en-place.*

———. Series M, Police. 1 M 175–177. Political sedition.

———. Series M, Police. 1 M 347. 1 M 366–369. Royal festivals.

———. Series M, Police. 4 M 632–635. Seized printed matter.

———. Series T, Theater. 4 T 81. Police of the theaters.

Bibliothèque Nationale, Paris (Richelieu: Salle des Estampes). Tb mat 1 and Tb mat 1a. Prints featuring scenes from Molière's *Tartuffe.*

———. Registre. Etats de Dépots de la Librairie, 1815–1830.

Museum of the National Archives, Hôtel Soubise, Paris. AEV, various. Actual seditious objects corresponding to police dossiers.

National Archives, Paris. BB 22 12–14; 15–23. Minister of Justice, political pardons.

———. CC 499–534. Procès politiques de la Cour des pairs, 1815–1820.

———. F2 I 135. Minister of the Interior, departmental administration, reports on *Mise-en-place.*

———. F7, Police. F7 3784–3798. Police bulletins, 1815–1829.

———. F7, Police. F7 6692–6693. Theater, departments, 1815–1830.

———. F7, Police. F7 6704–6706. Seditious writings and objects, 1814–1830.

———. F7, Police. F7 6727. *Gardes du corps.*

———. F7, Police. F7 6729. *Colporteurs.*

———. F7, Police. F7 6738–6739. Coronation of Charles X.

———. F7, Police. F7 6742. Newspapers.

———. F7, Police. F7 6745–6746. Louvel Affair (1820).

———. F7, Police. F7 6767–6772. Political situation in departments, 1815–1830; prefect reports.

———. F7, Police. F7 6779–6784. Political situation in departments after 1830; gendarmerie reports. For a useful inventory of the very important subset of police files, F7 6678–6784, see Chaline Chaumié, *Objets généraux des affaires politiques, F7 6678–6784: Inventaire et table*. Paris: Imprimerie Nationale, 1954.

———. F7, Police. F7 9792–9794. Correspondence regarding the Missions to the Interior.

———. F7, Police. F7 9890. Anniversaries of January 21 and October 16, 1815–1830.

———. F7, Police. F7 9897–9898. Kings' Saint Days, 1814–1830.

———. F18 551. *Imprimerie, Librairie, Presse,* Censorship: Peddlers.

———. F19. Minister of Religion. F19 5549. Procession of the Fête-Dieu and Vow of Louis XIII, 1814–1830.

———. F19, Minister of Religion. F19 5561. Establishment of mission crosses.

———. F19, Minister of Religion. F19 5566. Prayers, festivals, and public ceremonies, Restoration and July Monarchy.

———. F19, Minister of Religion. F19 5599. Sacrilege Law, Restoration.

———. F19, Minister of Religion. F19 5601. Political attitude of clergy, July Monarchy.

F21. Beaux-Arts. F21 966–998. Censorship of theater.

———. F21, Beaux-Arts. F21 966–995. Procès-verbaux of censorship in Paris, organized by theater.

———. F21, Beaux-Arts. F21 997–998. Censorship in the departments, including correspondence with local officials.

———. F21, Beaux-Arts. F21 1104. Odéon Theater.

———. F21, Beaux-Arts. F21 1214. Correspondence regarding departmental theaters.

Books and Articles

Andrieux, François Guillaume Jean Stanislas. *Molière: Comédie Episodique.* Paris: Chez les Marchands de Nouveautés, 1828.

Bayard, Jean François Alfred, et Auguste Romieu. *Molière au théâtre,* comédie en une acte et en vers. Paris: J. L. J. Brière et Barba, 1824.

Bulletin des Lois.

Cénac-Moncaut, Justin Edouard Mathieu. *Avant et Pendant: Comédies Politiques en vers et imitées de Molière.* Paris: Comptoir des Imprimeurs Unis, 1850.

Collection complète des Lois, decrets, ordonnances, Réglemens, avis du Conseil-d'état. Vol. 20. 2d Ed. Paris: A. Guyot et Scribe, 1837.

Le Colporteur au Village. l'Abbé . . . . 3d ed. Tours: Ad. Mame. et Cie, 1849.

Le Constitutionnel.

Croy, Gustave, Maximilien, Juste, Prince de. *Instruction Pastorale et ordon-*

nance de S. A. Mgr. l'archevêque de Rouen, primat de Normandie. Rouen: Méjard Imp., in-4, 19 Mar 1825.

Cuvillers, Le Baron D'Henin de. *Des Comédiens et du clergé, suivi de reflexions sur le mandement de Mgr. L'Archevêque de Rouen.* Paris: P. Dupont Delannay, et les marchands de nouveautés, 1825.

Dumersan, Théophile Marion. *La Mort de Molière.* Paris: Barba, 1830.

Garnier, François. *Le Mariage de Molière ou le Manteau du Tartuffe.* Paris: J. N. Barba; Lyons: Cambit, fils, Oct. 1828.

Hubert, Le Toile (pseudonym of Philippe-Jacques Laroche). *Le Faux Mentor ou Encore un Tartuffe.* Paris: Dondez-Dupré, 1820.

Journal de l'Empire.

Marx, Karl. *The 18th Brumaire of Louis Bonaparte.* New York: International Publishers Co., 1963; orig. 1852.

Molière, Jean Baptiste Poquelin de. *Tartuffe.* Translated into English verse by Richard Wilbur. New York: Harcourt, Brace & World, 1961.

———. *Tartuffe.* Avec de nouvelles notices historiques, critiques et littéraires par M. Etienne. Paris: C. L. F. Panckoucke, Editeur, 1824.

———. *Tartuffe.* Paris: Baudouin Frères, 1825. Preface signed C. L., attributed to Claude Langlois in other versions.

———. *Tartuffe.* Paris: Imprimerie et Fonderie de J. Pinard, 1825. Unsigned "Discours Préliminaire."

Moniteur Universel.

Pradel, Eugène de. *Un Trait de Molière: Prologue de Tartuffe en vers.* Paris: chez Ladvocat, Librairie au Palais Royal, et chez Barba, 1821.

Samson, Joseph Isidore. *La Fête de Molière.* Paris: J. N. Barba, 1825.

Sand, George. *Molière: Drame en cinq actes.* Paris: E. Blanchard, 1851.

Scènes imitées de Molière, facéties politiques extraites du Figaro, du Revenant, du Corsaire, de la Caricature, du Charivari, et du Bridolson. Paris: Bibliothèque de M. le Baron Taylor, 1847.

Scribe, Augustin Eugène, et Michel Nicolas Balisson de Rougemont. *Avant, Pendant, et Apres.* Paris: Bezou et aimé andré Librairies, 1829.

Simon, Henri. *Ninon, Molière, et Tartuffe.* Paris: Barba, 1815.

Stendhal, *Le Rouge et le Noir.* Paris: Gallimard, 1972; orig. 1830.

Translation into verse from Comedies of Molière and Casimir Delavigne to which are added original poems, imitations, school exercises, and the Magic Lantern, a satire. E.-F. Paris: A. and W. Galignani, 1829.

Secondary Sources

Agnew, Jean-Christophe. *Worlds Apart: Market and Theater in Anglo-American Thought, 1550–1750.* Cambridge: Cambridge University Press, 1986.

Agulhon, Maurice. *Marianne au Pouvoir: L'imagerie et la symbolique républicaine, 1880–1914.* Paris: Flammarion, 1989.

———. *Marianne into Battle: Republican Imagery and Symbolism in France, 1780–1880.* Translated by Janet Lloyd. Cambridge: Cambridge University Press, 1981.

———. *The Republic in the Village: The People of the Var from the French Rev-*

olution to the Second Republic. Translated by Janet Lloyd. Cambridge: Cambridge University Press, 1982.

———. *La Vie Sociale en Provence Intérieure au lendemain de la Revolution.* Paris: Société des Etudes Robespierristes, 1970.

Agulhon, Maurice, Gabriel Désert, and Robert Specklin. *Histoire de la France Rurale,* Vol. 3: *Apogée et crise de la civilisation paysanne, 1789–1914.* Paris: Editions du Seuil, 1976.

Alexander, Robert. *Bonapartism and Revolutionary Tradition in France: The Fédérés of 1815.* Cambridge: Cambridge University Press, 1991.

Alméras, Henri D'. *Le Tartuffe de Molière.* Paris: SFELT, 1946.

Backscheider, Paula R. *Theatrical Power and Mass Culture in Early Modern England.* Baltimore: Johns Hopkins University Press, 1993.

Barrows, Susanna. "Laughter, Language, and Derision: Seditious Speech and Popular Political Culture in Mid-Nineteenth-Century France." Unpublished manuscript.

Baschera, Marco. *Théâtricalité dans l'oeuvre de Molière.* Biblio 17–108. Papers in Seventeenth-Century Literature. Tubingen: Gunter Narr Verlag, 1998.

Bastid, Paul. *Institutions politiques de la monarchie parlementaire française, 1814–1881.* Paris: Sirey, 1954.

Beach, Vincent. *Charles X of France.* Boulder, Colo.: Pruett, 1971.

Beecher, Jonathan. *Charles Fourier: The Visionary and His World.* Berkeley: University of California Press, 1986.

Berenson, Edward. *Populist Religion and Left-wing Politics in France, 1830–1852.* Princeton, N.J.: Princeton University Press, 1984.

Bertier de, Sauvigny Guillaume de. *Le Conte Ferdinande de Bertier, 1782–1869, et l'énigme de la Congrégation.* Paris: Presses Continentales, 1948.

———. *La Restauration.* Paris: Flammarion, 1955.

Boulard, F., and J. Rémy. *Pratiques Religieuse urbaine et régions culturelles.* Paris: Les Editions Ouvrières, 1968.

Boutry, Philippe. "'Le Roi martyr': La Cause de Louis XVI devant la cour de Rome (1820)." *Revue d'histoire de l'Eglise de France* 76 (1990): 57–71.

Brooks, Peter. *The Melodramatic Imagination: Balzac, Henry James, Melodrama and the Mode of Excess.* New Haven: Yale University Press, 1976; reprint, New York: Columbia University Press, 1985.

Brown, Frederick. *Theater and Revolution: The Culture of the French Stage.* New York: Vintage Books, 1989.

Burke, Peter. *The Fabrication of Louis XIV.* New Haven: Yale University Press, 1992.

Burns, Michael. *Rural Society and French Politics: Boulangism and the Dreyfus Affair, 1886–1900.* Princeton, N.J.: Princeton University Press, 1984.

Chaline, Nadine-Josette. "Une Image du Diocese de Rouen sous l'Episcopat de Monseigneur Le Croy (1823–1844)." *Revue historique de l'Eglise de France* 58 (1972): 53–71.

Chartier, Roger. *The Cultural Origins of the French Revolution.* Translated by Lydia G. Cochrane. Durham, N.C.: Duke University Press, 1991.

———. *The Culture of Print: Power and the Uses of Print in Early Modern Eu-*

rope. Translated by Lydia G. Cochrane. Princeton, N.J.: Princeton University Press, 1989.

Cholvy, Gérard, and Yves-Marie Hilaire. *Histoire religieuse de la France contemporaine, 1800–1880*. Toulouse: Privat, 1985.

Collins, Irene. *The Government and the Newspaper Press in France, 1814–1881*. London: Oxford University Press, 1959.

———. Editor. *Government and Society in France, 1814–1848*. London: Edward Arnold, 1970.

Confino, Alon. *The Nation as a Local Metaphor: Wurttenburg, Imperial Germany, and National Memory, 1871–1918*. Chapel Hill: University of North Carolina Press, 1997.

Corbin, Alain. "L'Agitation dans les théâtres de province sous La Restauration." Pp. 93–114 in *Popular Traditions and Learned Culture in France from the Sixteenth to the Twentieth Century*. Edited by Marc Bertrand. Stanford, Calif.: Anma Libri, 1985. Also translated into English by Jean Birrell, "Agitation in Provincial Theaters under the Restoration." Pp. 39–61 in *Time, Desire, and Honor: Towards a History of the Senses*. Cambridge: Polity Press, 1995.

Corce, Pierre de la. *La Restauration: Louis XVIII*. Paris: Plon, 1926.

Cordonnier-Detrif, Paul. "Imagerie et Colportage." Extrait de *La Revue Historique et Archéologique du Marne* 3 (1953): 3–51.

Corney, Frederick. "Writing October: History, Memory, Identity, and the Construction of the Bolshevik Revolution, 1917–1927." Ph.D. dissertation, Columbia University, 1997.

Crubellier, Maurice. *Histoire culturelle de la France, XIXe et XXe siècles*. Paris: Armand Colin, 1974.

Cubitt, Geoffrey. *The Jesuit Myth: Conspiracy Theory and Politics in Nineteenth-Century France*. Oxford: Clarendon Press, 1993.

Dansette, Adrien. *Religious History of Modern France*. Vol. I: *From the Revolution to the Third Republic*. New York: Herder and Herder, 1961.

Darnis, Jean-Marie. *Les Monuments expiatoires du supplice de Louis XVI et Marie-Antoinette sous l'Empire et la Restauration*. Paris: J. M. Darnis, 1981.

Davis, Natalie Zemon. *Society and Culture in Early Modern France*. Stanford, Calif.: Stanford University Press, 1975.

De Certeau, Michel. *Practices of Everyday Life*. Translated by Steven Randall. Berkeley: University of California Press, 1984.

Desan, Suzanne. "Crowds, Community, and Ritual in the Work of E. P. Thompson and Natalie Davis." Pp. 47–71 in *The New Cultural History*. Edited by Lynn Hunt. Berkeley: University of California Press, 1989.

———. *Reclaiming the Sacred: Lay Religion and Popular Politics in Revolutionary France*. Ithaca, N.Y.: Cornell University Press, 1990.

Les Droites françaises De la Revolution à nos jours. Sous la direction de Jean-François Sirinelli. Paris: Gallimard, 1992.

Eagleton, Terry. *Ideology: An Introduction*. London: Verso, 1991.

Fellows, Otis E. *French Opinion of Molière (1800–1850)*. Providence, R.I.: Brown University, 1937.

Fliegelman, Jay. *Declaring Independence: Jefferson, National Language, and the Culture of Performance*. Stanford, Calif.: Stanford University Press, 1993.

Fogel, Michel. *Les Cérémonies de l'information dans la France du XVIe au milieu du XVIIIe siècle*. Paris: Fayard, 1989.

Ford, Caroline. "Violence and the Sacred in Nineteenth-Century France." *French Historical Studies* 21, 1 (Winter 1998): 101–12.

Fourcassié, Jean. *Villèle*. Paris: Fayard, 1954.

The French Revolution and the Creation of Modern Political Culture. Vol. 1: *The Political Culture of the Old Regime*. Edited by Keith Michael Baker. Oxford: Pergamon Press, 1987.

———. Vol. 2: *The Political Culture of the French Revolution*. Edited by Colin Lucas. Oxford: Pergamon Press, 1988.

———. Vol. 3: *The Transformation of Political Culture, 1789–1848*. Edited by François Furet and Mona Ozouf. Oxford: Pergamon Press, 1989.

Garnier, J. P. *Le Sacre de Charles X et l'opinion publique en 1825*. Paris: Jouve, 1927.

Gibson, Ralph. *A Social History of French Catholicism, 1789–1914*. London: Routledge, 1989.

Giesey, Ralph E. *The Royal Funeral Ceremony in Renaissance France*. Geneva: Librairie E. Droz, 1960.

Goldstein, Robert Justin. *Censorship of Political Caricature in Nineteenth-Century France*. Kent, Ohio: Kent State University Press, 1989.

Guillemin, Henri. *Histoire des Catholiques français au XIXème siècle, 1815–1905*. Geneva, Paris, Montreal: Editions du Milieu du Monde, 1947.

Habermas, Jurgen. *The Structural Transformation of the Public Sphere: An Inquiry into a Category of Bourgeois Society*. Translated by Thomas Burger. Cambridge, Mass.: MIT Press, 1993.

Hammond, Paul. "The King's Two Bodies: Representations of Charles II." Pp. 12–48 in *Culture, Politics, and Society in Britain, 1660–1800*. Edited by Jeremy Black and Jeremy Gordon. Manchester: Manchester University Press, 1991.

Hartman, Mary S. "The Sacrilege Law of 1825 in France: A Study in Anticlericalism and Mythmaking," *Journal of Modern History* 44, 1 (1972): 21–37.

Hemmings, F. W. J. *Culture and Society in France, 1789–1848*. New York: Peter Lang Publishers, 1987.

———. *The Theater Industry in Nineteenth-Century France*. Cambridge: Cambridge University Press, 1993.

Hermon, Rita. "Fêtes révolutionnaires, fêtes républicaines: une tradition retrouvée." *Nouvelle Revue Socialiste* 53, (1981): 42–56.

Higgs, David. "Discursive Shouts: Marginals and Bonapartism in Restoration Toulouse." Paper presented at the Annual Meeting of French Historical Studies, Vancouver: March 1990.

———. *Ultra-Royalism in Toulouse: From Its Origins to the Revolution of 1830*. Baltimore and London: Johns Hopkins University Press, 1973.

Hobsbawm, Eric, and Terence Ranger. Editors. *The Invention of Tradition*. Cambridge: Cambridge University Press, 1983.

Hunt, Lynn. Editor. *The Family Romance of the French Revolution.* Berkeley: University of California Press, 1992.

———. "The Many Bodies of Marie Antoinette: Political Pornography and the Problem of the Feminine in the French Revolution." Pp. 108–30 in *Eroticism and the Body Politic.* Edited by Lynn Hunt. Baltimore and London: Johns Hopkins University Press, 1991.

———. *Politics, Culture, and Class in the French Revolution.* Berkeley: University of California Press, 1984.

Jackson, Richard A. *Vive le Roi!: A History of the French Coronation from Charles V to Charles X.* Chapel Hill: University of North Carolina Press, 1984.

Jardin, André, and André-Jacques Tudesq. *Restoration and Reaction, 1815–1848.* Translated by E. Forster. Cambridge: Cambridge University Press, 1983.

Jones, Allison K. "Deliver us from evil: Maréchal Pétain and Extreme Right-wing Politics Cast in an Expiatory Mode during Vichy Regime France." Master's thesis, University of Florida, 1999.

Kantorowicz, Ernst H. *The King's Two Bodies: A Study in Medieval Political Theology.* Princeton, N.J.: Princeton University Press, 1957.

———. "Mysteries of State: An Absolutist Concept and Its Late Mediaeval Origins." *Harvard Theological Review* 48 (January 1955): 65–91.

Kieswetter, James. "Law of Sacrilege." P. 606 in Vol. 2, *Historical Dictionary of France from the 1815 Restoration to the Second Empire.* 2 vols. Edited by Edgar L. Newman. New York and Westport, Conn.: Greenwood Press, 1987.

Krakowitch, Odile. *Hugo Censuré: La Liberté au Théâtre au XIXe siècle.* Paris: Calmann Levy, 1985.

———. *Le Théâtre soumis à la censure, 1815–1830.* Paris: National Archives, 1982.

Kroen, Sheryl T. "Revolutionizing Religious Politics during the Restoration." *French Historical Studies* 21, 1 (Winter 1998): 27–54.

Kselman, Thomas. *Miracles and Prophecies in Nineteenth-Century France.* New Brunswick, N.J.: Rutgers University Press, 1983.

———. "Popular Religiosity." Pp. 812–17 in Vol. 2, *Historical Dictionary of France from the 1815 Restoration to the Second Empire.* Edited by Edgar L. Newman. New York and Westport, Conn.: Greenwood Press, 1987.

Langlois, Claude. *Le Catholicisme au féminin: les Congrégations françaises générale au XIXe siècle.* Paris: Editions du Cerf, 1984.

———. "De la violence religieuse." *French Historical Studies* 21, 1 (Winter 1998): 113–24.

Le Bras, Gabriel. "La Religion dans la société française." In *Aspects de la société française.* Edited by André Siegfried. Paris: Librairie Générale de Droit et de Jurisprudence, 1954.

Ledré, Charles. *La Presse à l'assault de la monarchie, 1815–1848.* Paris: A. Colin, 1960.

Le Roy Ladurie, Emmanuel. *Le Territoire de l'historien.* Paris: Flammarion, 1973.

Lewis, Gwyn. "The White Terror of 1815 in the Department of the Gard." *Past and Present* 58 (1973): 108–35.

Lyons, Martyn. "Fires of Expiation: Book-Burnings and Catholic Missions in Restoration France." *French History* 10, 1: 1–27.

McMahon, Darrin M. *Enemies of the Enlightenment: The French Counter-Enlightenment and the Birth of the European Right, 1778–1830.* Forthcoming, Oxford University Press, 2001.

McPhee, Peter. *The Politics of Rural Life: Political Mobilization in the French Countryside, 1846–1852.* Oxford: Oxford University Press, 1992.

———. "Popular Culture, Symbolism, and Rural Radicalism in Nineteenth-Century France." *Journal of Peasant Studies* 5 (1978): 238–53.

———. "The Seed-time of the Republic: Society and Politics in the Pyrénées-orientales, 1846–1851." *Australian Journal of Politics and History* 22 (1976): 196–213.

———. *Social History of France, 1780–1880.* London: Routledge, 1992.

Margadant, Jo Burr. "The Duchesse de Berry and Royalist Political Culture in Postrevolutionary France." *History Workshop Journal* 43 (Spring 1997): 23–52.

Margadant, Ted W. *French Peasants in Revolt: The Insurrection of 1851.* Princeton, N.J.: Princeton University Press, 1979.

Marin, Louis. *Portrait of the King.* Minneapolis: University of Minnesota Press, 1988.

Martin, Jean-Clément. *La Vendée de la mémoire (1800–1980).* Paris: Editions du Seuil, 1989.

Mason, Laura. *Singing the Revolution.* Ithaca, N.Y.: Cornell University Press, 1997.

Maza, Sarah. "The Diamond Necklace Affair Revisited (1785–1786): The Case of the Missing Queen." Pp. 63–89 in *Eroticism and the Body Politic.* Edited by Lynn Hunt. Baltimore and London: Johns Hopkins University Press, 1991.

———. *Private Lives and Public Affairs: The Causes Célèbres of Prerevolutionary France.* Berkeley: University of California Press, 1993.

Mellon, Stanley. *The Political Uses of History: A Study of Historians in the French Restoration.* Stanford, Calif.: Stanford University Press, 1958.

Ménager, Bernard. *Les Napoléon du peuple.* Paris: Aubier, 1988.

Merrick, Jeffrey W. *The Desacralization of the French Monarchy in the Eighteenth Century.* Baton Rouge: Lousiania State University Press, 1990.

Merriman, John. *The Agony of the Republic: The Repression of the Left in Revolutionary France, 1848–1851.* New Haven and London: Yale University Press, 1978.

———. Editor. *1830 in France.* New York: New Viewpoint, of Franklin Watts, 1975.

Mosse, George. *Nationalization of the Masses.* Ithaca, N.Y.: Cornell University Press, 1975.

Muel-Dreyfus, Francine. *Vichy, et l'Eternel féminin.* Paris: Seuil, 1996.

Newman, Edgar. "The Blouse and the Frock Coat: The Alliance of the Common People of Paris with the Liberal Leadership and the Middle Class During the Last Years of the Bourbon Restoration." *Journal of Modern History* 47 (March 1974): 26–59.

———. "Lost Illusions: The Regicides in France During the Bourbon Restoration, 1815–1830." *Nineteenth-Century French Studies* 10 (1981–1982): 45–74.

———. "Republicanism During the Bourbon Restoration in France, 1814–1830." Ph.D. dissertation, University of Chicago, 1969.

———. "Republicans." Pp. 882–86, Vol. 2, *Historical Dictionary of France from the 1815 Restoration to the Second Empire*. New York and Westport, Conn.: Greenwood Press, 1987.

Newman, Simon. *Parades and the Politics of the Street: Festive Culture in the Early American Republic*. Philadelphia: University of Pennsylvania Press, 1997.

Nora, Pierre. Editor. *Les Lieux de Mémoire*. Vol. 1: *La République*. Paris: Gallimard, 1984.

O'Brien, Patricia. "Michel Foucault's History of Culture." Pp. 25–46 in *The New Cultural History*. Edited by Lynn Hunt. Berkeley: University of California Press, 1989.

Ong, Walter J. *Orality and Literacy: The Technologizing of the Word*. London and New York: Routledge, 1982.

Outram, Dorinda. *The Body and the French Revolution: Sex, Class and Political Culture*. New Haven: Yale University Press, 1988.

Ozouf, Mona. *Festivals of the French Revolution*. Translated by Alan Sheridan. Cambridge, Mass.: Harvard University Press, 1988.

Parent-Lardeur, Françoise. *Les Cabinets de Lecture: La lecture publique à Paris sous la Restauration*. Paris: Payot, 1982.

Phayer, J. Michael. "Politics and Popular Religion: The Cult of the Cross, 1815–1840," *Journal of Social History* 11, 3 (Spring 1978): 346–65.

Pierrard, Pierre. *La Vie quotidienne du prêtre français au XIXème siècle, 1801–1905*. Paris: Hachette, 1986.

Pilbeam, Patricia. *The Revolution of 1830 in France*. New York: St. Martin's Press, 1991.

Ponteil, Felix. *Les Institutions de la France de 1814 à 1870*. Paris: Presses Universitaires de France, 1966.

———. *La Monarchie parlementaire, 1815–1848*. Paris: Colin, 1949.

Price, Roger. Editor. *Revolution and Reaction: 1848 and the Second French Republic*. London: Croom Helm; New York: Barnes and Noble Books, 1975.

Ravel, Jeffrey S. *The Contested Parterre: Public Theater and French Political Culture, 1680–1791*. Ithaca, N.Y.: Cornell University Press, 1999.

Rémond, Réné. *L'Anticlericalisme en France de 1815 à nos jours*. Paris: Fayard, 1976.

———. *The Right Wing in France from 1815 to De Gaulle*. Philadelphia: University of Pennsylvania Press, 1966.

Resnick, D. P. *The White Terror and the Political Reaction after Waterloo*. Cambridge, Mass.: Harvard University Press, 1966.

Richards, Jeffrey. *Theater Enough: American Culture and the Metaphor of the World Stage, 1607–1789*. Durham, N.C.: Duke University Press, 1991.

Rosanvallon, Pierre. *Le Moment Guizot.* Paris: Gallimard, 1985.

―――. *La Monarchie Impossible: Les Chartes de 1814 et de 1830.* Paris: Fayard, 1994.

Rousso, Henry. *The Vichy Syndrome: History and Memory in France since 1944.* Translated by Arthur Goldhammer. Cambridge, Mass.: Harvard University Press, 1991.

Sahlins, Peter. *Forest Rites: The War of the Demoiselles in Nineteenth-Century France.* Cambridge, Mass.: Harvard University Press, 1994.

Salomon, Herman Prins. *Tartuffe devant l'opinion Française.* Paris: Presses Universitaires de France, 1962.

Salvan, Paule. "Le Tartuffe de Molière et l'agitation anticléricale en 1825." *Revue de la Société d'Histoire du Théâtre* 12 (1960): 7–19.

Sanson, Rosamonde. *Les 14 Juillets, fêtes et conscience nationales, 1789–1975.* Paris: Flammarion, 1976.

Schneider, Robert A. *The Ceremonial City: Toulouse Observed, 1738–1780.* Princeton, N.J.: Princeton University Press, 1995.

Sennett, Richard. *The Fall of Public Man.* New York: W. W. Norton, 1977.

Sevrin, Ernest. *Les Missions religieuses en France sous la Restauration, 1815–1830.* Vol. 1: *Le Missionnaire et la mission.* St. Maudé: Procure des Prêtres de la Miséricorde, 1948; Vol. 2: *Les Missions, 1815–1820.* Paris: Librairie Philosophique J. Vrin, 1959.

Sewell, William, Jr. *Work and Revolution in France: The Language of Labor from the Old Regime to 1848.* Cambridge: Cambridge University Press, 1980.

Southerland, D. M. G. *France 1789–1815: Revolution and Counterrevolution.* London: Collins, 1985.

Spitzer, Alan B. "The Ambiguous Heritage of the French Restoration: The Distant Consequences of the Revolution and the Daily Realities of the Empire." Pp. 208–26 in *The American and European Revolutions, 1776–1848: Sociopolitical and Ideological Aspects.* Edited by J. Pelenski. Iowa City: University of Iowa Press, 1980.

―――. *The French Generation of 1820.* Princeton, N.J.: Princeton University Press, 1987.

―――. *Old Hatreds and Young Hopes: The French Carbonari Against the French Restoration.* Cambridge, Mass.: Harvard University Press, 1971.

Spurr, John. "Virtue, Religion, and Government: The Anglican Uses of Providence." Pp. 31–47 in *The Politics of Religion in Restoration England.* Edited by Tim Harris, Paul Seaward, and Mark Goldie. London: Basil Blackwell, 1990.

Stallybrass, Peter, and Allon White. *The Politics and Poetics of Transgression.* Ithaca, N.Y.: Cornell University Press, 1986.

Starobinski, Jean. *Jean Jacques Rousseau: La Transparence et l'obstacle.* Paris: Gallimard, 1971; orig. 1959.

―――. *1789: Les Emblêmes de la raison.* Paris: Flammarion, 1979.

Strong, Roy. *Splendor at Court: Renaissance Spectacle and the Theater of Power.* Boston: Houghton-Mifflin, 1973.

Tackett, Timothy. *Religion, Revolution, and Regional Culture in Eighteenth-Century France.* Princeton, N.J.: Princeton University Press, 1986.

Thompson, E. P. "Le Charivari anglais," *AESC* 27 (1972): 285–312.

Tilly, Charles. "How Protest Modernized in France, 1845–1855." Pp. 192–255 in *The Dimensions of Quantitative Research in History.* Edited by W. Aydelotte. Princeton, N.J.: Princeton University Press, 1972.

Tudesq, André-Jean. *Les Grands Notables en France (1840–1849): étude historique d'une psychologie sociale.* Paris: Presses Universitaires de France, 1964.

Van Gannep, Arnold. *Manuel de folklore français contemporain.* 9 vols. Paris: Picard, 1943–1958.

Van Kley, Dale. *The Damiens Affair and the Unraveling of the Ancien Regime, 1750–1770.* Princeton, N.J.: Princeton University Press, 1984.

———. *The Jansenists and the Expulsion of the Jesuits from France, 1757–1765.* New Haven: Yale University Press, 1975.

Vaulabelle, Achille De. *Histoire des Deux Restaurations.* 8 Vols. 3d ed. Paris: Perrotin, 1855–1857.

Vovelle, Michel. *Les Métamorphoses de la fête en Provence de 1750 à 1820.* Paris: Aubier-Flammarion, 1976.

Waldstreicher, David. *In the Midst of Perpetual Fetes: The Making of American Nationalism, 1776–1820.* Chapel Hill: University of North Carolina Press, 1997.

Waquet, Françoise. *La Fête royale sous la Restauration, ou l'Ancien Regime retrouvé.* Geneva: Groz, 1981.

Waresquiel, Emmanuel de, and Benoît Yvert. *Histoire de la Restauration, 1814–1830: Naissance de la France moderne.* Paris: Perrin, 1996.

Warner, Michael. *The Letters of the Republic: Publication and the Public Sphere in Eighteenth-Century America.* Cambridge, Mass.: Harvard University Press, 1990.

Weber, Eugen. *Peasants into Frenchmen: The Modernization of Rural France, 1870–1914.* Stanford, Calif.: Stanford University Press, 1976.

Williams, Raymond. *Marxism and Literature.* Oxford: Oxford University Press, 1977.

Wolloch, Isser. *The New Regime: Transformation of the French Civic Order, 1789–1820s.* New York: Norton and Co., 1994.

Index

Agnew, Jean-Christophe, 299–301
Agulhon, Maurice, 16–17, 19, 159, 312n33
Alexander, Robert, 13, 286, 309n18, 311n26
amendes honorables: in Missions to the Interior, 77, 102, 104, 107; Sacrilege Law, as part of, 113. *See also* eucharistic model of monarchy; expiation
anticlericalism, 5, 10, 202–228 passim, 259, 287, 293; carnival, the carnivalesque, and, 134, 149, 203, 208, 209–216, 291–292; clerical plot and, 5, 120; lax treatment of perpetrators, 150, 211, 259, 261, 272; missionaries and, 132–133, 134–141, 142, 175, 209–216, 260–284; missionaries, successes in controlling, 133, 134, 144, 145, 146–147, 148, 212, 213, 214, 246, 256; Montlosier pamphlet, 261, 309n22; morality of priests and, 3–4, 137, 205–207, 214–215, 232, 238–239; national movement, as, 138, 243, 259, 282, 334n60, 361n54; new Catholicism and, 3, 124, 203; participants, 134, 136–137, 139–140, 333n48; press, spreading, 150, 204, 215, 231, 234, 251–252; religious rigor and, 10, 32, 124, 148, 203, 204–209; religious versus political, 10, 202–203; song, 134, 205–206, 334n50, 352–353nn5–12; tactics, 141, 142,

204, 213. *See also* Brest; Eucharist; historiography; mission crosses; Missions to the Interior; sacrality, transfer of; sacred, struggles over; Tartufferie

Béranger, Pierre Jean de: "The Old Flag," 62, 322n84; seditious objects featuring, 191, 195 (figure 4)
Bertier de Sauvigny, Guillaume de, 13, 14, 308n16, 309n22
biens nationaux: attacked by missionaries, 77, 94, 95, 100, 102, 103, 111, 114–115, 122–123, 128, 129, 146, 148, 204, 217; defended by state, 103; song criticizing missionaries' attack on, 135. *See also* laws (Restoration)
Bonapartism, 200–201; 15 August, 164–165, 177, 180; placards, 164–165, 168, 169, 177, 178; prints, 190, 192 (figure 2); republicanism, blurring with, 287, 293, 311n26; seditious cries, 167, 175; songs, 62, 182, 184; unofficial politics and, 200. *See also* politics (unofficial)
Brest: 1819, opposition to missionaries, 134–141, 199, 278; 1826–1827, opposition to missionaries, 260–284. *See also* anticlericalism; Tartufferie

carnival, carnivalesque, 164, 209–216; economic, material concerns regarding, 209–210; *mise-en-place* and, 320n62;

carnival, carnivalesque (*continued*)
missionaries and, 91, 145–146, 204,
207–208, 209; Revolution of 1830,
in and after, 291–292; state officials'
sympathy for, 209–212; use as anticlerical tactic, 149, 174, 203, 208,
209–216, 291–292. *See also* festivals
(popular); Missions to the Interior;
sacred, struggles over

Catholic Church (Old Regime): Counter-
Reformation and, 31–32; dechristianization, 31–32, 326n19, 358n11;
monarchy and, 30–35, 111–112

Catholic Church (Restoration): missionaries' support for, 88, 92–93, 125,
131, 138–139, 143, 151–152, 204,
327n45; regime's ceremonial support
for, 116–120; regime's legal support
for, 110–116; state of during, 83–84,
326n17. *See also* church-state relations
(Restoration); Missions to the Interior;
sacrality, transfer of; sacred, struggles
over

Catholicism, new. *See* anticlericalism;
Missions to the Interior

censorship. *See* laws

charivari: against missionaries in Brest,
134, 136, 175, 199, 213; efforts to
control, legally, 208, 354n24; Revolution of 1830, in and after, 291–292.
See also anticlericalism; carnival, carnivalesque; festivals (popular); sacred,
struggles over

Charles X: coronation, 4, 118–119,
163, 169–170, 231, 235; jesuit-king,
as, 10, 13, 160, 194–195, 203, 217,
223–227, 285; missionaries and, 126;
Papal Jubilee and, 119–120; Revolution of 1830 and, 285; seditious acts
against, 166–168, 178, 217; Tartuffe,
as, 302. *See also* clerical plot; eucharistic model of kingship; kings' days;
sacred, struggles over; Tartufferie

Charter. *See* laws (Restoration)

church-state relations (Old Regime): mu-
tually supportive, 30–32; strains in,
32–35, 121–122. *See also* Catholic
Church (Old Regime)

church-state relations (Restoration), 7;
ceremonies illustrating, 116–120, 133,
149–150; chronology defining, 115–
116, 121–122, 125; church hierarchy
defending missionaries against state intervention, 80–81, 97–98, 125, 138–
139, 141, 148, 151–152; comparison
with Old Regime, xii, 111–115, 121–

122, 125; laws defining, 110–116;
laws used by state against missionaries,
110, 121, 127–132; leniency of state
toward critics of missionaries, 150,
211, 261, 272; long-term consequences
of regime's disciplinary measures toward missionaries, 121, 152–153,
203, 283–284, 287–290, 295, 296;
missions, negotiations over, defining,
82, 120, 121–126, 133, 138–141,
144–153, 259- 284; secular legacy of
Revolution of 1789, consolidated in,
11, 121–126, 202–203, 283; state
support for missionaries, 143, 149–
150; state tactics to control missionaries, 126, 145, 260–261, 288–290,
335n83, 336n86. *See also* Catholic
Church (Restoration); clerical plot;
laws (Restoration); Missions to the
Interior; sacred, struggles over

church-state relations (Revolution of
1830): church hierarchy defending mission crosses, 289; July Monarchy as
successor to Restoration regime's disciplining of church, 11, 152, 187–190.
See also Catholic Church; clerical plot;
Missions to the Interior

clerical plot, 206, 216–221 passim, 283,
291, 302; 1825 as key turning point in,
4, 116–117, 119–120, 216–218; billets in theater evoking, 268; Charles X
and, 4, 10, 116, 203, 217–227; crisis
of legitimacy and, 10, 216; jesuits as
grounds for fearing, 216, 279, 282,
284, 356n50; June Ordinances of 1828
in response to fears of, 115; legal versus ceremonial trappings of monarchy
and, 116–117; local perception of in
Rouen, 239–240; missions as evidence
of, 82, 108, 133, 152–153; Papal Jubilee and, 119, 226; placards: 176–
177, 178, 239; political anticlericalism
and, 10; Sacrilege Law and, 9, 113,
216. *See also* Charles X, jesuit-king, as;
church-state relations (Restoration)

commemoration, 297–298; expiation
and, 8, 96–108, 153, 294, 298, 302;
forgetting (*oubli*) and, 7–8, 20, 39–
75, 153, 294, 298, 302; improvisation
and, 294, 298; laws dictating, 42–43,
63–64. *See also* expiation; forgetting
(*oubli*), politics of; laws; *mise-en-place*;
Missions to the Interior; monarchy;
regicide

Concordat, 111, 121, 127–129, 131;
missionaries' attitude toward, 94, 99;

used against missionaries, 127–132, 274; used to defend missionaries, 272
Constant, Benjamin: seditious objects and, 191
Corbin, Alain, 19, 173–174, 227, 270, 310n22, 367n153
coronation (Old Regime), 25–27, 28
coronation (Restoration): Charles X, 4, 118–119, 163, 331n18; local celebrations, occasions for seditious acts, 169–170; Louis XVIII, avoidance of, 118; Tartufferie in response to, 4, 230–231, 243, 248. See also Charles X; Louis XVIII; monarchy (Old Regime); monarchy (Restoration); Tartufferie
crisis of legitimacy of Restoration, 5; clerical plot as expression of, 10, 203, 216, 227–228; jesuit-king as embodiment of, 223–227; July Monarchy, in relation to, 291–293; missionaries and, 132; resolution through Tartufferie, 11, 227–228; Revolution of 1789 and, 6–7, 302; seditious acts exposing, 9, 203; struggles between church and state and, 7, 153; Tartuffe as expression of, 37–38; use of theater to expose, 174, 227–228. See also Charles X, jesuit-king as; Tartufferie; sacred, struggles over
Croy, Archbishop Le, of Rouen, 205–207, 215; Tartuffe of Seine-Inférieure, 229–242

Davis, Natalie Zemon, 208, 219, 295, 354n20
Desan, Suzanne, 158–159, 370n17

Enlightenment: anti-Enlightenment of eighteenth century, 309n22, 329nn57, 65; Good Book Society and, 186–187; mandement condemning, 101, 185; missionaries' assault on in Restoration, 79, 90, 100, 101–102, 112, 153, 186, 310n23; pamphlet wars and, 186–187; opposition press publicizing, 185, 187; seditious objects popularizing, 188, 191; songs defending, 134, 334n50. See also expiation; Missions to the Interior
Eucharist, 114; attacks on, 219–220, 294; effigy of king as equivalent to, 25–26; kings' two bodies and, 24, 105–108, 114; missionaries and, 90, 91, 105–108; portrait of king as equivalent to, 26–30; ritual re-consecrating

of in support for missionaries, 220, 294; Sacrilege Law and protection of, 9, 113–114, 218. See also Charles X, jesuit-king, as; eucharistic model of kingship; monarchy; sacrality, transfer of; sacred, struggles over; symbol(s) (Christian)
eucharistic model of kingship, 8, 27–30, 104, 105–108, 221–222, 225–227, 294–295; amendes honorables and, 78, 105–108; funeral ceremonies of Renaissance kings, 25–26, 107; jesuit-king and, 194–195, 203, 222–227; mission crosses expressing, 78; Missions to the Interior and, 78, 104–108, 153, 218–219; opposition to, 219–227; Papal Jubilee and, 218; Revolution of 1789, in relation to, 36; Sacrilege Law and, 9, 113–114, 218–219. See also expiation; Marin, Louis; Missions to the Interior; monarchy, portrait of the king
expiation, 8, 20, 99–101, 159, 294, 298; mise-en-place and, 55–56; missionaries and, 73–74, 76–83, 96–108, 133, 153; regicide, the state, and, 64–65, 70–74. See also commemoration; eucharistic model of monarchy; Missions to the Interior; regicide; sacred, struggles over

festivals (popular), 172, 209–213; Catholic Church and, 31–32; Concordat, suppression of, 208; mise-en-place described as, 50, 51. See also carnival, carnivalesque; politics (unofficial); sacred, struggles over
festivals (revolutionary), 117, 208; bishop of Strasbourg and, 98–99, 101; missionaries' assault on, 98–101; oaths, contrast with 21 January, 67–68; Restoration law affirming sanctity of Sundays and holidays, 112; transfer of sacrality to secular republicanism, 35–36, 158–159, 202. See also Missions to the Interior; Ozouf, Mona; sacrality, transfer of; sacred, struggles over
festivals (royal), 117, 163, 170
Forbin-Janson, Charles de, 76, 81, 84, 250;
forgetting (oubli), politics of, 39–75, 153, 159; Conciergerie and, 71–74; failure of, 9, 58–62, 201; ideological purpose of, 49, 56–58, 62, 64; legal framework for, 40–41, 322n87; missionaries undermining, 100, 108, 122,

forgetting (*oubli*), politics of (*continued*)
153. *See also* commemoration; *mise-en-place* ceremonies; regicide

general will, 67, 137, 140, 213
Giesey, Ralph, 25–27
Guyon, Père, 77, 86, 88, 105, 261, 274

historiography: on anticlericalism, 10, 13, 309n20, 309–310n22; on church-state relations (Old Regime), 30–35; on democracy, 14–15, 16, 18, 19; on legacy of French Revolution, 16–17, 159–160; on Missions to the Interior, 14, 19, 83, 309n22, 310n23; on monarchy, 17–18, 19, 20, 23–36; on political culture, 10–15, 157–160; on Restoration, 12–19, 308n16, 313n49; on Revolution of 1789, 157–159; on Revolution of 1830, 285–293
Hundred Days, 5, 85, 118; fédérés supporting Bonaparte throughout Restoration, 13, 286, 309n18; *mise-en-place* ceremonies and, 41–42, 50, 52; songs evoking, 182
Hunt, Lynn, 36, 158–159, 296, 301, 302, 316n47, 321n68

jesuits: Charles X, figured as, 194–195, 203, 217–227; missionaries and, 79, 86, 326n25; Ordinances of June 1828 and, 115; plot of, as evoked by attorneys in Brest, 1827, 274, 276, 277–278, 279–280, 282, 303; protests against, 213, 261; seditious objects featuring, 191
jubilee. *See* Papal Jubilee

Kantorowicz, Ernst, 23–35; Louis Marin in relation to, 314–315n21. *See also* king's two bodies
kings' days (Saint Louis and Saint Charles), 163, 166–169, 173, 178, 210, 242, 258
king's two bodies: demise of in eighteenth century, 34–35; Renaissance kings and, 23–27, 107; Restoration (missionaries), 77–78, 105–108; Restoration (state), reluctant commemoration of regicide and, 63, 67–68, 118, 331n17; Revolution of 1789 and, 35–36; Sacrilege Law, defining the Host as the body of the king, 114, 218. *See also* Eucharist; eucharistic model of kingship; expiation; Missions to the

Interior; monarchy; regicide; sacred, struggles over

La Mennais, Abbé Félécité de, 91–92, 326n26
laws (Old Regime): censorship, 33–34, 112; clerical, 30–35, 111; defining citizenship in relation to Catholicism, 33, 111; sacrilege, 34, 111
laws (Restoration): announcement of, 163, 176; censorship, 101, 112, 141, 151–152, 184, 187, 189; Charter, 129, 132, 134, 135, 139, 140, 161, 167, 184–185, 191, 278, 280, 282; clerical, 8–9, 112, 115, 120; forgetting, politics of, 40–41, 63–65, 322n87; missionaries, attacking Charter and other laws, 123, 128, 146; missionaries, laws protecting, 98, 135, 139, 142–143, 144, 151–152, 161; missionaries, laws used to discipline, 99, 110, 121, 126–132, 133, 146–147, 274; missionaries, ordinance legalizing, 85–86, 131; Ordinances of June 1828, 115, 120; Penal Code, application of Article 201, 128; Sedition (11 November 1815), 42–43; typical acquittals for sedition, 141, 150, 197, 222, 261, 272. *See also* church-state relations (Old Regime); church-state relations (Restoration); monarchy (Old Regime); monarchy (Restoration); Sacrilege Law (1825)
Limoges, 1828, 141–144
Louis XVIII, 112, 116; coronation, 118; Missions to the Interior and, 84–86, 126; sedition against, 165, 167, 168, 177, 178. *See also* kings' days; monarchy

Marin, Louis, and the portrait of the king, 26, 29–30, 221–227, 314–315n21
Marx, Karl, 299, 307n1
Maza, Sarah, 373n41
Merrick, Jeffrey, 32–35, 121–122
mise-en-place ceremonies, 7, 39–62; creating symbolic battleground of Restoration, 190–191; dates chosen for, 50, 55; expiatory message as compared to missionaries, 55–56; failure of compulsory amnesia, 58–62, 201; ideological logic of, 49, 56–58, 62, 317n16, 321n68; laws establishing, 40–43; local initiatives, 42, 51; monarchical and Christian symbols erected in, 54–55; national campaign, 42–45; objects

destroyed in, 52–53; practices against revolutionary reminders, 48–49, 51, 190; reception, 49, 51, 58–60; religious message of, 55–56; Revolution, Empire, and Hundred Days represented in, 53–54, 56; speeches during, 53–54, 56; typical ceremony, 49–50; use of seditious revolutionary symbols against, 194. *See also* commemoration; forgetting (*oubli*), politics of; symbol(s)

mission crosses: attacks on during Restoration, 10, 195, 220, 294; attacks on after 1830, 286, 287–288, 309n20, 320n23; disputes over placement, 147, 336n85; eucharistic conception of monarchy and, 78, 218–221; funding for, 147–148, 221; policy regarding during Restoration and July Monarchy, 148; replacing revolutionary symbols with, 100, 102. *See also* Eucharist; expiation; Missions to the Interior; monarchy; sacred, struggles over; symbol(s)

Missions to the Interior, 76–108; constitutional priests, attacks on, 94, 95–96, 100, 102–103, 329n71; Enlightenment, attacks on, 79, 90, 100, 101–102, 112, 310n23; eucharistic model of kingship in, 8, 78, 104–108; expiatory message of, 8, 77–78, 96–104, 298; jesuits and, 79, 82, 86; Louis XVIII, initial support for, 84–85; Marseilles, 1820, as example, 76–83; Missionaries of France, 84–86, 93, 103; missionary, typical, 87; monarchy, attacking secular foundations of, 96–98, 122–124; monarchy, staging of, 7, 82–83; number, geography of and participation in, 87–88, 94, 327nn31, 32, 328n50; ordinance supporting and defining organization of, 85–86, 110, 131; policing of, by the state, 80, 127–132, 258–259, 288–290; political message of, 87, 94–95, 98–101, 159, 202, 218, 292, 328n52; regional, local support for, 87; relationship to established church, 88, 93, 327n45; religious message of, 83–84, 89–94, 124. *See also* anticlericalism; carnival, carnivalesque; charivari; church-state relations (Restoration); Eucharist; eucharistic model of monarchy; expiation; festivals (popular); festivals (revolutionary); mission crosses; monarchy; sacrality, transfer of; sacred, struggles over

Missions to the Interior, acts against, 133, 204; firecrackers, stink bombs, 78, 142, 212, 261, 267; masquerades, costumes, 212; placards, 78, 142, 261; sacraments, mockery of, 203, 207–209; songs, 261; symbolic violence, 213, 219–220, 261; Tartufferie, 278, 283, 260–284; violence, 213

Missions to the Interior, expiatory ceremonies, 8; autos-da-fés, 100, 101–102, 153, 310n23; confessions, individual, 102–103; confessions, mass, 103, 104; erections of mission crosses, 77, 104, 218–221; 21 January, 77, 104, 105, 145, 146, 216

Missions to the Interior, new Catholicism of, 91–94, 203–209; attitudes toward carnival, popular festive culture, 78, 91, 93, 145–146, 204, 207–208, 209; counter-reformation, relation to, 94; pastoral letters and, 92, 204–207, 232, 241; refusal of sacraments, 93–96, 204, 207, 328n54

Missions to the Interior, tactics, 90; canticles, 107, 138, 182, 191; church services, choirs, 89–91; fire-and-brimstone sermons, 77, 91, 92; selling of trinkets, 90, 191; symbolic refurbishing of landscape with Christian and monarchical emblems, 78, 107, 220

Molière, Jean Baptiste Poquelin de. *See* Tartuffe

monarchy (French Revolution): ceremonial interregnum, 35–36; *mise-en-place* as effort to efface, 62

monarchy (Old Regime): ceremonial interregnum, 25, 26; ceremonies under Louis XIV, 26–30; Christian (by the grace of God), 30–35; desacralization of, 6, 32, 34, 35, 315n41; portrait of the king, 26–30; Renaissance funerals, 25–27; secularization of, 33–35; symbols of, 28; *Te Deum*, 27–28, 117, 314n16; touching for scrofula, 24–25, 119. *See also* Catholic Church (Old Regime); Eucharist; eucharistic model of monarchy; festivals (popular); king's two bodies; symbol(s)

monarchy (Restoration): ceremonial interregnum, *mise-en-place* as effort to efface, 62, 283; ceremonial trappings of, 7, 17–18, 63–75, 98, 116–120; Christian, missions and staging of, 81–83, 96–98, 104–108, 109–110; Christian, state and staging of, 116, 118; legal foundations in Restoration,

monarchy (Restoration) (*continued*)
8–9, 110–116, 218–219; negotiations
over, 7, 9, 11, 132–133; portrait of the
king, 27–30, 221–227; secular versus
Christian, 8–9, 82–83, 97, 109–153,
114, 115, 120, 284; staging of, 109–
110; *Tartuffe* and, 37–38. *See also*
church-state relations; crisis of legitimacy of Restoration; commemoration; coronation; eucharistic model
of kingship; laws; regicide; symbol(s);
Tartufferie
municipal council: as revolutionary instrument of protest, 134, 136, 139–
140, 161

Newman, Edgar Leon, 310n26, 363n95
Nora, Pierre, 17, 71

Ozouf, Mona, 8, 35–36, 98–101, 158–
159, 202, 208, 292. *See also* festivals
(revolutionary); Missions to the Interior; sacrality, transfer of; sacred,
struggles over

pamphlet literature, 185–189; battle of
books encouraged by missionaries,
186; difficulty controlling, 141; legal
briefs popularizing trials, 137–141,
276, 348n131; spreading anticlericalism, 134, 137–141. *See also* Enlightenment; Tartufferie; politics (unofficial)
Papal Jubilee, 4, 116, 163, 216; Charles
X and, 119–120; protests against,
213, 355n35; Tartufferie, 243, 248–
249; 260–284
Pilbeam, Pamela, 13–14, 286–288
placards, 142, 169, 176–180, 198, 202,
217, 237, 238, 269. *See also* anticlericalism; political (unofficial); Tartufferie
politics (official), 13, 14; Bertier de Sauvigny's definition of, 309n21; Charter's
definition of, 161; court's definition
in Brest, 1827, 272–273; Pamela Pilbeam's definition of, 286
politics (official), calendar defining:
21 January, 63, 65, 163; 16 October,
63, 163; kings' days, 163, 166–169,
173; Papal Jubilee, 163
politics (unofficial), 9, 13, 161–201 passim, 293, 297; humor in, 195–196;
ideological content of, 162, 200; justification for clerical plot and, 283; justification for legal defense of, 274, 275,
284; national quality of, 16, 89, 164,
170, 200; people involved in, 10,

171–172, 196–200, 237, 351n168,
351n170, 351n176; people involved
in, colporteur (peddler), 171, 183,
190, 196; people involved in, liberal
plot theory and, 196, 237, 251–252,
359n26; political culture and, 15–20;
practices of, 10, 162, 197; practices of,
placards, 142, 176–180, 207; practices
of, seditious speech, or symbolic sedition, 180–181, 190–195; practices of,
songs, 181–184, 232; press, role of in,
172, 184–185. *See also* pamphlet literature; placards; song(s); symbol(s)
politics (unofficial), calendar defining, 10,
163–170; 14 July, 164, 201; 15 August, 164–165, 177, 180, 201; 21 January, 58, 165–166, 177; carnival, 163,
164; coronation, local celebrations
of, 169–170; missions, 89; patron
saint days (of localities), 13–14,
164, 211; saint days of Louis XVIII
and Charles X, 163, 166–169, 173,
178, 210, 242, 258; visits of royal
family, 169
politics (unofficial), geography of, 10,
12–13, 170–175; cafés, cabarets, 172,
180–181; churches, 175; marketplace,
fair, 170–172; private homes, 175,
199–200; streets, 175; theater, 172–
174, 180
Protestants, 113, 128, 131, 139, 243,
247, 255, 309n19, 336n88

Rauzan, Jean-Baptiste, 84, 85
regicide (of Louis XVI and Marie Antoinette in 1793), commemoration of:
emigrés and coins representing, 74; local civil celebrations of, 66, 68; missionaries and, 70, 77, 80, 104–107,
129, 146, 216; state and coins representing, 8, 70, 74–75; state and politics of forgetting, 7–8, 63–75; state as
opposed to missionaries, 70, 107; state
ceremony on 21 January and 16 October, 65–66, 68–70; state monuments and, 64, 70–74, 118, 322n87,
324n111; 21 January and 16 October
as occasions for sedition, 58, 68,
165–166. *See also* commemoration;
eucharistic model of monarchy; expiation; forgetting (*oubli*), politics of;
kings' two bodies; Missions to the
Interior; politics (official); politics
(unofficial)
republicanism, 62, 164, 167, 193, 200,
287, 293

republican tradition: in nineteenth century, 16, 17, 159; in Restoration,
310n26
Revolution of 1789: crisis of legitimacy
of Restoration and, 5; legacy of, attacked by missionaries, 8, 94–96, 99,
102–104, 392n71; secular legacy of,
consolidated in Restoration, 11–12,
114–115, 126–132, 160; struggles of
transposed to Restoration, 20, 157;
symbolic legacy, 36, 157. See also crisis
of legitimacy; expiation; Missions to
the Interior; republican tradition;
sacrality, transfer of; sacred, struggles
over; symbol(s)
Revolution of 1830, 11–12, 13–14,
285–293; anticlericalism in relation to
Restoration, 11, 152–153, 203; mission crosses and, 11, 221
Rouen. See Tartufferie
Rousseau, Jean-Jacques: advertisements
for pamphlet versions of, 185; missionaries attack on, 90, 101; press publicizing battle with missionaries, 185; songs
defending, 135

sacrality, transfer of: from Christian kingship to secular nation, 34–35; from
Christian kingship to secular republicanism during Revolutionary decade,
35–36, 98, 158–159, 202; missionaries reasserting Christian kingship during Restoration, 8, 96–101, 157,
159–160, 202, 218–228, 292. See also
Eucharist; eucharistic model of monarchy; festivals (revolutionary); Sacrilege
Law; mission crosses; Missions to the
Interior; Ozouf, Mona; symbol(s)
sacred, struggles over, 158–160, 205,
209, 216–221, 290–291, 294–295,
356n57; attacks on sacred symbols
(Host, crosses, vessels), 150, 195, 219–
220; failure of mise-en-place to inspire,
59, 321–322n76; mockeries of sacraments, 203, 207–209. See also anticlericalism; carnival, carnivalesque;
Catholic Church (Old Regime); Catholic Church (Restoration); church-state
relations; crisis of legitimacy; Eucharist; eucharistic model of monarchy;
Missions to the Interior; monarchy;
sacrality; politics (unofficial)
Sacrilege Law (1825), 4, 112–114, 116,
133, 142–143, 216, 218, 287; seditious acts related to, 4, 148, 191, 231,
235, 247; use of to defend mission-

aries, 113, 133, 142–143. See also
Charles X; church-state relations;
clerical plot; Eucharist; eucharistic
model of monarchy; laws; sacred,
struggles over
Sahlins, Peter, 208, 291–293
sedition. See laws; symbol(s)
song(s), 181–184; against missionaries,
134, 135; canticles, missionaries' use
of revolutionary tunes for, 182; censorship efforts, 47; difficulty in controlling, 183–184; disseminating news,
181; disseminating news of mandement, 232–233; organizing protest,
236–237, 359n25; pamphlet versions,
186; revolutionary tunes recast, 181–
182, 236; spreading Tartufferie, 253–
254, 364n102. See also anticlericalism;
Béranger, Pierre Jean de; politics (unofficial); Tartufferie
symbol(s) (Christian) attacks on, 150,
195, 212, 219–220; crosses, 54, 55,
100, 102, 105, 149, 159, 320n61; missionaries and, 78, 90; statues of Christ,
54, 55. See also Eucharist; mission
crosses; Missions to the Interior;
sacred, struggles over
symbol(s) (monarchical), 28, 39–40, 78,
90, 107, 159; attacks on, 168–169,
178–179, 194–195; bust/portrait
of king, 54, 168, 190, 194; concealing Napoleonic, 191–193, 352n179;
fleur-de-lis, 53, 54, 58, 75, 190, 194;
missionaries and, 78, 90; white flag/
cockade, 48, 54, 55, 58, 166, 168–
169, 194, 319n34. See also Charles X,
jesuit-king, as; Missions to the Interior;
monarchy; politics (unofficial)
symbol(s) (revolutionary and imperial),
7, 16–17, 36, 39–40, 49, 159,
312n33, 312n35; busts of Napoleon,
171, 191; everyday objects and traffic
in, 44–45, 47, 61–62, 171, 175,
190–193; guillotine, 74, 77, 100, 175;
ideology and, 57, 159; imperial eagle,
52, 54, 60, 191; laws defining as seditious, 42–43; liberty cap, 53; liberty tree, 46, 53, 55, 100, 147, 175,
320n61; mise-en-place ceremonies and,
7, 39–62, 190–191; missionaries encouraging, 191; seditious use of, 61–
62, 169, 175, 193–194; tricolor, 46,
48, 49, 52, 53–54, 60–61, 169, 170,
192–193, 319n34, 322n84. See also
crisis of legitimacy; festivals (revolutionary); forgetting (oubli), politics of;

mise-en-place ceremonies; politics (unofficial); republican tradition; Revolution of 1789

Tartuffe: anticlericalism after 1825, focus of, 3–4, 138, 243, 258, 259–260, 334n60, 361n54; broadsheets popularizing, 253, 254 (figure 7); censorship of, 233, 365n121; court of Louis XIV and, 3, 5–6, 20, 37, 301; framework for understanding Restoration, 1–2, 3–5; Molière and, 1; monarchy depicted in, 5–6, 37; pamphlet versions sold in Restoration, 4, 186, 252–253; plot summary, 2–3; portrait of the king, 37; press and publicity for, 189, 251–252, 253; priests, missionaries as "Tartuffes," 3–4, 237–240; rise and fall of monarchy and, 37–38; vaudeville versions, 253, 255

Tartufferie, 1–2, 11, 229–285, 295; geography of, 243–244 (chart), 257 (map); participants in, 237, 242, 243, 246, 247, 250–256, 272, 281–282, 359n26; police action against, 258–259; tactics employed, 235–237, 250–255, 261. *See also* anticlericalism; Charles X; clerical plot; crisis of legitimacy; Missions to the Interior; politics (unofficial); *Tartuffe;* theatricality

Tartufferie, by city, 257 (map); Angers (1829), 246, 361n58; Angoulême (1826), 198, 246, 256; Beauvais (1825), 245; Besançon (1826), 178; 249; Bordeaux (1825), 246–247; Bordeaux (1827), 246–247; Bordeaux (1828), 255; Brest (1819), 134, 138, 199, 334n60; Brest (1826–1827), 246, 249, 260–284; Carpentras (1829), 251; Clermont-Ferrand (1826), 250–251; Colmar (1825), 247; Epinal (1827), 250; LaRochelle (1825), 250–251; Lyons (1825), 247; Lyons (1826), 198, 248–249; Nancy (1825), 250; Nantes (1825), 243, 245; Nimes (1825), 148, 243, 246, 247–248, 361n58; Marseilles (1820), 78–79; Marseilles (1826), 249; Rouen (1825), 198–199, 229–242, 243–245; Rouen (1826), 246; Toulon (1825), 243, 245; Toulouse (1826), 250

Tartufferie, consequences of: critical perspective, even of civil officials, 258,

266–271; long-term impact, 256; missionaries restricted to interior of churches, 148; national anticlerical movement, 138, 243, 258, 259–260, 272–282, 334n60, 361n54; political rights defended in courtrooms, 11, 259–260, 271–282

Tartufferie, provocations: coronation, 4, 243, 248, 361n56; kings' days, 242, 258; missionaries, 246, 247; Papal Jubilee, 4, 178, 198, 243, 248–250, 260–284; religious rigor, 3–4; Sacrilege Law, 231, 235, 247

Tartufferie, spreading: broadsheets featuring scenes from *Tartuffe,* 4–5, 253, 254 (figure 7); pamphlets reproducing trials, 137–141, 276; pamphlet versions of *Tartuffe,* prefaces and, 4, 252–253; press, 189, 251–252, 253; songs, 4, 235–236, 253–254, 364n102; vaudeville versions of *Tartuffe,* 253–255

theater: missionaries, in relation to, 174; seditious uses of, 2, 168, 172–174, 176, 180; used by regime for public festivities, 168, 173

theatricality: as critique of capitalism, 299–301; as critique of missionaries, 79, 137–138, 174, 178, 203, 214–216, 302, 334n50; as critique of Old Regime, 2, 7, 37, 372n39; as critique of Restoration regime, 37–38, 174, 203, 224–228, 283–284, 302; democracy, in relation to, 12, 299–305; perspective adopted by civil officials, 215, 266–271. *See also* Charles X, jesuit-king, as; clerical plot; crisis of legitimacy; Tartufferie

transparency, 301, 372n39

Van Kley, Dale, 32–35, 121–122
Vaulabelle, Achille de, 317n16, 320–321n62
Voltaire: inflammable!, 187; missionaries' attack on, 90, 101; pamphlet versions of, 101, 186; press advertising publications of, 185–187; press publicizing struggle with missionaries over, 185; songs defending, 135

Waquet, Françoise, 17, 117, 331n15
White Terror, 5, 79, 100, 123, 131, 247, 286, 309n19

STUDIES ON THE HISTORY OF SOCIETY AND CULTURE

Victoria E. Bonnell and Lynn Hunt, Editors

1. *Politics, Culture, and Class in the French Revolution,* by Lynn Hunt

2. *The People of Paris: An Essay in Popular Culture in the Eighteenth Century,* by Daniel Roche

3. *Pont-St-Pierre, 1398–1789: Lordship, Community, and Capitalism in Early Modern France,* by Jonathan Dewald

4. *The Wedding of the Dead: Ritual, Poetics, and Popular Culture in Transylvania,* by Gail Kligman

5. *Students, Professors, and the State in Tsarist Russia,* by Samuel D. Kassow

6. *The New Cultural History,* edited by Lynn Hunt

7. *Art Nouveau in Fin-de-Siècle France: Politics, Psychology, and Style,* by Debora L. Silverman

8. *Histories of a Plague Years: The Social and the Imaginary in Baroque Florence,* by Giulia Calvi

9. *Culture of the Future: The Proletkult Movement in Revolutionary Russia,* by Lynn Mally

10. *Bread and Authority in Russia, 1914–1921,* by Lars T. Lih

11. *Territories of Grace: Cultural Change in the Seventeenth-Century Diocese of Grenoble,* by Keith P. Luria

12. *Publishing and Cultural Politics in Revolutionary Paris, 1789–1810,* by Carla Hesse

13. *Limited Livelihoods: Gender and Class in Nineteenth-Century England,* by Sonya O. Rose

14. *Moral Communities: The Culture of Class Relations in the Russian Printing Industry, 1867–1907,* by Mark Steinberg

15. *Bolshevik Festivals, 1917–1920,* by James von Geldern

16. *Venice's Hidden Enemies: Italian Heretics in a Renaissance City,* by John Martin

17. *Wondrous in His Saints: Counter-Reformation Propaganda in Bavaria,* by Philip M. Soergel

18. *Private Lives and Public Affairs: The Causes Célèbres of Prerevolutionary France,* by Sarah Maza

19. *Hooliganism: Crime, Culture, and Power in St. Petersburg, 1900–1914,* by Joan Neuberger.

20. *Possessing Nature: Museums, Collecting, and Scientific Culture in Early Modern Italy,* by Paula Findlen

21. *Listening in Paris: A Cultural History,* by James H. Johnson

22. *The Fabrication of Labor: Germany and Britain, 1640–1914,* by Richard Biernacki

23. *The Struggle for the Breeches: Gender and the Making of the British Working Class,* by Anna Clark

24. *Taste and Power: Furnishing Modern France,* by Leora Auslander

25. *Cholera in Post-Revolutionary Paris: A Cultural History*, by Catherine J. Kudlick

26. *The Women of Paris and Their French Revolution*, by Dominique Gondineau

27. *Iconography of Power: Soviet Political Posters under Lenin and Stalin*, by Victoria E. Bonnell

28. *Fascist Spectacle: The Aesthetics of Power in Mussolini's Italy*, by Simonetta Falasca-Zamponi

29. *Passions of the Tongue: Language Devotion in Tamil India, 1891–1970*, by Sumathi Ramaswamy

30. *Crescendo of the Virtuoso: Spectacle, Skill, and Self-Promotion in Paris during the Age of Revolution*, by Paul Metzner

31. *Crime, Cultural Conflict, and Justice in Rural Russia, 1856–1914*, by Stephen P. Frank

32. *The Collective and the Individual in Russia: A Study in Practices*, by Oleg Kharkhordin

33. *What Difference Does a Husband Make? Women and Marital Status in Germany*, by Elizabeth Heineman

34. *Beyond the Cultural Turn: New Directions in the Study of Society and Culture*, edited by Victoria E. Bonnell and Lynn Hunt

35. *Cultural Divides: Domesticating America in Cold War Germany*, by Uta G. Poiger

36. *The Frail Social Body and Other Fantasies in Interwar France*, by Carolyn J. Dean

37. *Blood and Fire: Rumor and History in East and Central Africa*, by Luise White

38. *The New Biography: Performing Femininity in Nineteenth-Century France*, edited by Jo Burr Margadant

39. *France and the Cult of the Sacred Heart: An Epic Tale for Modern Times*, by Raymond Jonas

40. *Politics and Theater: The Crisis of Legitimacy in Restoration France, 1815–1830*, by Sheryl Kroen

41. *Provisional Notes on the Postcolony*, by Achille Mbembe

42. *Fascist Modernities: Italy, 1922–1945*, by Ruth Ben-Ghiat

Compositor: G&S Typesetters, Inc.
Text: 10/13 Sabon
Printer: Thomson-Shore, Inc.
Binder: Thomson-Shore, Inc.